Egypt's Culture Wars

Egypt is the cultural centre of the Arab world and sets a lot of the intellectual agenda for the rest of the region. The strain between secular liberals, an authoritarian state and Islamists is reaching boiling point in Egypt and mirrors to some extent similar pressures elsewhere in the Arab world.

This ground-breaking work presents original research on cultural politics and battles in Egypt at the turn of the twenty-first century. It deconstructs the boundaries between "high" and "low" culture, drawing on conceptual tools in cultural studies, translation studies and gender studies to analyse debates in the fields of literature, cinema, mass media and the plastic arts. Anchored in the Egyptian historical and social contexts and inspired by the influential work of Pierre Bourdieu, it rigorously places these debates and battles within the larger framework of a set of questions about the relationship between the cultural and political fields in Egypt.

Egypt's Culture Wars is a valuable contribution to the often neglected and ignored subject of cultural politics and battles for representation in Egypt. Detailed and insightful, this innovative interdisciplinary volume allows us to understand what has been happening in the sphere of public debate in Egypt. As such, it will be of interest to scholars and students from the literary field, cultural studies, political science, Middle East studies, sociology and gender studies.

Samia Mehrez is Professor at the Department of Arab and Islamic Civilizations, American University in Cairo, Egypt.

Routledge advances in Middle East and Islamic studies

1 **Iraqi Kurdistan**
  Political development and emergent democracy
  Gareth R. V. Stansfield

2 **Egypt in the Twenty First Century**
  Challenges for development
  Edited by M. Riad El-Ghonemy

3 **The Christian–Muslim Frontier**
  A zone of contact, conflict or cooperation
  Mario Apostolov

4 **The Islamic World-System**
  A study in polity-market interaction
  Masudul Alam Choudhury

5 **Regional Security in the Middle East**
  A critical perspective
  Pinar Bilgin

6 **Political Thought in Islam**
  A study in intellectual boundaries
  Nelly Lahoud

7 **Turkey's Kurds**
  A theoretical analysis of the PKK and Abdullah Ocalan
  Ali Kemal Özcan

8 **Beyond the Arab Disease**
  New perspectives in politics and culture
  Riad Nourallah

9 **The Arab Diaspora**
   Voices of an anguished scream
   Zahia Smail Salhi and Ian Richard Netton

10 **Gender and Self in Islam**
   Etin Anwar

11 **Nietzsche and Islam**
   Roy Jackson

12 **The Baha'is of Iran**
   Socio-historical studies
   Dominic Parvis Brookshaw and Seena B. Fazel

13 **Egypt's Culture Wars**
   Politics and practice
   Samia Mehrez

Egypt's Culture Wars
Politics and practice

Samia Mehrez

LONDON AND NEW YORK

First published 2008
by Routledge
2 Park Square, Milton Park, Abingdon, Oxon, OX14 4RN

Simultaneously published in the USA and Canada
by Routledge
711 Third Avenue, New York, NY 10017

Routledge is an imprint of the Taylor & Francis Group, an informa business

First issued in paperback 2011

© 2008 Samia Mehrez

Typeset in Times by Wearset Ltd, Boldon, Tyne and Wear

All rights reserved. No part of this book may be reprinted or reproduced or utilized in any form or by any electronic, mechanical, or other means, now known or hereafter invented, including photocopying and recording, or in any information storage or retrieval system, without permission in writing from the publishers.

British Library Cataloguing in Publication Data
A catalogue record for this book is available from the British Library

Library of Congress Cataloging in Publication Data
A catalog record for this book has been requested

ISBN10: 0-415-42897-1 (hbk)
ISBN10: 0-415-66687-2 (pbk)
ISBN10: 0-203-92900-4 (ebk)

ISBN13: 978-0-415-42897-2 (hbk)
ISBN13: 978-0-415-66687-9 (pbk)
ISBN13: 978-0-203-92900-1 (ebk)

To the memory of Magda al-Nowaihi (1958–2002)

Contents

List of plates	xi
Acknowledgements	xii
Introduction	1
Prologue: Take them out of the ball game – Egypt's cultural players in crisis	14

PART I
Inside the literary establishment: power struggles and dreams of autonomy — 23

1 Dr Ramzi and Mr Sharaf: Sonallah Ibrahim and the duplicity of the literary field — 25

2 Children of our alley: the AUC Naguib Mahfouz Award and the Egyptian literary field — 41

3 The big one: the intellectual and the political in modern Egyptian literature — 58

4 The value of freedom: the writer against the establishment — 72

PART II
Remaking culture: emerging institutions, discourses, icons and metaphors — 89

5 Lost in globalization: education and the stranded Egyptian elite — 91

6 Translating gender between the local and the global — 107

Contents

- 7 Where have all the families gone? Egyptian literary texts of the 1990s — 123
- 8 From the *hara* to the *imara*: emerging urban metaphors in the literary production on contemporary Cairo — 144

PART III
The bounds of change: state, street and self-censorship — 169

- 9 Taking the soap out of the opera: the case of Hagg Mitwalli's Family — 171
- 10 The new kid on the block: *Bahibb issima* and the emergence of the Coptic community in the Egyptian public sphere — 188
- 11 *Found in Cairo*: the limits of representation in the visual field — 208
- 12 Literature and literalism: the *Al-Khubz al-hafi* crisis reconsidered — 229
- Epilogue — 251

Appendices — 253
Notes — 276
Bibliography — 314
Index — 325

Plates

8.1	Heliopolis main street	154
8.2	Heliopolis: Man in balcony	154
8.3	Heliopolis Laundry	155
8.4	The train	155
8.5	Along Tariq el Nasr Road facing Manshiyyat Nasir	156
8.6	Cairo Rooftops I	156
8.7	Cairo Rooftops II	157
8.8	Wash in Nile	157
10.1	Naʿim at barred window, *Bahibb issima*	196
10.2	Adli praying, *Bahibb issima*	196
10.3	Angels greet Naʿim at cinema, *Bahibb issima*	197
10.4	Adli bruised after State Security handling, *Bahibb issima*	197
10.5	Family fight in church during wedding, *Bahibb issima*	198
10.6	Naʿim and Adli play at the beach, *Bahibb issima*	198
10.7	Adli having a stroke while cycling with Naʿim, *Bahibb issima*	199
11.1	Shoe moulds I	218
11.2	Shoe moulds II	219
11.3	Shoe moulds III	219
11.4	Shoe moulds IV	220
11.5	Shoe moulds V	220

Acknowledgements

Putting this volume together has proven to be a learning experience for me. Its individual chapters were not originally written with a view of bringing them together, for they represented work in different areas of the Egyptian cultural field that have never been brought together before, specifically the textually oriented field of Arabic literature in its relationship with other forms of cultural production. Most of my earlier work had concentrated on literary texts and the conditions and contexts in which they emerge. It is only recently that I have started writing about other cultural subfields like cinema, mass media and the visual arts. However, I was not necessarily conscious of the connections that were already being written into my work between these different fields nor was I necessarily aware of the reasons behind the choices I was making in writing about specific moments in the Egyptian cultural field at large.

Many people have contributed to the various stages of this learning experience. Initially, it was my colleague Martina Rieker with her sharp eye who saw some of the relationships that were embedded in part of the work included here. Joseph Massad's enthusiasm for the initial proposal for this book was tremendously important in helping me further sharpen the structure of the volume. Elliott Colla with whom I also shared the early stages of this project has made me define what exactly lay behind the work itself. His comment that I was writing a book about my friends has been crucial in making me understand what I was doing, the position from which I was undertaking it, and why it all mattered so much.

Indeed, this book is about my friends at both a literal and symbolic level. All of the writers and artists included here are or have become my friends to whom I am indebted for their creative energy and output that constitute the very *raison d'être* of this volume. My friendship with many of these cultural producers whose works, vision and positions are represented in the chapters of this book is cemented through the inspiring models of *being* within the cultural field with which they continue to provide me. I have learned to write the history of the cultural field "through the back door" from Sonallah Ibrahim's literary life project; I have tried to emulate Huda Lutfi's remarkable attention to detailed layering in her art work, and to represent Cairo from its rooftops and its streets like Randa Shaath in her photographs of the city. I have learned to celebrate the "mediocre" from Usama Fawzi and Hani Fawzi's fine work in cinema; I have acquired new "languages" from the worlds depicted in the works of Hamdi Abu Golayyel and Ahmed Alaidy and I have been inspired by Ibrahim Issa's sharp and gutsy critical humour. I remain grateful to all these friends and many more whose work is represented here for teaching me *how* to write about our friendship.

I am also equally indebted to several colleagues who have read and commented on various parts of this work. Diane Singerman's careful reading of the entire manuscript has been an enormous help in revising and expanding the various chapters. I know that this final version still falls short of some of her important recommendations. Barbara Harlow's perceptive and encouraging comments on a later draft helped me sustain the energy during the more difficult period of final revisions. I am equally grateful to Ferial Ghazoul and Nicholas Hopkins not just for reading and commenting on various chapters but for all the support they continue to offer me beyond the bounds of this book. I also wish to thank my graduate student assistant, Amira Abou Taleb, who has read the manuscript many more times than she may have ever imagined as she carefully and attentively helped me with various aspects of formatting.

Some of the chapters included here were presented in earlier versions at colloquia and conferences in Lebanon, Turkey, Cairo and the US and were subsequently published in different places. I am grateful to all those who invited me and commented on these earlier versions. The Prologue to this volume was previously published in *Middle East Report*, no. 219 June/July 2001, pp. 10–11. Chapter 1 was initially presented as a paper at the Colloquium on the Politics of Culture in Arab Societies in an Era of Globalization at Princeton University in May 1997 that was organized by Walter Armbrust and was subsequently published in *Literature and Social Transformations*, Wael Hallaq (ed.), Brill, Leiden: 2000, pp. 262–283. Chapter 2 was presented at NYU in the context of a conference on Naguib Mahfouz's work organized by Philip Kennedy in May 2002. It was later published in *Al Jadid*, Fall 2002. Chapter 3 is based on a paper delivered at MESA 2000 and was subsequently expanded and published in *MIT EJMES*, Vol. 4, 2004, pp. 30–40, while Chapter 4 was initially a short article written for *Al-Ahram Weekly*, 30 October 2003.

Other chapters represent new directions in my work that were brought about through equally new venues of participation. Chapter 5 was initially a working paper presented at the Cultural Sovereignty: The Humanities and Globalization workshop organized by the Interdisciplinary Center for the Study of Global Change at the University of Minnesota in May 2004. I am grateful to Ragui Assad and Iman Ghazalla for their hospitality and for providing me with an important comparative context in which to think through crucial questions surrounding the study of the humanities in general and within Egypt in particular. Chapter 6 is an expanded version of the keynote address I delivered at AUC for the international conference on Gendered Bodies, Transnational Politics: Modernities Reconsidered in December 2003, upon the invitation of the late Cynthia Nelson, Director of the Institute for Gender and Women's Studies at AUC who challenged me, as she has more than one generation of scholars, into articulating important concerns with regard to gender studies between local and global contexts. A version of Chapter 6 has been published in *Journal of Middle East Women's Studies*, Indiana University Press, Vol. 3, no. 1 2007. Chapter 7 was initially presented at the Arab Families Working Group organized by Suad Joseph, one of the most fun and risky conversations I have had as a literary critic with a group of social scientists concerning representations of the Arab family in literature. This paper was expanded and published in *Arab Studies Journal*, Summer 2002, pp. 31–49.

I was very fortunate to be part of several interdisciplinary events that enabled the kind of comparative work that informs this volume. Chapter 8 was inspired by my participation in the Cairo Papers Symposium at AUC on Transformations in Middle Eastern Urban Landscapes: From Modernism to Neoliberalism held in May 2005 and organized by Iman Hamdi, the editor of *Cairo Papers in Social Science* in collaboration with the S*hehr Comparative Urban Landscapes Network* which is co-ordinated by Martina Rieker. I wish to thank them both for inviting me to think about the representation of urban space in literary texts. Chapter 9 developed out of a much shorter version that was presented in Beirut in April 2002 at a regional cultural event organized by Christine Tohmé, art curator, founder and Director of Ashkal Alwan: The Lebanese Association for Plastic Arts. It was subsequently published in Arabic in *Homeworks: Cultural Practices in the Arab Region*, Beirut, 2002, pp. 82–87. Chapters 10 and 11 are the fruit of presentations at two consecutive workshops organized by Alev Cinar, Maha Yahya and Srirupa Roy from which I benefited enormously. The first was on Secularism, Religious Nationalism and the Public Sphere in Comparative Perspective at Bilkent University, Ankara, Turkey, in October 2004 and the second in Beirut on Secularism, Religious Nationalism and the State: Visual Practices and Public Subjects during April 2005 at AUB. A short version of Chapter 10 was published in *ISIM Review*, 15, Spring 2005. Last, but not least, Chapter 12 was published in Arabic in a shorter version upon the invitation of Samah Idris, editor of the *Al-Adab* cultural journal in Beirut for a special issue on censorship in Egypt. I am grateful to Samah for providing me with the opportunity to rethink my position within the academy through the testimony I wrote for *Al-Adab*.

I am also indebted to my anonymous readers for their encouraging comments and enthusiasm about this project at a stage when the manuscript still left much to be desired. I have tried to incorporate as many of their perceptive comments as possible and hope that this final version has moved in the directions they anticipated. I owe special thanks to Huda Lutfi for allowing me to reproduce images from her exhibit *Found in Cairo*, Randa Shaath for her beautiful photographs of Cairo, Jean-Pierre Ribière who at a last-minute request sent me his excellent photos of Cairo's *ashwa'iyyat*, and the Arab Production and Distribution Company for allowing me to reproduce images from the film *Bahhib issima*.

There are some very dear people who have willingly granted me the space I desperately needed to finish this project. I wish to thank my parents for their enormous patience and understanding as I gradually disappeared from their life into a cocoon. Knowing that I have their support and love despite my shameful absence on so many important occasions has been a life-saver for me. I am also very grateful to my smart son Nadim for his tremendous sympathy and warmth as the book was being finalized.

Finally I want to acknowledge the importance of the domestic conversations that have been crucial in shaping this book. I want to thank my husband Richard Jacquemond for having first introduced me to the work of Pierre Bourdieu thereby providing me with a new lens through which to read the Egyptian cultural field. Richard is a French Arabist who, like me, is a specialist in Arabic Literature; however, we obviously occupy substantially different positions vis-à-vis our object of study: I as an insider; he as an outsider to it. Our domestic conversations, arguments, differences and agreements about our object of study are at the very core of my writing. Indeed, as will become clear from the chapters themselves, Richard's work punctuates my own. But beyond these domestic conversations Richard has patiently cohabited with this project for perhaps too long during which time he has provided unwavering support, encouragement, and sympathy. For all this and more I remain utterly grateful.

Introduction

The time of dissent

On 16 June 2005 Egyptian writers, artists, journalists and other pro-reform and democracy advocates gathered at the Journalists' Syndicate in downtown Cairo to commemorate the death of Sheikh Imam Issa, the blind composer and singer who put to music the political protest poems by leading vernacular poet Ahmad Fuad Nigm, and who, as part of the duo Imam-Nigm, had become *the* icon of political dissident during the 1970s. On this politically charged occasion, on the eve of the Egyptian presidential elections of September 2005, Nigm read the founding statement of the Writers and Artists for Change movement that, only two weeks earlier, had joined the ranks of a host of pro-reform groups and movements that had mushroomed in Egypt to protest against yet another six-year mandate for President Mubarak. The text of the statement began by reaffirming the historic role and responsibility of Egypt's writers and artists, as the spearhead for change in the country, since the nineteenth-century *nahda* (cultural renaissance). The signatories of the statement declared their solidarity with other democracy groups and activists such as the popular political movement Kifaya (Enough), the Popular Campaign for Change that was constituted through a coalition of judges, journalists, university professors and professional syndicates, the Youth for Change movement, human rights activists and others, all primarily demanding the end of Mubarak's rule and opposed to the possible succession of his son Gamal.

The most significant aspect of the Writers and Artists for Change statement was the relationship it constructed between the call for political change (democracy, equality, transparency, the right to protest, etc.) and the call for freedom of literary, artistic, and academic work and the refusal of all forms of censorship and intimidation. For this nascent movement, political freedom *is* cultural freedom and no regime can claim to be democratic without according freedom of opinion and expression in all fields of knowledge and creative endeavour. Such was the crux of the movement's statement, delivered ceremonially by one of Egypt's most popular poets, at a moment when the Egyptian state is under international pressure to implement democratic reforms. The signatories of the statement included some of Egypt's most prominent writers, artists, critics,

2   Introduction

filmmakers, script-writers and actors in a show of remarkably organized solidarity and force. On 2 August 2005 Writers and Artists for Change organized their first peaceful demonstration on Tal'at Harb Square in downtown Cairo where, surrounded by riot police who blocked access to the square, they held banners calling for reform and paraded posters of such seminal cultural icons as the dean of Arabic letters, Taha Hussein; Egypt's diva, Umm Kulthum; the popular composer Sayyid Darwish; the theatre pioneer Nagib al-Rihani; and the leading vernacular poets Salah Jahin and Fuad Haddad, while chanting the political songs of the 1970s by the poet Ahmed Fuad Nigm and Sheikh Imam.

During the summer of 2005, the Writers and Artists for Change movement held weekly meetings at the offices of Miret publishing house, a budding private enterprise that, over the past decade, has published some of Egypt's foremost literati and avant-garde writers who have chosen to distance themselves from state-run publishing in order to ensure a wider margin of freedom and better production work. In an interview published by the *Al-Ahram Weekly*, Adil al-Siwi, one of the most distinguished contemporary Egyptian painters and a founding member of the Writers and Artists for Change movement, explained the *raison d'être* of this nascent and collective cultural movement:

> Intellectuals have long been attempting to wage a battle against the official cultural authority, but they have consistently failed to achieve real gains.
> (…)
> The cultural movement has always been sporadic, it never has a set strategy. … The oppositional scene had been monopolized by religious currents, especially the Muslim Brothers, for too long. But Kifaya has finally carved out a different space for dissidence, and in so doing it has paved the way for other alternatives, not all of which are necessarily overtly political.
> (…)
> [W]e stand for change, not reform. Reform implies partial change to policy. We are rather about dramatic change.
> (…)
> The space for imagination, the creative drive, has been terribly limited, so has the opportunity for genuinely critical research. It's unbearable.… Another problem is book banning, which occurs annually at the Cairo Book Fair – it's a phenomenon intellectuals have yet to tackle.[1]

Not surprisingly, the movement has been at the forefront of angry protests that took place in the aftermath of the Beni Soueif Cultural Palace disaster of 5 September 2005, where a fire caused by a candle on stage led to the death of at least 46 of Egypt's young generation of drama students and actors as well as noted drama specialists and critics who were trapped inside the locked, unattended and fire-hazardous auditorium. Members of the movement issued a statement condemning state corruption and negligence, calling for the resignation of the Minister of Culture, Faruq Husni, and demanding that those responsible for the catastrophe – primarily the Ministers of Culture, of the Interior and of Health –

should be brought to Justice. However, to the great dismay of members of the movement and other protesting groups, President Mubarak reinstated the Minister of Culture who, in a strategic move to contain angry popular sentiment, had in fact tendered his resignation.

It is important to note that Egyptian writers and artists have rallied together before in moments of crisis (for example, after the attempt on Naguib Mahfouz's life in 1994), however, as al-Siwi rightly pointed out, such rallies were always sporadic and crisis-driven and therefore never attained the level of sustained battle to which the Writers and Artists for Change movement aspired. Indeed, the re-emergence of a unified writers' and artists' movement is testimony not only to the fact that the problems, interests and battles of these diverse cultural actors are one and the same, but that the cultural wars themselves are part and parcel of the political ones.

This volume will map out some of the most significant cultural battles in Egypt focusing specifically on the Mubarak era (1981–) that has witnessed significant and often contradictory changes within the cultural field in an increasingly globalized context. Much has been written about recent developments in the economic, social and political fields in Egypt; however, the cultural field, its politics and battles, as well as the structures and frameworks within which these develop, remains, despite some valuable contributions in the field of cultural politics and representations, highly understudied.[2] Moreover, the Egyptian cultural field is the oldest in the Arab world, with an early hegemony over cultural production and dissemination through literature, performing and visual arts, cinema and mass media and has historically been at the forefront of debates about modernity and national identity as they are elaborated through cultural representations.[3] Furthermore, the contests over cultural meanings and the institutional boundaries of culture have been at the centre of many key debates, scandals and court cases in Egypt throughout the twentieth century and more specifically during the last 25 years, steadily thrusting the cultural field into the centre of political struggles.

Indeed, the Mubarak era, as will be argued in the Prologue and demonstrated through several other chapters, has witnessed the Egyptian state's renewed active involvement in the cultural field if compared to late President Sadat's marginalization of the field and its actors.[4] Control of the cultural field has been the state's consistent strategy in countering the rising influence of the Islamist movement and groups (a legacy of the Sadat policies) as well as the more amorphous and deeply rooted "Islamic Trend", to use Gregory Starrett's formulation to describe how civil society and public space have been penetrated by the discourses of religion through the school, the media and the market.[5] Moreover, in order to compensate for the loss of control over the political and economic fields that are increasingly dominated by international global forces as well as step up its domination of both the religious and cultural fields the Egyptian state has adopted contradictory strategies in its simultaneous attempts to recapture a modern secular image while aiming to establish itself, through its increasing investment in Islamic symbols, as the sole moral and religious authority. Finally, in its obsession with the game of power and its own self-preservation the state has exasperated civil society and civil institutions and has had to deal with dramatic manifestations of what seems to be a new culture of dissent.

The elephant in the room

Indeed, the hot summer of 2005 marked a historic mobilization of civil society organizations and groups of which Writers and Artists for Change was but one example. Under the general umbrella of the "Egyptian Movement for Change" Cairo witnessed an unprecedented movement of protest from groups across the political and civic spectrum whose unifying slogan was Kifaya (enough).[6] Equally historic has been the sustained solidarity and collaborative action between these civil society groups and the Muslim Brotherhood, Egypt's officially banned Islamist organization that, because of its religious ideology, its position on vital issues such as democracy and the Coptic community, as well as cultural politics, was not necessarily viewed by these secular actors as a reliable ally. However, the state's sustained oppression and violence against all members of its opposition across the political spectrum, its corrupt neo-liberal policies as well as its massively contested regional and global ones specifically with regard to Palestine, Iraq and Lebanon, not to mention its sheer contempt and indifference for the welfare of its citizens as can be amply demonstrated through multiple examples (the Beni Soueif fire being just one), has yielded momentous and unexpected solidarities.[7]

From among this generalized movement of dissent within universities, unions, syndicates, human rights organizations and youth groups the Muslim Brotherhood is the only group that has been able to accede to Parliament with 88 seats out of 454 in the parliamentary elections of December 2005; a historic victory despite fraudulent ballots and persistent state violence against its members. Since 1984, the members of the Muslim Brotherhood have run for parliament as independents to circumvent the government's ban on the group's political activities. Given the weak performance of the legal secular opposition parties (only nine seats), the Muslim Brotherhood was suddenly propelled into the forefront of the political landscape as the only real opposition against the ruling National Democratic Party. Intent on gaining the trust of other ideologically unsympathetic constituents, the Muslim Brotherhood changed its strategy from attacking the state on the softer terrain of the latter's cultural politics (which regularly antagonized the secular players, as will be demonstrated in the Prologue to this volume) to a head-on confrontation on political, economic, social and environmental issues and reform. By adopting new discursive and pragmatic strategies the Muslim Brotherhood was able to represent other unrepresented or underrepresented voices politically within the political spectrum.[8] Hence the Muslim Brotherhood was able to transform its own historic image since it was founded by Hasan al-Banna in 1928 "from [being] a religious mass movement to what looks very much like a modern political party".[9]

Observers of the tumultuous summer of 2005 held their breath as the Muslim

Brotherhood ascended to this new and potentially threatening (for both the state and the secular cultural producers) political visibility. True their 88 seats do not allow them to pass parliamentary bills; however they have still been able to mobilize other constituents in Parliament on more than one count. For example, the Brotherhood rallied to oppose a proposed extension of the emergency law that has been in effect since 1981. They also protested, along with Kifaya members and other pro-reform parliamentarians and groups, against the state's disciplinary action against judges Hisham al-Bastawisi and Mahmud Makki who exposed the fraudulent parliamentary elections of 2005. Furthermore, they supported the Judge's Club version for a new judicial authority law that would guarantee the independence of the judiciary. Despite this mobilization however, the Egyptian Parliament voted a two-year extension of the emergency law in April 2006 and the Judge's Club proposed law reforms were not passed.[10]

Moreover, the Brotherhood incurred massive arrests in the ranks of its members, before, during and after the 2005 elections, which included some of its most influential leaders like the dynamic and pragmatic Isam al-Iryan, head of the Brotherhood's Political Committee, and Muhammad Mursi, head of the Parliamentary Committee.[11] However, it persisted in its new confrontational politics, announcing that it planned to constitute a political party.[12] The state's meditated response to this new development did not come as a surprise. In November 2006 President Mubarak gave his initial consent for Parliament to amend article 76 of the Egyptian constitution (which had already been amended and ratified by a popular referendum in 2005 allowing for the first time ever multi-candidate Presidential elections). The new and widely contested amendments passed in 2007 stipulate that only parties with 5 per cent seats in Parliament can run for Presidential elections.[13] Given the state's control over the other weak political parties, the proposed amendment is perceived by the opposition as a way to close the already very limited window for independents and to create a smoother entry for the ruling party's expected candidate, Gamal Mubarak. As for a political party for the Muslim Brotherhood, that too was brushed aside given that Egyptian law forbids the establishment of political parties on the basis of religious platform. Despite all these tactics of containment, the Muslim Brotherhood remains the state's biggest headache because of its effective grassroots mobilization. Massive demonstrations in December 2006 at Cairo, Ain Shams and Al-Azhar universities by thousands of Muslim Brotherhood student activists and adherents protesting against the state's interference in student union elections bear testimony, despite the Brotherhood's calculated distance from the militia-like demonstration at Al-Azhar, to the impact of the group on the expanding levels of political dissent.[14]

On the other hand, the fact that other pro-reform groups do not have the Brotherhood's political, structural or organizational strategies and outreach has made them easier targets for the state's overt and covert violence, especially since unlike the Brotherhood they lack a broad-based popular and populist movement. This has been the case with Ayman Nur, the leader of Al-Ghadd

6   *Introduction*

(Tomorrow) party who garnered 8 per cent of the 2005 Presidential election and who is currently serving a five-year prison sentence for allegedly forging signatures to form his party.[15] This has also been the fate of Egypt's young and savvy bloggers whose consistent global exposure of the state's violence has subjected several of them to detention and torture.[16] Despite the state's relentless oppressive tactics and measures, there is no denying that dissent has become the name of the game.

Paradox in the cultural field

As many of these civil society groups continue to contest and resist state violence, corruption and oppression, the Writers and Artists for Change movement that was so ceremoniously launched in June 2005 slowly dwindled and disappeared. Its gradual collapse was not much of a surprise given the continued differences in interests, ideological orientations and generational aspirations of the various cultural producers. Furthermore, as will become apparent through several chapters in this volume, the cultural producers maintain the most ambiguous relationship with the state that is at once their patron and their persecutor. Their reputed secular leftist leanings have pitted them against religious forces in society in general, often pushing them into dubious alliances with the state. These alliances have impacted the prospects of the autonomy of the cultural field at large and have allowed the state to manipulate the cultural producers in its own game of power. It has also meant that, in their wars against the state, cultural producers have remained locally isolated within their own marginal and dominated constituency.

Indeed, both the movement's founding rally of June 2005 and Adil al-Siwi's statements about its agenda underline the paradoxical position of the cultural producers. On the one hand al-Siwi had declared: "[W]e stand for change, not reform. Reform implies partial change to policy. We are rather about dramatic change." But on the other hand, in their rally, the voices of these cultural producers seemed to come only from the past, reproducing the state's official "Enlightenment" discourse about the nineteenth-century *nahda* while parading icons of the dead – Taha Hussein, Umm Kulthum, Salah Jahin, among others and chanting Ahmad Fuad Nigm's political poetry of the 1970s. The cultural producers profess their concern for "the space for the imagination" and "the creative drive" as al-Siwi argued; words that seem to gauge the question of the autonomy of the cultural field. Yet, in their statement at the June 2005 rally they reaffirmed their historic role and responsibility as the spearhead for change in the country: an affirmation that recasts them in a political reformist role of which they have been stripped not just by the state but by the Muslim Brotherhood who, as al-Siwi acknowledges, have "monopolized" the oppositional scene "for too long".

Not only does the state understand the paradox inherent in these positions but it uses them to cultivate its own global image as the patron of the secular cultural producers. In doing so, it thrusts the marginal and dominated cultural field

Introduction 7

into the centre of the political one. These tactics were symbolically captured through the state's hijacking of the Egyptian Nobel laureate Naguib Mahfouz's funeral. Unlike any of Egypt's national and cultural icons whose funerals are attended by thousands of Egyptians, Mahfouz, who died on 30 August 2006 at the age of 94, was given a highly mediatized state military funeral attended only by President Mubarak and Egypt's political elite with much pomp, ceremony and thousands of black-clad security but in the total absence of the cultural elite itself.

However, despite the visible centrality of state control over the cultural field at the local level, the latter has not been insular to the general flux of global capital and privatization policies, nor to the struggles over "democratization", and civil society movements that have all marked Egypt under Mubarak.[17] These new realities have impacted the economic context as well as the symbolic values of the cultural field itself whose dependence on state employment and the state's cultural apparatus is being reshaped by a growing private sector in the world of publishing and translation, film and media production, as well as private galleries and global art markets. Such developments have provided new conditions for cultural production and for cultural players to carve out new sites of resistance to state domination. Indeed, these emerging venues of global dissemination have provided cultural producers with the space to develop counter-strategies that would check, expose and subvert not just the state's domination of the cultural field but the mounting Islamic trend as well. Throughout this volume the expression "street censorship" (*raqabat al-shariʿ*) will be used to refer to this rising Islamic trend and its interventions in the cultural field at large. "Street censorship" is the expression coined by the cultural players themselves to describe interventions by non-state actors who try to constrain and contaminate the intrinsic values of the cultural field by imposing dominant conservative religious ones on the secular players. The fact that cultural players refer to all such intervention as "street censorship" is revealing for it helps them define the parameters of the field and its values through the exclusion of all other actors from outside the field (religious authorities, journalists, lawyers, civil servants in the state apparatus, etc.). The strategies and impact of "street censorship" on both the cultural players and the political field itself and the ways in which they were resolved are explored in several chapters in this volume through different crises that have erupted in the cultural subfields. Moreover, contests over new global contexts of cultural production that may provide venues for freer artistic expression away from state and street constraints have laid bare the internal battles among the cultural players themselves, exposing the "orthodox" and "heretical" positions that various actors occupy within it.[18] The terms "orthodox" and "heretical" are used by Pierre Bourdieu in his analysis of the academic field in order to characterize the different relationships of domination and subordination within the academy. Those who have dominant positions hold "orthodox" views that seek to reproduce the structure of power within the academic field. "Heretical" actors on the other hand occupy subordinate positions and seek to transform the power structure that the "orthodox" actors defend and maintain. These relationships of power and domination among the cultural players as well as their historically interested dependence on the state implicate them in the bounds of many cultural battles and the constraints and setbacks they have entailed over the past twenty-five years.

Stories from the cultural field

This volume explores the values, paradoxes and battles that have shaped the Egyptian cultural field at both the local and global levels at the turn of the century. Several chapters have been developed in conversation over a period of time and have either been published in shorter versions or presented in various places. Given the nature of its development, this volume does not pretend to be all-inclusive or exhaustive: rather it provides a spectrum of the constraints and problems but also the risks and opportunities that cultural actors encounter and confront in Egypt today. The individual chapters deal with different aspects of both the cultural and the educational fields including literature, film and mass media as well as the academy. Bringing these individual pieces together in the context of this volume provides for an overview of the cultural politics in Egypt as well as the contests over power, legitimacy, knowledge, language and representation.

Pierre Bourdieu's complex and wide-ranging theoretical work on the socio-historical ground for cultural production informs the questions and issues raised in many of the following chapters. In particular, Bourdieu's work on the cultural field, its internal structure, values, and battles and its relationship to the economic, political and religious fields frames the entire volume. More specifically, the Prologue and Part I draw on Bourdieu's *Les règles de l'art* and his analysis of the emergence of an autonomous literary field in nineteenth-century France, where he focuses predominantly on the work of Gustave Flaubert as a high point in this autonomy.[19] For Bourdieu any given field is constituted of the diverse positions of domination and subordination over which different agents or actors in the field compete. Within the literary field and the cultural field at large this competition is structured around notions and values of honour, recognition, prestige, reputation and consecration. Unlike the rules of competition and recognition in the economic field, none of these values constitutes economic capital. They do however constitute what Bourdieu calls symbolic capital and hence authority within the cultural field. Indeed, Bourdieu argues that the cultural field is an economic world in reverse for, contrary to the rules that govern the economic field where the actors' positions of domination and subordination are measured through their economic capital, within the cultural field power is amassed through forgoing economic gain for a symbolic one. Hence, the "social miracle" as he formulates it, that within the cultural field "he who loses wins".[20] Bourdieu's theory of the literary field therefore takes into consideration the literary/cultural products themselves as well as their producers whose positions within the field are determined by their lack of interest in values (political and economic) not intrinsic to the field itself. Moreover, Bourdieu analyses the position of the literary field within the more general field of power looking at its relative autonomy or domination by other fields (political, economic, religious, etc.). For Bourdieu literary, cultural and artistic production in general is inherently related to a complex network of institutions (inside and outside the cultural field) that enable or impede, empower or delegitimize it and its actors.

Bourdieu's key analytical concepts are at once applied and embedded in the Prologue and Part I (four chapters) of this volume that focus on the literary establishment and its values as well as its internal and external struggles with other fields of power. These are crucial to understand, since they are emblematic of parallel and similar battles in other cultural subfields, as will become clear in Part III where case studies from cinema, mass media, the visual arts and the academy are analysed. The initial focus on the secular literary establishment is justified since its relationship to the fields of power (both political and religious) dates back to the nineteenth-century *nahda* and, as such, has the longest and most complex history. Since the time of Muhammad Ali (1805–49), the Egyptian state, with its need for secular civil institutions and servants, has been responsible for producing and administering the modern literary establishment. The secular literati, who are products of this establishment, have therefore been historically dominated by the political field and have consistently been dependent on it for status and power, especially in their (and the state's) competition with the religious field that continues to hold an increasingly strong sway over the Egyptian street.

The first four chapters take the reader inside the Egyptian literary field and explore its dominant values and how they and the positions of the literary producers themselves are being renegotiated within new global contexts. The four chapters also dwell on the nature of the relationship that binds the secular literati to the state and the mechanisms through which their dependent status is maintained. Throughout these four chapters, the figure of the Egyptian writer Sonallah Ibrahim looms large as a model of autonomy within an otherwise dominated literary field. His symbolic capital and "honour" within the field is juxtaposed against other "dishonouring" values (both aesthetic and economic) that contaminate and "threaten" the field's doxa (i.e. its taken-for-granted conventions and assumptions) that allows the new players to accede to legitimate positions within it. Chapters 1, 2 and 3 provide examples of such "dishonouring" values from the point of view of the consecrated actors in the field who seek to conserve and reproduce its doxa. Hence the chapters analyse the mechanisms of inclusion and exclusion that regulate the field at multiple levels based on nationalist ideology, gender relations and, most importantly, the field's dominant literary conventions and aesthetic values. Furthermore, the chapters investigate the extent to which the intrinsic or extrinsic values of the field materialize within the literary production itself, reading the literary works of writers like Sonallah Ibrahim, Gamal al-Ghitani, Ibrahim Issa and others not as examples of individual artistic accomplishment but rather as instances of how these texts and their aesthetic values are socially and historically constituted.

Part II, which comprises four chapters, shifts attention to the levels of state

10   *Introduction*

intervention in the cultural field through its adoption and propagation of "modernist" discourses and institutions that would ensure its secular image in a global context upon which it has become increasingly dependent. Chapters 5 and 6 raise questions about cultural sovereignty and explore the contradictions and challenges that confront the Egyptian state and its cultural apparatus as it introduces new values, concepts and institutional structures in line with global interests and capital flux, while maintaining more traditional ones that ensure its local moral or ethical authority. The fields of education and gender studies, both of which continue to receive international attention and are saturated with global investment, constitute the focus of these two chapters. Through a reading of the changes that have occurred in the increasingly privatized and globalized elite educational system in Egypt Chapter 5 problematizes the Egyptian public's relationship with Arabic language and culture as well as liberal education at a moment when the state's "modernizing" strategies are being resisted and contested by the Islamist movements and the Islamic trend in general. Furthermore, both chapters explore the boundaries and limitations encountered by the state in its attempt to *translate* itself in a global market with vested global interests that seek increasingly internationalized socialization in local contexts. At this level, Chapter 6, in particular, addresses key questions surrounding the linguistic and political debates that characterize the *translation* of the term "gender" and its application(s) within the Egyptian context in relationship to national and transnational agendas and translations. In contrast, Chapters 7 and 8 expose the "modern" façade of the state through literary works and representations at the turn of the century. These are characterized by a general resistance to and contestation of the state's dominant icons of family and nation that ensure its control over the community's imaginings of itself. The literary works of the 1990s by young women and men analysed in Chapter 7 provide examples of the changing economic and political contexts of literary producers and literary production as well as emerging aesthetic conventions that announce a rupture with dominant metaphors of family and nation within the literary text. Likewise, through readings of substantially different literary representations of the city of Cairo, Chapter 8 explores how writers have engaged the various contradictions of modern urban space and have remapped and rewritten Cairenes' experiences in their "globalized" city.

In Part III, the final four chapters travel to other cultural subfields – mass media, cinema, the visual arts and the academy respectively – and provide instructive parallels with the chapters in Part I that deal exclusively with the literary establishment. Unlike other studies that have persistently separated "high" and "low" culture, the literary establishment and popular culture, this volume reads the cultural field as a whole in order to render a larger, more comprehensive and comprehensible picture of the cultural politics and politics of culture in Egypt today. The final four chapters represent censorship cases across the cultural field revealing the extent to which "high" and "low" culture share the same problems of state, "street" and self-censorship. Indeed Part III probes several issues that cut across the boundaries between the different cultural subfields: the state's visible and invisible strategies and practices, the changing profile of cultural producers and its impact on cultural production itself, the complex relationship between writers or artists and the state, and the struggles for power, legitimacy and recognition within the cultural field in an increasingly global context, as well as the contest over language, icons and freedom of expression. All four chapters foreground transgressive texts and moments in the various cultural subfields under study. They also provide a close reading of cultural and academic "scandal" in an attempt to understand how these crises develop, what constitutes these moments of transgression, the strategies used to fuel them, the counter-strategies that ensue to surpass them and the price paid and lessons learned in the process.

By exploring the strategies of contestation and resistance that cultural players have used in their cultural wars in Egypt these case studies also unsettle the dominant representation of the binary relationship in which an authoritarian state is pitted against a dominated cultural field.[21] The growing and globally oriented private sector in mass media, cinema and the art world has provided new venues (satellite television, private art galleries, international exhibitions, biennales, international festivals, new funding opportunities and conditions of production) that have allowed cultural producers to renegotiate their relationship with the political field. At another level, these case studies reveal that the rules of the game of censorship no longer lie solely with the political field but that the autonomy of the cultural field is under threat of contamination by extrinsic religious, aesthetic and social values and mores that have come to dominate Egyptian society at large during the past quarter of a century. As will be seen in Chapters 10 and 11, the state seems to have ceded public space to religious authorities (both Islamic and Coptic) and non-state actors allowing them to censor cultural and artistic works. However, a closer look shows that the state maintains its dominance by recognizing the religious capital of religious authorities and communities (both Islamic and Coptic) while at the same time manipulating them and confining their position to one of subordination. It must also be recognized that these strategies on the part of the state, as is demonstrated in Chapter 10, have increasingly strengthened the interventions of the religious field in the cultural one and have threatened the political field's "winning" position in the game.

Standing inside the cultural field

This volume marks a change in my general orientation as a literary critic whose primary concern was the literary text and the conditions of its production, to a broader more culturally orientated investigation of other texts and their respective contexts. It also coincides with a change in geographic and professional location: from being there (in the US) to being here (in Egypt) from being a spectator of the cultural field in Egypt to becoming an actor within it. Being here has meant direct involvement with the cultural players themselves and has implicated me in many cultural battles during which I have taken sides and participated in different levels of mobilization and public debate about issues of freedom of expression and autonomy. Hence my choice of the object of study in this project (i.e. the cultural field) bears the mark and contradictions of my position as subject within it. Since my return to Egypt in 1990 I have steadily moved from being in a subordinated "heretical" position to a relatively more powerful one within both the cultural field and the academy. My "heretical" views and "subversive" vision of the Arabic literary language and "canon" are the focus of Chapter 12: a personal testimony on the crisis surrounding my teaching of Mohamed Choukri's controversial literary autobiography *Al-Khubz al-hafi* in one of my literature courses at the American University in Cairo in December 1998. I believe that the crisis with *Al-Khubz al-hafi* was a defining moment for my research orientations, general concerns and understanding of the cultural field and its battles, something I have come to realize in retrospect as I started to look back on the nature of what I had written since then. Following the *Khubz al-hafi* crisis, and thanks to the local and global interventions in that battle over academic freedom, I have moved steadily to a relatively more consecrated but perhaps equally contested position within the field. This newly acquired symbolic power is represented through my position as chair of the AUC Naguib Mahfouz Literary Award as well as my participation in 2005 on the panel of judges for the newly established Sawiris Literary Award. The AUC Naguib Mahfouz Award (discussed at length in Chapter 2) has symbolic monetary value but comes with the promise of translating the award winning-novel into English; the Sawiris Literary Award on the other hand, which is offered by Egypt's biggest business tycoon awards yearly prizes that total more than £E300,000, a hefty economic gain for both consecrated and avant-garde writers in Egypt (£E = approximately US$5.50). Both prizes continue to be viewed by some within the literary field as threats to its doxa and praxis of "disinterest" in the economic world as well as challenges to the social miracle of "he who loses wins". My service on these two committees is one indication that I have moved from the margin to the centre and has implicated me (this time from a position of power) in heated contests over the representation of the Arabic literary "canon" both locally (through the Sawiris Award) and globally (through the AUC Award).

Furthermore, being here has also meant a change in the parameters of my object of study. Standing inside the cultural field meant that I could no longer deal with the literary field in isolation from other cultural subfields whose conditions of production, values and battles intersect with many in the literary field. Indeed being here has showed me just how fluid and artificial the "boundaries" between the cultural subfields are, ones that impede crucial interdisciplinary and comparative work. This volume traverses those disciplinary boundaries, travelling among more than one theoretical approach, as will be seen through the chapters themselves, from Bourdieu's sociological model of the cultural field to the fields of cultural studies, translation studies and gender studies. As is the case with my reading of the literary field, the choices I have made from within these other subcultural fields of cinema, mass media and art are ones that coincide with my own "heretical" position. All of them are cases that seek to transform rather than reproduce the doxa of the cultural field; all are attempts at elaborating counter-languages that would unsettle the dominant political and religious ones.

Finally, my position within the Egyptian cultural field is marked by my past and present location within the American academy (as both student and teacher) and the very language in which I reconstitute the field. Writing in English about the Egyptian cultural field casts me in the role of the translator and involves me in the act of rewriting the original text into a target-language. In fact, at a more literal level I have indeed translated and to a great extent written in English two chapters that had originally been published in Arabic elsewhere (Chapters 9 and 12). The act of translation that provides the focus of Chapter 6 is never innocent for it is conditioned and shaped at one level by the translator's own history, ideology and values. My *translation* of the Egyptian cultural field into English is no different and should be read as such. At another level, translating the Egyptian cultural field into English places this local and localized text alongside a larger global one, situating it in the heart of debates of global magnitude not just local circumstance. All of the issues that surround my discussion of the cultural field in Egypt must be understood and read within the context of this global text, a new world order of which the Egyptian case is but one manifestation: the alarming levels of state violence in both the US and Europe in the name of national security; the rise of fundamentalism, neo-conservatism and the religious right worldwide; the increasing violation of civil liberties and civil society specifically in the aftermath of "9/11"; the censorship of cultural expression as a means for increased political control and moral guardianship and the surveillance and policing of educational institutions in the name of patriotism and homeland security.[22] Similarly, my discussion of the crisis of higher education in Egypt and the internationalization of school curricula (Chapters 5 and 12) echo critiques of the same globalizing educational processes elsewhere; my concerns for liberal education and the increasing commercialization of the academy conjoin debates on the contemporary university worldwide that has forsaken its historic role of promoting and protecting national culture and has turned into a transnational corporation.[23] Indeed, the readability of my translation of the Egyptian cultural field in English will depend primarily on the readers' ability and willingness to situate themselves between these two texts: the local Egyptian text and the larger global one.

Prologue
Take them out of the ball game – Egypt's cultural players in crisis

On 2 January 2001, newly elected parliamentary deputy and Muslim Brother Gamal Hishmat submitted an enquiry to Minister of Culture Faruq Husni concerning the publication by the General Organization for Cultural Palaces (GOCP) of three novels containing what the MP described as "explicitly indecent material amounting to pornography".[1] Within two days of the submission of the enquiry, the Minister of Culture ordered an investigation, whereupon his legal adviser conducted an "interrogation" of those responsible in the absent minister's office. The outcome was the formal dismissal of Muhammad al-Bisati – editor of Literary Voices, the GOCP series responsible for the publication of the three novels, and one of Egypt's leading writers – along with his managing editor, the poet Girgis Shukri. Both men had already tendered their resignations before the parliamentary crisis, owing to bureaucratic disputes within the GOCP. The next day, the Prime Minister Atif Ibid officially sacked Ali Abu Shadi, head of the GOCP, a man deemed by his peers, and by Faruq Husni himself, to be one of the most respected members of the institution. The first half of the latest match between Egypt's political and cultural players was over before the opposing team had a chance to suit up.

Defending his actions, Husni – whose title in the media since his appointment as Minister of Culture in 1987 has been *"al-fannan Faruq Husni, wazir al-thaqafa"* (the artist Faruq Husni, Minister of Culture) – joined the Muslim Brother Hishmat in labelling the three novels "pornographic". After withdrawing the three novels from circulation, Husni dismissed media concerns about freedom of expression and the implications of his actions for proponents of fundamentalism in Egypt, saying: "Is everything the Islamists say wrong? I must defend society from cheap writing. My fundamental responsibility is to protect society's values from pornographic works."[2] In less than five days, Husni conducted over 20 interviews on local and regional satellite television, on the radio and in newspapers. He reiterated his position as guardian of societal morality, challenged anyone who could allow his sister, his wife or his daughter to read such indecencies, reminded intellectuals that Egypt is not Europe, invited those writers who persisted in flouting societal values to go elsewhere and vowed not to publish any book or novel that contests religion or violates the values of society. This valiant stance in defence of morality won the artist/minister the complete support of the cabinet, as well as the blessings of the Islamists, who concluded that "the minister has repented".[3]

The second half

These radical punitive measures do not seem to have taken Egyptian intellectuals completely by surprise. Yasir Shaʿban, one of the three authors charged with corrupting millions of young readers, saw the penalty coming. In a prophetic passage from the offending novel, Shaʿban's narrator/writer satirizes the current logic and politics of censorship by incriminating himself:

> I am so terrified of this game that I reread my novel, *Abna' al-khata' al-rumansi* (Children of Romantic Error), which I have yet to finish, and found in it what they can use as proof of Satanic worship. They will reduce everything to having sex in graveyards in the presence of the dead. Hence I will become a Satan worshipper. I will become the talk of the town. I will cause a lot of clamour. Even those who do not read will read me. It will be great, smashing, wild. The most important thing is to be part of the frenzy before it's over.[4]

All three authors became part of the frenzy, despite one literary critic's conclusion that "anyone excited by the prospect of reading these three novels in order to get a pornographic kick will be very disappointed".[5]

With the ball on their side of the field, the literati mounted a vigorous attack on Faruq Husni, whose ministerial tenure is punctuated with foul plays from which he has always risen unruffled. Immediately following the outbreak of the crisis, a group of Egyptian intellectuals issued a statement entitled "Against Oppression and Censorship", criticizing the minister's position and declaring their intended boycott of the cultural activities at the Cairo International Book Fair scheduled to open on 24 January 2001. This threat was understood by the minister as blackmail since the Book Fair has become the icon of the alliance between the political and intellectual fields. A number of prominent Egyptian writers announced their resignation from positions in the Ministry of Culture, in solidarity with Abu Shadi and al-Bisati. *Sawt al-Umma*, the independent weekly newspaper, published the minister's abstract paintings, some of which are laden with phallic symbolism. Gamal al-Ghitani, editor-in-chief of *Akhbar al-Adab*, and one of the fiercest critics of Husni's ministerial policies, revealed that the ministry was withholding from publication two parts of the *diwan* (collected poems) of Abu Nuwwas, the controversial Abbasid poet, and that it has burnt large quantities that were already published.[6] Responding to Husni's demand that writers who do not abide by society's values should go elsewhere, the veteran striker Gamal al-Ghitani levelled: "No, minister. We shall remain and you will leave!"[7]

16 *Prologue*

The referee

On 24 January date of the annual presidential meeting with Egypt's prominent intellectuals at the Book Fair, the President Hosni Mubarak blew his whistle, ending the game in Faruq Husni's favour, and confirming the minister's media image as a professional player (*wazir la'ib*). Mubarak, who on previous occasions had sought to appease the literati by declaring that there is no censorship in Egypt, showed the rowdy cultural players a yellow card, reminding them of the rules of the game. While he encouraged intellectual freedom, Mubarak said, writers should also keep in mind "traditions, morality and religious considerations". He concluded that there was no need for such a fuss over the sexual content of the novels, because the ministry would be more cautious in the future, adding that private publishing houses were free to publish whatever they liked as long as they remained within the boundaries of the law.[8] Game over. The losers went home, while the cheerleaders for public morality proceeded to pillage the Book Fair, confiscating books they deemed inappropriate, despite local and regional protests.

Name of the game

This moment of confrontation between political and cultural figures in Egypt encapsulates the nature of their mutually dependent relationship since Muhammad Ali's modernization project (1805–49) and the ensuing years of the *nahda* – the cultural "awakening" in Egypt and the Arab world. To transform Egypt from an Ottoman province into a modern regional power, Muhammad Ali initiated a series of modern Western institutions within a traditional, Islamic cultural context that had been dominated by its religious rite the *ulama*. From the start, the modernist paradigm in Egypt was dictated by the interests of political power: a military man's expansionist dreams whose armies required a modern infrastructure to support them.[9] Over the past two centuries, those modern cultural institutions have produced the secular players within the cultural field. Their effectiveness, welfare and status have largely depended on the government's degree of commitment to the modernization project. Religious conservatives have continued to be a force for the political field to contend with given their historic access to and influence on "the masses", whose participation in the modernist paradigm was, and remains, not only absent but totally undesirable. In its attempt to weaken the traditionalists, the "modernist" political power could not afford to abandon the *ulama*'s pre-modern paternalistic attitude toward the people. With the logic of "if you can't beat them, join them", the political field confirmed the dichotomy between the elite and the masses. Under Nasser, the state formally institutionalized and monopolized the cultural and the religious, adding an economic/ethical dimension to the symbolic relationship between the parties because both secular and religious players were transformed into civil servants.[10]

For Egyptian cultural figures, this history has meant that the cultural is the handmaiden of the political and must always abide by its rules. The cultural has always been placed in a reactive position depending largely on the space it is granted by the political field in the latter's own calculations of power. The end result, of course, is the weakness of a modernist paradigm that is developed, produced and sustained from within the cultural field itself. Rather than seek independence from political players, cultural figures have sought protection; rather than spearhead criticism, they have demonstrated compliance. The cultural players become the protégés of the state so long as they are intelligent enough to respect the unpredictable boundaries of the political game. Those who do not, and they are less than a handful, are considered *hors jeu*.

Inversely, the accelerated control of civil society and civil liberties on the one hand, and the largely cosmetic political institutions on the other, have rendered the political field dependent on the cultural to articulate its semblance of modernity to the world. With its refusal to develop beyond modernization to modernism – beyond modern signs in concrete to concrete signs of modernity – the political field needs the cultural as the most important icon of its claim to be modern. Hence, the relationship between the political and cultural fields may veer from a semblance of partnership to one of total control, but within this framework the prospects of autonomy for the cultural field remain minimal. So long as the political field remains obsessed with its own power to the detriment of its own development, the cultural players will continue to be reminded – should they forget – that the cultural is political. This is the name of the game.

Preparing the playing field

Faruq Husni is the perfect heir to this long history. His carefully chosen title, the artist/minister, itself embodies the relationship between the cultural and the political fields. The position Husni has taken during the crisis surrounding the three Egyptian novels demonstrates his perfect understanding and acceptance of this *double casquette*: not "the artist vs. the commissar", as Ferial Ghazoul had put it in her critique of the minister's position but rather the artist *and* the commissar, for within this framework they are one.[11]

It is not haphazard that Faruq Husni was handed the Ministry of Culture at the moment when the political and cultural fields began to warm up to one another. The Sadat period (1971–81) had been marked by mutual *froideur*. The valorization of "village ethics" (*akhlaq al-qariya*) over the modernist paradigm led to the revival of conservative Islamist ideology. Sadat himself paid the highest price for his cultural politics, but there were also grave repercussions in both the political and cultural fields: the assassinations of the parliamentary speaker Rifʿat al-Mahgub (1990) and the liberal intellectual Farag Fuda (1992), the attack on the Egyptian Nobel laureate Naguib Mahfouz (1994), the Nasr Hamid Abu Zayd apostasy case (1993–96) and the assassination attempt on President Mubarak in Ethiopia (1996), not to mention the various terrorist attacks all over the country. In its efforts to constrain the Islamist onslaught, above and beyond massive detentions, the political field attempted to reconstruct its gravely damaged global image and its seriously shaken internal one through the old ally: the secular players in the cultural field. The latter, targeted by the Islamists and infiltrated from within, accepted the alliance. Husni, the cool and unconventional artist/minister, was the ideal architect of the political designs to reaffirm that the cultural is political.

The 1990s witnessed a face-lift for Nasserist cultural institutions. The very fact that the Mubarak regime decided to revive, rather than rethink, Nasser's defunct cultural machinery – which had practically collapsed under Sadat – indicates the political field's real designs for the cultural one. Faruq Husni enlisted the country's major cultural players under the banner of enlightenment against obscurantism: a hasty and empty copy of the nineteenth-century *nahda* project that is, first and foremost, the political agenda of the day. State enlightenment, to use Nasr Hamid Abu Zayd's term, was set in motion. The General Egyptian Book Organization launched "The Family Library", an affordable series of reprints of major *nahda* figures under the patronage of the First Lady. The Higher Council for Culture was resurrected, taking a lead role in the reintegration of cultural players within the institution. The GOCP and the ministry's cultural publications were revived. Prominent literary and cultural figures were appointed to editorial and managerial positions within the ministry. All this activity was crowned in 1986 with the annual presidential meeting with the literati at the Book Fair. No wonder that the artist/minister has, on more than one occasion, congratulated himself for having gathered all the intellectuals, except a few, back into the "coop".

The explosion in size of the dysfunctional Nasser-era cultural institutions generated a host of contradictions. In its dependence on its cultural players for a modernist image, the political field distanced itself from the role of the official censor while encouraging cultural figures to be their own censors. The boundaries of freedom of expression seemed to expand, but covert levels of censorship, motivated by political intimidation and rivalries among the secular civil servants within the cultural field itself, mushroomed and multiplied. The new *laissez-faire* nature of these institutions – with expanded budgets and privileges – led to an internal, informal privatization that parallels the regime's disastrous economic programme. Secular cultural players were neutralized vis-à-vis the political field, they were mobilized in the latter's battles over power and, last but not least, they were polarized against each other.

Last season's box scores

It is against all this background that the Haydar Haydar affair that exploded in Egypt during April–May 2000 must be read.[12] Two factors came together to ignite the unprecedented controversy. *Al-Shaʽb*, the now defunct weekly newspaper of Egypt's Socialist Labour Party that, for purposes of survival, had struck an alliance with the outlawed Islamists, had an axe to grind with the political field: three of its reporters had been arrested on charges of slander against Egypt's then powerful Minister of Agriculture, Yusuf Wali. In the meantime, the disgruntled writer Hasan Nur, whose works were being held up in GOCP's

Prologue 19

bureaucratic machinery, wrote a review of Haydar's *Walima li a'shab al-bahr* (*Banquet for Seaweed*) – then just reprinted in its eleventh (and first Cairo) edition by one of the GOCP literary series – accusing the text and its author of blasphemy against Islam.[13] The timing was perfect: *Al-Sha'b* used the crisis within the cultural field as a riposte to the government's oppressive measures against it and as a way to contest the regime's respect for public morality and societal values. *Al-Sha'b*'s campaign began with Muhammad Abbas's inflammatory, sermon-like article, "Who Pledges to Die with Me?" urging Muslims to rise up in defence of their faith and demanding no less than the Minister of Culture's head, along with the heads of those responsible for the publication of the "blasphemous" novel.[14] The campaign led to a brutal confrontation between riot police and hundreds of student demonstrators from Al-Azhar, Egypt's historic Islamic university, who had not so much as seen the "blasphemous" novel, let alone read it. The cultural players inevitably got caught in the middle of the showdown between the Islamists and the political field.

In this fast-moving game, the political field launched a series of impressively calculated strikes that evidently bore the imprint of lessons learned from Sadat's fatal strategies. Rather than crushing all other players at once, the political field opted for alternating strikes, thus ensuring its control over both the left and right wings of the field. The artist/minister, in the centre field, first withdrew the "blasphemous" novel from the market and appointed a committee of experts to investigate the charges against it. Then, despite the experts' acquittal of the novel and its author, the artist/minister, under pressure from parliament, forwarded the novel to no less of an authority than the head of Al-Azhar, Sheikh Muhammad Tantawi. Capitalizing on the chance to extend his purview beyond religious matters, Sheikh Tantawi condemned the novel and its author, holding the minister responsible and demanding that Al-Azhar oversee the ministry's publications in the future. It was a long shot. Stealing the ball from the Islamists, the State Security Department called in the editor and managing editor of GOCP's Literary Horizons – the series that had published *Walima li a'shab al-bahr* – and formally charged them with blasphemy. The final strike came from the government's Committee for Parties Affairs, which orchestrated a rather transparent contest over the Labour Party leadership, leading to the suspension of the party, the closure of its newspaper *al-Sha'b* and perhaps even the untimely death, in late March 2001, of Adil Husayn, the ex-Marxist Secretary General of the Labour Party, editor-in-chief of *Al-Sha'b* and foremost attack player on the Islamist team.

Last but not least, the controversy has instilled fear within the hearts of all the minister's men. The atmosphere of intimidation is movingly captured in Hamdi Abu Golayyel's testimony after his visit to the State Security Department:

> Since that day I have considered myself a criminal, a runaway criminal who expects to be arrested at any moment in an ambush. Fortunately, or unfortunately, ambushes in my case are well-known: they amount to what one writes or what one publishes. So, since that day I have tried to evade

ambushes. I reread any story I write several times. Given the number of prohibitions and my inability to determine them I have resorted to a legal adviser, a young lawyer who is my neighbour. He reads every story I write and every book I publish especially when written by a naive writer. My agony begins as soon as the book enters the print shop: the book contains a scene of a woman sitting with a man, the book contains someone who thinks, the book contains someone eating with appetite, the book contains people, and wherever there are people, there is sin. I dream, I hallucinate, and I am submerged in nightmares. Once my wife caught me completely dressed, at four o'clock in the morning, at the door of our apartment. I had imagined that one of the books in the print shop contained an indecent scene and was on my way out to stop the printing before morning.[15]

Lessons from seasons past

Besieged by an economic collapse, a stalemate in the so-called "peace process" and the prospects of unsettling parliamentary elections, the political field spent the hot summer of 2000 expanding its alternate strikes and isolating other potentially dangerous players, one after the other. First came the arrest and renewed detention of Saad Eddin Ibrahim, professor of sociology and pro-democracy activist, with a mind-boggling list of charges that included embezzlement and espionage (the perfect inhibition for defenders of civil society and human rights). Then came the daily detentions of "Islamists" prior to the "free" parliamentary elections (not a bad lesson for the suspended Labour Party and its paper). In all of this heat, the cultural players kept their cool, watching in almost total complacent silence, as civil liberties, basic human rights and freedom of expression were smashed.

In the meantime, the artist/minister, aligning himself with the cultural politics of the day, redefined the rules of the game: schedules of publication within the ministry were stalled and new forms of surveillance on the literary series were instated. In fact, the latest crisis surrounding the three Egyptian novels erupted precisely because al-Bisati, editor of Literary Voices, sidestepped the minister's new, unwritten emergency laws and published the three novels on the basis of merit, not on the basis of the ministry's "waiting list" policy.[16]

The arrival during autumn 2000 of 17 of the outlawed Muslim Brothers in Parliament commenced a new game in cultural politics that was to leave the cultural players completely divided and disarmed after the crisis over the three Egyptian novels. The successful policies of polarization of the minister's men duly served the minister and discredited his men. Indeed, the same players that had stood in defence of the minister during the Haydar Haydar crisis, arguing that a work of art must be read and judged in its totality, were now describing the sexual passages in the three novels, taken out of context, as "blatant". Those who had defended the ministry's role in guaranteeing "freedom of expression" were now writing against it, calling for "responsible freedom of expression" that is informed by the writer's responsibility towards the law. The Writers' Union, which had issued a statement in support of Haydar's *Walima*, issued another one condemning the three novels. Those who supported the Egyptian writer Salah al-Din Muhsin against charges of blasphemy in March 2000 remained silent after he was sentenced to three years' imprisonment in January 2001.[17]

The irony in all of this is that no one reads these books. The thousands of works printed yearly in editions of 3,000 copies all would have remained in the ministry's warehouses had it not been for the diligent door-to-door distribution by the writers themselves to immediate friends, editors and critics. One journalist wrote a satirical piece telling writers that they should be grateful for the repeated crises surrounding books since it is the only way to expand the circle of readers beyond two: the writer and the censor. This dismal situation means that Mubarak wasn't playing fair in his comments to the literati at the 2000 annual meeting. Not only is private publishing completely crippled with problems of cost and distribution, but it is certainly far more vulnerable than the ministry to the arsenal of laws that govern publication in Egypt, not to mention the recently renewed emergency laws that have been in effect since 1981. In this last crisis, Mubarak displayed his competence as veteran referee: his initial warning to the cultural players was followed by his announcement that there will be no changes in the cabinet, an uncontested ruling that Gamal al-Ghitani's violent shot on goal "No, minister. We will remain, and you will leave!" had fallen out of bounds.

During the crisis over the three Egyptian novels, Dawud al-Shuryan wrote an editorial in *Al-Hayat* highlighting Egypt's weight in regional cultural politics and rightly arguing that:

> The Arab cultural model is linked to the Egyptian one that continues to allow the public sector to dominate the written word, arguing that the private sector is not an alternative and cannot protect culture, when at the same time the private sector is entrusted with protecting the economy and the loaf of bread.[18]

Al-Shuryan asks whether the time has not come for the political field to renounce its jurisprudence over the written word. Given the nature of the game and the position of the cultural players within the field, the answer is a simple and straightforward no. The cultural is political.

Part I
Inside the literary establishment
Power struggles and dreams of autonomy

1 Dr Ramzi and Mr Sharaf

Sonallah Ibrahim and the duplicity of the literary field

January 1997 marked the end of the expected intervals between Sonallah Ibrahim's past and most recent novels.[1] *Dhat* had appeared in May 1992 and, with the advent of 1997, Ibrahim's Egyptian and Arab audiences greeted the new year with the publication of the opening chapters of his new novel *Sharaf*, serialized, for the first time ever in Ibrahim's 30-year career as a writer, on the pages of Cairo's weekly literary paper, *Akhbar al-Adab*.[2] An eventful new year indeed, for it marked a crucial change in Ibrahim's politics and strategies of publication; a change which this chapter will read attentively as a revelatory moment in recent developments of the literary field in Egypt today, and as an instructive episode where the field's internal structure, positions and battles are concerned.

Those among us who have followed Ibrahim's publishing history know that this development had been unthinkable. It was unthinkable that Ibrahim's work would appear on the pages of a state-run paper, given what he writes and the history of its reception (or lack thereof) by the state apparatus.[3] Whereas his first novel *Tilka l-ra'iha* (1966; English translation *The Smell of It*, 1971) was published with a small publisher, requiring his financial collaboration, and was subsequently banned, his last novel, *Dhat* (English translation, *Zaat*, 2001) appeared through Dar al-Mustaqbal al-Arabi, an established leftist, Nasserist, private Egyptian publisher, with acknowledgements by the author to three lawyers "who graciously provided advice and guidance"[4] concerning the lethally critical manuscript. All the first editions of his other works have been published outside Egypt, by Arab publishers, with the exception of *Bayrut Bayrut* (1984), which marked the beginning of his collaboration with Dar al-Mustaqbal. With the publication of *Sharaf*, first in serialized form (a few opening chapters in *Akhbar al-Adab*) and subsequently the publication of the complete manuscript (March 1997) by Egypt's reputedly liberal, state-run Dar al-Hilal, an establishment of considerable history and intellectual weight, the impossible marriage indeed occurred. It is important to note that Ibrahim was courted by both *Akhbar al-Adab* and Dar al-Hilal and that he was initially wary of their commitment. But, they both took the risk and delivered. How is it then that this new alliance is made possible? Why is it so important that we attend to it? How does it bespeak the cultural politics that govern the cultural field in Egypt today? And how does it impact on Ibrahim's position within it?

The literary field: an economic world in reverse

In an earlier article entitled "Sonallah Ibrahim's *Dhat*: The Ultimate Objectification of the Self" I argued that the history of the publication and reception of *Dhat* attested to the emergence of a relative autonomy within the literary field in its relationship with that of power. More importantly, the very existence of the text *within* Egypt pointed to the fact that such autonomy was being recognized by the field of power itself, since the novel that vehemently attacked the workings of the state, its apparatus and institutions was published without any attempts at banning or censorship. Moreover, I also argued that the nomination of *Dhat* for a national book award (The Cairo International Book Fair Award), and the prompt withdrawal of this nomination on the eve of the award ceremony, seemed to reconfirm what the French sociologist Pierre Bourdieu has called "the social miracle" in which, as he puts it, "he who loses wins". I had relied on Bourdieu as a conceptual and methodological aid, especially in his work *Les règles de l'art* (English translation, *Rules of Art*, 1996) in which he looks at the emergence of an autonomous literary field (*le champ littéraire*) in nineteenth-century France, focusing predominantly on the work of Gustave Flaubert as a high point in this autonomy. I had noted that the nature of the developments which had taken place within the literary field in Egypt were substantially different from those which surrounded its emergence in nineteenth-century France. However, I did suggest that Bourdieu's theoretical framework provided an inspiring model that can be rethought and used to serve as an analytical tool for the study of the changes within the social space in modern Egypt, focusing on developments in the cultural field, in particular.[5]

The purpose of this chapter is to examine some of the values and dynamics within the literary field in Egypt as they become evident through a close reading of one text and one episode in the recent history of the field: Gamal al-Ghitani's laudatory editorial that accompanied the appearance of the first chapters of *Sharaf* on the pages of *Akhbar al-Adab*. I will argue that this document is of crucial importance for it is written by one of the most influential pens in Egypt today and is published on the pages of the most widely distributed and read literary journal in the Arab region. It is of paramount importance to note that, like Ibrahim, Gamal al-Ghitani made his debut in the mid-1960s and, like him again, al-Ghitani has risen to a different but equally prominent position within the literary field today.[6] However, the 30 years or so that mark the professional development of the two men, as artistic producers, and subsequently the space which each has come to inhabit within the literary field sets them apart: as Ibrahim continues to work in the margins, refusing to take up any public occupation other than writing, al-Ghitani consolidates his public career as journalist, becoming editor-in-chief of a widely influential literary weekly within the field. These elements, in addition to the circumstances surrounding the publication of *Sharaf*, give occasion to explore more fully the Bourdieu model that I had suggested would be instrumental in understanding some of the developments in cultural life in Egypt today.

According to Bourdieu, the division of labour within the social space during the modernization process has led to the emergence of subfields of production (*sous-champ de production*) within the social space itself, each with its own history, its own values, its own internal relationships of production and its relative autonomy in face of the field of power (*le champ du pouvoir*). Among these subfields of production Bourdieu identifies the political field, the economic field, the cultural field which, in turn, is constituted of subfields: the scientific field, the artistic field, the philosophical field and the literary field. Each and every one of these subfields is a heterogeneous structure characterized by a set of constitutive objective relations that orient the battles or conflicts that seek to conserve or transform the field.[7] Moreover, the relations of production within each of these subfields can be understood only with reference to the field of power (*le champ du pouvoir*) which, Bourdieu warns, is not to be confounded with the political field (*le champ politique*). The field of power is defined as the space where relationships of power between agents or institutions that own the necessary capital (political, economic, religious) get played out. This dynamism, within the field of power, allows the various owners of capital to occupy dominant positions in the different subfields of production thereby contaminating their values and the relationships of production within them. Hence, all subfields of production are in a dominated or subordinate position to the field of power that for ever controls their degree of autonomy. Autonomy for Bourdieu is not independence: given the existence of the field of power and its dominant position, the autonomy of the subfields is always menaced by its interventions and contamination.

As for the literary field in particular, the focus of our attention here, it acquires relative autonomy with the accumulation, over time, of symbolic capital by several successive generations. This accumulation allows the cultural producers, indeed forces them, to ignore the demands of temporal power for the sake of principles and norms internal to the literary field itself. In other words, those who enter the literary field have every interest to be disinterested.[8] This disinterest is what allows Bourdieu to define the literary field as an economic world in reverse where the fundamental law is internal independence vis-à-vis any external demand outside the field. The economy of praxis in the literary field is based on the inversion of the fundamental principles of the economic world. This inverted economic logic creates the social miracle of "he who loses wins".[9] However, the various positions of the agents within the literary field are always traversed by the values of the field of power, i.e. economic or political profit. Hence there will always be internal conflict, within the field, between two principles: the heteronymous principle (agents that dominate the literary field economically or politically) and the autonomous principle (agents that distance themselves from economic or political profit).[10]

Sharaf Sonallah Ibrahim: he who loses wins

If Bourdieu's model remains somewhat too theoretical, I trust that Gamal al-Ghitani's editorial, significantly entitled "Sharaf Sonʿallah" (Sonallah's

Sharaf/Honour), will, to a great extent, provide an exemplary elucidation of the model.[11] Through its discourse on Ibrahim and its representation of other players in the field, the editorial maps out the relationships of production within the literary field in Egypt, the conflicting and contradictory positions within it, its contamination by various agents from the field of power (both political and economic) while developing, through its very representation of Ibrahim himself, a vision of the ideal literary field, the ideal internal norms and values that should govern it, and its ideal relationship with the field of power.

The very title of the editorial already bespeaks one of the most important attributes of the ideal cultural producer. The word *Sharaf* (honour) in the title of the editorial obviously performs a double role. First, *Sharaf* is a reference to the title of the new novel (also the name of the protagonist, who, like the female protagonist of Ibrahim's previous novel, *Dhat* (self), is gradually emptied of that initial identity). On a second level the word *sharaf* (honour) is an attribute of the author himself: the honour of Sonallah Ibrahim. Those familiar with Ibrahim's *démarche* will take this attribute very seriously and will indeed agree that, as a cultural producer, he is Bourdieu's disinterested ideal, occupying a position of the writer most antagonistic to the field of power, and bearing a hefty badge of honour, a crucial symbolic capital that he diligently accumulated over at least thirty years within the literary field through both his independence from and outspokenness against the field of power. By constructing this attribute as a positive value, however, al-Ghitani, author of the editorial, produces another interesting and crucial effect: recognizing and upholding honour as a value, even when attributed to Ibrahim alone, makes of that value a shared symbolic capital among those who inhabit a similar position within the field. Hence it becomes not only a value bestowed on Ibrahim but one that is upheld by the author of the article himself. Even if the two men are not close friends, even if they meet but on rare occasions, even if their respective writing careers develop in different directions (details which the editorial is keen on noting), their relationship is cemented through this positive and shared value of *sharaf*/honour.

Al-Ghitani's article opens with a return to the mid-1960s, a return to the first moment that earned Ibrahim his badge of honour. The flashback is to *Tilka l-ra'iha* and its eventful publication and immediate banning. The opening of the editorial positions itself at a transformative moment within the autonomy of the literary field in Egypt: "It was clear then that the writer [Ibrahim] was challenging both unwritten and uncharted prohibitions that had settled within the writers themselves in what may be referred to as conventions."[12] In this opening paragraph al-Ghitani reconstructs the internal battles of the field during the mid-1960s. Sonallah Ibrahim and other new agents, among them al-Ghitani himself, were engaged in a battle or conflict not simply with the political authorities, as we have all grown accustomed to represent it, but with other participants within the field itself, other writers who had settled into certain "conventions". It is by reading these lines as a description of a transformative moment that we can reread many of the lashing comments that the writers of the 1960s received at that moment in time. It is only natural therefore for earlier agents within the field, who have acceded to various dominant positions, guardians and propagators of certain symbolic values, to combat the new arrivals, in the following terms:

> This young generation that does not read (Taha Hussein), that does not study (Muhammad Hasanayn Haykal), that does not seek depth (Ahmad Baha al-Din), this generation of bureaucrats that does not know its own classics, nor the classics of others, what will it write?[13]

The dominant symbolic values of the mid-1960s are more than clear as enumerated above: heritage, education, world classics, high culture, etc. The new agents, like Ibrahim, represent the absence/lack or even inverse of those symbolic values. More seriously these new agents seem to bring into the field values that are alien to it: "they" do not know the classics, do not ready, do not study, do not seek depth! The relationship between these two positions was, and had to be, antagonistic, for the literary field is a battle field of forces acting on the participants, in various ways, depending on the position they occupy within it.

When *Tilka l-ra'iha* first appears it is banned by the political authorities for political reasons (Ibrahim's political *not* creative past).[14] However, it is also lashed at from within the literary field itself. The late Yahya Haqqi's well-known attack on the novel makes much more sense when understood as a battle over competing values that tend to conserve (through Haqqi's position) or transform (through Ibrahim's intervention) the literary field.[15] As al-Ghitani notes, Sonallah Ibrahim's work contributes to a change of the dominant language rendering it "neutral" and "devoid of ornamentation or excess". In the editorial, *Tilka l-ra'iha* is deemed "a mark of considerable creative courage" (notice *creative* not political), it marks "the beginning of a new trend in the development of the Arabic novel". However, Haqqi's evaluation of the novel was negative: it is vulgar, foolish, with a flawed sensibility and without taste.[16]

Al-Ghitani's editorial reveals new battles over values within the field today. By providing the reader with a profile of Sonallah Ibrahim, al-Ghitani in effect provides a list of the ideal symbolic values within an ideal literary field and proceeds to pit them against other values, negatively represented within the article. Of Ibrahim al-Ghitani writes:

> Sonallah's career can be summed up in two words: dedication and asceticism. Sonallah's dedication to literature is unparalleled: he has devoted his entire life to literature, abandoning every other work or job that he had occupied. He has lived at a minimal level of subsistence that would ensure persistence.... He applied himself to reading and writing in his small apartment on the sixth floor in Heliopolis ... living with his small family in isolation, rarely appearing in the cultural events that crowd Cairo.[17]

Ibrahim's life, as constructed in this passage, is indeed a direct application of Bourdieu's definition of the literary field as an economic world in reverse: he acquires value within the field by adopting ones that are in direct opposition to those within the economic world. He seeks no material gain, an ascetic who contents himself with a minimal level of subsistence; he lives in a small apartment in Heliopolis on the sixth floor (and may I add with no elevator); he has renounced any form of material occupation or job; he lives in isolation not seeking the spotlights, connections etc. that may enhance his position, all this for the sake of "persistence" (at the level of creative production) and "dedication to literature". In the economic world Sonallah Ibrahim is certainly a loser, but within the literary field, Bourdieu would argue, "he who loses wins". And he is obviously recognized as a winner and is admired, perhaps also envied for this "unparalleled" position. Despite Ibrahim's "isolation", al-Ghitani tells us, "Sonallah is forever sought out by every Arab writer, every Arabist who arrives in Egypt. He receives many invitations to world famous universities and international conferences."[18] This international recognition is directly related to the position Ibrahim occupies within the field, the symbolic value that he has accumulated over thirty years and his awareness as a cultural producer of the necessity of ignoring the demands of temporal power for the sake of principles and norms internal to the field itself. It is Ibrahim's complete disinterestness that brings him so close to the figure of the prophet in Bourdieu's model: as a writer he adopts a similar attitude from the "worldly" and the "profane" (economic or political profit).[19] And indeed, al-Ghitani's further rendition of Ibrahim, on the pages of *Akhbar al-Adab*, envelopes him in the garbs of a prophet:

> During my travels with him I have learned to appreciate his simplicity in everything and his contentment with what is on hand, and what is possible, be that with regard to food or accommodation; I have learned to appreciate his humour and sarcasm despite his visible depression and his hidden grief [due to the general state of the country, the region, and the world at large].[20]

In 1994 both Sonallah Ibrahim and Gamal al-Ghitani were invited to attend a conference on Arabic literature in Tunisia, organized by the UNESCO. The organizers had imposed the presence of an Israeli writer during that event, an act that produced various reactions among the Arab writers present. The editorial is critical of the nature of the positions taken by two Arab writers who had attended and turns to Ibrahim's reaction during the event as a model, once more endowing him with prophetic qualities:

> Sonallah's position was clear and firm, unblemished by any considerations that seek to court a prize, or an authority in France, or a ministry in the United States, or a university in England. Sonallah defended the values of Arab culture and the principles of national identity to which adhering has become a matter of sarcasm for some.[21]

It is obvious here that Ibrahim is constructed as the autonomous writer par excellence. Not only is his life a model of the inverted economic world but it is also one that combats and distances itself from the field of power (*le champ du pouvoir*) in general, a distance that safeguards his symbolic value from the owners of capital: political, economic and cultural. This construction by al-Ghitani of a prophet-like writer, autonomous in every way is "unparalleled", as he himself notes in his editorial. However, the author of the editorial will use this exception to combat other positions and other values, those of "the market and business world", of "traffickers" and "mercenaries" that are "creeping into our literary and cultural life". It is important to recall that al-Ghitani constructs the values and positions within the literary field from the vantage point of *his* position, which, we must be aware, is a very powerful one given his public role as an editor-in-chief of a widely read literary weekly that provides an important forum for various contentious national and intellectual debates. Herein lies the importance of this document and the necessity of understanding all its ramifications, as well as its double discourse.

Al-Ghitani is conscious of both his double discourse and his implied readers: there are those for whom the article addresses general values and ethics (the general readership) and there are others, from within the field, for whom these seemingly general values can be decoded on a far more particular level. Those of us who live in close proximity to the "Triangle of Horror" (*muthallath al-ru'b*) to use Sonallah Ibrahim's description of the dens of Egyptian intellectuals in downtown Cairo: Sulayman Pasha Street, *Zahrat al-Bustan* coffee shop and the Cairo Atelier – had been following a series of debates prior to the appearance of *Sharaf* on the pages of *Akhbar al-Adab*.[22] In order to decode al-Ghitani's double discourse we need to review some of these debates. I will therefore take a moment to explain what might appear to be a missing link in the editorial.

Two important events need to be brought to the fore. In November 1996 Ibrahim Abdel Meguid, author of several important novels and a late comer to the field (even though quite close to al-Ghitani's age bracket – the former was born in 1946, the latter in 1945 – he published his first short stories in the early 1970s) had been invited to the United States to attend the MESA (Middle East Studies Association) Conference. Upon his return Abdel Meguid published an article in the Nasserist paper *Al-Arabi* with the "blasphemous" title "Amrika umm al-dunya" (America Mother of the World) in which he reviewed some of the phenomena that impressed him during his stay in the United States.[23] This was followed, in December, by yet another event that further stigmatized Abdel Meguid: the names of the recipients of the Naguib Mahfouz Literary Award, sponsored by the American University in Cairo, were announced. They were two: the late Latifa al-Zayyat for her 1960 novel *Al-Bab al-maftuh* (*The Open Door*) and Ibrahim Abdel Meguid for his 1991 novel *Al-Balda l-ukhra* (*The Other Place*). The two winners received a symbolic honorarium and their respective works were translated into English, and published by the American University Press. It is perhaps important to note here that the prize received by Abdel Meguid was initially destined to Sonallah Ibrahim who, in perfect keeping with his image, refused it.[24]

32 Inside the literary establishment

For several weeks, I imagine Ibrahim Abdel Meguid did not sleep. His article in *Al-Arabi*, the American University Award and the prospective translation of his work by its press all became a public debate on the pages of *Akhbar al-Adab* in which he was basically portrayed as having dishonoured the literary field by seeking global recognition through the Imperial American cultural machine. This debate culminated in a short reply, by Abdel Meguid, on the pages of the same paper, a piece that sums up both the accusations hailed upon him and his rather timid defence:

> I followed, with attention, what my friend the critic Dr Sayyid al-Bahrawi wrote concerning the Naguib Mahfouz Literary Award sponsored by the American University in Cairo.
> (...)
> Dr Sayyid's second article about the prize suggests that the prize is an indication of dependency, among other things and considers my article that was published in *Al-Arabi* about my trip to America, further confirmation of that. I would like to clarify that my article expressed admiration for some of the characteristics of American life; this does not mean admiration for American policy; both my opinion and position on the latter are known, the article itself includes direct passages that address this issue.
> (...)
> Accepting a prize from the American University does not mean conceding to American politics. After all, the prize does bear the name of Naguib Mahfouz and the university counts many respected Egyptians and other nationals among its faculty, whose patriotic positions are well known.
> (...)
> The title of my article was about freedom, time, public opinion, but the editor in *Al-Arabi* chose the title "Amrika umm al-dunya" [America Mother of the World] perhaps for the sake of sensationalism, not more.
> (...)
> Finally, to move from one trench to another, Dr Sayyid, is not such a simple matter. I wish to assure you that our trench is solid and unshakeable.[25]

Abdel Meguid's defence merits a study all to itself however, this is not the purpose of my chapter. What I would like to draw attention to, in general, is the fact that Abdel Meguid's reply actually introduces (quite hesitantly and timidly) certain values that collide with some of the more generally accepted ones within the field: looking to the other (an Imperial Other), seeking "global" attention (prizes, translations, conferences) etc. In al-Ghitani's representation of the literary field, Abdel Meguid will find himself in close quarters with the other two Arab writers, involved at the UNESCO conference in Tunisia in 1994, whose values (as described by al-Ghitani) seem to be closer to Abdel Meguid's than to Ibrahim's or his own, for that matter. The battle of "us" (nationalist, disinterested, honourable writers) against "them" (globally dependent, unpatriotic, fame and fortune seekers) is relaunched through the disinterested image of Ibrahim:

[Sonallah] receives many invitations to world-famous universities and international conferences, some of which he accepts without ever seeking to promote his image or boast about himself and the recognition he received to the exhausted, worn-out reader, even though Sonallah is well deserving of recognition.
(...)
It [*Sharaf*] is perhaps a hot beginning for 1997, one that confirms the firm stability of beautiful creative values in face of mushrooming phenomena in our literary life that warn of alarming corruption and the widespread fickle and facile values of traffickers (*tuggar shanta*). The same values we have come to know in the market and business world are creeping into our literary and cultural life, but here is not the place to elaborate on this.[26]

When the disinterested writer becomes interested

What happens to the disinterested writer when he decides to become interested? In what does he become interested? And is it all worth his interest? What is the fate that awaits "Sharaf Sonallah", to use al-Ghitani's editorial title? Here I wish to return to the opening of this chapter to examine two crucial points: Ibrahim's motifs in publishing with both *Akhbar al-Adab* and Dar al-Hilal, and the implications of his decision on his position as a disinterested writer.

One of the most crucial elements in Bourdieu's theory concerning the literary field, in particular, is his attention to the economic praxis within the field itself. After having described the literary field as an economic world in reverse he is quick to add:

> this does not mean that there is no economic logic to this economics of charisma that is based on a sort of social miracle...
> (...)
> Within this logic one would have to analyze the relationship between writers or artists and their publishers or their gallerists. These double personas ... must possess essentially contradictory dispositions: economic ones that are for some sectors of the field, quite alien to the producers and intellectual dispositions close enough to those of the producers whose work they can only exploit if they know how to appreciate and endow it with value.[27]

The relationship that had bound Sonallah Ibrahim to his earlier publishers especially perhaps his Egyptian, private publisher Dar al-Mustaqbal al-Arabi was one premised on much of Bourdieu's analysis. I will focus particularly on Dar al-Mustaqbal with whom Ibrahim has had a long history and who actually features in his acknowledgements at the end of the Dar al-Hilal edition of *Sharaf*. In my article "Sonallah Ibrahim's Dhat: The Ultimate Objectification of the Self" I had already tried to suggest the importance of the relationship between author and publisher, noting in my description of their alliance, the centrality of their close intellectual or ideological dispositions:

It is no coincidence that *Dhat*, like *Bayrut Bayrut*, should be published by Dar Al-Mustaqbal al-Arabi (a leftist, Nasserist publisher) and not Dar al-Shuruq for example (an Islamist, commercial, conservative publisher).
(...)
The text opens with the author's list of acknowledgements that ... ends with the names of three lawyers.... This page is followed by the publisher's intervention, which inscribes the essence of the lawyers' guidance and advice.
(...)
[These] interventions point to the position both author and publisher occupy within the literary field.... This is the story of a distinguished professional writer (and perhaps he is the only one we have) who enters into an alliance with one of Egypt's important publishing houses, headed by Muhammad Fayiq, a former Nasser-era minister of information and the man who currently presides over the Human Rights Organization in Egypt.[28]

The risk-taking on both sides of the alliance pays off: not only do author and publisher reap symbolic profit (rave reviews and articles) but, as Bourdieu suggests, they are able to transform this symbolic profit into an economic one (*Dhat* enters into a second edition within six months of releasing the first one).

It is at this high point of his career, at this prophet-like, untouchable position, that Ibrahim is courted by both *Akhbar al-Adab* and Dar al-Hilal, whose positions within the field are certainly contaminated by the field of power. To the great dismay of Dar al-Mustaqbal, Ibrahim enters into a new alliance, a partnership that essentially represents a rupture with the autonomous praxis described by Bourdieu. There are obvious reasons why this alliance of opposites should be possible at this particular historical juncture, reasons that will force us to read the field of power (*le champ du pouvoir*) as being itself a dynamic and heterogeneous structure, like all other subfields of production that it dominates. I will return to this point later on in the chapter.

With the release on the pages of *Akhbar al-Adab* of the first chapters of *Sharaf* all hell broke loose. The few chapters that had been published begin to tell the story of Sharaf (Ashraf Abdel Aziz Sulayman), born in 1974 to a middle-class family whose existence is deformed by the alarming privatization policies and the myth of globalization. Throughout the text Sharaf monologues, dreams and thinks in imported trademarks and designer labels, pitting them against possible local "options" whether that concern food, clothes, gadgets or cigarettes. He is a high-school drop-out and like millions of his generation roams the streets of downtown Cairo, with empty pockets and on an empty stomach, feeding on the glittering world that Cairo boutiques, movie theatres, fast food stands and women (local and foreign) may have to offer the hungry eye. The first chapter is set in downtown Cairo with Sharaf's back ironically turned to the statue of Talaʿat Harb.[29] Sharaf meets John, from Australia, in front of a movie theatre. After Sharaf accepts his invitation to the movie, John takes him home, tries to seduce and attempts to rape him. Struggling to live up to his name, or rather in defence of it, Sharaf murders John and ends up in prison. Sharaf's prison world is a mirror image of the outside world divided into haves and have-nots, with bribes and tips to pay for every meal, and every move he, and others, make in jail. Thus begins Sharaf's journey and *Sharaf*'s problems.

Rumours circulated within the literary milieu to the effect that Sonallah Ibrahim had plagiarized from another work. Soon *Al-Arabi* published a brief article that confirmed the rumours:

> **Writer Fathi Fadl Accuses:** ***Sharaf*** **Sonallah Ibrahim is copied from** ***The Cell***
> Novelist Fathi Fadl is now preparing to sue novelist Sonallah Ibrahim and will appeal to the Writers' Union to strip the latter of his membership.
> (...)
> This has triggered an enormous amount of surprise and disbelief in the literary and cultural milieux given the alleged accusation against a writer of Sonallah Ibrahim's stature. According to Fathi Fadl, the plagiarism concerns the content, setting, timeframe, protagonist, events and characters, besides 42 paragraphs copied, verbatim, from the original novel, *Al-Zinzana* (*The Cell*), without any acknowledgement.[30]

But the question remains, who is Fathi Fadl? Fathi Fadl (owner of a print-shop) was the third party sentenced to eight years' imprisonment in December 1991, along with Alaa Hamid (a virtually unknown writer and author of a novel deemed "blasphemous" by Al-Azhar) and Madbuli (Cairo's most renowned bookstore owner). All three did not serve the eight year sentence since, after massive protest by Egypt's intellectuals, the Presidential decree that would have put the sentence into effect was never signed. However, Fadl still spent 40 days in prison after which he recorded his memoirs of that experience in *Al-Zinzana* (*The Cell*), the alleged "original novel" from which *Sharaf* had been copied.

Despite Sonallah Ibrahim's "stature", he found himself involved in what appeared to be a literary/ethical scandal that quickly took on tabloid dimensions; a scandal very different from that which, 30 years ago, had greeted *Tilka l-ra'iha* and had earned him the badge of honour (*sharaf*), bestowed upon him only two weeks earlier by al-Ghitani, in his editorial. The give and take between plaintive and accused on the pages of several Egyptian papers, together with the rumours circulating in the "Triangle of Horror" not to mention those elaborated beyond such borders (Ibrahim had told me then that *Al Haya al-Jadida*, a Palestinian paper in Ramallah, had published an article claiming that he had offered to publish *Sharaf* with Fadl as co-author!), all this called for a serious investigation of the case.

Wa'il Abd al-Fattah of the *Ruz al-Yusuf* weekly produced a reasonable report entitled: "*Sharaf* Sonʻallah Ibrahim fi *l-Zinzana*" (Sonallah Ibrahim's *Sharaf*/honour in *The Cell*).[31] The badge of honour was now in question; on trial. Ibrahim's very credibility as a writer at all suddenly erupted; his laudatory history, as constructed by al-Ghitani, was transformed into a series of accusations which the *Ruz al-Yusuf* article reports: "He has earned more than what he deserves", "the Egyptian Left made him a star". Evidently, the accusations stabbed exactly where expected: all were directed towards his "unparalleled" position within the field as avant-garde, autonomous and disinterested.

In an interview with Sonallah Ibrahim after the publication of *Sharaf*, I probed him on the reasons why he opted for publication with two state-run outfits. His response was revelatory, in so far as it recognized the field of power as a dynamic, heterogeneous structure that does in turn impact on his autonomous, disinterested position. Ibrahim basically argued (and here I am paraphrasing him) that even if *Akhbar al-Adab* and Dar al-Hilal held heteronymous positions within the literary field they still had within them elements with whom he was willing to collaborate (Gamal al-Ghitani, editor-in-chief of *Akhbar al-Adab*, and Mustafa Nabil, editor-in-chief of the well established *Riwayat al-Hilal*, both of whom solicited Ibrahim's manuscript, both fully aware of the potentially explosive nature of his work and both of whom delivered as promised). However, the existence of such "risk-taking" elements in heteronymous positions within the field is a recent development, immediately related to the newborn alliance between the state and the Egyptian liberals and leftists in its attempt to contain the Islamist position within the social sphere.[32] This is obviously an interesting shift in the field of power: given its own dynamism and heterogeneity, today it is willing not only to recognize some of the values which characterize Ibrahim's position but to actually adopt them itself, through its domination or contamination of the literary field. Al-Ghitani's editorial in *Akhbar al-Adab* therefore at once constructs the values of Ibrahim himself as well as those of the institution that publishes him; a kind of rapprochement of values that is certainly in the interest of the field of power that dominates the literary field. What we may have considered to be contradictory positions all of a sudden come to look alike. But this is just one side of the coin.

In entering this new alliance with state-run institutions, Ibrahim cannot himself escape the lookalike aspect of this new position. As these institutions hope for his values to rub off on them, theirs will inevitably rub off on him. One of the most attractive prospects of Ibrahim's new alliance with *Akhbar al-Adab* and Dar al-Hilal was their market, their distribution and their readership. The former is reputed to publish an estimated 10,000 copies while the latter publishes 5,000 copies and both distribute on a regional level. These figures (whose exact accuracy cannot be ascertained, since both outfits deal with distribution figures as if they were military secrets) cannot be compared to the 3,000 copies that take years to sell with a private publisher. Beyond this, working with both *Akhbar al-Adab* and Dar al-Hilal seemed to provide Ibrahim with both symbolic and economic profit. *Akhbar al-Adab* sells for £E1.50 and can certainly ensure the symbolic profit for *Sharaf* (a series of five chapters that become a kind of sample for a large public). As for the Dar al-Hilal edition, it is sold at £E8.50 (compared to £E1.50 until recently) with 12.5 per cent of the sales to the author. Certainly not a fortune, but an economic profit none the less.

However, all these calculations enforce the rules of the economic world, a world whose values are a direct inverse of the economics of charisma within which Ibrahim's autonomous position had been shaped and consolidated. No longer is this the social miracle of "he who loses wins": rather this new alliance, these new values come to confirm that within the literary field "he who wins loses". As soon as Ibrahim seeks to win the market, adopting its logic and values, he has to succumb to and is also measured by those same values.

Anyone familiar with Ibrahim's work knows that the document, or the docufictional element is an integral part of his work. In fact, it is precisely his original use of documents that has set him apart from all other writers and has earned him his role of "leadership" in developing one of the trends in the modern Arabic novel. Ever since his second work, *Al-Lajna*, 1981 (English translation *The Committee*, 2001), Ibrahim has always relied on external documentary sources that become an integral part of the very structure of his fictional work. *Sharaf*, of course, is no exception. In all instances the author has provided a long list of sources and acknowledgements at the end of each work. His publishers (and this is indeed an important factor) have always diligently reproduced these pages. In the case of *Akhbar al-Adab*, however, the logic of the serial (itself a commercial logic) into which both Ibrahim and the paper are interlocked does not take heed of such ethical or literary considerations that are quite alien to the values of the market (especially an unregulated one as is the case in Egypt). For the first time ever Ibrahim commits an oversight: the chapters, which *do* draw on some of the details in Fathi Fadl's description of his prison experience are published without acknowledgements (even though these appear later in al-Hilal's edition of *Sharaf* with a host of other acknowledgements to a handful of authors and sources).[33] But is it an oversight? Or is it a confirmation of the fact that indeed the praxis of the economic world dominated the entire episode of publication? In either case, the commercial, serial introduction of *Sharaf* in the literary field allowed a quasi-anonymous element (Fathi Fadl) to be identified, in the papers, as a "novelist" (when he is not), on a par with no other than Sonallah Ibrahim himself. In short, Fathi Fadl gains symbolic profit at the expense of Ibrahim's accumulated symbolic capital, and he is quoted as having said, at the peak of the entire episode, "I am living the happiest days of my life." Ibrahim's reaction was equally telling: "I discovered that I have no friends", he said, over the phone, commenting on reactions against him within the literary field.

Dr Ramzi and Mr Sharaf: the ultimate subjectification of the self

The irony is that the novel itself seems to foretell much of the circumstances that surrounded its publication. As I had said earlier, the chapters published in *Akhbar al-Adab* introduced the reader to Sharaf's ordeals in captivity. With the complete Dar al-Hilal edition the readers continued this journey inside Egyptian prisons. We move from the *anbar miri* (military ward), for the have-nots of the prison world, to the *anbar malaki* (regal ward), for the affluent prisoners. Those who are acquitted from the former are those who can afford to pay for the latter. In both wards, the reader is introduced to a phenomenal number of prisoners with crime cases ranging from petty theft, murder, violence, to more serious crimes of corruption at every level: construction, food, medicine, espionage, etc. All of the characters portrayed in the novel are based on documentary material that the author "fictionalizes" and integrates into the larger world of the prison that he creates with amazing detail and ability.

Within captivity Sharaf acquires a narrative voice that will alternate with that of the omniscient presence in narrating the 19 chapters of the novel. The omniscient narrator in *Sharaf* resembles, to a great extent, the satiric presence which puppeteers the characters' lives in *Dhat*. Again like Dhat, Sharaf's voice is contained, constrained, limited and naïve, rendering him a chronic recipient of others' actions, a young man who carries a name too big for him, a premonition that is fulfilled at the end of the novel when he consciously and quietly agrees to shave his body hair in preparation for a same-sex relationship with another prisoner.

After a period of long hardship in the military ward, Sharaf is finally transferred to the regal ward when his mother's short, unwelcome but necessary visits, with her modest, local provisions, allow for such a move. In the regal ward, Sharaf's social and economic stature again places him at a disadvantage. He circulates, within the prison, in a world beyond his means, populated by ambassadors, fat cats, doctors, smugglers etc. He quickly occupies a position similar to that he had occupied outside of the prison: the closest one in the ward to the bucket of urine.

In the regal ward, Sharaf encounters his counterpoint in the novel: Dr Ramzi Butrus Nasif. Dr Ramzi is, on all levels, Sharaf's other. He is of a middle-class Coptic family, a successful graduate of pharmacology, a witness to the grand national dreams of the 1950s and early 1960s, a patriot and Nasserist, despite his father's depressive attitude towards that. He is both cultured and progressive, a successful professional and a critical mind. He is a man of the world, travelling in the Middle East, Europe, Latin America and back; a multinational, corporate executive with an Achilles heel: his ambitions for the Third World, his critique of multinationals and his extreme awareness of the politics of globalization, especially as they impact on Third World economies, societies and general welfare. When he tries to take on the evils of multinationals alone, he is framed by his colleagues, in a fabricated bribery case, and ends up in jail.

Dr Ramzi's character occupies a substantial space in the novel, splitting it down the middle. However, this space will recede when he is placed inside a solitary cell towards the end. A whole section is set apart for the newspaper clippings which he carefully collects and hides in a plastic bag in prison. These clippings represent his continued preoccupation with the corruption in the outside world at both a national and a global level. Eventually, with the collaboration of Sharaf, the prison authorities seize this little treasure along with a lengthy self-defence that Ramzi himself had prepared, in anticipation of his own trial.

The draft of the self-defence is an impressive, encyclopaedic piece of research that Ibrahim weaves from an amazing number of sources and documents all listed and acknowledged in the appendix to the novel. From these documents Ibrahim constructs Ramzi Butrus Nasif's life-account, presented to the reader in another first-person pronoun that becomes a counterpoint to Sharaf's. This self-defence, however, turns into an obsessive dismantling and critique of multinationals and globalization.

From the start, Dr Ramzi has a grain of the saviour about him: as a student he believed in free medicine for all, as a corporate manager he worked against the ideologies and policies of the multinationals that employed him. Even as a prisoner he incessantly advised fellow prisoners on what to eat and what not to. In his sincere mission to enlighten and save, he writes and directs a subversive puppet show for the prisoners. In it he attempts to recanvass all the network of relations that bind the United States with Israel, with the multinationals, with globalization, with corruption, with injustice etc. Ignorant of its contents, the prison authorities allow Dr Ramzi to stage his show in celebration of the 6 October Victory (in the 1973 war against Israel). At the end, the entire event is transformed into a riot. The prison authorities take matters into control, penalize the prisoners and lock up Dr Ramzi in solitary confinement. Dr Ramzi spends the rest of his existence on the pages of the novel yelling proclamations from his solitary confinement to awaken his fellow prisoners and incite them to rebel, to no avail. Ramzi's appeals are met with total disinterest and contempt. *Sharaf* closes with Dr Ramzi alone in his cell, unheeded and unheard as Sharaf stands under the shower, shaving his body hair.

Ibrahim's readers will find themselves quite familiar with Dr Ramzi's character. He is a déjà vu, much like the protagonists in *Tilka l-ra'iha*, *Al-Lajna*, *Najmat Aghustus*, *Bayrut Bayrut* and even *Dhat* (Ibrahim's only female protagonist, who locks herself up in her bathroom and cries, sitting on the toilet seat). They are all the self against the world; the self oppressed, disillusioned, defeated, alone, unheard and crushed. And they all resemble their creator: their idealism, concerns and dreams for a better, more just world echo Ibrahim's own lifetime positions. But who is Sharaf who acquiesces to a same-sex relationship in prison in order to survive when he initially entered prison because he had refused that very idea; Sharaf (honour) who is basically stripped of the signification of his name and identity because he willingly commits an act of (dis)honour? Indeed, Sharaf commits the very act that has for long haunted and obsessed most of Ibrahim's narratives where his protagonists entertain the idea of same-sex "dishonourable" relationships without ever fulfilling the act.

In my earlier reading of *Dhat* I had argued that Ibrahim's use of both an omniscient narrator and a female protagonist, for the first time ever in his novels, had allowed him to achieve "the ultimate objectification of the self". Rather than adopting a first-person narrator who is implicated in the action as he had done so far in all his earlier works, in *Dhat* Ibrahim chooses an omniscient voice that rises above the characters' lives and adopts a distant and sarcastic view allowing him a detached and objective perspective on Dhat (self) and her mediocre world. In *Sharaf*, again for the first time, Ibrahim uses two first-person narrators: Sharaf (too small for his name) and Ramzi (too big for the world); two selves that see, narrate and occupy the world of the prison quite differently. Indeed, the novel pits the two first-person accounts (Dr Ramzi's and Sharaf's) against each other rendering them simultaneously opposite and complementary; two sides of the same coin. Can one now ask: is this doubling of the "I" in the text, with such totally antagonistic positions, a sign of the self, divided? Is *Sharaf*, in contrast to *Dhat*, Ibrahim's novel that represents the ultimate *subjectification* of the self where the author, rather than soaring above his characters' world through the voice of an omniscient narrator, decides to descend into the dark corners of selfhood through two first-person narrators? In other words, do Dr Ramzi and Sharaf represent the two divided sides of Ibrahim himself specifically with regard to the market decisions he made about the publication of *Sharaf*? Can we begin to read Dr Ramzi's position in the text as parallel to Ibrahim's economics of charisma (he who loses wins) and Sharaf's final acquiescence to the act that he had initially so vehemently resisted as parallel to the economics of the market in which Ibrahim found himself entangled? Indeed, the compromising circumstances that surrounded *Sharaf*'s publication in *Akhbar al-Adab* and Dar al-Hilal served Ibrahim as a lesson in the risks of adopting the economics of the market on the one hand, and the virtues of returning to the economics of charisma on the other, leading him to re-cement his partnership with the private, leftist publisher Dar al-Mustqbal al-Arabi.

Finally, beyond Ibrahim as a writer and his conflicted and compromised position within the literary field during that particular juncture, do not Dr Ramzi and Sharaf represent the duplicity of the literary field itself; a field torn between the economics of charisma (disinterest in the economic and political fields) that have secured Sonallah Ibrahim's "unparalleled position" and those of the market that have been so disapprovingly exposed by Gamal al-Ghitani in his attack on the "traffickers" and "mercenaries" who have contaminated the literary field with global market values? Indeed, the reactions to the alleged "plagiarism" scandal surrounding *Sharaf* is a case in point: Ibrahim's "honour" and disinterested position were swiftly smeared by those who envied the much desired but realistically unattainable "prophet-like" autonomy of the writer dragging him down into the increasingly dominant world of the market where most are *dishonoured*, within the literary field, by the economic formula, he who wins loses. Hence, in many ways, *Sharaf* becomes not just the ultimate subjectification of the individual self of the author but also the ultimate subjectification of the Egyptian literary field itself.

2 Children of our alley
The AUC Naguib Mahfouz Award and the Egyptian literary field

In this chapter I will use Naguib Mahfouz's 1959 novel *Awlad haratina* (English translation *Children of Our Alley*, 1996) and its representation of the status of the scribe of the alley as an extended metaphor (the alley as the nation) to look at the literati themselves and the politics and battles that permeate the constrained and globally dependent literary field in Egypt through a reading of the American University in Cairo (AUC) annual Naguib Mahfouz Award over the past 11 years. By focusing on the nature of the battles that erupt yearly after the announcement of the prize, I will explore issues of class and gender, as well as cultural and national belonging that on the one hand circumscribe the literary field and on the other situate it within a global context. As will be seen from the nature of the battles that follow the announcement of the AUC Naguib Mahfouz Award, many of the questions surrounding the ideal literary producer that lay at the heart of Chapter 1 are ones that are intricately linked to these yearly debates as well. I am particularly implicated in this chapter since I currently chair the AUC Naguib Mahfouz Award, a position I have occupied since 2003 after my colleague Ferial Ghazoul of the Department of English and Comparative Literature, who had chaired the committee since the award was established in 1996, stepped down.

The first scribe of the alley

In 1959 Naguib Mahfouz (1911–2006) published his controversial novel *Awlad haratina* in the pages of the Egyptian daily paper *Al-Ahram*.[1] This work represented a clear departure from the historical and realistic modes that dominated Mahfouz's earlier work until the completion of his *Al-Thulathiyya* (*Trilogy*) on the eve of the 1952 revolution in Egypt. *Awlad haratina* came after seven years of literary silence most uncharacteristic of a disciplined and prolific Mahfouz. However, it has been repeatedly argued that this silence was becoming of a writer at the high point of his career, observing a turning point in the social and political reality that he had been depicting through his texts. Not only is *Awlad haratina* an initial marker in Mahfouz's ambitious experimentation with the symbolic mode, but it is also a crucial moment of assessment of his role as a writer after some 30 years of consistent literary production.[2]

42 *Inside the literary establishment*

The story of *Awlad haratina* is told from the point of view of a narrator/writer, himself one of the children of the alley. We first encounter him in the short, but intriguing, opening section of the text. The narrator is the man entrusted, by the alley, to put in writing its rich history. Unlike all the other characters whose stories he tells, the narrator remains nameless throughout. Given the symbolic nature of the entire text, this opening section merits an attentive reading. Indeed, I will argue that the last two paragraphs that close this *iftitahiyya* (preface; literally, opening) represent Mahfouz's reading of his own position as a writer within the literary field in Egypt, one that continues to be relevant, in fact, crucial, for our understanding of the field today, 50 years after this nameless narrator/writer so eloquently described it in *Awlad haratina*. The closing section of the opening chapter reads as follows

> I have witnessed the recent period in the life of our alley, and lived through the events that came about through the coming of Arafa, a dutiful son of our alley. It is thanks to one of Arafa's friends that I am able to record some of the stories of our alley. One day he said to me, "You're one of the few who know how to write so why don't you write down the stories of our alley? They've never been told in the right order, and even then always at the mercy of the storytellers' whims and prejudices; it would be wonderful if you wrote them carefully, all together so that people could benefit from them, and I'll help you out with what you don't know, with inside information."
> (…)
> I was the first in our alley to make a career out of writing, though it has brought me much contempt and mockery. It was my job to write the petitions and complaints of the oppressed and needy. Although many wretched people seek me out, I am barely better off than many of our alley's beggars, though I am privy to so many of the people's secrets and sorrows that I have become a sad and brokenhearted man.
> But – I am not writing about myself or my troubles, which amount to nothing compared with those of our alley – our strange alley with its strange stories![3]

Not only does this passage encapsulate Mahfouz's own position and history within the field but it also defines the very *raison d'être* of the writer within it as the conscience of the nation and the recorder of its collective memory and underground history. As the scribe of the alley, one among the few who can write, and the first to make of writing a profession, the narrator/author in the passage is entrusted with a formidable task: to set down the story of the alley in a trustworthy book in order to counter the storytellers who twist it in their own way. Not only will the narrator/writer supply the written truth about the complaints of the oppressed but, more importantly, he will be aided with inside information and stories of people's secret sorrows, i.e. an underground, unwritten history of the alley. Despite this formidable task however, the scribe of the alley is unable to raise himself above the level of its beggars, and his chosen job as scribe earns him only great scorn, mockery and sarcasm. However, this economic and social under privilege is irrelevant as a concern at the end of the day for the scribe's own troubles are nothing if compared to those of the alley. His material loss is compensated by symbolic gain: his written record is of benefit to the children of his alley.

Almost fifty years later, Mahfouz's opening passage in *Awlad haratina* continues to represent both the material and symbolic position that characterizes our alley's scribes today. This is the *hara* (alley) that the American University in Cairo Press decided to walk into with its Naguib Mahfouz Award.

Celebrating the best scribe of the alley

On 11 December 1996, on the occasion of Naguib Mahfouz's eighty-fifth birthday, the American University in Cairo Press inaugurated the Naguib Mahfouz medal for Literature to "recognize an outstanding contribution to Arabic writing" and to confirm "the AUC Press continuing and expanding commitment to bring the best Arabic literature to the attention of the widest possible English language audience throughout the Middle East, Europe and North America".[4] AUC's commitment to the translation of Arabic works into English is not new: for the past 25 years the AUC Press has contributed quite systematically to the growing number of titles available on the international market before and after the Naguib Mahfouz Award. What is new, however, is the decision to select one work and to declare it publicly, in a highly publicized ceremony, both nationally and regionally, as the *best* Arabic literature. This declaration of merit is further legitimated through the name of the scribe of the alley, the Nobel laureate himself. Even though Mahfouz never attended the ceremony in person, his yearly videotaped messages to the recipients and the audience enforced his position as godfather of the Arabic novel. Further, Mrs Mahfouz's dedicated presence on this occasion, even after his death, certainly confers upon the evening feelings of family and of genealogy. In its endeavour to select the best texts in Arab literature, the AUC Press is aided by a permanent and distinguished panel of judges who represent both AUC and other national universities and whose contribution to the Arab literary field at large is uncontestable.[5]

Despite the award's symbolic monetary compensation ($1,000), the AUC Mahfouz medal has become one of the most coveted in the region. The worldwide, cumulative distribution figures of Mahfouz's works, announced yearly by the Director of the AUC Press (more than one million copies to date), have elicited dreams of fame and fortune from the truly disadvantaged writers of the Arab world who, since Mahfouz's own description of their status in *Awlad haratina*, almost 45 years ago, still have to contend with the alley's scorn and sarcasm. A glaring example of this situation is the award ceremony of the year 1999 that witnessed the very well attended decoration of the "phenomenal al-Kharrat", to use one of the jury's descriptions of the renowned recipient.[6] Edwar al-Kharrat is one of Egypt's most prominent and prolific writers, "a man for all seasons and all generations", "a renaissance man: open to all disciplines and civilizations with solid roots in his own community and culture";[7] his novel *Rama wa l-tinnin* (1980)[8] was awarded the AUC Naguib Mahfouz Prize and was praised for being "a break through in the literary history of modern Arabic fiction".[9] That year, the AUC Press decided to celebrate the award around an elaborate Ramadan *iftar* (fast-breaking meal) since Mahfouz's birthday coincided with the Holy month. After the ceremony, *Al-Ahram al-Arabi* reported sarcastically that Egyptian intellectuals flocked to "the American banquet of the All-Merciful" (*ma'idat al-rahman*, now an established tradition of a free *iftar* provided by the rich, for the poor of Egypt, during Ramadan) much to the embarrassment of their AUC hosts who did not expect this large number of scribes. To make things worse, the yearly guest of honour, the Minister of Culture Faruq Husni, a great *fidel* to the Mahfouz Award ceremony, spent his congratulating word referring to the 75-year-old godfather of the Egyptian avant-garde as Edwar *al-Khayyat* rather than Edwar *al-Kharrat* (not once, not twice, but three times) to the embarrassment and dismay of al-Kharrat's fellow scribes and admirers in attendance.[10]

Not only does the prize bear the name of Naguib Mahfouz, but it also comes with the unique opportunity of immediate translation. Given the unfavourable situation with both private and state publishing, the retreat of the literary product, the near to total absence of readership and the increased number of crises surrounding freedom of expression, this golden promise of translation and worldwide distribution is both economically and symbolically attractive. The one million copies of Mahfouz's works that have been sold worldwide may not sound impressive in global market terms; however, they are astronomical when compared to sales figures in the Arab world, which only in very rare cases exceed five thousand copies. Somaya Ramadan, the 2001 recipient of the medal, succinctly describes this dismal situation in the following terms:

> The creative writer in our societies does not achieve material gain from writing. Some private publishing houses ask the authors to pay for the publication of their work. As for the state-run outlets, writers have to wait their turn that could last for four or five years. After all this hardship, they risk being labelled apostates.[11]

Since its establishment, the AUC award has steadily gained importance, edging closer and closer to the centre of the local literary scene, and has provoked a yearly heated debate. Announcing the name of the winner has systematically become a declaration of war within both the Egyptian and the Arab cultural fields. The AUC Naguib Mahfouz Award has become an important factor in fuelling the schism within Egyptian literary and critical circles and is accused of creating a generation of writers who write with an eye on the west and on translation. Even more contentious is the declared role that the AUC Press has assigned itself in presenting the *best* Arabic literature worldwide, a role that is perceived as a potential "deformation" of the representation of the modern Arab literary field at large.

Moreover, the fact that the Naguib Mahfouz Award is given to one text has generated a host of questions concerning literary merit and aesthetic value. Literary awards in general are of two kinds: ones that are given to a life time achievement (for example: the Nobel, the King Faysal Prize, the Sultan al-Uways Prize,[12] the Egyptian State Merit Prize), and others that are awarded to a single text (for example: the Booker, the Goncourt, the State Encouragement Prize, the Cairo International Book Fair Prize, the Sawiris Literary Award). Whereas the first category is given to established or senior names in the field, the second is generally intended to draw attention to new talents within it. The different nature of the selection process for the two kinds of prizes makes the latter far more controversial, always open to potential contestation. This is the fate of the Naguib Mahfouz Award.

In 1996, AUC's Ferial Ghazoul, Professor of Comparative Literature and former chairperson of the panel of judges of the award, announced that the Naguib Mahfouz medal had an "additional dimension". Not only was it to honour new talents in Arabic literature but it was to acknowledge and make known established writers whose works have not yet been translated into English – a double take that was deemed "intelligent" since acknowledging established writers also meant bestowing legitimacy on this newly established prize within the literary field. Hence, over the years, the Naguib Mahfouz medal has been awarded to established writers as well as recent names in the field, to pioneering texts as well as works of the avant-garde from the entire Arab world. To date, the medal has been awarded to the following writers: in 1996 Ibrahim Abdel Meguid's *Al-Balda al-ukhra* (*The Other Place*) and the late Latifa al-Zayyat's *Al-Bab al-maftuh* (*The Open Door*); in 1997 Mourid Barghouti's *Ra'aytu Ramallah* (*I Saw Ramallah*) and the late Yusuf Idris's *Qissat hubb* (*City of Love and Ashes*); in 1998 Ahlam Mosteghanemi's *Dhakirat al-jasad* (*Memory in the Flesh*); in 1999 Edwar al-Kharrat's *Rama wa t-tinnin* (*Rama and the Dragon*); in 2000 Hoda Barakat's *Harith al-miyah* (*The Tiller of Water*); in 2001 Somaya Ramadan's *Awraq al-narjis* (*Leaves of Narcissus*); in 2002 Bensalem Himmich's *Al-Allama* (*The Polymath*) in 2003 Khairy Shalaby's *Wikalat Atiyya* (*The Lodging House*); in 2004 Alia Mamdouh's *Al-Mahbubat* (*The Loved Ones*); in 2005 Yusuf Abu Rayya's *Laylat urs* (*Wedding Night*); and in 2006 Sahar Khalifeh's *Sura wa ayquna wa ahdun qadim* (*The Image, the Icon, and the Covenant*).[13] A total of 13 recipients: six women, seven men; seven Egyptians (two of whom have received the award posthumously), two Palestinian, one Lebanese, one Algerian, one Moroccan and one Iraqi have been awarded the prize. By honouring one text, the Naguib Mahfouz Award panel of judges not only extended the legitimacy of established writers in the field to the international level but they have taken upon themselves the more risky role of conferring legitimacy on new ones. In other words, AUC has taken on the role of identifying and naming the *best* scribes of the alley. Having walked into this minefield, AUC has consistently found itself subject to the rules of the alley and its few scorn-ridden scribes and has been described as "represent[ing] a reality of its own making".[14] It is thus deemed "a great danger to the Arab novel" and to the "literary field in the Arab World", indeed the "entire Arab future!"[15]

The true scribes of the alley

The initial history of the AUC Mahfouz award remains an unwritten one. The first award was intended for Sonallah Ibrahim, one of the alley's most prominent and "trustworthy" scribes, in recognition of his highly acclaimed novel *Dhat* (*Zaat*).[16] But, Ibrahim, whose unique autonomous position within the field is an exceptional anomaly,[17] and who, as a staunch leftist and nationalist, has always had a problematic relationship with AUC as an American institution in Egypt, discreetly declined the award, arguing politely that it should go to younger and less established talents.[18] This refusal constituted an initial blow to the legitimacy of the award that will conveniently serve yearly debates surrounding succeeding nominations. Even though Ibrahim's discreet refusal represented his personal position towards the American University, it was used by those opposed to the award to represent its "anti-national" nature, thereby stigmatizing the annual recipients. Hence, Ibrahim's refusal of the award became a measure of who the "true" scribes of the alley really are, and allowed for the yearly reprimand of the recipients on national and nationalistic grounds. Indeed, every year a group of the alley's scribes launches a public call to boycott the award that inevitably turns into a war against both the award-conferring institution and the award-winning recipient. Only a few of the recipients have been spared the firing squads, notably the two posthumously decorated pioneers Latifa al-Zayyat and Yusuf Idris whose selection by the AUC judges, given the two writers' historic national stature, was deemed an act of "co-option". These yearly battles have inadvertently exposed the vying scribes and the secrets of their alley.

Indeed, the debate that took place in the aftermath of the announcement of the first Naguib Mahfouz medal in 1996 amply demonstrates the national or nationalistic discourse engendered by the AUC prize. It is important to note that the establishment of the Naguib Mahfouz Award dovetailed with anti-American sentiments that were accentuated by the American-led war against Iraq and the US's unwavering support for Israel. When in its first year the award was split between the novelist Ibrahim Abdel Meguid and the veteran leftist and activist Latifa al-Zayyat, who was decorated posthumously and had never during her lifetime accepted invitations to AUC, much ink was spilled between the attacking and attacked scribes.[19] The campaign against the award was launched by Sayyid al-Bahrawi, Professor of Arabic Literature at Cairo University, and distinguished literary critic, himself both a leftist and activist and a close lifetime friend of the late Latifa al-Zayyat who headed the Committee in Defence of National Culture (opposed to normalization with Israel) of which al-Bahrawi is a member. In an article published by *Akhbar al-Adab*, the literati's widely distributed weekly journal, al-Bahrawi declared that he personally believed that had Latifa al-Zayyat been awarded the prize during her life time she would have refused it. He argued that the name of the American University in Cairo that is attached to the annual award smeared the award, the Arab novel and Arabic literature in general given, as he claimed, the institution's "political agenda and its well-known intelligence role" in Egypt and "its antagonistic position toward Arab national culture".[20] In a clear reference to Sonallah Ibrahim's as yet unpublicized refusal of the prize, al-Bahrawi warned that the AUC was actually "using the name of Naguib Mahfouz" in order to "seduce" the scribes of the alley through the promise of translation that combined both symbolic and material gain and that "even though some have refused this year's award, such an option will not be possible in the coming years given the growing cultural crisis in Egypt and the Arab World".[21] Al-Bahrawi concluded by saying that, given his life time friendship and comradeship with Latifa al-Zayyat, he felt it was his duty to stop the attempt to deform the values that she and her works represented and to resist transforming her into a symbol of values adverse to her own.[22] It is note worthy that Latifa al-Zayyat's *Al-Bab al-maftuh* (*The Open Door*) that won the award is considered a national and feminist classic in modern Arabic literature that was described by the award committee as a "majestic novel" that interwove gender, class and nation where "the question of women's liberation ... is essentially the liberation of the national will".[23]

Needless to say, al-Bahrawi's article, which he followed up with another,[24] generated several responses from both within and outside AUC.[25] In his second article, al-Bahrawi attacked the other recipient Ibrahim Abdel Meguid whose novel *Al Balda al-ukhra* (*The Other Place*) was described by the award committee as the "season of migration to the South", thereby establishing a strong relation between its uniqueness in representing the lives of immigrant workers in the Gulf and that of Tayeb Saleh's classic *Season of Migration to the North*. al-Bahrawi insinuated that Ibrahim Abdel Meguid had been co-opted: on the basis of an article written by the latter upon his return from the US entitled "*Amrika Umm al-dunya*" (America Mother of the World), al-Bahrawi accused Abdel Meguid of becoming a peddler who flirted with the West.[26] Interestingly, Ibrahim Abdel Meguid who was the first to accept the award, despite the stigmatizing taboos that surrounded it, responded to al-Bahrawi by confirming the national or nationalist role of the scribes of the alley and their historic responsibility as the conscience of the nation.[27] Even though Abdel Meguid began his rebuttal on the defensive, he concluded, directly addressing Sayyid al-Bahrawi as a fellow nationalist, with the declaration: "Moving from one trench to the other is not that simple, Dr Bahrawi. Rest assured that our trench is solid and unshakeable", a clear reference to the nationalist values that bind them despite Abdel Meguid's acceptance of the award.[28]

The nationalist mode that was launched by al-Bahrawi against the Naguib Mahfouz Award became central to the annual wars that precede and accompany the announcement of the winner. For example, in the year 2000, the award went to the distinguished Lebanese writer, Hoda Barakat for her novel *Harith al-miyah* (*The Tiller of Water*), which was described as "spellbinding" for its multi-layered narrative, its rich texture and the author's ability to "spin the universe on her narrative loom".[29] That year, a group of the alley's scribes, led

48 *Inside the literary establishment*

by the novelist Salwa Bakr, issued a statement that was released to the press, with the announcement of the winner, calling upon the recipient to boycott the award in solidarity with the Palestinian people in their *intifada* and in protest against Israeli atrocities and American biased policies.[30] Hoda Barakat, who had lived through war torn Beirut and who is incontestably recognized and respected as a major Arab writer, stood firm. The situation backfired on to the attackers when the boycott statement collected only four signatures. Salwa Bakr, who has published with the AUC Press and has actually been invited to teach a course in that institution, retracted on the pages of *Akhbar al-Adab*: "Why should I be jealous of Hoda Barakat?"[31] But, Salwa Bakr's interviewer responded with another relevant question: "Why was there *no* objection to the prize when it was awarded to *Ra'aytu Ramallah* (*I Saw Ramallah*) [by Palestinian poet Mourid Barghouti, 1997] during the peak of the Palestinian *intifada*?"[32]

In 2004, the Iraqi novelist Alia Mamdouh who lives in exile in Paris was awarded the Naguib Mahfouz Prize for her fifth novel *Al-Mahbubat* (*The Loved Ones*). This novel is a deeply moving, polyphonic and symbolic narrative of displacement and nomadism that can be read as a hymn to friendship; a captivating celebration of difference and of bonding. *Al-Mahbubat* tells the story of Suhayla, a comatose middle-aged Iraqi exile, through fragments of conversations, memories and letters pieced together and (re)membered around her sickbed by her son, Nadir, and her women friends. Mamdouh's acceptance speech at the award ceremony visibly moved the audience when she spoke of the plight of the Iraqi people and drove many of the attending scribes, as well as members of the award committee, to tears and was deemed an act of courageous confrontation with "America" on its own grounds – i.e. the American University in Cairo. Grieving over the unburied dead who fill the streets and mosques of Iraq, Mamdouh said:

> No writer has been able to stop wars. That is why I try to catch up with my country, racing it, lest the city should die as I write it.
> (...)
> Iraqi cities are being annihilated as if there is no ethical contradiction between submission to silence and coercion into sullied speech ... Iraq is disappearing before our very eyes. It is as if the American Administration has come to cleanse Iraq of the Iraqis. The barbarism has pushed us all to the limits of our existence.[33]

But, even Alia Mamdouh, who should have represented an ace for the awarding committee given the general anger and horror at the Iraqi tragedy and her established career as an important Arab writer, was not shielded from the nationalist wars of the scribes: she was accused of being a "Ba'thist" and of having left Baghdad for political reasons, charges which she denied publicly in all of the interviews she conducted after the award.

The real significance of these nationalist wars, however, remains that the award recipients are made to fail Mahfouz's model of the scribe: the trustworthy, or selfless son/daughter of the alley, recorder of a collective underground reality whose record is of benefit, not to his or her individual self but to all the children of the alley.

Who's who in the alley

Though it is true that the award ceremony of the Palestinian poet Mourid Barghouti who won the prize for his memoir, *Ra'aytu Ramallah* in 1997 did not meet with the usual nationalist objections levelled every year, it still raised new protests from the scribes who decried the choice of a poet, not a novelist, for the award! Obviously, Barghouti's position within the literary field in Egypt protected him from the usual nationalist accusations: he is one of the most prominent Palestinian poets in exile, with more than ten collections to his name, and is an adopted son of the alley whose literary relationship to Egypt is cemented through his marriage to one of its leading intellectual figures, Radwa Ashour: academic, creative writer, leftist and activist. *Ra'aytu Ramallah* is the memoir of Mourid Barghouti's first homecoming in the 1990s to his city, Ramallah, since the Israeli occupation of the West Bank in 1967. Published in 1997, the memoir won almost instant acclaim for its dense, poetic rendition of Ramallah then and now; as well as its intense and highly moving account of exile, of memories, and of reminiscences. Edward Said's foreword to the English translation by Ahdaf Souief described it as "an important literary event.... One of the finest existential accounts of Palestinian displacement that we now have." The scribes of the alley could not disagree with that, but, literary event or not, they were still dismayed that the award went to an "autobiography" – some called it "travel literature" – by a poet, when the award was, from their perspective, earmarked for a novel. Some said that "Mourid has prove himself as a poet but not as a novelist", and therefore his book "doesn't deserve the prize".[34] In contrast, the award committee described Barghouti's text as a work "which joins elements of autobiography to sophisticated narrative techniques with remarkable aesthetic power"; a work "populated with different types of characters, constituting simultaneously a novel, a personal story and a collective drama".[35] Nevertheless, the distinguished Palestinian poet Mourid al-Barghouti was seen as an intruder into an alley that was already overpopulated with unrecognized scribes.

Tellingly, the quietest year of the AUC Naguib Mahfouz Award was 2002 when the prize went to the Moroccan Bensalem Himmich for his novel *Al-Allama (The Polymath)*, which recast the life of Ibn Khaldun, the Arab philosopher of history, into fictional form. The quiet that surrounded the AUC annual ceremony had to do more with the alley's conceited indifference than with its customary objections. The scribes' remarkable calm on that occasion encapsulated, with the exception of a handful of well-known literary figures from North Africa, the historic imbalance in the relationship between the literati of the *maghrib* (Morocco, Tunisia, Algeria, Lybia), and those of the *mashriq* (from Egypt to the Gulf). Egypt's historic position as the cultural heart of the Arab world together with North Africa's colonial past have always allowed the scribes of the *mashriq* to claim a leading role in Arabic letters, and to relegate the accomplishments of the *maghrib* to the margin. In addition to this general historic situation, Bensalem Himmich is not really just a scribe. Both his symbolic and material position set him apart from the scribes of the alley as represented by Naguib Mahfouz in *Awlad haratina*: Himmich is a scholar of Ibn Khaldun with a doctoral degree on the medieval period in the Maghreb from the Sorbonne in France. He is currently Professor of Philosophy at Mohamed V University in Rabat, a consultant of the Moroccan Academy and the vice-president of the Writers' Union. Surely not the same profile of many of the Egyptian scribes who attended AUC's *ma'idat al-rahman* (the banquet of the All Merciful) during Ramadan 1997 on the occasion of Edwar al-Kharrat's decoration. Hence, given both the historic past and the individual profile, the scribes of the alley felt unthreatened by Himmich's sudden appearance on the scene. Indeed, after the ceremony, *Al-Ahram Weekly* reported that "This year ... reactions have been subdued: perhaps the award has taken observers by surprise as many in Cairo are not quite up to date with *maghribi* literature".[36] It was therefore not surprising that Bensalem Himmich was congratulated several times during the ceremony as "Salem Benhimmich" by the attending representative of Egypt's Minister of Culture.

The prodigal daughters of the alley

The most ruthless yearly attacks were reserved for the Algerian Ahlam Mosteghanemi and the Egyptian Somaya Ramadan, the most recent arrivals among the children of the alley whose rites of passage expose not only the sexual/textual battles among the scribes but their class and nationalist defences as well. Whereas Mosteghanemi's bestselling first novel *Dhakirat al-jasad* (*Memory in the Flesh*) was described as belonging to "the popular literature of Mexican soap operas",[37] Ramadan's initially well-received *Awraq al-narjis* (*Leaves of Narcissus*) was deemed, upon its nomination to the award, a "national disaster", the "death certificate of [Mahfouz's] prize!"[38] Mosteghanemi was accused of "falsifying history" by selling herself on the jacket of the book as the first Algerian woman to write in Arabic,[39] while Ramadan was accused of writing an "anti-Nasser", "anti-national" text.[40] Mosteghanemi's style was deemed melodramatic and laden with antiquated clichés,[41] while Ramadan's text was labelled "beginner's literature" replete with "grammatical mistakes" that massacre our "beautiful Arabic language".[42] Both were ostracized for their absences from the alley: Mosteghanemi was made to pay for her life in exile away from Algeria, between France and Beirut; Ramadan for her years of study in Ireland. The former sold "the cause" for "a materially comfortable marriage" away from the Algerian tragedy;[43] the latter belonged to the "aristocracy", well known for its "collaboration with colonialism".[44] As women writers, decorated for their first novels, both Mosteghanemi and Ramadan were stripped of the very ability to write. The success of their first works was explicated through baseless and vicious allegations about their personal relations with established male figures in the field. On the one hand, questions were raised around the "illicit genealogy" of Mosteghanemi's novel strongly suggesting that the text (and by implication its author) bore the intimate mark (both textual and sexual) of the Lebanese poet Nizar Qabbani and/or the Iraqi poet Saʻdi Yusuf.[45] On the other hand, Ramadan's pre-award positive reception was explicated not by the beauty of the text but by the beauty of the author![46] To discredit them altogether Mosteghanemi was judged to be "conceited", full of her self-image and thankless to those who encouraged her,[47] and Ramadan was deemed "trivial", a writer whose "only access to Egyptian reality came from television".[48] By juxtaposing the two cases against each other, despite the three years that separated their awards, the strategies of rejection, especially with regard to recent women's writing, become glaringly apparent.[49]

It is note worthy, however, that such literary assassination was not directed against Hoda Barakat, who had also received the Naguib Mahfouz Award. The difference between Barakat's award (2000) and both Mosteghanemi's (1998) and Ramadan's (2001) is that Hoda Barakart had already established herself in the field on both a literary and nationalistic level: she had two widely acclaimed novels to her name while in the case of Mosteghanemi and Ramadan theirs were the first novels in their career as writers, and she was a survivor of the Lebanese civil war which she witnessed first hand. Equally instructive is the fact that both works had already been in circulation prior to the Naguib Mahfouz Award and had been received very positively by the critical establishment. In Mosteghanemi's case, *Dhakirat al-jasad* had already gone through several reprints since it was first published in 1993; Somaya Ramadan's *Awraq al-narjis* had also received a considerable amount of enthusiastic attention in Cairo's cultural circles during more than one roundtable discussion. Mosteghanemi and Ramadan were welcome as newcomers but certainly not as decorated descendants of *the* scribe of the alley, whose works, as AUC chose to phrase it, represent the *best* of modern Arabic literature.

The post-award antagonism to which both women writers were subjected despite the three years that separated their respective decoration, may also be read as an objection to the hybrid profile they share. If Mourid Barghouti was seen as an intruder by genre, Mosteghanemi and Ramadan were seen as intruders by culture. Both women are products of colonial language school systems and have subsequently earned Ph.D. degrees abroad: Mosteghanemi has a Ph.D. in sociology from the Sorbonne in France and Ramadan a Ph.D. in literature from Trinity College in Ireland. It was therefore not a coincidence that the same charge was levelled against them: they do not know how to write in their own language, for one uses "clichés" and the other makes "grammatical mistakes". For their peers, the years the two women writers spent away from the alley disqualified them from fulfilling the most important role of the scribe: that of the underground historian of the alley's secret stories and sorrows. This in spite of the award committee's judgement that Mosteghanemi's novel was "able to represent five decades of Algerian history, from the 1940s through the 1980s, as they interweave through the characters' trajectories and memories", embodied convincingly "through a male voice who constructs this extraordinary tale of passion",[50]

52 *Inside the literary establishment*

and their assessment that *Awraq al-narjis* by Somaya Ramadan was "like the accounts of Tawfik al-Hakim, Taha Hussein, and Tayeb Saleh ... about a young Arab [woman] student going West in search of education"; a captivating novel that "displays rare virtuosity in evoking and interlacing literary motifs".[51]

It is instructive to compare the negative reception of Mosteghanemi and Ramadan to the overwhelmingly positive one that greeted another hybrid: Ahdaf Souief and her first novel *In the Eye of the Sun*. Souief, who lives in England and writes in English, was reclaimed by the scribes of the alley, upon the international success of her first novel, as one of them. Indeed, *In the Eye of the Sun* was described by Sonallah Ibrahim himself as "*The* Great Arab Novel". There is no denying that Souief's *In the Eye of the Sun* is a masterpiece, but at the same time, from the point of view of the embattled scribes, it also represented a dream come true: an Egyptian writer, besides Naguib Mahfouz, who has become part of "the international republic of letters". This attitude was further confirmed when Ahdaf Souief's second novel, *The Map of Love*, did not receive the Booker Prize for which it was short-listed. On that occasion, the literati's journal, *Akhbar al-Adab*, accused the Booker jury of prejudice, declaring that even though the jury denied Souief the Booker Prize, for them the Egyptian literati she was still the real winner.[52]

The sages of the alley

In 1999, the Naguib Mahfouz Award went to *Rama wa l-tinnin* (*Rama and the Dragon*) by Edwar al-Kharrat, the most decorated Arab writer with the exception of Mahfouz himself. Not only have several of al-Kharrat's works been translated into several languages, but he is also regularly invited to speak and write about modern Arabic literature abroad, and he had already been awarded several prestigious prizes: the State Merit Prize (1972), the Arab French Friendship Prize (1991), the Sultan al-Uways Prize (1996), and the Cavafy Prize (1998). Just as Mahfouz is considered the father of realism in modern Arabic fiction so is al-Kharrat regarded as the father of the "new sensibility" in modern Arab letters. Indeed in his acceptance speech al-Kharrat made sure to foreground the centrality of the "new sensibility" in modern Arabic literature:

> I consider this prize [the Naguib Mahfouz Award], which I hold in great esteem and for which I have the utmost respect, a certificate of merit for the new sensibility in Arabic writing ... one which invents its own laws ... seeks new knowledge, and, through questioning, acquires its own aesthetic values.... Such, I believe, is the case with *Rama wa l-tinnin*.[53]

But such celebration of the "new sensibility" of which Edwar al-Kharrat is both a pioneer and a shepherd, earned him the scorn of some fellow scribes who argued that his very acceptance of the Naguib Mahfouz Award, whose work is generally seen as more conventional than al-Kharrat's, if not in direct opposition to it, was an act of reneging on the latter's own life time literary convictions.

Moreover, attackers argued that al-Kharrat had already received his share of fame and fortune and should not have been selected for this symbolic prize; may "someone else receive some attention", argued the scribes.[54]

Indeed, during Edwar al-Kharrat's ceremony, the name of "someone else" was whispered widely between the scribes; that of the other forgotten sage of the alley: Khairy Shalaby, veteran writer, with at least twenty novels to his name, none of which had been translated into English and who, despite his prolific and widely appreciated contribution to the secret stories and sorrows of the alley, remained on the margin of literary stardom. The alley's scribes took issue with the judges' choices of the works selected for translation for, from their point of view, they reflected global rather than local literary genealogies, pointing specifically to Edwar al-Kharrat's avant-guardist "new sensibility" (which in terms of local sales did not fare so well)[55] in comparison to Shalaby's more popular and populist storytelling. Indeed, Khairy Shalaby's novel, *Wikalat Atiyya* (*The Lodging House*), had won unanimous praise from his fellow scribes when it first appeared in 1992, confirming his role as an underground historian of the alley. *Wikalat Atiyya* escorts the reader on an underworld journey of epic dimension: an underground city, the home of the town's marginal and underprivileged characters whose lives immerse us in the myths, logic and language of the popular imaginary. Like most of Shalaby's works, *Wikalat Atiyya* chronicles an unwritten history and contributes to the alley's repertoire of tales about the marginalized, the oppressed and the disadvantaged. In 2003 *Wikalat Atiyya* received the Naguib Mahfouz Award and was celebrated as "the gem that crowns Khairy Shalaby's long and prolific history as one of Egypt's most distinguished storytellers".[56] Shalaby expressed his joy at being decorated after such a long career as a writer in the following terms:

> This award has come to me. I did not seek it. It is a badge of honour inscribed with the name of Naguib Mahfouz like a precious stone, bearing the scent of his noble, humanistic spirit.
> (…)
> Today I can finally celebrate the wedding night of my preferred daughter, my novel *Wikalat Atiyya*, after thirteen years of waiting for a long lost lover, waiting with love and with certainty for his blissful arrival.[57]

These exaggerated words of joy came from the very same Khairy Shalaby who, when asked, only two years earlier, what he thought of the AUC Naguib Mahfouz Award had said sarcastically and condescendingly, referring to the previous recipients: "I reckon that its value lies in the happiness of the *children* who are awarded it"[58] (my emphasis).

The "*futuwwa(s)*" of the alley

But the onslaught does not stop at the recipients of the Mahfouz award. Members of the awarding committee have also come under increasing shelling over the years. Their role, in the scribes' minds, has come to resemble that of the *futuwwa* (the thug, the boss, the authority, the bouncer) in Mahfouz's alley. Like the *futuwwa* in *Awlad haratina*, the panel of judges of the Naguib Mahfouz Award is accused of unjust and unequal distribution of the *waqf* (estate) among the children of the alley. The lexicon that is used repeatedly in the attack on the AUC judges is telling of the extent to which they are perceived as an illegitimate authority that exercises its power to the detriment of the welfare of the alley. In one instance, the judges are accused of selecting works below standard that do not reflect the literati's choices for that literary season;[59] in another, they are made responsible for deforming Arabic literature at the global level where international readers will stop reading things Arabic because, given the choices the judges make for English translation, Arabic literature will be seen as "a beginner's literature" with names of major writers such as Muhammad al-Bisati, Ibrahim Aslan, Bahaa Taher, Khairy Shalaby (who had not yet been awarded the prize), Muhammad Mustagab etc. absent from the list.[60]

In addition, there have been calls for "transparency" in the selection process, as well as accusations of "ineptitude" and "clientalism". Demands have been made for the change of the panel of judges in order to ensure the representation of the alley's "indigenous" aesthetic values not those of hegemonic cultural institutions. In face of these repeated allegations and accusations the judges have responded:

> Literature has nothing to do with age. Sometimes one text by a recent author is much better than twenty by an established writer. We do not consider the cumulative output of a writer (...). Since the importance of the prize stems from the translation of the work into English, the judges steer away, as much as possible from writers whose works have already been translated into English.[61]

Translating the alley

It is precisely because the Naguib Mahfouz Award guarantees translation into English that it has become the target of the scribes' attention and contempt. Despite its symbolic material value, it is the only prize in Egypt and in the region at large that comes with the promise of translation and, in the scribes' minds, also guarantees them a space in the international republic of letters where their participation continues to be highly underrepresented, misrepresented or, at best, simply constrained.[62] Indeed, the scribes' ambition to accede to the international republic of letters and to emerge from a nationally dependent and globally marginalized literary field like Egypt's can be a way for the scribes to acquire a new role: not just that of the conscience of the nation but that of a new conscience of the globe which, given the geo-political economy of translation, has seldom occasion to hear their voice. For, as Lawrence Venuti cautiously envisaged in "Translation, Community, Utopia":

A translation becomes the site of unexpected groupings, fostering communities of readers who would otherwise be separated by cultural differences and social divisions yet are now joined by a common fascination ... a translation can also create a community that includes foreign intelligibilities and interests, an understanding in common with another culture, another tradition.[63]

Ideally, then, translation can enable cross-cultural imagined communities. Such a positive role for translation seems to be especially urgent in the context of the Arab region where it can unsettle and question dominant global misrepresentations. Just as the scribes of the alley take seriously their nationalist role as the conscience of the alley or nation even though they remain "barely better off than many of [the] alley's beggars", so do they aspire to become part of the global translation market where they can, and at times have, established new symbolic solidarities.

Moreover, the symbolic global capital acquired by the scribes through translation is compounded by the new material opportunities that the international republic of letters has to offer. For the global market and readership, even if minimal for Arabic literature in translation, remains a far more desirable and profitable one at the economic level when compared to the local conditions of literary production and consumption. It is perhaps precisely for these reasons that, even though Sonallah Ibrahim had declined the Naguib Mahfouz Award when it was first established, he still signed a contract with the AUC press for the translation of his novel *Dhat* (*Zaat*), which was initially the first candidate for the prize, a position which testifies to his understanding of the importance of translation and his awareness of the limited venues available to Arab writers (both symbolic and material) in the international republic of letters no matter how autonomous and established they are. Indeed, in a presentation at the Cairo International Book Fair, Mark Linz, the director of the AUC Press, announced some very disheartening statistics in this regard:

> Translations represent only 10% of the world's annual new publications, but of the 50,000 translations published annually less than 1% come from the Arab world and only a few dozen important literary works are translated from the Arabic every year.[64]

What seems to emerge as the core of the problem from these global figures as well as the actual political, material and symbolic position of the scribes of the alley is the extent to which the Egyptian literary field is dominated both locally and globally. Indeed, this situation places the scribes of the alley in a double bind. Because the Egyptian literary field is dominated locally, the scribes are bound to seek recognition (both material and symbolic) in the global village or international republic of letters. At the same time, given their self-appointed role as the conscience of the alley or nation and representatives of the collective rather than individual good, they are bound to define themselves despite their global dreams on a national or nationalist level. This double bind is simply irresolvable so long as the literary field remains dominated both locally and globally.

Furthermore, given the hegemonic relationship between the global north and the global south, the idea that translation can create cross-cultural imagined communities remains a utopia that has yet to exist. In reviewing the politics of translation and reception of Arabic literature in the West, several scholars, including Richard Jacquemond, Amal Amireh and Magda al-Nowaihi, have come to the conclusion that, rather than facilitating cross-cultural imaginings, translation, in many instances, and with the best possible intentions, has in fact, depending on the context of reception, entrenched cultures in already fixed positions and has come to justify dominant misrepresentations and misperceptions.[65] Hence the scribes' aspiration to accede to the international republic of letters may not always help realize the utopian dream of cross-cultural imagined communities. On the contrary, it may in fact contribute further to their difference and their otherness.

All these local and global factors confirm that the mechanisms involved in translating the alley and "distributing the *waqf*" do not simply lie with the *futuwwa* (i.e. the Naguib Mahfouz awarding committee and institution) but lie in a global context over which the *futuwwa* may have no control. Even though the awarding committee is charged with selecting the "best" of Arabic literature, it has no control over the reception of these works in the international republic of letters. Indeed, the awarding committee's selections, if looked at from the global reception perspective, may not be the "best" after all. The mind-boggling and overwhelming global success of Alaa al-Aswany's *Imarat Ya'qubyan* (*The Yacoubian Building*), which was not nominated for the Naguib Mahfouz Award but has become a bestseller in the Arabic original as well as in its English, French, Italian and other translations (selling close to 200,000 copies worldwide) is a case in point. Within the Egyptian literary field, al-Aswany, a dentist by profession, is perceived as a writer of "popular" and not avant-garde fiction; his first novel, *Imarat Ya'qubyan* is considered "scandal literature" that appeals to the literate masses but not the literary elite.[66] Nevertheless, al-Aswany's novel has been globally received as a "chef-d'oeuvre du roman arabe contemporain" (a classic of contemporary Arabic literature), a veritable heir to Naguib Mahfouz's realistic works of the 1940s and 1950s.[67] Much to the veteran scribes' dismay, al-Aswany's spectacular success came to confirm that the way into the international republic of letters may depend not on the scribes' local status in the alley but rather on the global village and what *it* deems to be a "classic". Indeed, the comparison between Sonallah Ibrahim's *Dhat* and Alaa al-Aswany's *Imarat Ya'qubyan* is an instructive one: both writers deal with more or less the same period (the latter half of the twentieth century) and both vehemently expose and critique the multiple levels of corruption and decadence in Egyptian society since the 1960s. Sonallah Ibrahim's chef d'oeuvre *Dhat* is actually the most successful of his works in translation. However, its sales figures (upward of 15,000 copies in the French translation which, with the exception of Naguib Mahfouz, is extraordinary for Arabic literature in translation) remain minuscule when compared to *Imarat Ya'qubyan*, which dominated the best seller charts in France for several months with more than 130,000 copies sold. One way of explaining the stunning success of a novice like al-Aswany over a veteran scribe like Sonallah Ibrahim is the mode in which each text is written: *Dhat* belongs to an avant-garde tradition of experimental fiction that requires, in fact demands, the active creative participation of its readers while *Imarat Ya'qubyan* navigates within the boundaries of classical realism that appeals to a much wider spectrum of uninitiated readers in the global village.

As long as the dominated position of the Egyptian cultural field both locally and globally (within the international republic of letters) persists, the scribes of the alley will continue their yearly battles. So, like Naguib Mahfouz's narrator/writer in *Awalad haratina*, one can only record "the heart-breaking knowledge of many [scribes'] secret sorrows", wait for the announcement of next year's winner and brace oneself for yet another battle between the scorn-ridden scribes. As Mahfouz would have said: "Amazing little alley with amazing events."

3 The big one
The intellectual and the political in modern Egyptian literature

This chapter will trace the development of the relationship between the intellectual and the political fields in Egypt since the post-1960s through their representation in Egyptian literary texts from the 1960s to the present. I will focus specifically on two examples: *Al-Zayni Barakat* by Gamal al-Ghitani[1] and *Maqtal al-rajul al-kabir* (*The Assassination of the Big Man*) by Ibrahim Issa.[2] Whereas *Al-Zayni* is written very early on in al-Ghitani's appearance within the literary field, *Maqtal al-rajul al-kabir* is written after some 15 years in Ibrahim Issa's career as a journalist and creative writer. Hence, not only do the texts reflect different historical junctures between the intellectual and the political in Egypt but they equally bespeak the respective experiences of the two writers as actors within the literary field, as well as their understanding of their relationship with the political one.

While *Al-Zayni* is today considered one of the landmarks of the 1960s, *Maqtal al-rajul al-kabir* is more of an underground text that continues to be circulated and read within the Egyptian literary milieu. Despite the difference in subgenre, one that this chapter will situate within a political context (*Al-Zayni* being a historical allegory that deals with the present by casting it in the past, while *Maqtal al-rajul al-kabir* is a satirical political thriller that immerses the reader in the details of current local and global politics) between them, these two texts map out some 30 years of the relationship that binds the intellectual field to the political power structure in the country. At the heart of this relationship, as depicted in the texts, is the contest over knowledge and truth: both sought by the intellectual and masked and/or mystified by the political apparatus. Both texts present the reader with substantially different understandings and hence representations of a "Big One": a political power against which the figure of the intellectual in the text is juxtaposed. The very nature, manifestations and workings of this Big One will be analysed, moving from the all-powerful, all-oppressive, self-contained police state of the 1960s, to a weakened, transparent and more globally dependent one in the 1990s.

Al-Zayni Barakat re-visited

It is perhaps important to say that my reading of *Al-Zayni Barakat* in this chapter constitutes a revisitation of a text that lay at the heart of my graduate work in the early 1980s: a moment that represented the auspicious beginnings of Gamal al-Ghitani's career. It marked his ascent from the underworld of the literary field to the position of a major actor in the generation of the 1960s that today dominates the key literary and cultural positions and institutions of the 1990s. The early 1980s equally represented al-Ghitani's growing affiliations with the field of power: it is during the early 1980s that al-Ghitani becomes an established journalist in the daily *Al-Akhbar*, responsible for its weekly literary pages that have paved the way to his much coveted position as editor-in-chief of *Akhbar al-Adab*, the most widely distributed literary review in the Arab world today. This turning point in al-Ghitani's position within the literary field coincided with my own entry into it. My understanding and reading of the text then was shaped by these important elements.

Today, however, my re-visitation of *Al-Zayni* is informed by Richard Jacquemond's reading of the same work in the late 1990s in his Ph.D. dissertation *Le champ littéraire égyptien depuis 1967*,[3] a reading that coincided with al-Ghitani's consolidation of his position within the field of power to the detriment of his position within the literary one. Even though both readings understand *Al-Zayni* as a kind of "*education sentimentale*" of the author, Jacquemond's reading, unlike my much earlier one, introduces a prophetic dimension to the text that was simply absent 20 years ago when al-Ghitani's career and relationship to both the literary and political fields was still in the making. Jacquemond explains the "miracle" of *Al-Zayni Barakat*, the "chef-d'oeuvre" written by a mere beginner at the age of 25, by reading it *à la* Bourdieu in his study of Flaubert's career, *Les règles de l'art*, i.e. as a "lucid instance of the 'objectification of the self' that not only explains the past trajectory of its author but further announces, with exactitude, the turn it will take in the future".[4] This prophetic element constitutes a crucial moment in my rereading of the representation of the political field within the novel as well as the various roles of the actors in the text, specifically that of the young protagonist Sa'id al-Juhayni.

Published in Damascus in 1974, Gamal al-Ghitani's *Al-Zayni Barakat* parodies the Egyptian police state of the 1960s through the representation of Mamluk Egypt in the sixteenth century, a strategy that is both legitimate and effective in bypassing censorship or direct confrontation with the political field of the 1960s. It is set on the eve of the Ottoman invasion of Egypt and draws upon Ibn Iyas's sixteenth-century chronicle of that same moment in history, *Bada'i' al-zuhur fi waka'i' al-umur*, not only for the archaisms of the language and the docu-fictional forms it uses but also for its central and enigmatic character, the absent/present in the novel, Al-Zayni Barakat himself, the *muhtasib* (supervisor of trade and prices) of Cairo who in both the medieval chronicle and al-Ghitani's modern novel remains a controversial character. As many critics have already pointed out, and as al-Ghitani himself confirmed, there exists an analogy between the medieval police state that we read about in *Al-Zayni* and the modern Egyptian one. The factors that contributed to the Ottoman invasion in 1517 and the Egyptian defeat in 1967 were not dissimilar. We know that the historian

60 *Inside the literary establishment*

Ibn Iyas was very critical of the Sultan and his corrupt administration and held them responsible for the defeat. In both cases (the medieval and the modern Egyptian states) we have administrations that failed to live up to their images. And in both cases we have regimes that tried to mask the reality of defeat from the people for as long as possible.

Even though the novel traces the emergence of Al-Zayni, his rise to power and his success at remaining in power after the fall of the Mamluks and the advent of the Ottomans, it does so without him ever appearing in the text. Al-Zayni consolidates his power through an alliance with Zakariyya ibn Radi, the supreme *shihab* (chief of the police and spy force). Saʿid al-Juhayni is the young student of Al-Azhar who is initially infatuated by Al-Zayni and is ultimately manipulated and destroyed by the alliance between the controversial *muhtasib* and the supreme *shihab*. In painting Saʿid al-Juhayni as the young upcoming intellectual in the text, al-Ghitani infuses him with key autobiographical elements that bring him unmistakably close to the author himself. Like al-Ghitani, Saʿid is a *Saʿidi* (Upper Egyptian) from the village of Juhayna (al-Ghitani's own village). He is of modest background but is a potential social climber who is intent on transcending his marginal position through both the cultural (namely Al-Azhar and his close relationship with Sheikh Abu l-Saʿud whose daughter he is secretly in love with) and possibly through a naive belief in the political (an initial support for and belief in the *muhtasib*, Al-Zayni Barakat ibn Musa).

This portrait of the young man in the novel is a mirror of that of the young author in his twenties as an "apprentice intellectual". Owing to the family's limited financial means, al-Ghitani was forced to abandon dreams of a university degree and worked as an apprentice carpet designer in order to support his siblings. However, he was able to transcend this marginal position through creative writing. The publication of his first collection of short stories, *Awraq shabb asha mundhu alf am* (1969), earned him immediate recognition within the cultural field and a permanent, even though modest, position in the daily *Al-Akhbar*. Further, Saʿid's relationship with Al-Zayni is not unlike al-Ghitani's own initial naive relationship with the late Egyptian president, Gamal Abdel Nasser: a relationship of infatuation and support that is later transformed into disillusionment and compromise. As it turns out, in both cases, that of the young character, Saʿid, and that of the young author, al-Ghitani, it is the political field that will determine their respective relationship to and position within the cultural one.

In the beginning Saʿid divides the world between the good (Al-Zayni) and the bad (Zakariyya, the supreme *shihab*). As the text progresses, and with the reoccurrence of controversies surrounding Al-Zayni, this clear-cut understanding of the world collapses. When Saʿid's suspicion of Al-Zayni's manipulative intentions are confirmed, when he finally knows "the truth" and dares to utter it in the text, confronting Al-Zayni at a public appearance in a mosque and calling him a liar, he is arrested by Al-Zayni's guards and is surrendered to Zakariyya who imprisons, tortures and co-opts him. Zakariyya's agenda is unambiguously stated towards the end of the text: "the step by which a man crosses our threshold should be a clear line of demarcation separating two eras. That moment should divide a man's life into two parts in such a way that the man comes out of here, bearing the same name, but, in reality, a different person."⁵ Indeed, when two years later Saʿid is finally released, he becomes that different person: a collaborator, employed by Zakariyya to spy on his own spiritual mentor, Sheikh Abu al-Saʿud, a radical outspoken critic of Al-Zayni:

> We know, Saʿid that you wish to see your mentor. This is your right, of course. And need I remind you "He who taught me one letter makes me his slave"? You said his name several times in your sleep ... Go to him. Don't be afraid. On the contrary, we want you to resume your relationship with him exactly as it was before. We want you to enjoy his confidence. Don't alienate him. Go to him, prostrate yourself at his feet. Cry. Shed real tears. He will ask you, "Where have you been since your return?" Tell him, "They forbade me, but I don't care about that anymore. I have disobeyed them and come to you." Curse us, Curse our grandfathers! Pray to God to ruin us! Say whatever you want, Saʿid. You must revive his confidence in you.... We know you can do it. Otherwise, we wouldn't have come to you. We are asking for your help, Said. You are close to us; you are one of us. You are ours. You are one of us. You are ours.⁶

Indeed, Saʿid's anguished monologues and reflections at the end of the text mark the beginning of a new era: "Oh, there is no turning back."⁷ "Aaah, they have made me rot, they have destroyed my forts."⁸

Like Saʿid, al-Ghitani was detained in October 1966 by the same regime he had supported, during a purge against the "pro-Chinese" communists. He was released from the Citadel prison in March 1967 upon the intervention of Jean Paul Sartre and Simone de Beauvoir. *Al-Zayni Barakat* represents the fictionalized narrative of that experience and announces, through Saʿid's final lines in the novel, the beginning of a new era for the young author himself. Again, like Saʿid, al-Ghitani acquires a new understanding of the political field that will redefine his relationship to it. This is perhaps the decisive moment in his career that will gradually change his position within the literary field from that of the apprentice intellectual (who divides the world into the good and the bad) to becoming, as Jacquemond succinctly puts it, the "intellocrat" whose position within the literary field is contaminated by his relationship with the political one.⁹

Al Ghitani's representation of the field of power in his novel *Al-Zayni Barakat* is further manifestation of his own "apprentice" position in relation to that field. All the narrative strategies and techniques he uses reinforce this idea. Al-Zayni, the main figure who represents the field of power, remains invisible, inaccessible, and elusive, throughout. The text is constructed out of the constant juxtaposition of public and secret docu-fictional forms (memoirs, spy reports, public announcements, royal decrees, etc.) that generate two levels of reality in the text: a reality for popular consumption and another that circulates among those in power. Some of the docu-fictional spy reports are at times labelled "Top

Secret" and made unavailable even to the reader who predominantly occupies a far more informed and privileged position than that of the other characters in the text. In all of this Sa'id, the young student of Al-Azhar, remains the naive outsider, with no real grip on the inner dynamics of power, or on his relationship to it, until of course he dares to tell "the truth" and is arrested. The political field is depicted as opaque, all knowing, all-powerful, both efficient and effective, a force that will crush when it fails to manipulate.[10]

In the late 1960s, al-Ghitani was promoted to the position of military correspondent of *Al-Akhbar*. But he was soon punished for signing the manifesto of 1973, spearheaded by the noted Egyptian intellectual figure Tawfik al-Hakim, and signed by more than 100 Egyptian intellectuals in solidarity with the student movement of 1972 that demanded of the late president Anwar Sadat a military confrontation with Israel.[11] Al-Ghitani was first dismissed for eight months from *Al-Akhbar* and then brought back, "put away" in its offices and forbidden to write on its pages. There he will remain until the mid-1980s when, with a change in the administration of *Al-Akhbar*, he will be given the responsibility of its literary pages. From then on the journey to becoming the intellocrat begins.

The assassination of the small man

In contrast, Ibrahim Issa's trajectory stands in diametrical opposition to that of al-Ghitani. Born in 1965, he graduated in Mass Communication in 1985 and was appointed journalist in the weekly *Ruz al-Yusuf* where he rose to become managing editor until 1995. Unlike al-Ghitani, Issa began as a professional and not as an apprentice quickly gaining ground inside the political kitchen. In *Ruz al-Yusuf* he established himself as an articulate satirist and excelled in his attack on the Islamists. In 1995 he was only 30 when chosen to be editor-in-chief of Cairo's popular, privately owned weekly *Al-Dustur*, which boasted its non-partisanship to opposition parties and some 60 prominent contributing journalists and intellectuals representing the Egyptian right, left and centre. Despite the apparent expansion of the boundaries of freedom of the press in the Mubarak era, *Al-Dustur* was closed down by the state in 1998 for its attack on Coptic businessmen in Egypt.[12]

When compared to al-Ghitani, Issa's career represents another miracle, but in the opposite direction: at the age of 30 he is already at the heart of the field of power with direct access and information to its workings and a singular position to understand, demystify, denude and satirize it. He accedes to the literary field through the back door – journalism – and will continue to have problems legitimating his position within it. Even though his first novel, published in 1989, was very favourably reviewed by al-Ghitani himself, Issa will continue to be regarded by many within the literary field as an intruder, a journalist who uses his profession to write "quick" novels: a professional political satirist yes, but an "apprentice" within the literary field none the less, despite the seven novels and three collections of short stories that he has published, predominantly at his own expense. Ibrahim Issa's novels are considered by many of the literati as a paler version of the popular works of Ihsan Abd al-Quddus (1919–90): daring in content but conventional in form, technique and language, certainly not to be compared with the avant-garde narrative forms of the 1960s or the experimentation of the 1970s.

With the closing of *Al-Dustur* in 1998, under the eyes and complicit silence of Egypt's intellectual elite, Issa falls between two stools: he becomes an outcast of both the political and literary fields. Published in 1999, after the crackdown on *Al-Dustur*, *Maqtal al-rajul al-kabir* represents Issa's attempt at coming to terms with this crisis. The novel is at once a suicidal severing with the field of power that totally exposes and ridicules it and an audacious attempt at a laissez-passer into the literary one through its successful manipulation of an uncharted literary genre in modern Arabic literature, namely the satirical political thriller. Issa wrote the manuscript of *Maqtal al-rajul al-kabir* in the US, where, according to him, he could distance himself from all kinds of censorship and maximize the limits of what he could write. He completed in two months the writing of the novel that distils his experience within the field of power. He left one copy with a friend in the States, and flew back with the other, having calculated the unpredictability of Egyptian cultural politics and the very real possibilities of censorship. Issa published the novel at his own expense and gave it to *Al-Ahram* for distribution. According to Issa, upon orders from State Intelligence *Maqtal al-rajul al-kabir* was not distributed. After negotiations with *Al-Ahram*, Issa's copies of the novel were returned to him; they were sold out at a reception he held at the Greek Club, Cairo's most recent downtown den for the intellectual milieu. Despite, or perhaps because of, the banning, *Maqtal al-rajul al-kabir* was reportedly read by the president of the republic himself.

Maqtal al-rajul al-kabir is set in the present and without ever naming the place or the actors is able to evoke through the constant use of familiar episodes, incidents and characters the tragi-comic reality of the contemporary Egyptian field of power both locally and globally. The novel opens with the discovery that the president of the republic has been stabbed to death in his own bed with a dagger that had been hanging on the wall in his bedroom. The president's private secretary summons key members of the cabinet for consultation. As they arrive at the presidential palace, their inner thoughts and consciousness are revealed to the reader in a series of flashbacks that expose the corruption, mediocrity and ridicule of the political apparatus as well as the ministers' anxieties and fears for their fragile positions within the political field. In a long sequence of hilarious fictional episodes that bear unmistakable resemblance to reality, Issa provides the reader with his insider's view of the wheeling and dealing of the field of power. Each chapter represents a satiric parody of current Egyptian political realities: the president's plans for a total change of the cabinet members that terminates in the dismissal of the prime minister with no change at all; the failed assassination attempt against the president at the zoo; the cowardly and complicit role of the press, the parliament, and the media; the orchestrated false elections, the propping up of the president's son as heir to the presidency, the

64 *Inside the literary establishment*

dubious role of the powerful and power-hungry businessmen, *bref*, the entire system, all based on Issa's direct knowledge of the political kitchen.

The central question that preoccupies the cabinet members in the novel is not who killed the president but rather how to preserve the system and their power despite the president's death. To the people, they announce that the president has died a natural death. To the American ambassador, they tell the truth! The role of big brother that is assigned to the United States in the text is another satiric testimony from Issa's long experience within the political field. Upon the orders of the president of the United States, a "fact finding" committee is set up to investigate the circumstances surrounding the president's murder. Its "findings" are meant not for the consumption of the people (who believe their president has died a natural death) but for the democratic political kitchen in the US that does not want to be caught red-handed, or uninformed, should the story of the assassination be discovered and aired. The committee is constituted with the membership of two intellectuals: the blasé, disengaged and silent Egyptian law Professor Yusuf Radwan, and the naive, committed and rather hysterical Arab American Professor of Middle East Studies, Rita McKurby (an Americanization of her original name, of Arab origin, al-Maghrabi). In their short lived search for "truth" it is Rita, the catalyst and alter ego, who draws Yusuf Radwan out of his silent disengagement and ultimately becomes responsible for his tragic end in an asylum accused, by the local press, of being a "necrophile", "a grave thief", "head of a gang whose weird pastime is to dig up graves", "caught naked inside a women's graveyard".[13]

As an intellectual, Yusuf embodies the modern history of his country: he is the grandchild of an Islamist (on his father's side) whose torture he had witnessed as a child, and a communist (on his mother's side) who, after being released from the detention camp, entered in the service of the state and died denouncing its corruption and oppression. The experience of his grandfathers leads to his total disillusionment with the field of power. When he is handpicked to serve on the fact finding committee he repeatedly explains to Rita, who firmly believes in her heroic role as "fact finder", that they were brought only to complete paperwork and files and not to search for "the truth" that may prove to be disastrous, if discovered. As the clues to the president's assassination begin to unravel, Rita abandons the search for "truth" and seeks refuge in a Sufi order, leaving Yusuf obsessed with what he had so wisely been disengaged from: the search for "truth". When Yusuf begins to deduce that the president, his cook and the president's swimming pool engineer had all been poisoned by a "foreign expert" and proceeds to act on his deductions, he is denied audience by the authorities who had so far been "co-operative", he is checked out of his hotel, he is stripped of all the files related to the crime and is finally arrested and put in a madhouse for attempting to conduct an autopsy of the bodies of the cook and the engineer.

Unlike al-Ghitani who in his first novel *Al-Zayni Barakat* shields himself from his contemporary police state by representing it in the past, Issa's *Maqtal al-rajul al-kabir* is submerged in the current, everyday political reality. If al-Ghitani uses parody in order to fend off censorship, Issa confronts that very same possibility head on. But could Issa have written *Maqtal al-rajul al-kabir* during the 1960s? The answer, I believe, is a categorical no. The very representation of the political field in both novels and the respective protagonists' attitude toward it attest to the extent to which these two authors' fictional imaginings are products of very specific historical moments. In *Al-Zayni* power is concentrated in the hands of two individuals: the *muhtasib*, Al-Zayni Barakat, and the supreme *shihab*, Zakariyya ibn Radi, whose reign of terror permeates the entire text. Together they represent a highly centralized political power that rules with a confident, ruthless, impenetrable iron fist, an awe-inspiring parody of the Egyptian political field in the 1960s. In contrast, *Maqtal al-rajul al-kabir* represents a political field that has been stripped of its power and whose workings are ridiculously transparent and exposed. Unlike al-Ghitani's text, Issa's depicts a political vacuum and a political field dominated by the dictates of the market whose interests are dependent on *the* global power that ultimately manipulates the entire narrative. Not only is the representation of the political field radically different in the two texts, but also the very mode and language of that representation are equally poles apart. Whereas al-Ghitani uses an archaic and Sufi-like classical Arabic language, Issa works with the spoken Egyptian dialect pushing it to the most colloquial, at times "foul" level. Whereas the omniscient narrator in *Al-Zayni* deprives the reader of certain levels of information (top secret reports, covert relationships between characters) thereby increasing the opaqueness of the system, the reader of *Maqtal al-rajul al-kabir* is privy to the most intimate, private, and denuding conversations between the president and his men. The president's comments with regard to the change of cabinet members during a meeting with his prime minister is just one example:

> Listen, everyday I read about poor services in hospitals and people who end up dying.... What do people think? Do they think that if they go to hospital they won't die? How idiotic! How greedy! They think that because we have hospitals no one will die. Ungrateful half-wits! That's why I want for the future minister of health, even if he's a ticket collector, to write on the entrance of every hospital the Qur'anic verse "Everyone shall taste death." And let's see who will dare object to divine will.[14]

Issa's *Maqtal al-rajul al-kabir*, like al-Ghitani's text, may be read as his own objectification of his trajectory in the field of power. The satiric mode in which the entire novel is written allows him to distance himself from his experience while establishing an intimate and complicit relationship with the reader. The back cover of the novel semiotically attests to Issa's determination to break free from the constraints of both the political and literary fields: an image of the author on the Hudson river in New York with the city in the background, his head turned towards a flock of seagulls, flying across a blue sky. Printed against this image is a series of recommendations and directions to the reader:

Advice before you purchase this novel:
1   Reading is an individual responsibility.
2   The novel may cause you depression.
3   The novel is for adult readers only.
4   Do not leave any evidence that you own a copy.
5   Do not buy this novel.

Directions for Reading:
1   Watch the news before you read this novel.
2   Do not read it at your workplace or where you suspect people's intentions towards you.
3   Reading dosages: 20–30 pages. You may increase the dosage if you can bear it.
4   Do not try to compare between the events in the novel and real life. The author does not wish to be responsible for any similarities.
5   Keep your copy out of sight; preferably in the refrigerator.

Furthermore, the end of Yusuf Radwan's search for "truth" is not unlike Issa's own. *Al-Dustur* was closed down for daring to cross the red line and speak the truth about prominent and powerful businessmen in Egypt. Like Yusuf Radwan, Ibrahim Issa, the editor-in-chief of *Al-Dustur*, paid the price: he found himself put away, out of grace, totally marginalized within the field he had so comfortably come to occupy. The tragedy remains, however, that Issa's suicidal severing with the field of power did not win him a substitute place within the literary one. Not only was *Maqtal al-rajul al-kabir* banned by the political authorities but it was equally "banished" from grace within the literary one, despite Issa's original and successful distribution of the three thousand copies in a very short period of time. Suddenly boy wonder is transformed into a madman, an outlaw in both the political and literary fields.

Two examples will situate the radically different positions of al-Ghitani and Issa today. As the crisis surrounding Haydar Haydar's novel *Walima li-a'shab al-bahr* (*A Banquet for Seaweed*) was at its peak,[15] and as *Akhbar al-Adab* (the main battle ground) braced itself to defend the issue of freedom of speech and expression with weekly editorials by al-Ghitani denouncing terrorist or fundamentalist discourse against the novel, its author, the publishers and the minister of culture (a long-standing enemy of al-Ghitani against whom he conducted a national battle both in the Egyptian courts and on the pages of *Akhbar al-Adab*), Ibrahim Issa begged the right to differ with everyone. In one of the issues dedicated to Haydar's defence, *Akhbar al-Adab* published an article by Ibrahim Issa entitled: "I Beg Your Pardon ... I Disagree with You: What Haydar Haydar Wrote Has Nothing to Do with Freedom of Speech!" The article can be read as Issa's riposte to his marginalization within the literary field. He accuses the Egyptian intellectuals of hypocrisy for suddenly inventing a "classic" out of a "mediocre novel" and for condoning Haydar's "attack" on Islam while condemning his own attack on the president, in his banned novel. He concludes with an outright cry that encapsulates his compromised position on all fronts:

> Finally, one could have just put one's tongue inside one's mouth and shut up and avoided this controversy altogether and let you all go to hell ... Islamists and leftists alike. For none of you lent a helping hand or wasted a drop of ink to rescue a banned and persecuted writer for whom they have closed seven papers and whose novel has been banned by national security without any of you dashing to republish it in defiance of power or the sultan. I could have kept quiet and spared my self your disdain for my words but had I been among those who kept their tongues in their mouths I would not be where I am today.[16]

Ironically, it is precisely because of this sense of banishment that Ibrahim Issa was able to step out of line and publicly defend Professor Saad Eddin Ibrahim in his crisis with the field of power, a crisis over which the Egyptian cultural field has, at best, remained silent when not in perfect alignment with the incriminating position of the political one.[17] Al-Ghitani's ruthless editorial after Ibrahim's release, which he concludes by calling for Ibrahim's boycott, is a perfect example of this dominant unsympathetic position.[18]

In stark contrast is Issa's defence of Ibrahim, where he unleashes his wrath and disdain for both the transparent political field and the complicit literary one. He denudes, questions and mocks the alleged official accusations levelled against Ibrahim and bewails the reactions within the intellectual milieu concluding with a defence of the victim that bespeaks Issa's understanding of their shared position, one that is identical to that of Yusuf Radwan in *Maqtal al-rajul al-kabir*: the "mad man" who dared to seek and speak the truth:

> I say I am defending Saad Eddin Ibrahim because I believe he is a political victim in this case. I hope that our intellectuals – no matter how different their views – will come to realize that Saad Eddin Ibrahim is being assassinated both politically and psychologically because he dared to demand impartial elections and national democracy and because he allowed himself to invite every one of the people to "Be a Partner and to Participate".[19]

Despite Al-Ghitani, and Issa's different public positions on issues that preoccupy the intellectual field, their respective fictional representations in their novels of the status of the intellectual in his relationship with the political field are ominously identical. It is true that *Al-Zayni Barakat* and *Maqtal al-rajul al-kabir* present the reader with substantially different understandings and hence representations of a "Big One": a political power against which the figure of the intellectual in the text is juxtaposed. It is equally evident that, between them, the two texts map out the very nature, manifestations and workings of this Big One, moving from the all-powerful, all-oppressive, self-contained police state of the 1960s, to a weakened, transparent and more globally dependent one in the

1990s. However, the invariable element in the two texts remains the place and fate of both protagonists Saʿid al-Juhayni and Yusuf Radwan, whose search for truth leads to their destruction by two political powers whose nature and structure is substantially different. Even though Saʿid is initially the innocent, naive and uninitiated young man and Yusuf is the blasé, experienced and all-knowing intellectual, they both end up in the same place: crushed, marginalized, scandalized and irrelevant to the workings of political power. The very last words uttered by both characters in the two novels are the same: Saʿid al-Juhayni's anguished cry at the very end of *Al-Zayni Barakat* "Aaah, they have made me rot, they have destroyed my forts"[20] is identical to Yusuf Radwan's equally tormented last utterance in *Maqtal al-rajul al-kabir* when, after a long period of complete silence in the asylum, all that he can say is: "Aaah, Aaah, Aaah."[21] These agonized and besieged cries by both protagonists who represent the intellectual in the respective texts are all we are left with at the end. A very disarming position indeed when we consider the time that separates the two works, the transformations that have occurred over that time with regard to the political field, and finally the radically different trajectories of both authors within the intellectual field.

The comeback kid

In its October 2005 issue, the English-language weekly *Cairo Magazine* ran a cover story with a full front-page picture of Ibrahim Issa entitled: "The Last Laugh: How Egypt's Most Controversial Newsman Came out on Top". The story basically chronicled the resurrection of Ibrahim Issa and his journey from being the "bête noire" and "persona non grata" of Egyptian journalism to becoming, the editor-in-chief of Egypt's two most popular opposition weekly papers namely *Al-Dustur* (which had been closed down in 1998) and *Sawt al-Umma*.[22] Similarly, *Akhbar al-Adab*, on whose pages Issa had attacked the Egyptian literati for their silence with regard to his censored novel *Maqtal al-rajul al-kabir*, ran a long interview with him in which he discussed his literary career and his more recent novel *Ashbah wataniyya* (*Nationalistic Ghosts*). A miraculous double comeback for Issa therefore in both the political and literary fields.

What is ironic about Issa's comeback story is the extent to which he owes this spectacular return, after both his political and literary suicides, to the very same centrally disempowered political field he had represented so sarcastically and transparently in his banned novel *Maqtal al-rajul al-kabir*. A number of elements have converged to bring about Issa's gradual reinstatement: in the first place the late 1990s witnessed not only the proliferation of political parties and independent papers (of which the closed *Al-Dustur* had been an example) but more significantly the increase in the number of privately owned satellite television channels that provided an alternative and considerably more independent arena from state institutions. These new realities, given the general context of increasing US pressures for reform, freedom of expression, democracy and good

The big one 69

governance, also meant that dissenting voices, unwelcome by the state and constrained by its immediate power and control, could find themselves a space beyond such control, namely through satellite television. Ibrahim Issa is one such example. After *Al-Dustur* had been closed down and *Maqtal al-rajul al-kabir* banned, Issa basically became a pariah: no paper would publish his work. It is through satellite television, specifically the Egyptian, privately owned Dream TV that Issa was able to relaunch his career with a series of engaging and highly popular shows that, despite initial pressures of censorship, actually reimposed him in the political field as one of the most controversial, outspoken, and interesting voices.[23] Ibrahim Issa anchored several programmes on Dream TV: *Ala l-qahwa* (*At the Coffeeshop*), a current affairs show, *Kalam garayid* (*News Talk*), a political news programme, *Allahu a'lam* (*God Knows Best*), a programme on religious issues, *Rigal ba'd al-rasul* (*Men After the Prophet*), a historico-religious programme and *Min awwil il-satr* (*The Beginning of the Line*) a cultural programme that he currently presents. A truly impressive menu of debates, questions and controversies conducted with openness and an accessible spoken Arabic that rendered Issa's programmes some of the most popular shows on satellite television with a vast local and regional spectatorship. Through satellite television Ibrahim Issa simultaneously succeeded in positioning himself beyond state control and above the limited and closed circle of the Egyptian literati. At the same time, in 2001, the final verdict from the Supreme Administrative Court ruled that *Al-Dustur* be republished. This verdict was finally put into effect in 2004 with Ibrahim Issa as re-instated editor-in-chief.

Since his return to *Al-Dustur* Ibrahim Issa's editorials have been scathing in their critique of the regime and of President Mubarak himself, frequently crossing the red lines that are generally observed within the profession, ones that Saad Eddin Ibrahim had crossed just a few years earlier and had been made to pay dearly for. *Al-Dustur* has also been able to forge a new language, more in tune with a younger reader, using idioms and metaphors from the street and engaging the young with issues that directly concern them. As the *Cairo Magazine* put it, "*Al-Dustur* has come back with a vengeance" with its readership at once dazzled by its audacity and puzzled by the fact that it continues to be tolerated. On the literary front, Ibrahim Issa has been just as daring. He serialized his own banned novel *Maqtal al-rajul al-kabir* on the pages of *Al-Dustur* during the summer of 2005, has republished it through Merit, the leading private publisher in Egypt, and it was sold at the 2006 Cairo International Book Fair without any visible problem.

In 2005 Ibrahim Issa published his latest novel *Ashbah wataniyya*, which like *Maqtal al-rajul al-kabir* stepped out of line with the dominant literary genres in the field. *Ashbah wataniyya* is another thriller; a symbolic horror novel highly influenced by its western cinematic counterpart and as such is a newcomer to the Egyptian literary genres. As was the case with *Maqtal al-rajul al-kabir*, *Ashbah wataniyya* was received not as a literary text but rather as an impostor, a pale copy of western thrillers that was too closely entangled in real characters and real histories.[24] Issa's response to this accusation is particularly telling and instructive since he immediately compares himself and his intervention in the literary field to Gamal al-Ghitani and *Al-Zayni Barakat*:

> Consider a novel like *Al-Zayni Barakat* that is set during the Mamluk period but draws on contemporary reality and real characters enveloped in the writer's fictional imagination. Why is it permitted [to represent reality] when you set it seven hundred years ago and it is not permitted when I choose to represent the past seven months? There is another point that has to do with the fact that in my capacity as a journalist I have come very close to the world of power: as an observer, as an opposition figure, and as an editor. I have seen what many among my writer colleagues have not: they have seen the oppressed, they have seen the officers who beat them up, but I saw those who employ these same officers.... Why should they be permitted to write about the world of the oppressed and I be denied the right to represent the world of power?[25]

Issa's riposte to the literati is multi-pitched and scores several points at once: primarily it is an attack on his critics from among the writers who, according to him, continue to "write the same novel", i.e., in critiquing their contemporary reality without confronting censorship, have resorted to the historical, the symbolic and the metaphoric, and have consequently avoided and scorned other literary genres like the detective novel or the thriller with the excuse that they are too immediate, too facile or too direct. At the second level, by authoring such marginal and marginalized genres in the literary community, Issa, the journalist who has access to the world of power, argues that he has been able to better represent reality than many others since they only saw "the officers who beat them up", but he had access to "those who employ these same officers". At the third level, by comparing himself to al-Ghitani and his chefs d'oeuvre, *Al-Zayni Barakat*, Issa claims more knowledge about the workings of the world of power than was ever available to al-Ghitani when he represented that same world before him. Finally, Issa's choice of writing the contemporary thriller becomes, from his point of view, a way of creating a space for freedom of expression: "We need this kind of novel.... I wish to say that it is not important that there be a margin of freedom for writing, for it is possible for writing to create that margin of freedom."[26] Hence, the same confrontational strategies that have become Ibrahim Issa's blue print in journalism have also come to characterize his reinstated position within the literary field. *Ashbah wataniyya* comes to reconfirm these confrontational strategies at both the political and literary levels.

The novel begins with the sudden appearance of huge imposing ghosts, clad in black, with green head covers, who appear to a group of Egyptian yuppies on their way to an exclusive summer resort on the northern coast of Egypt in their Cherokee loaded with alcohol and drugs. The narrative develops through alternate sequences: those of horror scenes where the young members of the group are attacked by the pursuing ghosts and those that recount the personal histories of these characters whose arrogance and corruption are promoted and protected by their even more corrupt and powerful parents who are actually the reason for the very existence of these horrific creatures and their unrelenting hunt of the young group, their mutilation, and their ultimate murder. The ghosts' only request is carved out on the chest of one of the dead yuppies; the simple sentence "Say we're sorry". The ghosts have also recorded a message on tape making the same demand:

> What happened to you tonight ... is a message for you from creatures that pursue you, haunt you, and torture you; creatures from your past or your present. Perhaps they seek revenge for what you have committed. But perhaps they only want your apology. Think well, for this may lead to your salvation. The heavens only want to hear your apology, to witness your repentance.[27]

But no apology was forthcoming. Not from the young crowd as it was being chased and hunted down, or from their parents, none of whom sheds a tear after the collective murder that in the absence of "concrete" evidence of an actual murderer was considered group suicide. No one ever says "we're sorry"; no one responds to the ghosts' only request.

In many ways *Ashbah wataniyya* translates Ibrahim Issa's comeback, indeed his resurrection. Like the ghosts in *Ashbah wataniyya*, Issa returns from the world of the dead to haunt the political field that had literally assassinated him professionally. But his comeback remains that of a ghost. His scathing editorials, his critical satellite shows, his confrontational literary texts represent his own search for the very same simple request that his own ghosts in *Ashbah wataniyya* make: "Say we're sorry." And like his ghosts, he remains incapable of extracting that simple request, for no apology has been forthcoming. Instead, Ibrahim Issa now confronts a case in court for slandering President Hosni Mubarak.[28] Indeed, the ghosts in *Ashbah wataniyya* are not just a trope for Issa's own individual relationship with the political field, but they can be read as a metaphor for the relationship of the whole intellectual field to the political one where the latter, obsessed with its own power and longevity, continues to deal with all forms of dissence not as a force to which it is answerable but rather as one that is and should be part of the world of the dead.

4 The value of freedom
The writer against the establishment

Speaking truth to power: a snapshot

The Egyptian Opera House, Small Hall, Wednesday 22 October 2003, 7 p.m. This is the closing ceremony of the second International Conference on the Arab Novel. By way of hurried tribute this year's conference was dedicated to the late Edward Said. Tonight Egypt will honour one of the Arab world's most distinguished novelists. The winner will walk away with £E100,000 awarded by the Egyptian Higher Council for Culture, under the auspices of the Minister of Culture Faruq Husni. The auditorium is packed with Egyptian, Arab and international guests, all awaiting the outcome of the panel's deliberations.

The president of the panel of judges, the celebrated Sudanese writer Tayeb Saleh, reads the report. He enumerates the winner's distinguishing features within the literary field: he is an ascetic, both on the material and creative levels, he has lived his life outside state institutions, a guardian of "the sacred temple of Art", he has dedicated his life to writing, a champion of justice and truth. A wave of whispers in the auditorium: "Sonallah ... Sonallah." Finally, Saleh announces the name of the winner. It is indeed Sonallah Ibrahim, well known for his unique position within the Arab cultural field, his determined and constant distance from the state apparatus, an exceptional and much envied position within the field itself.

Sonallah makes his way to the podium amidst rising applause. We await his speech and marvel at the blatant contradiction. Another wave of whispers in the auditorium: How can he accept this award? Didn't he refuse many others? Didn't he just boycott a conference in Morocco to protest an Israeli minister's visit there? He begins his speech with familiar satiric humour, distancing himself from official language and official discourse: "I am incapable of competing with Dr Gabir's [Gabir Asfur, secretary general of the Higher Council for Culture] improvisational skills." Applause and laughter. He tells us that he has therefore written a few words that express his own feelings. As I listen I find myself remembering the nameless protagonist in Sonallah's novel *Al-Lajna* (*The Committee*): in the text the protagonist does not speak the same "language" as the committee before which he is summoned. Yet he still has to make himself heard and understood in front of the head of the committee who is practically blind and half-deaf.

With customary modesty Sonallah proceeds to read an inventory of literary comrades all "more deserving" of this award: an impressive list of Arab writers, deceased and alive, men and women, young and old, writing in Arabic and in English, with whom he shares a committed literary project. He salutes the distinguished panel of judges and singles out Mahmud Amin al-Alim from among them: his mentor and companion in prison (1959–64) who taught him "true national values". He reads his own selection by the panel as a tribute to "serious and dedicated work" that will always find recognition without the need for "public relations" or "compromised principles" or "buttering up to official institutions" from which he (citing himself as an example) has diligently sought distance. More whispers in the auditorium. Sonallah has just struck a sensitive chord: the dependence of the cultural field on the political one. In the Arab world cultural figures are predominantly civil servants of the state, hence its protégés, so long as they are intelligent enough to respect the unpredictable boundaries of the political game. Such is the dominant model to which Sonallah is an exemplary exception. It is precisely his distance from this dominant model that has allowed him to assume his "responsibility" as an Arab writer whose creative work is engaged, indeed saturated with, "contemporary individual and national issues".

At the podium Sonallah continues with an elegy of the Arab world that "once upon a time was Arab". Initially, his tone is contained, his voice sad. Gradually it rises: loud, powerful, angry and passionate. It resonates in the auditorium and unites with feverish, incessant applause from some of the members of the jury themselves to the younger generation of writers who had, on various occasions, including this conference, declared a "rupture" with the elders and their worn out "grand cause":

> At this very moment Israeli forces continue to occupy what remains of Palestinian land (…) executing, with concise precision and method, a genocide against the Palestinian people … But the Arab capitals continue to receive Israeli leaders with open arms…

As I listen I am reminded of the epigraph to *Tilka l-ra'iha* (*The Smell of It*), Sonallah's very first pseudo-autobiographical novel that was published in 1966 upon his release from five years in political detention and that was subsequently banned. The epigraph was taken from James Joyce's *A Portrait of the Artist as a Young Man*: "This race and this country and this life have produced me … and I shall express myself as I am."

In 1986, twenty years after the initial publication of *Tilka l-ra'iha* and its subsequent and repeated banning, Sonallah wrote an introduction to the first complete and uncensored edition in which he highlighted some of the issues that haunted him in writing this critical narrative:

> The Arab community, with Egypt in the lead, was engaged in a fierce confrontation with American imperialism and its stepdaughter Zionism, not to

mention the emergence of Arab nationalism. Naturally I was plagued by the question of whether, under those circumstances, I was harming my country with this work.[1]

Indeed, Sonallah's unresolved dilemma as articulated above attests to his acute awareness of the constraining relationship between the cultural and the political, and his early attempt to come to terms with the position of the intellectual vis-à-vis power. Not only do these issues "plague" him at a theoretical level but they equally haunt him throughout all his fiction. Sonallah's protagonists are actors of his own drama: they are all writers or citizens whose works or deeds never see the light of day because they refuse to produce or comply with what is "acceptable" and therefore compromising. In *Tilka l-ra'iha* (1966) the narrator, alienated by the bourgeois literary aesthetics of the time, gives up writing and contents himself with masturbation. In *Najmat Aghustus* (1974) the fate of the young journalist's revealing report on the High Dam remains unknown. In *Al-Lajna* (1981) the protagonist sits at his desk and literally eats away at his own body, in accordance with the verdict passed upon him by the members of the committee who confiscated his study. In *Bayrut Bayrut* (1984) the Egyptian writer in the text leaves war-torn Beirut and returns to Egypt with his manuscript unpublished. In *Dhat* (1992) Sonallah's only female protagonist locks herself up in her bathroom and cries after all her attempts at protest are defeated. In *Sharaf* (1998) Dr Ramzi is placed in solitary confinement inside the prison where he spends the remaining pages of the novel yelling unheeded and unheard proclamations to his fellow prisoners, inciting them to rebel against the prison authorities, to no avail. In *Warda* (2000) the Egyptian protagonist is forced to leave Oman after he has unearthed documents about Warda, the Omani woman with whom he was in love as a young man and who died during the thwarted Omani armed rebellion of the 1960s. And finally *Amrikanli* (2003) ends with the exiled Egyptian history professor's failed attempt at love making with his American student in San Francisco.

This gallery of fictional portraits, with compromised destinies directly related to their desperate attempts at the production of an alternative knowledge, parades before me as Sonallah proceeds to denounce, in public, not in fiction, Egypt's normalization with Israel, the American occupation of Iraq, the impotence of our foreign policy, the widespread corruption and the absence of human rights. I listen and think to myself: here he is, fulfilling the dream expressed in the epigraph of his very first, banned novel: "I shall express myself as I am." And naturally, he turns his critical attention to parallel failings in the cultural field: "We have no theatre, no cinema, no research, no education. We only have festivals and conferences and a boxful [referring to Egyptian television broadcasting] of lies." The auditorium goes wild. People applaud him and nod their heads in agreement with this unprecedented confrontational speech. More whispers from the crowd: Courageous words, but they remain just words.... Suddenly, Sonallah dumbfounds his audience and transforms the words into action: "I publicly decline the prize because it is awarded by a government that, in my opinion, lacks the credibility of bestowing it."[2] He descends from the podium amidst cheers of support, tears of joy and deafening applause. He begins to leave the auditorium accompanied by his wife. The younger literati, at the back of the auditorium are the first to prance upon him. They block his exit. They shower him with kisses and envelop him with embraces. "You have given us hope", they say to this small and seemingly fragile man of monumental stature. This is the real tribute to Edward Said from Sonallah Ibrahim, an intellectual who thoroughly understands the price and value of freedom.

The truth, the whole truth and nothing but the truth

In April 2005 Sonallah Ibrahim was invited to deliver the George Antonius Memorial Lecture at St Antony's College in Oxford. In his talk, which was entitled "The Development of an Egyptian Writer", Ibrahim traced the various political, literary, and aesthetic circumstances and influences that shaped his vocation as a writer. Throughout the text of the lecture the central question that seems to have haunted him from the start is the question of truth. He begins his lecture by informing his audience that his arrest and detention in 1959 along with leading personalities of the communist movement and the left in general "was the most important experience in [his] life" for, as he stated, "Prison is a good school for a writer. Time there is long; long, which allows him to think, doubt, come nearer to human fragility and become himself more human."[3] He explains that it is in prison that he was transformed from being a political activist to becoming a creative writer:

> I was twenty-two years old, full of romantic visions and envisaging a future of militant political engagement. I soon realized that I lack many characteristics, which are components for such a career. The freedom endowed in literary expression captured my imagination. That is how I decided to become a novelist.
>
> It was not an easy endeavour. I started with some short stories, written in my head only because paper and pens were forbidden. When circumstances allowed I was able to put down some of them on the fine small paper of cigarettes (normally used in preparing manual joints of tobacco or Marijuana). Then I started a diary, which contained some of my observations, some projects, and excerpts from my readings. The overwhelming theme in all this was the problems of writing, how to write and what to write about, the role of the writer, the different concepts of art and literature.[4]

This prison diary which Ibrahim has published under the title *Yawmiyyat al-wahat* in 2005 (*Oasis Diary*, in reference to the Oasis detention camp where Ibrahim had spent six years) becomes the record of how the political activist was transformed into a writer, one whose political commitment became the defining element for the very *raison d'être* of the writer.[5] Hence committed writing became central to Ibrahim's creative project at the level of both content and form. The prison diary is filled with entries about the different manifestations of such commitment and the persistent search for the true role of the artist. The sketchy notes on cigarette paper included entries from the post-Stalinist Russian poet Yevgeni Yevtushenko "The poet has to mercilessly surrender himself to the truth. He is not allowed to cheat.... When Rimbaud became a slave merchant and his behaviour contradicted his poetic ideas he stopped writing"; from Ernest Fischer "we firmly demand an art which seeks the truth and portrays the different sides of reality"; from Naguib Mahfouz "the only main commitment in art is to tell the truth", and others. After his release in a general amnesty in 1964, Ibrahim's so far theoretical ideas about the role of the writer were put to the test in his first, ground-breaking novel *Tilka l-ra'iha* (*The Smell of It*) which he published at his own expense in 1966. *Tilka l-ra'iha* became Ibrahim's way of "find[ing] the essential in reality and the form to express it"; "[i]t recorded in a simple language and stark frankness the impressions and experiences of the weeks following [his] release from prison",[6] all of which were "truthful" and critical at the political, social, and aesthetic levels. The novel was immediately banned in Egypt.[7]

Ibrahim's obsession with telling "the truth" as a writer, despite this first encounter with censorship, led him to exercise new creative strategies that would enable his vocation. This led him to constitute his own archive of "the truth" through over half a century of collecting and rearranging newspaper clippings that have become an integral part of his creative work and the hallmark of his following novels:

> During my teen years I became fond of collecting pictures of semi nude actresses. At that time, half a century ago, complete photos of nudes were not easily available. With the growth of my consciousness other material found its way to my modest archive beside the famous legs of Betty Grable, the great bust of Jane Russell and the swimming agility of Ester Williams. Over the years this hobby became an obsession. It was also enlightening. Scrutinizing the media over an extensive period, one may discover the intricate play of power and exploitation, the manipulations, the secret interconnected relationships. Arranging them in an artistic way while following the destiny of live characters may give a literary work a certain depth.[8]

Ibrahim's lifetime search for "the truth" has also been responsible for his choice to maintain a distance from the state and its institutions which he continues to view as the main fabricator of the "boxful of lies" to which he referred in his rejection speech of the Arab Novel Award in 2003 at the Opera House. It has also been responsible for his position as an autonomous anomaly within the Egyptian cultural field that is predominantly dominated by the state. This has perhaps also allowed him to align himself globally with others outside the Egyptian context with whose positions on the "truth" he could identify, thus rendering his own individual struggle part of a collective and universal one. In his lecture at St Antony's College he draws up a long list of such others who, like

The value of freedom 77

himself, and the Indian writer Arundhati Roy whom he quotes at length, "must consider [themselves] at war":

> Three years ago, the Portuguese Nobel prize-winner Saramago stood among fellow writers beside the entrapped Palestinian leader Yasser Arafat in Ramallah, denounced the Zionist occupation and defended the rights of the Palestinian people.
> A year later, the known Iraqi Poet Saadi Youssef, who lives in exile, abstained from returning, along with other confused intellectuals, to his occupied native country.
> The following year I was awarded a state prize. I rejected it in public and used the event to deplore the policy of dependence and corruption followed by the Egyptian regime.
> Writers in Morocco and Britain refused to receive prizes or tributes from the state organs in protest against anti-popular policies. At the World Social Forum in Mumbai last year, the young Indian novelist Arundhati Roy called for global resistance to the U.S. occupation of Iraq and the Israeli occupation of Palestine.
> (...)
> Seeking the truth, and acting in accordance, is no longer a privilege for writers alone. At the beginning of this year the Egyptian ambassador at Venezuela resigned his post in protest against the capitulating foreign policy of Egypt and its internal corrupted one.
> Last month Britain's Association of University Teachers, with 40,000 members, called for boycotting two Israeli universities in solidarity with an Israeli professor, who was persecuted for demanding an end to the occupation of Palestine.
> Although this call is under dispute, it has pointed to something extremely important.... That it is not any more difficult to define the truth.... The whole truth and nothing but the truth.[9]

Hence, Sonallah Ibrahim's "bombshell" at the Opera House needs to be situated in a context larger than his own literary career and work. It should be read not as an individual act of defiance but rather as Ibrahim's own response and contribution to a global war for truth.

Sonallah Ibrahim: between the heroic and the anti-heroic

Ibrahim's refusal of the Arab Novel Award "because it is awarded by a government that ... lacks the credibility of bestowing it", and his dramatic exit from the ceremony followed by the vast majority of those present, left the Minister of Culture along with the members of the jury who had all lined up on stage practically alone in the auditorium surrounded by a handful of journalists. This prompted the minister to make three retaliatory statements that were meant to deflate the euphoria that accompanied Ibrahim's speech and his "heroic" stance

78   Inside the literary establishment

as well as score points for the Egyptian state and its cultural policies: first the minister argued that Ibrahim's public refusal and his scathing speech were a badge of honour for the Egyptian regime and that they represented solid proof of democratic practices and freedom of speech.[10] Second he accused Ibrahim of hypocrisy for having accepted the $50,000 al-Uways Award in 1993 insinuating that Ibrahim refused the Egyptian one because of its modest monetary value when compared to the heftier Gulf dollars,[11] and third he declared Ibrahim's refusal of the award an insult, not to the Egyptian government (which Ibrahim had trashed) but to the esteemed members of the jury, all prominent Arab writers and intellectuals who had independently selected Ibrahim for the award.[12] The Minister's statements set the parameters of the battle that was to ensue between Ibrahim and his defenders on the on hand and the state and its cultural institutions on the other.

By turning down the considerable economic gain (£E100,000) he could have collected from the Arab Novel Award Ibrahim obstinately clung to the symbolic capital amassed from his lifetime commitment to "truth" as a politically engaged writer. It became critical for the state cultural machinery to counter this symbolic victory. It is therefore no surprise that in an interview with Gabir Asfur, almost two years after Ibrahim's rejection of the award, the secretary general of the Higher Council for Culture teasingly insisted that:

> From a legal point of view, Mr Sonallah Ibrahim accepted the award (repeated twice) and turned down the monetary compensation.... He accepted it when I called to tell him, he accepted it when he came to the ceremony, he accepted it when he shook hands with all the members of the jury, he accepted it when he received the certificate and the medal from the Minister of Culture.... All these are indications that the man received the prize and accepted it, from the practical point of view (laughingly). If you do not accept the prize, then why shake hands with the members of the jury and thank them? Why accept the certificate from the Minister? All this has one meaning: acceptance of the prize.[13]

The strategies adopted in the battle waged against Ibrahim were familiar ones that had been used in other instances of reprisal against dissenting intellectuals which essentially cast them as isolated and irresponsible ones who stand against the nation as a whole. Despite the obvious differences between such voices of dissent, the arsenal of character assassination, anti-national accusations and allegations of collaboration with foreign powers are the same and are regularly used strategies: from the notorious case of Saad Eddin Ibrahim, who was sentenced to seven years in prison, to the more recent case of the presidential candidate, Ayman Nur, who is currently serving a five-year sentence.[14] The reaction to Ibrahim's confrontational act, at once cultural and political, was received with the almost identical arsenal of accusations and comparable fears of possible retaliatory measures.

The instant polarization of the literati, immediately following Ibrahim's refusal of the award, not only revealed the losses and the gains for each group but equally exposed the internal battles and contradictory positions within the cultural field as well. On the one hand, those closest to the centre of power (in this instance the Minister of Culture and the Higher Council for Culture) along with their clients, were all bound by the role they were expected to play, as defenders of the state cultural machinery and critics of Ibrahim's "irresponsible" act. On the other hand, Ibrahim's defenders were constituted of an interesting and significant mix of consecrated and marginal intellectuals who, because of their own symbolic capital (in the former group's case) or lack thereof (in the latter's), found themselves united against the institution despite their different ulterior motives. The spectrum of reactions within the cultural field allowed one journalist, defending the institution, to assert: "The democratic climate and the wide margin of freedom that Egypt enjoys during the Mubarak era can only be denied by the ungrateful." The author of the article proceeded to describe Ibrahim as one example of a writer who has actually thrived on this kind of freedom since his works, all critical of the state, have never been censored. Rather, despite his outspoken criticism, he was selected for the Arab Novel Award. Furthermore, he continued, Ibrahim delivered his scathing speech and went home safely without anyone obstructing his way. Had the same thing happened, the author of the article added, during times past, "[Ibrahim] would not have descended from the stage on his feet, he would not have gone home, but rather he would have gone to the darkness of prison".[15] However, it is precisely these strategies of seeming plurality and calculated allowances for freedom that have characterized the state's game of cultural politics during the Mubarak era and have become its means to maintain its secular façade and "democratic" facelift against global pressures. As Steve Negus of the *Cairo Times* succinctly put it in his editorial after Ibrahim's bombshell:

> The regime can be quite subtle in how it uses these institutions – it generally expects only the slightest of compromises in exchange for patronage.... Maybe you can write whatever you want in your novels, as long as you show up once a year to be televised exchanging a kind word and a handshake with the minister. You're not expected to advocate state policies, you're not even expected to tone down your criticism very much – you merely lend your name to state institutions and add just that little bit of implied legitimacy to the regime's claim that it represents, not just a narrow set of political interests, but the nation as a whole.[16]

However, Ibrahim's public snub of the state that dominated the media and flew over the internet thereby becoming "the most exciting thing going on in Egyptian politics",[17] upset the rules of the patronage game and unmasked its true face. Hence it called for immediate retaliation.

Among the most noteworthy reactions within the institutional camp was that of the secretary general of the Higher Council for Culture, Dr Gabir Asfur, Professor of Arabic Literature at Cairo University, who was single handedly responsible for the resurrection of the Council, its expanded budget, its

80 *Inside the literary establishment*

ambitious National Translation Project (one thousand titles to date) and its flurry of well-funded and systematically oversized national, regional and international cultural activities that have, over the past ten years or so, drawn not only most of Egypt's literati, both old and young, but also the most noted Arab intellectuals, as well as distinguished European and American Arabists, thus becoming the symbol of Egypt's renewed position as the throbbing heart of the Arab world.

The relationship between Asfur and Ibrahim up until the day the latter rejected the prize was more than an amiable one based on mutual respect and recognition. Indeed, prior to that eventful night, Asfur had published a series of laudatory articles about Sonallah Ibrahim's oeuvre in his weekly column in the Saudi-owned daily *Al-Hayat* newspaper during the period from June to October 2001. However, when Ibrahim rejected the Council's prize, Asfur, one of the Arab World's most distinguished literary critics and a great enthusiast of Ibrahim's career and work, deemed the latter's act "a cheap performance",[18] and a "grave insult to both Egyptian and Arab intellectuals".[19] Most of the Egyptian and regional papers quoted Asfur saying that Ibrahim has the right to accept or reject the prize but that he should have found a more "civilized" way to do so especially that Asfur himself had called him up to break the news and that Ibrahim had expressed his happiness and gratitude: "He could have turned down the prize when I first informed him and then issued a statement explaining his reasons and motives instead of this performance that has harmed all the Arab and Egyptian intellectuals."[20] Like the Minister of Culture, Asfur reiterated the same incriminating question: "Why did Ibrahim refuse the Arab Novel Award when he had accepted the al-Uways?"[21]

Beneficiaries of the patronage of the Higher Council for Culture were quick to align themselves with the institution but not without exposing the inherent contradictions in their constrained and compromised positions as clients of the state cultural apparatus. For example, in one interview, the Egyptian writer Salwa Bakr declared, at one and the same time, that "I am not employed by the institution nor am I one who benefits from it", but that: "I sometimes benefit from the Council when I obtain a ticket to attend a cultural event abroad. This is a good thing because I believe that the Ministry of Culture's money is my own." Indeed, Bakr described the Higher Council for Culture as an "enlightened institution" and the Minister of Culture as "an artist and an intellectual" whose views are "no different from those of Sonallah Ibrahim" for, she adds, "Who among us wants to see the Israeli flag flying under our skies?" This level of duplicity toward the patronage of state cultural institutions is echoed in her reaction to Ibrahim's rejection of the award. At one moment she declared: "Sonallah Ibrahim's position expresses not only that of the Egyptian intellectuals but that of the Arab ones as well. My only reservation is that it created a confrontation with an Egyptian cultural institution that represents us." At another moment she accused Ibrahim of elitism:

> Sonallah Ibrahim represents an elite that snubs Egyptian cultural life as well as daily problems and their complexity. They prefer to critique everything

behind closed doors. This attitude – despite my wholehearted support for him – is an elitist one.... The conference that he did not attend and did not participate in was very valuable because it was able to bring together Egyptian and Arab intellectuals in dialogue.[22]

There were also those who, genuinely taken by the euphoria of the evening, simply forgot, at least momentarily, their position as clients of the institution, thus revealing the double weight that state patronage represents in the cultural field: at once abhorred and needed, hated and desired. The reaction of the Nubian writer Idris Ali who was seated in "the back seats" among "the slave progeny" (as he described himself and other non-consecrated literati attending the ceremony) is a case in point. In a repenting article published on the pages of the weekly *Al-Qahira*, which is owned by the Ministry of Culture, Idris Ali depicts himself as one who was spellbound by Ibrahim's "performance": "I jumped from my seat. I applauded insanely. A wave of madness overtook the entire auditorium. Even the members of the jury who had just received the blow applauded." However, when he "regained the sanity" that he had lost in a moment "beyond the bounds of logic" Idris Ali discovered that he had placed himself "in the wrong trench". He asked himself: "Does Dr Gabir Asfur deserve this blow?" "How can we be so ungrateful?" "Indeed, Sonallah ... chose the cheapest way to stardom and false glory." The lexicon of tribalism that emerges in Idris Ali's repentant article is precisely what defines the relationship between the state as patron and the intellectuals as clients: you are either with us or against us and each should calculate the losses and the gains. For Idris Ali, those seem to have become clear overnight. Hence Ibrahim, the hero of an evening past, who literally swept him off his feet, is transformed into an ungrateful, irresponsible ideologue, incapable of recognizing the merits of the Mubarak regime that has "shielded us from fighting lost wars".[23]

Not only did Ibrahim's "bombshell" expose the Egyptian literati but it further implicated Arab intellectuals (regular invitees of the Egyptian cultural institution) as well. For, the same jury (with the exception of three members)[24] that selected Ibrahim on the basis of his unique autonomous profile was the first to critique him for his act of autonomy. This contradictory position was clearly exemplified by the Sudanese writer Tayeb Saleh, who presided over the jury and who had, in his awarding speech at the ceremony, described Ibrahim as "an ascetic, both on the material and creative levels, he has lived his life outside state institutions, a guardian of 'the sacred temple of Art', he has dedicated his life to writing, a champion of justice and truth". Saleh's reaction to Ibrahim's snub was yet another indication of the power of state patronage in seaming discord among the literati and exposing the contradictory positions they find themselves obliged to take. Saleh described Ibrahim's act as "childish" and "outdated", an act "devoid of decorum and *asala* [a sense of belonging]", "a stupid", "theatrical act".[25] Interestingly, in its 2004 exceptional round,[26] the Arab Novel Award went to Tayeb Saleh himself. He accepted it with gratitude.

On another level, if the state's position vis-à-vis Ibrahim's act was symptomatic of its strategies towards dissent, so was the reaction of defenders of the author symptomatic of the opposition's limited manoeuvring space and their inability to counter actively and effectively the state's compromising cultural patronage. While it is true that Ibrahim's rejection of the Arab Novel Award amassed spectacular solidarity, received unprecedented coverage in the media and was deemed inspiring by his admirers and supporters, young and old, no concrete collective measure was taken, not to honour him (for that was obviously not his point) but to protest against the regime's cultural politics, the criticism of which was enthusiastically applauded by the vast majority of the people in the auditorium who were mesmerized by Ibrahim's daring speech. A typical reaction came from a group of Egyptian intellectuals and writers signatories of a statement of support entitled "Egyptian People's Prize for Sonallah Ibrahim" that was carried by several papers and eventually posted on the internet. This group formed the Friends of Sonallah Ibrahim Society in order to "protect him from possible retaliatory measures by the authorities".[27] They also announced that he would be awarded the "Egyptian People's Prize during a public ceremony to honour his courageous stance". What is indeed instructive in this reaction from supporting leftist intellectuals is the extent to which the legacy of the all-powerful authoritarian, overtly oppressive state continues to dominate the literati's imaginary when all the elements surrounding Ibrahim's eventful selection for, and rejection of, the Arab Novel Award point to the fact that the rules of the game have changed. It is true that initially there was some concern over retaliatory measures that might be taken against Ibrahim, and many doubted that the local media would actually dare publish the text of his entire rejection speech. Ibrahim himself expressed similar concern: in more than one interview he talked about the absolute secrecy with which he prepared his speech and his fear that his phone might be bugged. He also said that he delivered his speech as quickly as he could lest he should be interrupted, or that they unplug the microphone or the electric current.[28] However, given his literary and symbolic stature, and the careful, calculated wording of the speech, Ibrahim himself was perhaps the most certain among us that despite his "performance", aired live on several satellite channels, he would remain untouchable. He too had mastered the rules of the new game. As for the promised "people's prize" and the "public ceremony to honour his courageous stance", to date no such award or celebration has been forthcoming. Not that Ibrahim had counted on it, for in his rejection speech he had already warned: "I will not ask you to issue a condemnation statement, for that is futile. I will not ask you for anything. For you know, better than I, what needs to be done." But nothing was done! The only act remained his own: he symbolically placed it, during his lecture at St Antony's College, in the context of a global war for truth.

Americanli (Amri kan li) and the global war for truth

Sonallah Ibrahim's "bombshell" overshadowed the appearance earlier in 2003 of his novel, *Amrikanli* (Amri kan li) an ambitious and painstakingly researched and documented work that, while trying to answer the question "how has all this happened to us and how has Egypt come to this?", interrogates the very nature of history. The title itself is a play on words and supports more than one meaning: it may be broken down to constitute three Arabic words that mean "my affairs were once in my hands", and, at the same time, it can mean "Americanish" or "American-like" in reference to US hegemony over not just Egypt but the entire world. Put together, the two possible significations of the title encapsulate Egyptian history, past and present.

The narrator, Shukri, is an Egyptian professor of history who, persecuted and depressed because of his controversial book on the Arab conquest of Egypt, is invited by an old student to teach a seminar on history in the US. On the first day of the seminar he tells his students: "I started my life [as a child] by tearing up history books.... I do not recall when I first tried to read these books and perhaps I never did."[29] This introduction to his first class becomes the first moment of the autobiographical text of the narrator which constitutes one of the main axes of the text. As he teaches his seminar on world history and historical methodology, assigning different historical projects, moments and problems to his students of different ethnic origins, Shukri ends up writing his own history and that of the entire globe. The vastness of the novel's project prompted one reviewer to say: "Sonallah Ibrahim's latest book gives the impression that the author felt that he had one last chance at writing all he had to say",[30] or, as Ibrahim himself had put it in his lecture at St Antony's College, "the truth, the whole truth, and nothing but the truth". Unlike Ibrahim's earlier novels where most of the protagonists are frustrated writers in search of an elusive truth, the protagonist in *Amrikanli* is made to occupy the position of power represented by the historian or soothsayer, which enables him to create his own truth thereby subverting the very title of his novel *Amri kan li* (my affairs were once in my own hands) and reclaiming possession of these "affairs", their history and their representation. Indeed, in writing this novel about history, Ibrahim, like the Uruguayan writer Eduardo Galeano in his *Memory of Fire Trilogy* (1982–88) – a politically engaged literary epic about the making of the New World that combines historical research and creative writing to provide "a sound reading of history",[31] and is used by one of the students in *Amrikanli* as her research project for the protagonist's seminar – patiently, but demandingly engages the reader in his global war for truth.

Moreover, at a certain level, *Amrikanli* can be read as a sneak fictional preview of Ibrahim's real public "performance" on 22 October 2003 that actually falls short of imagining the impact of such a "performance". As customary in his earlier novels, many of the autobiographical details that we read about Shukri, the protagonist in *Amrikanli* are actually details about the author's life. Generally speaking the lives of Ibrahim's protagonists resemble his own and his readers can compare his autobiographical essay, *Cairo from Edge to Edge*,[32] or his more recent *Yawmiyyat al-wahat* with many episodes and moments in his fictional texts. In fact, the relationship between him and his fictional characters is so deliberately blurred that parts of Shukri's life are actual episodes that have taken place in Ibrahim's. Inversely, some passages from Ibrahim's George Antonius Memorial Lecture about his own development as a writer are lifted, verbatim, from Shukri's autobiographical narrative in *Amrikanli*.[33] The blurred boundaries between the fictional and the real, Shukri's life and Ibrahim's, ultimately allow for a unique moment of impersonation where the author becomes his fictional character, thereby uniting the creative endeavour and actual life, the writer and the political activist. In the novel, Shukri is invited to attend a conference on Arab culture funded by an Arab prince. In the presence of a great number of distinguished Arab intellectuals, Shukri decides not to read his paper about freedom of expression. Instead, he improvises a speech that dismantles the relationship between intellectuals and the state throughout history, and exposes the implications of the distinguished guests' presence at the conference funded by their patron prince:

> Attempts have been made to consolidate the relationship between the intellectuals and the prince instead of cementing the one between them and the revolutionary. Many among the avant-garde have become tutors to a crown prince, or advisers to a king, or sultan, or spokespersons for a president.
> (...)
> Intellectuals are, after all, human: they get hungry, they get scared, they get anxious, like everyone else...
>   So we must not expect them to perform superhuman acts...
>   The problem, however, is that we can only look to them for hope.[34]

Shukri's critical speech in *Amrikanli* leaves the auditorium silent. No one applauds him as they did all the other speakers at the conference. His words fall on deaf ears. When Ibrahim decided to imitate *Amrikanli*'s fictional character during the ceremony at the Opera House, he expected a similar morose reaction for which he had already prepared himself through the fictional reception of Shukri's confrontational speech: "I was expecting those present to respond to me with cold resentment."[35] The scenario he had prepared at home with his wife, Layla Uways, was that before the last line of the speech she would begin to move towards the stage and wait by the steps, then they would leave the auditorium together as soon as he ended his speech.[36] But Ibrahim's homemade scenario was not meant to be, for the reality of the "performance" outdid both his fictional imaginings (in *Amrikanli*) and his theoretical ones (at home). It seems that, like most, if not all, of his protagonists, Ibrahim had imagined that he too would become the outcast; that like them, he would be the only undesired and unwelcome voice of discord. However, the stunning reaction of writers and intellectuals, specifically the young among them who remain on the margin of state institutions, placed him squarely at the very heart of Egyptian and Arab cultural politics. Instead of a silent, morose auditorium he was confronted with an auditorium that went wild:

> it was somewhat surprising to be met, all of a sudden, with such joyful gratitude – hugs and tears, people kissing my hand and climbing over my shoul-

ders. Since then I haven't been able to sleep with the phone ringing almost continuously with calls not only from Egypt but from every corner of the Arab world and beyond, people telling me that my position has resuscitated cultural and political life.[37]

Between the theatrical and the carnivalesque

Ideas of "performance", of "acting" of "drama" and theatricality in general are ones that enveloped the lexicon surrounding both the Arab Novel Award ceremony and its outcome. But in fact, if there was a "performance" to begin with, it was that prepared by the state's cultural institutions at both the real and symbolic levels. The whole ceremony took place on a stage at the Opera House (a performance space, par excellence) where the various actors moved and spoke according to a carefully choreographed plan. Initially, many of the spectators understood the scene to be that of the return of the prodigal son to the forgiving arms of the father in exchange for his symbolic repentance and a change in the direction of his life. This was actually Ibrahim's own reading of the upcoming "performance" as well, for he told his interviewers (referring to the Minister of Culture's claim that he has brought back all the intellectuals to the barn): "They told me [about the award] two days ahead of time to find out if I was going to enter the 'barn'. They wanted me to become part of the herd to which I never belonged."[38] But this déjà vu performance was transformed by Ibrahim into a veritable counter "show" as he described it,[39] one charged with genuine and ingenious creative energy that united Ibrahim's fictional and real worlds and turned tables on the institution and beat it at its transparent game. Indeed, Tayeb Saleh's awarding speech and his dramatic description of Ibrahim as "an ascetic, both on the material and creative levels, he has lived his life outside state institutions, a guardian of 'the sacred temple of Art,' he has dedicated his life to writing, a champion of justice and truth" could almost be read as the ominous words of a soothsayer in a Greek drama whose words are not reality but prophecy.

In a brilliant reading of the performative signification of the entire ceremony, Ferial Ghazoul, Professor of Comparative Literature at AUC and one of the three members of the jury who were reprimanded by the Minister of Culture for departing from her "role" and applauding Ibrahim's dramatic rejection of the prize, perceptively reads Ibrahim's counter-show as a live and unique instance of the resistance implicit in the Bakhtinian carnivalesque:

> The carnivalesque relies on sarcasm that is directed towards the institution. It overturns the hierarchy of power so that the rogue is crowned a king, and the scoundrel, a ruler i.e. an inversion of the status quo that ridicules all that is above criticism; an expression of the prohibited, the forbidden and the silenced.... We [in the Arab world] do not have the freedom of the carnivalesque; we do not have a tradition of the carnivalesque as understood in European civilization. However, through his unique act, Sonallah Ibrahim ably translated this carnivalesque dimension. Only now can we begin to

understand Bakhtin, for Sonallah Ibrahim has rendered him in Arabic more eloquently than any of his translators and critics (myself included).[40]

As for the more immediately political reading, the Minister of Culture's claim that Sonallah Ibrahim's "cheap performance" was a badge of honour for the Egyptian regime and its democratic practices was countered by the writer and journalist Ibrahim Issa, editor-in-chief of two of Egypt's most popular weekly papers, *Sawt al-Umma* and *Al-Dustur*, who declared: "It is precisely because of the lack of democracy that Sonallah Ibrahim was forced to do what he did."[41] Issa's perceptive comment actually responds to the question that many supporters of the institution had trumpeted in an attempt to dismiss Ibrahim's act as a personal quest for stardom and glory: why didn't Ibrahim, in a more "civilized" manner, turn down the award in private, over the phone, when he was first notified?

Many already knew, however, that this was not the first time that Ibrahim had been denied an award or had turned down a prize in a "civilized" manner. In 1993, at the very last minute, the nomination of Ibrahim's *Dhat* as the novel of the year at the Cairo International Book Fair was withdrawn when it was brought to the attention of the head of the selection committee that the text vehemently discredits the state.[42] In 1996 Ibrahim turned down, in private, the AUC Naguib Mahfouz Award, an episode that remained in the realm of rumour until he confirmed it publicly in the media some years later. Again, in 1998, Ibrahim's *Sharaf* was selected as the novel of the year at the Cairo International Book Fair. He did not show up for the ceremony, which is attended by President Mubarak, for he chose to be hospitalized for an operation on the same day; he never received the award, never sent someone to receive it in his lieu, and never sent apologies. All three instances, whether Ibrahim was denied the prize or opted to reject it, are examples of his position against the political and cultural establishment. However, no formal, historical record of these moments exists; no written trace of the reasons behind them. Explaining the need for his public "performance" at the Opera House Ibrahim says:

> When I was informed that I was selected to receive the award.... I didn't sleep for three days thinking, and discussing with my wife, the best way to make my refusal public; and then drafting and redrafting the speech to make it as accurate and precise as I could. If that same speech had been issued as a statement they might have denied that I was offered the award in the first place. And people might not believe me. I had to go, to make the best of the opportunity to declare my position.[43]

Ibrahim's public rejection of the award therefore becomes, in and of itself, a moment of truth, for no one could now erase it from collective memory. It became history and part of the public record, even if the daily state paper *Al-Ahram*, as the writer Bahaa Taher pointed out, remained completely silent about the entire event.[44] It is as if Ibrahim's rejection speech, like *Amrikanli*, was his one last chance at saying all he had to say; not in fiction, but for real.

The prison house of the institution

The gates of Egyptian prisons carry the sign: "Prison: Discipline and Reform". We encounter this sign in Ibrahim's *Sharaf* (1997) when the protagonist, Sharaf, whose name means "honour", enters the prison for having killed an Australian male expatriate who tried to sexually assault him. Ironically, the novel ends with Sharaf still in prison, having shaved his body hair in preparation for a voluntary same-sex encounter with a fellow prisoner.[45] Perhaps, the symbolic signification of this ending does not require further commentary. However, what require closer reading are the parallels that can be drawn between this fictional plot and the real one with which Ibrahim has had to wrestle.

During the weeks that followed Ibrahim's rejection of the Arab Novel Award, the parallels that began to emerge between the prison and state cultural institutions became central in the post-ceremony media. The Minister of Culture himself was caught making the comparison when he was quoted saying: "Sonallah Ibrahim has destroyed himself.... If he has behaved inappropriately, we will not cast him out. Rather, we will try to redress his position and redirect him."[46] The disciplinary lexicon used by the minister prompted the veteran writer Gamal al-Ghitani, known for his heated battles against the Minister of Culture, to write an editorial entitled "The Ministry of Culture: Redress, Discipline and Reform",[47] which he concluded with the following:

> How can one redress and redirect a writer who has chosen to remain outside the barn? This is a serious and novel issue which we should not allow to pass lightly. In fact, I fear the moment when my turn will come to be redressed and redirected. Till then, I suggest that Faruq Husni's ministry ... adopts a new slogan, more appropriate for future times: the ministry of culture: redress, discipline and reform.[48]

Suddenly, the Minister's "barn" and the state's prison become one and the same; the divide between the cultural lexicon (barn) and the political one (prison) collapses making the Minister of Culture's declaration that since his appointment to the ministry he has tried his best to dissociate between the cultural and the political ring ironic.[49] Indeed, the Minister's declaration unearths the true motives of the state cultural apparatus with regard to political expression. It is precisely because Ibrahim understands these true motives that he attempts to recapture the historic role that has been denied the Egyptian intellectual during the second half of the twentieth century. As writer Bahaa Taher reminds us:

> Intellectuals have played a prominent role in issues of national unity, national independence, and social justice. They are now excluded and have been condemned to silence. When they do speak, they are ignored by the media that is dominated by civil servants and makeshift intellectuals. Genuine intellectuals have become strangers and estranged in their own country.[50]

88 *Inside the literary establishment*

By daring to speak truth to power, as the late Edward Said had put it, Sonallah Ibrahim exposed the prison house of the institution and reclaimed the public role of intellectuals that state cultural politics have calculatedly and systematically denied them. Indeed, in *Representations of the Intellectual*, as Said considers the universal role and responsibility of intellectuals, he asks a set of basic questions: "how does one speak the truth? What truth? For whom and where?"[51] On 22 October 2003, Sonallah Ibrahim effectively answered all these questions.

Part II
Remaking culture
Emerging institutions, discourses, icons and metaphors

5 Lost in globalization
Education and the stranded Egyptian elite

In June 1999, in keeping with its twice-yearly tradition, the American University in Cairo (AUC) awarded Edward Said an honorary doctorate. On that occasion, Said delivered a commencement address that focused on the idea of a university to the very last class of the twentieth century.[1] He dispelled the notion that liberal education is a European or western mode of study and reminded his audience that the principle of *ijtihad*, i.e. the central role of individual effort in study and interpretation, constituted the core of the Arab-Islamic culture and that in the past the *madrasa* (school) attached to the mosque, whose students practised *ijtihad*, was the locus of liberal thinking and education. He proceeded to note the special status that every society assigns to the academy "whether it exempts it from intercourse with the everyday world or whether it involves it directly in that world".[2] Said argued that it is this special status accorded to the university that produces "a sense of violated sanctity experienced by us when the university or school is subjected to crude political pressures".[3] Said proceeded to advance his own model for academic freedom one that is in perfect harmony with his own personal and professional histories: the model of the migrant or the traveller:

> If in the real world outside the academy, we must needs be ourselves and only ourselves, inside the academy ... we should be able to discover and travel among other selves, other identities, other varieties of the human adventure. But most essentially, in this joint discovery of self and other, it is the role of the academy to transform what might be conflict, or consent, or assertion into reconciliation, mutuality, recognition, creative interaction.[4]
> (...)
> The image of traveller depends not on power, but on motion, on a willingness to go into different worlds, use different idioms, understand a variety of disguises, masks, rhetoric, and be free to do so, and to be critical, to think for oneself.[5]
> (...)
> Most of all, and most unlike the sultan who must guard only one place and defend its frontiers, the traveller *crosses over*, traverses territory, abandons fixed positions.[6]

92 Remaking culture

Said, of course, was speaking at the commencement ceremony of the only liberal education institution in Egypt. However, as can be clearly seen from his address, he felt compelled to defend, contextualize and historically situate the very idea of liberal education in an institution that has been operating in Egypt since 1919. Why does Said in this address strategically and deliberately situate liberal education at the heart of an Arab-Islamic tradition, establishing a continuum between the premodern religious *ijtihad* practised within the *madrasa* attached to the mosque and modern secular analytical knowledge? Why did Said, who grew up in colonial Cairo during the 1940s and who in his autobiography *Out of Place* has so meticulously documented the alienating effects of colonial education (of which AUC, as initially conceived, was definitely part), feel compelled to deliver a speech on liberal education and the idea of a university before an audience that assembled predominantly Egyptian graduating students, powerful and affluent parents, Egyptian ministers and distinguished international guests, AUC faculty and administration?[7] Has the space for liberal education along with the crucial role it plays, through its emphasis on critical and analytical thinking, debate and dialogue become endangered within AUC? How has the re-Islamization of Egyptian society impacted this secular institution? Have global market demands and new expansion plans within AUC redefined this receding space? How have changes in the educational system in Egypt at large influence the understanding of liberal education? What is the relationship between AUC and other Egyptian institutions of learning? How have agendas of globalization remodelled both national and private education leading to a schism within the country's educational system? How can Said's humanist model of a "traveller" who "crosses over, traverses territory" be read within the context of an increasingly globalized education market? All these questions become all the more pressing and relevant when we know that Said's commencement speech was tailored to respond to two consecutive censorship crises that besieged the American University in Cairo and brought it into direct confrontation with the Egyptian authorities and the Egyptian society at large.[8]

We of AUC

Before we proceed to explore all these questions it may be important to look at the changing faces of AUC in Egypt since its establishment in 1919. Initially AUC was intended to be an American, all-male, private Christian preparatory school and university that was conceived, as an idea, by a group of missionaries headed by Charles R. Watson, corresponding secretary of the United Presbyterian Board of Foreign Missions. AUC was modelled on other missionary schools in the region such as the Syrian Protestant College that was to become, during later years, the American University in Beirut. It had become clear, after half a century of Protestant school education in Egypt and given what the two other existing universities (the religious centre of Al-Azhar and the newly created private secular university of Fuad I, later Cairo University, both of which I will return to shortly) had to offer, that a third institution of higher education, with a focus on liberal education for Egypt's expatriate and Christian population, would be successful.[9] In April 1919 the deal was completed for the downtown Cairo site and AUC moved into the Gianaclis building that had previously been rented by the Egyptian University.[10] Bachelor degrees were first issued in 1928, a year that also witnessed the enrolment of the first female student in the university. Analogous to the establishment of the College of Arts and Science was the establishment, in 1921, of the School of Oriental Studies (initially a non-degree Arabic language instruction unit that eventually awarded M.A. degrees and was subsumed in 1956 under the College of Arts and Science as the Center for Arabic Studies). At the outset, therefore, Egyptian society was insular to this newly conceived liberal arts college that catered first and foremost to Egypt's minorities (Greeks, Jews, Armenians and Italians). However, as Donald Malcolm Reid has shown, the increasing American influence on Egyptian education gradually increased with the eclipse of British power and presence in Egypt after 1952 when "Egypt needed a big-power sponsor in the post colonial (or, perhaps, neo-colonial) age, and the US vied with the Soviet Union for the post".[11] Indeed, Reid's statistics show that, in 1953, 21 per cent of Egyptian scientists and technicians held American doctorates compared to 45 per cent from Britain and 28 per cent from Egypt, with a parallel increase in Egyptian publication in American scientific journals. By the 1960s Muslim enrolments at AUC surpassed Christian ones while the AUC Arabic-language *Journal of Modern Education* preached American liberal arts education ideals to a larger public.[12]

It is important to note that, from the start, AUC had set itself a dual mission: one was a commitment to propagating American educational principles of liberal arts and the other was to teach the language and heritage of the Arab world within this new liberal context. This latter engagement was a long-standing practice within the American Protestant missions who were schooled in Arabic and employed Arab scholars.[13] The dual commitment to liberal education and to the "revitalization of Arab culture" is reflected in AUC's mission statements well into the 1990s that have always recognized that, given the institution's history and location, "Arabic language and Middle Eastern Studies are important parts of its offerings".[14] Likewise, in later years, the core curriculum mandated by the university for all of its students reflected this strong commitment to Arabic Studies, requiring all students to take a considerable number of courses in the field. Whether we choose to look at the rocky years of the 1960s, when AUC was placed under sequestration with its degrees not recognized by the Egyptian state,[15] or the auspicious 1990s that witnessed the restructuring of the university into three major schools – Business, Economics and Communication; Humanities and Social Science; and Sciences and Engineering – the institution continued to demand this dual commitment to liberal arts and Arabic language and culture from its students.

The tale of two universities

The establishment of AUC is historically only ten years down the line from the founding in 1908 of the Fuad I University (now Cairo University), the first national Egyptian university that was to produce the nation's secular intellectuals thus becoming the counterpart to the historic religious institution of Al-Azhar (today a fully fledged university in its own right) that produced the nation's *ulama* and continues to mandate religious studies for all of its students.[16] This historic concurrence between the establishment of an Egyptian secular national institution and an American liberal arts one meant, at least in theory if not in practice initially, that two institutions were now competing over the formation of the Egyptian and Arab elites in a modern secular educational context specifically with regard to these elites' own linguistic and cultural heritage. In addition, these two secular institutions, one national, the other American, were the fruit and logical extension of nineteenth-century educational policies that had been developed and implemented since the reign of Muhammad Ali (1805–48) and his family and until the British occupation of Egypt (1882–1923). The policies were meant to supply the Egyptian modern state with a cadre of bureaucrats, a skilled workforce and well-trained army officers. These new institutions were conceived as part of a modern educational "order" that would counter the apparent "disorder" that prevailed within traditional religious learning as represented by Al-Azhar.[17] They were modelled after modern European institutions and were superimposed on a traditional socio-economic and religious structure in Egypt. Hence they were perceived as repositories of colonial influence and domination. The two secular universities inaugurated at the beginning of the twentieth century were no exception. Under the Nasser regime of the 1950s both institutions succumbed to a series of containment strategies devised to strengthen the regime's control and domination of the educational system as a whole.

In order to understand the politics of education in Egypt during the 1950s and 1960s, it is important to look at the developments both in Cairo University and those at AUC. Indeed, the histories of AUC and Cairo University exhibit important parallel developments well into the 1960s, however, because the two institutions have always been looked at separately; seldom has this instructive parallelism been highlighted. Despite the enormous difference in enrolment figures (134 enrolled at AUC to 10,534 at Fuad I University in 1945–46;[18] 3,624 enrolled at AUC to 185,158 at Cairo University in 1998–99),[19] they came to represent two institutions that were responsible for the making of the Egyptian elite. In the 1950s, the Nasser regime was intent on reversing the influence and impact of colonial education as well as mobilizing education at all levels to propagate the new Arab nationalist and socialist ideology. To this effect, the regime devised a new "order" of control and surveillance of education through multiple "nationalization" measures. It is within this framework that the regime's sequestration of AUC during the 1960s should be read, for it resembled similar designs that had been mounted for the national university in Egypt. Like AUC, the Egyptian University, which had prided itself on its autonomy and had initially been created as a private liberal arts institution that sought "knowledge for its own sake",[20] was subjected to state control and containment.[21] In 1954 the university underwent an infamous purge whereby faculty perceived to be a threat to the regime were fired and replaced by staff more quiescent to its political and ideological agendas.[22] Likewise, while AUC's degrees were not officially recognized by the state because they were granted by a foreign institution, overt student political activities and student union elections were suspended at Cairo University.[23] Whereas, in the case of AUC, sequestration meant that the institution and its graduates would remain on the margin of national engagement, the purge of the national university and the regime's iron grip on its student body ensured that political conformity took precedence over intellectual excellence and critical thinking.[24]

The parallelism that characterized the regime's intervention in both institutions during the 1950s and 1960s subsequently developed into an acute polarization of the fate of the two institutions. In 1962 the Nasser regime declared university education a right and not a privilege, rendering it free for all. The 1960s also witnessed the proliferation of national universities and higher institutes that were meant to produce the cadres for a modern technological society to the detriment of the university's initial liberal, humanist vision.[25] By the time Nasser died, Cairo University had 50,000 students i.e. two and a half times as many as when he came into power.[26] Today, Egypt has one of the largest higher education systems in the developing world with 1.670 million students in 1999/2000 in national institutions that lack adequate financial, human and material resources[27] and provide poor-quality education that is at once mediocre, dogmatic and conservative.[28] In addition, the dramatic increase in enrolments in national university education has rendered the current system financially unsustainable.[29] With the advent of the 1970s and 1980s that witnessed Egypt's realliance with the US and its integration in a global market economy, it became evident that the national, public academy and its increasing decay could not respond to new market demands.

As the national university continued to sink into conservatism and self-preservation AUC rose to unprecedented visibility, attracting a new class of Egyptian *nouveau riches* for whom this American institution represented a window to the global future. Despite the fact that the language of instruction at AUC is English not Arabic as is the case in the national universities, it has steadily moved into the centre of the elite education market, boasting the formation of many of Egypt's (and the Arab world's) high-profile figures: intellectuals, executives, ministers, prime ministers, ambassadors, sons, daughters and spouses of political leaders and ruling families. With the state's official recognition of AUC's degrees in 1974, the institution's majority female student body of the 1960s gradually allowed for increasing numbers of Egyptian and Arab elite male students whose global professional opportunities were more solidly guaranteed through an American degree, not necessarily a national one any more.[30] This change also meant that AUC, where the language of instruction is English, became increasingly the target of national criticism for it was now *the* institution responsible for forming the affluent Egyptian elite, both male and female. Furthermore, the very fact that it is an American institution that schools the Egyptian elite in things western upholds liberal education principles and strives to protect academic freedom and its own autonomy, meant that it was bound to enter into various public confrontations. Given the rise of Islamism in Egyptian society, and the escalation of anti-American sentiments, it was only to be expected that the AUC's liberal education would be called into question, especially since the institution no longer occupied an insular position with regard to Egyptian society. In addition, it has indeed come to represent not just a microcosm of the contradictory and colliding values of the post-*infitah* social and economic Egyptian elite of Sadat's Open Door policies but the equally contradictory educational policies in Egypt as a whole.

The diversification and heterogeneity of the student body within AUC that was once a small, upper-class liberal arts college gave rise to challenging contradictions within the institution itself. The increasing plurality and diversity of the student body also meant that the institution now had to struggle with contending and conflicting values and ideas about its educational policies and process, ones that these incoming students brought with them from their different family and educational backgrounds. For example, starting in 1999 several unprecedented debates and crises surrounding the *niqab* (face veiling) erupted at AUC, with one woman student filing a case and winning it against the university for having been denied access to the university grounds because of her *niqab*.[31] In response to this incident, in 2001 AUC, whose female students are today almost equally split between veiled and unveiled women, issued a formal statement banning the *niqab*. The university backed its new policy by referencing the Ministry of Education regulation, upheld by a Supreme Constitutional Court decision declaring that "There should be a compromise between constitutional and legal rights on the one hand and the security perspective and aspects of the educational system on the other".[32] The AUC President declared that the ban on *niqab* was in line with the university's "educational philosophy", while the Vice President of AUC added: "for those who don't like it, there are many other universities they can attend".[33]

On another level, the growing and changing student body also meant that AUC's mission statement of the 1980s that reflected its strong humanities and social science components needed to be changed to reflect its expansion and restructuring to satisfy new client and market demands. Significantly, the new and highly demanded and demanding professional schools of Business, Economics and Communication and Sciences and Engineering, whose enrolment figures by far surpass those of the Humanities and Social Sciences, have tilted AUC towards professional technical education to the detriment of its liberal arts component. Moreover, given the traditional model for professional education provided through the national university, the very idea of liberal education which mandates a core curriculum for all students is predominantly looked upon by both the incoming students and their families with contempt.

Having moved to the centre of the educational map, AUC assumed its new Egyptian and regional role of "revitalizing" Arab culture by providing diverse educational opportunities to the less privileged but outstanding students. The most significant development in this vein has been the inauguration in September 2004 of the Leadership for Education and Development Program (LEAD) under the auspices of Egypt's First Lady and funded by the United States Agency for International Development and the Egyptian Ministry for International Co-operation. The LEAD programme offers full scholarships to 54 outstanding national high-school students annually – both male and female – from Egypt's governorates in order to "prepare [them] for the 21st century and qualify them to lead a positive vision of Egypt's future".[34] This new "order" within AUC seems to echo nineteenth-century strategies and policies of "modernizing" Egyptian subjects and actually takes place through similar strategies of surveillance and control. LEAD programme students are housed in the AUC dorms on a full-board basis and as a group attend special orientation sessions and seminars meant to integrate them into the university system as a whole. The first year of the programme is entirely dedicated to English language instruction to prepare LEAD students for the university curriculum. The ultimate professed goal is to produce the following:

> a student with the knowledge and skills that permit him/her to be employable and to actively participate in the development of the country; a student that has developed affiliation with the country and commitment to life-long community service, a student equipped with leadership skills and ethics of respect of the work, honesty, transparency, respect of the other and tolerance of differences; and finally a student that can compete internationally and integrate in the global world.[35]

Perhaps all these contradictions have best been captured by the blockbuster Egyptian comedy *Sa'idi fil-gami'a il-amrikiyya* (An Upper Egyptian at the American University in Cairo) that was released to enormous success in 1998. Khalaf, the protagonist in the film, is an Upper Egyptian student who wins a scholarship to study at the American University in Cairo where his traditional world view and values are brought into confrontation with AUC's elite and westernized students. The fact that Khalaf is a Sa'idi is highly significant since the Sa'id (Upper Egypt) is the poorest part of Egypt and a prime recruitment region for militant Islamist groups. At AUC, not only is Khalaf's identity reconstructed but his very language is equally changed. Indeed, one of the hit songs in the film is a take-off on the very language of AUC students: *Kajwiluh*, the Arabization of the English word "casual", is the title of the song that means "dress him casual". The song in the film is sung as Khalaf is escorted by some hard-won AUC student friends to one of Cairo's shopping malls where he abandons his outdated clothes for slick jeans and polo shirts. Even though initially it was rumoured that AUC planned to sue the filmmakers for using its name, it eventually dropped the idea when it discovered that the film ultimately depicted both the institution and its diverse students in a favourable if not nationalistic light. Yes, AUCians looked westernized in their general attire and mannerisms but they were also represented as nationalists, demonstrating for a free Palestine and burning the Israeli flag.

98 *Remaking culture*

The pot-pourri of AUC

In an attempt to understand who AUC students are and what educational values they might or might not have, I always open my introductory class on Modern Arabic Literature, a core requirement for all AUC students, with a set of very general questions that help me know and better guide the group of attending students during a given semester before I have them read the assigned literary texts. These questions, and the class discussions that ensue, are meant to reveal to me how these young people, who are voluntarily attending an elite, expensive, private, foreign, liberal arts institution in Egypt, understand education and how they relate to crucial academic principles of critical and analytical inquiry and thinking as well as freedom of speech and expression, the very core of the humanistic endeavour. What is a university? What is liberal education? What is the relationship between art and reality, the writer and society, literature and ideology? How do we read a literary text? How do we deal with questions of language, representation, interpretation and "truth" in the humanities? And ultimately, who is in my class? What kinds of reactions can I expect from them? How can we run a discussion in which all those present can participate? Responses to such questions have consistently confronted me with the challenging task that lies before us as educators within this institution in particular and within Egypt in general. Two striking examples from one of my classes may serve to reveal some of the challenges we confront as we try to understand the contending and contradictory educational values that coexist in one classroom.

The first example has to do with a discussion of a one-minute, obviously symbolic, scene in the contemporary Egyptian film *Al-Asifa* (The Storm) where the actress stands facing a mirror, with her back to the audience, hugging her naked torso, after having denied herself the prospect of marrying the man she loved, for the sake of her two grown sons. An Egyptian young man in the classroom declared that the scene, the actress and the filmmakers are all doubly sinful: first for actually producing this scene and second for having subjected him to viewing it, thereby implicating him in a sinful act. His verdict: the film should be banned and the cast and crew tried for corrupting the youth. The second example has to do with a discussion of a selection of contemporary Arab short stories, all of which are allegories against oppression and for freedom of expression. An Egyptian young woman in the class deemed the authors too blatantly political, their symbolism simplistic and their stories too direct. Her verdict: Arab writers are boring and do not speak to her as do Beckett, Sartre and Camus whose works, according to her, address larger, more universal, existential questions.

Polarized as they may appear to be, these two instances and reactions by students sitting in the same classroom point to an apparently different relationship to things Arabic that in the two instances informs their reactions to cultural representations in their society. I wish to argue that the reactions of the two students had to do with the *kind* of exposure they had had to Arabic language and Arab cultural curricula during their high-school education. That the Egyptian educational system can produce this spectrum of relationships to Arabic language and culture has become a norm rather than an exception. How are these apparently different but essentially identical reactions towards things Arabic produced? What is the nature of the educational landscape that produced them? How does these students' alienation from their surrounding cultural realities translate into an alienation from the realities of their language? What is the nature of their relationship to Arabic and how does alienation from one's language lead to an alienation from one's culture?

Arabic language and the knowledge society

On the metaphoric level and from an Arab nationalist point of view the Arabic language is not simply a tool for communication. Rather it is a symbol of group identity that "provide[s] the cultural and instrumental backbone of the group's legitimate objective of furthering its ethnocultural self-interest".[36] Hence the importance for Arab nationalists of calls to revitalize and modernize the Arabic language since the nineteenth century, for they thoroughly believed that "language ... is, in and of itself, both the medium and the substance of cultural delivery".[37] Maintaining a vital and vibrant Arabic language in face of inside and outside challenges seemed the most effective means of Arab cultural survival. The same concerns were articulated in the UNDP Arab Human Development Report, 2003[38] as well as the 2005 report by the ALECSO (Arab League Educational, Cultural and Scientific Organization i.e. the Arab UNESCO), which declared that the Arab world confronts major setbacks with regard to the Arabic language at a moment when globalization has become a threat to identity and specificity, as well as cultural and linguistic diversity.[39] However, the two extreme examples cited above of students reacting to their own culture seem to testify that something is amiss with the acquisition of the Arabic language itself, if we are to believe the Arab nationalist position that language is at once the medium and substance of cultural delivery.

In fact, the reactions of the two students may very well be read as examples of what Niloofar Haeri has called the Arabs' custodianship of their own language. In *Sacred Language Ordinary People*, Haeri asks the interesting question: "What does it mean to modernize a sacred language?" Indeed Arabic presents that very problem by virtue of its being at once the sacred language of the Qur'an and the official state language in the Arab world. If at the heart of the notion of modernity lies the arbitrary relationship between form and meaning, the signifier and the signified, how can one modernize the Arabic language when the relationship between the linguistic forms of the Qur'an and their corresponding meanings is believed by Muslims to be *non-arbitrary*?[40] To further complicate matters, Haeri argues in another context that classical Arabic "is a language with no native speakers. No one speaks it as a mother tongue. Different groups of Arabs speak various vernacular forms of Arabic that are quite different from their written language."[41] The vernaculars are owned by the people but classical Arabic has divine ownership: it is for the people to use but not to own. Hence they remain its custodians not its owners: "Only when custodians become owners of a language can they really turn it into something modern."[42] Simple and tidy as this may sound, Haeri's basic argument holds. True, the classical Arabic language has always undergone a process of modernization and revitalization since the *nahda* (Arab cultural renaissance) and up to our present day – in recent literary texts, the language of advertising, the press and the media, as well as information technology communication – but never without resistance and the accompanying guilt that somehow the human is "contaminating" the divine. This attitude can be readily supported by any haphazard reading of Arab newspapers that practically on a daily basis run an article or column bemoaning and bewailing what has befallen our beautiful Arabic language and the extent to which it has succumbed to various forms of "standardization", "simplification", "westernization" and outright "deformation". Furthermore, Arab reformists, and men of letters have throughout the nineteenth and twentieth centuries echoed more or less the same tune, maintaining that classical Arabic "embodies our long cherished glories", and that the *nahda* is in fact an endeavour "to perpetrate our imperial bond by means of the Arabic language as if we were revivifying with this bond our bygone empire".[43] Such fears of the "contamination" of classical Arabic on the one hand and its possible "erosion" on the other can be explained not only at a religious level by the sacred origins of Arabic but also, and of equal importance, at a political one through the nationalist and Islamist argument that maintains that ideas about language "are inseparable from those about the self, national identity, ... culture, nation and forms of governance".[44] Hence, the contamination of the language is a contamination of the self; its erosion is an erosion of national or Islamic identity. These assertions with regard to the Arabic language, Arab or Islamic national identity and Arab or Islamic sense of belonging are but a reconfirmation of Benedict Anderson's argument on the construction of imagined communities, national identities and the role he attributes to the emergence of national languages and national literatures in the invention of modern nations.[45] This brings us back to the two students whose reactions seem to expose a serious fracture in that sense of belonging that enables imagined communities. The question then becomes: how are these reactions constructed? And what is the context in which they develop and thrive?

Education and national security?

In *Transforming Education in Egypt: Western Influence and Domestic Policy Reform*, Fatma H. Sayed states that education in Egypt "has been referred to as a matter of 'national security' in every single presidential speech, ministerial press release, and official governmental statement addressing the topic since the beginning of the 1990s".[46] She goes on to point out that "In almost all his official statements on education, President Mubarak links educational reform to national security, espousing the broader definition of national security that encompasses political, economic, as well as military dimensions".[47] However, a quick glance at the actual educational landscape in Egypt today may actually reveal that education has become a national hazard!

The gradual collapse of the national system of education starting in the mid-1970s during the *infitah* period has meant that its fate, like that of the public sector, had become subject to an open-market economy that is dependent on global interests and global markets. The sheer numbers of the state-run, and run-down high schools that labour under a multitude of setbacks are alarming. Programmes in these institutions are dominated by didactic not interactive instruction with a drive to install loyalty, obedience, and support for the regime in power, besides being drenched in social inhibitions and religious taboos.[48] The antiquated and dogmatic curricula produce thousands who have a fossilized relationship to their own culture, and are suspicious of, if not antagonistic to, other cultures in the world. As is the case in many other developing countries, the Egyptian state had come to a point where it could no longer raise the funds required for educational reform and expanding demand for education. Hence the massive international intervention in the field of education in Egypt.

Since Egypt signed the Camp David Accords with Israel in 1978 it has topped the lists of development assistance recipients (much of which is earmarked for education) with 10 per cent of total world development assistance in 1991.[49] Contextualizing the reasons behind such exceptional amounts of funding, Fatma H. Sayed states that, with the end of the Cold War in the 1990s and the reshuffling of the world economic and political order, policy makers in donor countries had to rethink the very concept of development, giving more weight to the human aspect of development criteria. These criteria highlighted specifically the importance of education for "international socialization" whereby a set of values would be embedded and habitualized within Egyptian educational institutions to ensure Egypt's inclusion in the "international community" that is dominated by western organizations (World Bank, IMF, UNDP, UNESCO, among others) norms and interests.[50] This has meant that international donors practically mandate educational reform policies in Egypt starting from basic education all the way through to high school. As Sayed points out, the biggest unstated concern on international donor agendas is the radical Islamization of Egyptian society or,[51] to use Gregory Starrett's formulation, the "Islamic Trend" in Egypt especially in the wake of repeated attacks on tourists and the knowledge that Islamic groups are recruiting more and more among younger and younger high-school students.[52] Furthermore, it became apparent that contemporary Islam in Egypt was as much the result of the national educational system as it was of "traditional" texts and intellectual institutions like Al-Azhar:

> [T]he young men who bomb and shoot tourist buses, government ministers, and police tend also to be modern educated, with degrees and diplomas in technical subjects. In Egypt, many of them are from the largely agricultural regions of the south. Like the overwhelming majority of Egyptian youth, these would-be members of the overstaffed technical and administrative

classes are disturbed by the moral degradation of society and by its scarcity of economic and political opportunity, and believe that a new social framework based on Islamic law is the best solution.[53]

Starrett opens his book *Putting Islam to Work: Education, Politics, and Religious Transformation in Egypt* with a highly dramatic and disturbing scene: a raid on an apartment in Alexandria in August 1989 by the Egyptian Bureau for National Security Investigation where 20 young men, among them eight boys between the ages of four and ten, were arrested. The men were charged with "enticing the children with religious slogans and planting extremist ideas in their minds in preparation for transforming them into an extremist religious group".[54] Starrett argues that the central importance of the raid lay in its message to the Egyptian public: that children are at risk from "extremism":

> The fear that children can fall prey to unsanctioned religious ideas reflects a partial recognition of how deep are the cultural and institutional roots of the Islamic Trend. Recent news reports claim that groups like the Gama'a al-Islamiyya have moved beyond the indoctrination of children in private kindergartens, to use women and young people as couriers, messengers, arms buyers, lookouts, and bomb placers.[55]

Despite the US$4.6 billion in donor funds, Egypt is reputed to be "the black hole of development assistance", a statement often repeated by international development agency officials indicating the continued failure of aid agencies in accomplishing both their stated and unstated goals.[56]

Learn to speak a little bit of English

Concurrently, alongside international educational funding, in the 1980s Egypt witnessed a unique and regionally unparalleled privatization of the educational system at all levels and in different orientations. True, these recently established private schools represent fewer than 10 per cent of the total number of schools in Egypt; however, they have also become the Egyptian elite's way of dodging antiquated national curricula, avoiding overcrowded classrooms (at least forty students in a class), and circumventing the rote learning of the notorious *Thanawiyya Amma* national certificate that determines the future of high-school graduates. These alternative, globally oriented schools include the Cairo American College, which offers US curricula, the British International School, which offers UK curricula, the German School, which offers the German Abitur and the Lycée Français du Caire, which offers the French Baccalaureate. None of these schools mandates the national Arabic curriculum.

Egypt's open economy and the state's encouragement of private-education alternatives as well as the tax incentives and lax control over the curricula taught in newly approved private schools are all elements that have attracted entrepreneurs interested in getting into education, which is deemed by observers a growth industry in Egypt.[57] For example, the American International School in Egypt, established in 1990, is owned by a Syrian-born businessman; the Modern English School (1990) is owned by a Palestinian resident of Cairo; the International School of Choueifat, which is part of a worldwide network of colleges, is operated by Lebanese residents of Cairo; Ecole Oasis Internationale (2002) is an Egyptian venture. This is but a handful of the growing number of recent private schools in Egypt that offer a mind-boggling cocktail of national, American and British international certificates. The language of instruction in all these schools is either English or French. Again none of them mandate, the national Arabic curriculum. Moreover, in order to throw the widest net over increasing demand for private education in Egypt, some of these schools offer two separate national and international curricula among which the student body is split according to economic means (the international section being far more expensive). It is important to note that Egypt has always had a private language school system; however, all these language schools were "nationalized" in the 1950s, giving the state total control over their curricula, including Arabic and religion. In addition, their fees have remained affordable when compared to the more exorbitantly expensive fees of the globally oriented models of the 1990s that offer international curricula and certification.

Not only has the state's entrepreneurial policy towards all levels of school education generated chaos where high-school standards and diplomas are concerned but it has also meant that the study of the Arabic language, the official language of the state, has become an option, not a mandate. The study of foreign languages in private schools has taken precedence over the acquisition of Arabic since they constitute a vehicle for economic and professional capital and mobility. All this has recently translated into curricula that pay lip service to the Arabic language (and culture) almost across the board, producing more than one generation of linguistically, and therefore culturally, alienated youth within the Egyptian elite. Given the lack of knowledge of things Arabic, many of the students who graduate from these institutions have a phobic relationship to their culture and seek to emulate, imitate and parrot any other model available to them. Finally, not only have these schools widened the already existing gap between the haves and the have-nots but they have also exasperated social and ideological differences as well.

At the other end of the entrepreneurial spectrum in education lies the privatization of Islamic education. Sayed gives three categories of these institutions: the populist fundamentalist schools that are run by Islamic activists outside the purview of Al-Azhar (which the state has been trying to downsize) and the commercial and foreign-language Islamic schools that cater to a wider middle class and focus on teaching foreign languages (which are tolerated by the state).[58] The latter offer their students a combination of two worlds: a traditional Islamic education that makes conservative religious meanings and symbols part of daily practice and life meant to strengthen and regulate student belief and value systems as well as a modern education that would ensure their preparation for private, globally oriented institutions of higher education.[59]

The pot-pourri of AUC constitutes the receiving end of all these competing educational institutions and values. The classroom becomes a public display of the contradictions and pitfalls of the Egyptian educational system at large and the deep schism and antagonisms that are festering in the minds of the youth of the Egyptian elite. These are brought together within an institution that continues to maintain a mission statement that upholds liberal education and that declares its commitment to "prepare [the students] for the 21st century and qualify them to lead a positive vision of Egypt's future".[60]

The jungle of higher education

Not only is Egypt beset with problems internal to its educational system but it is also plagued with more recent questions of cultural sovereignty. Initially, as in the case of school education, some of the problems internal to the national system of higher education have been meekly addressed through two main venues: one was a 1996 presidential decree that allowed for the establishment of new private universities (the Sixth of October University, October University for Modern Sciences and Arts, Misr University for Sciences and Technology, and Misr International University, among others that continue to sprout);[61] the other was to implant within the national universities' otherwise collapsing system a new series of foreign affiliates within already existing departments and fields of study: for example, an affiliation with Harvard Law School within the faculty of law or an affiliation with French universities' departments of political science within the faculty of political science and economics.[62] These arrangements have meant elevated tuition fees for the students enrolled in these programmes. The new affiliates have the advantage of bringing to national universities international faculty in the various disciplines. Because of the rigorous demand for foreign languages (English and/or French) within these programmes, most, if not all, of their students come from private language schools and are selected for their outstanding academic performance. This new system of affiliation basically constructs a university within a university: one for the elite and another for the masses; one for the affluent, the other for the poor.

As for the question of cultural sovereignty that has become part of a heated and ongoing debate, one has to look at another form of partnership between Egypt and other foreign entities and countries. During the past decade alone the country has witnessed the establishment of several joint venture institutions of higher education where Egypt has entered into a partnership with another foreign country: hence the establishment of a British University, a French University, a German University and a Canadian University. All are expensive private professional and technical schools with no programmes in the humanities and no study of Arabic language or Arab culture. Even though enrolment remains in the thousands, it is expected, given the technical and professional orientation of these new universities, that they will attract both outstanding and affluent students. This basically means two things: students coming from schools that inculcate the traditional Islamic values will exit higher education into the professional world with those same values; as for Egyptian students who have opted for the international curricula in their private high schools where they can choose not to study Arabic (and their numbers are on the increase), they will not have done any Arabic since high school and until they graduate from the university. True, they all speak the vernacular, but for all intents and purposes they represent an illiterate elite where Arabic language and culture are concerned. What are we to expect from this sinister reality? What kind of future generation are we producing? How can an elite that has been robbed of its own cultural sovereignty enter into any global conversation? Granted, the conditions of linguistic exchange are, like the economic, ones unequal and the Arabic language, like its native speakers, is one that remains in a globally dominated position. However, what does a gradual erosion of Arabic tell us about the space remaining for us to occupy on a global map?

W(h)ither liberal education?

To date, AUC remains the *only* liberal education institution with a core programme in the humanities and a mandate for the study of Arabic language and culture. However, with the increasing competition from these new foreign private universities, the AUC administration has started to rethink its liberal education. Proposals have been put forth to cut back on the number of courses included in the core curriculum. These have actually reduced the number of courses mandated by the university in the Arab Culture component from three to two.[63] Concerned faculty and students from different departments including the Business and Engineering schools have signed an open letter to the AUC President protesting against these cuts and arguing that the proposed changes reflect "a new philosophy in education at AUC" that is contrary to its *raison d'être* as a liberal arts university, and is incompatible with the mission statement that "AUC considers it essential to foster students' appreciation of their own culture and heritage".[64]

Despite the resistance from concerned members of the AUC community it is already obvious that the university will move to accommodate its own demanding professional schools that are now competing with parallel ones in the new joint venture universities. These are indeed short-sighted measures if we but consider the two examples of students that I have used in this chapter and their already disturbing relationship to Arabic language and culture during their very first year in the university.

Inversely, and ironically, as Arabic language and culture take a plunge in private universities in Egypt, they come to experience an unprecedented boom on campuses in the United States! As the *Los Angeles Times* reported, since 11 September 2001 there has been a growing interest in the study of the language, so that Arabic has become "the fastest-growing spoken language of study at U.S. colleges and universities".[65] The paper more specifically cited a survey by the Modern Language Association showing the number of students studying Arabic at US colleges to have climbed 92.3 per cent – to 10,584 – between 1998 and

2002 and the number of undergraduate campuses teaching the language to have jumped 48 per cent, to 233. The article concludes by stating that "The importance of Arabic as a language is not going to go away, no matter what happens in the Middle East".[66] Unfortunately, the Egyptian system of education, whether private or public, seems oblivious to this important strategic fact. Even more disappointing is that AUC, whose history of liberal education and commitment to Arabic language and culture is almost a century long, can suddenly, and under global market pressure, lose sight of the *raison d'être* of its commitments – so eloquently charted by Edward Said in his commencement speech – and begin to contribute, despite its retailored mission statements, to the production of a stranded Egyptian elite.

6 Translating gender between the local and the global[1]

Translation theory and gender studies

In January 1991, I was writing an essay entitled "Translation and the Postcolonial Experience" when the First Gulf War broke out. In that piece, I was basically arguing that the plurilingual or pluricultural nature of postcolonial literature resists and ultimately excludes the monolingual and demands of its readers to be "in between", at once capable of reading and translating, where translation becomes an integral part of the reading experience.[2]

As I watched the deliberate escalation of the crisis leading up to the American-led Gulf War I could not help seeing the parallelism between this uniquely unequal war and my argument in the article. I added an after word to the essay in which I read the Gulf War as "the war of the monolingual", as a failure, indeed an intentional refusal, to understand the importance of being perpetual translators in a world that desperately needs to become plurilingual. I will spare you any further reflection on that after word as it relates to the American declaration on "the war on terror" and the ongoing American occupation of Iraq as well as the daily Israeli apartheid practices against the Palestinian people.

As I was preparing to write this chapter, my article, written more than a decade ago, thrust itself upon me. Once again I found myself calling upon translation theory but this time in order to speak about gender. There is perhaps good reason for the connections that were beginning to take shape between translation studies and gender studies as I approached my task. Both gender and translation permeate, define and shape our very identities. Just as we are gendered or gendering beings we are also translated or translating ones: our gestures, poses, movements, silences and language of course. Despite the fact that both gender and translation are basic to our collective human existence, our attempts to understand and theorize the processes that shape them are quite recent.

Both gender studies and translation studies are fairly new academic fields with international and interdisciplinary thrusts and implications. In both instances they have oriented themselves toward travelling across traditional academic disciplines to create transnational communities and cross-cultural communication. Given these general affinities, I thought it fitting to draw on some of the key theoretical formulations in translation studies to understand some of the challenges that face us in translating gender. This decision, on my part, will immediately implicate the reader in translating with me, as I move between gender and translation. Like any translator, I needed to situate myself between two specific texts and to make strategic choices of translation from one to the other. Given my own professional context, I have chosen to locate myself here: I will anchor myself in the nascent field of gender studies in Egypt and will try to read part of the text that unfolds before me, and to translate it both in local and in global terms.

As is the case with its counterparts in the "Third World", the emerging field of Gender Studies in Egypt is one with a double task. On the one hand, it is informed by and conversant with gender discourses, theories and activism elsewhere. On the other hand, it has the responsibility of elaborating, developing and disseminating its local translation(s) of gender issues in Arabic, and within the larger context of the Egyptian cultural field. Scholars in the western academy, engaged in gender research, within and about the Arab Islamic region, can today assume an interlocutor with whom they interact, i.e. engage, question, contest, reorient, redefine, in the same "language".[3] However, their counterpart colleagues in Egypt cannot necessarily claim the same interlocutor, or the same terms of engagement. Theirs is, first and foremost, the responsibility of translating gender locally. Without this local commitment, there would be no recognizable field of gender studies to contend with at the global level.

Translation theory tells us that translating a text means a rewriting of the original text no matter how invisible that process attempts to be. This act of rewriting does not happen in a vacuum. It is always conditioned and shaped by histories, ideologies, values, beliefs and representations that pre-exist the very act of translation in the target language. This relationship between a foreign text and a target language culture points to "the violence that resides in the very purpose and activity of translation":

> On the one hand, translation wields enormous power in the construction of national identities for foreign cultures, and hence it potentially figures in ethnic discrimination, geopolitical confrontations, colonialism, terrorism, war. On the other hand, translation enlists the foreign in the maintenance or revision of literary canons, dominant conceptual values, research and methodologies of the target-language culture.[4]

Despite this violence, however, translation, as a cultural political practice, can enable innovation and can generate new spaces for the development of individual societies and cross-cultural conversation. What I have been saying about the purpose and activity of translation is not a diversion. It is meant as an entry point into translating gender.

The history of the concept of gender in the Arab context is a history of cross-cultural communication and translation of knowledge. It is also a history of relations of power, at a specific historical juncture, between civilizations within that exchange. The entry for the noun *jins* (which currently signifies sex, kind or species in Arabic) in Ibn Mandhur's *Lisan al-Arab*, one of the most commonly used classical Arabic-language dictionaries, states that the word is considered *muwallad*, i.e. not truly old Arabic, introduced later into the language. Indeed, the word *jins* is simply absent from the Qur'anic text. The noun *jins* is derived from the Greek word *genus* (from which the word "gender" is also derived) and was brought into Arabic *as is*. *Jins* is basically a transcription rather than a translation of the Greek word. Once transcribed as *jins*, the noun takes on a new life that obeys the possibilities of the linguistic realm in which it now exists and becomes one of the living testaments of this early cross-cultural hybridization.

The fact that the Greek word *genus* morphologically resembles the basic Arabic triliteral root (*genus* is made up of three consonants like most Arabic roots) allows the word *jins* to "naturalize" itself more easily than other imported words. It begins to act as an "original" triliteral root and takes on, through the rich system of derivation in the Arabic language, a cumulative semantic life of its own. Hence, *jins* – the transcription of *genus* – is transformed into an Arabic triliteral root and becomes *janasa*. It proceeds to accumulate a whole range of new significations that do not necessarily coincide with the "original" word *genus* from which it is transcribed. Among the primary meanings of *jins* are: gender (as a grammatical category), kind, sort, species, category, class, sex (male, female) and race. The derivative forms from the triliteral root *janasa* have extended the word's field of signification beyond that of immediate categorization: *jinsiyy* means sexual; *jinas*, alliteration; *jinsiyya*, nationality; *tajnis*, naturalization; *tajanus*, homogeneity, etc. One of the lessons we should learn from translating *genus* into *jins* is the extent to which the histories of the two words are no longer identical, or antithetical, or complementary. Rather they are different.

Gender, translation and difference

Difference, as translation theorists have rightly insisted, is not necessarily a loss of the "original". Difference, in translation, is to be read as a gain. Translation emerges as "an active reconstitution of the foreign text mediated by the irreducible linguistic, discursive, and ideological differences of the target-language culture". Seen as such, difference does not become an element to overwrite for the sake of "transparency" and "homogeneity".[5] Rather, difference becomes the locus upon which we may construct enabling theoretical, textual and practical means of cross-cultural communication.

As I have pointed out earlier, in acquiring a different life, the noun *jins* becomes implicated in other histories and new genealogies, ones that feminists and gender studies specialists are now seeking to disentangle it from. How then do we translate gender? As a postmodern conceptual tool, gender has become "one of the busiest, most restless terms in the English language", "as slippery as it is indispensable" for it "draw[s] attention to the artificiality of what we think of as 'natural' behavior" that marks and legitimates the differences between women and men.[6] Indeed, the concept of gender develops from being a grammatical category for the classification of nouns into masculine and feminine during the eighteenth century to being a marker of sexual difference where, as Sherry Simon points out, gender becomes one lens through which differences of all orders (national, ethnic, class, race) are scrutinized:

> Emphasis is placed on the active nature of representational practices, which are seen to construct positions for subjects and to produce identities, binding people across diversities and providing new places from which they can speak. Cultural practices are central to the production of subjects, rather than simply reflecting them.[7]

If such are the complexities of the "original" modern signification of gender, how then can we translate it into the target-language culture, in a gender-sensitive language that would help us unsettle, rather than confirm, dominant masculine values and practices without submitting to "fluency", "transparency" and hence the power and dominance of the foreign text?

This problem is obviously not specific to the Egyptian, Arab or Islamic context for it exists also in other languages.[8] Each new context to which the term "gender" has travelled has endeavoured to translate its postmodern *conceptual* signification. The field of gender studies in Egypt is no exception. I wish to argue that a quick survey of some of the "solutions" to the problem of translating gender are telling of the juncture at which the field finds itself today. The various attempts at translating gender actually translate the position of gender studies within the larger context of the Egyptian fields of knowledge and practice. These "solutions" place us at the very heart of the politics of translation where language, as Gayatri Spivak rightly pointed out, should be seen as the process of "meaning construction".[9] I therefore believe that a reading of some of these translations of gender is in order.

Solutions to translating gender have ranged from attempts at "decolonizing" the concept to hybridizing solutions that are inspired by the historic relationship between the "original" Greek word *genus* and the "translated" Arabic root *janasa* as an exemplary instance of cross-cultural *transcription*. Between these two solutions emerged other combinations and neologisms depending on the fields of research engaged with the concept of gender as a category of analysis.

For example, in 1999, *Alif*, the journal of comparative poetics of the American University in Cairo, published a special issue on *Gender and Knowledge*. In the editorial, the reader is told that "after lengthy discussions with linguists, critics and poets" it was decided not to Arabize the term "gender" by giving it an Arabic pronunciation and script but rather to derive a new word from the root *janasa* that would correspond to the etymological significance of "gender". Hence, *Alif* proposed the neologism *junusa*, which corresponds morphologically to *unutha* (femininity) and *dhukura* (masculinity). This new coinage, the editorial explains, "incorporates notions of the masculine and the feminine as they are perceived in a given time or place, with all the ideological twists and politics that such a construction and vision imply".[10] The merit of this translation lies in the fact that it recognizes gender as a dynamic process rather than a static essence.

Despite this valiant effort, however, none of the contributors in the Arabic section in the journal's issue on *Gender and Knowledge* actually uses this neologism except the editor herself. Instead, we find a proliferation of other translations that either return us to the more essentializing lexicon of the Arabic language or dismiss the Arabic altogether as a language that is capable of translating modern conceptual configurations. These translations range from *dirasat al-jins* (which can be confounded with studies of sex, sexuality, race or nation), *dirasat al-naw'* (which can be confused with studies of biological kind, species, sort or nature). We also find the Arabization of the English word gender itself *dirasat al-jindar* (which alienates rather than communicates anything to an Arabic speaker and, given the hypersensitivity to "western" hegemonic discourses today, can result in combative nationalistic responses). Other, more recent publications that deal with women and gender studies use the more nuanced referent *dirasat al-naw' al-ijtima'i* (in which the category *naw'* i.e. kind, is grounded in the social, i.e. *ijtima'i*). Still, other formulations combine a translated version with a transcribed one, for example: *dirasat al-naw'/al-jindar*. On a positive note one can say that the proliferation of translations of gender points to a corresponding proliferation of discourse on gender issues. It suggests a young and dynamic field that is polyphonic and productive. However, a closer look at the choices and varieties of translation(s) themselves may suggest otherwise.

Meaning construction and gendered agency

I wish to return to the idea that language is the process of "meaning construction" and link that to the urgency of translation politics for gender studies in particular. If indeed, as Spivak succinctly put it, "the task of the feminist translator is to consider language as a clue to the workings of gendered agency",[11] then, the use of the essentialist nouns *naw'* (kind, species, sort) or *jins* itself to translate gender, given their history and current prevailing signification, reinforces notions of separation and difference. Both translations restation us in natural and fixed categories. Suddenly, ideas of socially constructed identities, of formation and of performance, all of which are packed into the concept of gender, as we understand it today, are lost. My question is: why? Why have we chosen to translate gender in the most essentializing terms when we have a language (Arabic) – and language is a process of meaning construction – that is far more open to creative invention as demonstrated by the example of the neologism *junusa* that was coined, but hardly ever used, by the editors of *Alif*? And since *junusa* never really gained currency what does this tell us about our relationship with translation?

The question of translation and the modernization of the Arabic language is one that has defined and shaped the very history of modern Egypt since the early nineteenth century and up to the present. It is also an issue that continues to meet

112 Remaking culture

with various forms of resistance by purist, more conservative elements in the intellectual field. Interestingly, the recent, controversial UNDP *Arab Human Development Report* 2003 dwells extensively on the centrality of language and translation for the global future of the Arab region at all levels and in all disciplines and fields of knowledge. It correctly concludes that:

> Arabic today, on the threshold of a new knowledge society, faces severe challenges and a real crisis in terms of theorization, teaching, grammar, lexicography, usage, documentation, creation, and criticism. The rise of information technology presents another aspect of the challenges to the Arabic language today.[12]

In addition, its authors make the crucial connection between the importance of a good command of one's mother tongue and the ability to learn foreign languages, a relationship that is indispensable for any global conversation or translation to take place.

For any student of modern Arab history and culture the observations listed in the *AHDR* with regard to language, translation and the dissemination of knowledge are practically identical to those made at the beginning of the nineteenth century when Muhammad Ali (1805–49) embarked on his modernization project in Egypt. At the heart of Muhammad Ali's modern infrastructure lay a massive project of translation from French into Arabic to instate linguistic, conceptual and technological modernity anchored in a local, indigenous Arab/Islamic culture. The *AHDR* takes note of this instructive and challenging moment in modern Egyptian history and upholds it as a model to be reproduced in the present. In the nineteenth century, translation became a social institution that contributed to a national project.[13] Not only did it create opportunities for the acquisition and transfer of knowledge but it also contributed to the elaboration of new values and new forms of empowerment.[14] Hence, to use Spivak's formulation once more, translation in nineteenth-century Egypt performed its ultimate goal of "meaning construction".

Are we, in Egypt, at a juncture parallel to that of the nineteenth century? Can the Egyptian regime's recent declaration of commitment to a "knowledge society" (a coinage the regime hijacked from the *AHDR*) be taken seriously? The panorama of the cultural realities surveyed by the *AHDR* leaves little room for hope. Like other countries in the Arab world, Egyptian education is dominated by the didactic not the interactive[15], and is inhibited by social and religious taboos. The sacred religious text remains outside the scope of history but is called upon to explicate and interact with historical realities.[16] The educational curricula are saturated with the glories of the past, and seek to install loyalty, obedience and support for the regime in power.[17] Institutions of higher learning lack autonomy and fall under the direct control of the ruling regime.[18] Freedom of thought and expression (two primary prerequisites for good-quality scholarship and intellectual development) are restricted.[19] Censorship prevails in all fields of knowledge, especially the humanities.[20] Researchers are monolingual

Translating gender 113

and inward-looking. Most Ph.D. holders study their own society rather than the "Other", and their participation in international symposia is markedly low.[21] In stark contrast to the nineteenth-century renaissance, there is an alarming regression in knowledge of foreign languages and consequently a serious decline in translated works specifically in the humanities.[22] It is not surprising, therefore, that we have no accumulated knowledge of the other.[23]

The more nuanced aspect of the *AHDR* is reserved for the central question of the Arabic language and its relationship to the assimilation and production of knowledge. One of the strongest and more urgent declarations in the report, considering our general focus here, has to do with the crucial importance of Arabic language in all levels of education for the future of the Arab region:

> Indeed, promoting and enhancing the Arabic language as a medium for acquiring and indigenising modern sciences is the surest way to achieve [dissemination of knowledge].[24]
> (…)
> the Arabization of university education and the teaching of Arabic … is no longer simply a matter of nationalism; it has become a prerequisite for developing the tools of thinking and the creative faculties of young minds.[25]
> (…)
> The re-birth of the Arabic language … is the core and crux of a new Arab renaissance centered on knowledge and human development.[26]

Despite the fact that, at certain moments, the language of the *AHDR* is itself steeped in the discourse of "the glories of the past" which it sets out to critique (note the use of *rebirth* and *new Arab renaissance* in the passage above), there is no denying that the status of the Arabic language and the importance of translation are indeed significant elements in the making of the Arab future at both local and global levels. Forging such a future will require creative and risk-taking strategies that would challenge the boundaries and limits of a conservative, taboo-ridden, religious and nationalist understanding of language and translation. The field of gender studies is no exception here.

Given the variety of translations of gender within the field, one has to question the venues of local, collective conversation between all those involved in creating a space for gender studies within the cultural, social, economic, scientific and political fields in Egypt. As I said earlier, the primary responsibility of the field of gender studies in any local context is to elaborate, develop and disseminate translations of gender that enable agency, ones that can break through the prison-house of language. Elucidating Spivak's understanding of the "ethics of translation", Sherry Simon notes:

> The translator, the agent of language, faces the text as a director directs a play, as an actor interprets a script. This cannot be the case when translation is taken to be a simple matter of synonymy, a reproduction of syntax and local colour.[27]

114 *Remaking culture*

Such an ethics of translation is an urgent task that we must assume collectively, in conversation and in dialogue: as colleagues, teachers, activists, journalists, policy makers and professionals. Such responsibility becomes all the more pressing as researchers and activists in gender studies accede to venues of public discourse and practice. We are no longer speaking to each other in "more or less the same language". Rather, we are translating gender to a wider audience of girls and boys, of women and men. This is not an exercise in philology. Rather, it is an exercise in communication, the very essence of translation. To understand Spivak's formulation of language as "meaning construction" requires, as the late sociologist Pierre Bourdieu rightly pointed out, that we be propelled into action:

> What are the historical mechanisms responsible for the relative dehistorisization and eternalization of the structure of the sexual division and the corresponding principles of division?
> (...)
> Posing the question in those terms marks an advance in the order of action. To point out that what appears, in history, as being eternal is merely the product of a labour of eternalization performed by interconnected institutions ... is to reinsert into history, and therefore to restore to historical action, the relationship between sexes that the naturalistic and essentialist vision removes from them.[28]

If we allow ourselves to be complicit and if we fail to understand translating gender as part of meaning construction we may find ourselves re-dehistorisizing the essentialist and essentializing categories of man and woman. This will deny us an understanding of ourselves as socially constructed identities with all the liberating and empowering possibilities such awareness entails. The challenge is enormous, especially as we compete for space, voice, visibility and impact with other conservative and neo-liberal discourses, both official and "oppositional", whose practices reinforce, institutionally, gender inequality and binary oppositions on all levels of individual and collective existence to ensure the continuing reign of the masculine.

A specifically telling example comes to mind when one speaks about the potentially disabling translation strategies that circumscribe the field of gender studies in Egypt. In December 2003 the Social Research Center at the American University in Cairo celebrated its Golden Jubilee at the Marriott Hotel where a summary of Egypt's Gender Assessment Report, co-sponsored by The World Bank and the National Council for Women, was presented. One day before the celebration, the Egyptian daily newspaper *Al-Ahram* announced the forthcoming event on its first page under the title *Taqrir Misr wa-l-naw' al-ijtima'i*, literally: "Egypt and the social kind report".[29] Since the translation of "gender" into "social kind" has no currency in modern standard Arabic except within highly limited circles, such a coinage would signify nothing to a lay Egyptian newspaper reader, or even an Arab one, for that matter. But this fact seemed irrelevant. The important point was that "gender" now had a safe, approved, institutional and official translation (*al-nawʿ al-ijtimaʿ*), rubber-stamped by the National Council for Women and The World Bank and hosted by the Social Research Center at the American University in Cairo. One day after the celebration, the regional Saudi-owned paper *Al-Hayat* reported the same event, again on its first page; only this time, the title read *Taqrir Misr wa l-tatawwur al-ijtimaʿi*, i.e. "Egypt and social development report".[30] Suddenly the whole notion that the report was about gender assessment in Egypt in the first place (and not about social development) disappeared! So intent were the translators of "gender" into Arabic on avoiding any derivation from the word *jins* (sex) lest the event be mistakenly associated with taboo subjects like sex, sexuality, sexual relations, sexual behaviour, sexual preference, *bref*, things sexual, that the readers of both *Al-Ahram*, which described the report as one on "social kind", and *Al-Hayat*, which described it as one on "social development", remained mystified as to the actual content and importance of the report.

Furthermore, at the event itself, it was brought to the attention of the panelists who conducted the summary presentation of the Gender Assessment Report by one of the discussants that most, if not all, the report focused on women and women's issues. Men, gender relations and gender-related issues in Egypt, in general, were hardly discussed. This glaring absence leads one to ask the question: do we, in Egypt, continue to understand "gender" as synonymous with "women"? What is the range of gender-related issues, problems and setbacks that are masked by equating gender with women? To what extent does such mistranslation contribute to the essentializing roles of man and woman? And finally, given the institutional power and authority of the parties involved in coining the translation of "gender" into Arabic (The National Council for Women and The World Bank and arguably the Social Research Center that hosted the event), what are the chances left for alternative, risk-taking, and potentially more empowering translations that subvert the eternal dichotomy man/woman?

Gender studies on trial

I wish to investigate further the problem of meaning construction as it relates to translating gender through an even more specific text: an interview published in Arabic, with Huda Elsadda, one of the founding members of the Women and Memory Forum in Cairo (a group of scholars and researchers whose main project is to rewrite Arab cultural history from women's perspective). In this interview Elsadda heroically and single handedly undertakes the responsibility of translating the field of gender studies to her interlocutors. Through a reading of the interview, I will, in turn, undertake to translate for the reader some of the problems the field encounters as they unfold through this text. The interview was conducted in writing with a group of specialists in the different disciplines of the humanities and social science: a philosopher, a sociologist, a literary theorist, a historian and an activist. Together they represent more than one generation, nationality, gender, ideological orientation, from the American University in Cairo and other institutions.

116 *Remaking culture*

The questions asked by the interviewers, together with Elsadda's salutary, though at times understandably exasperated answers, map out not just the location of gender studies within the larger Egyptian context but the sites of resistance and areas of misconception with which it has to contend as well. What is the importance of excavating women's histories? What is the conceptual understanding of gender? Isn't the concept itself a hegemonic idea imposed by the West? Why talk about gender when we should talk about human rights, citizenship and democracy? Can we measure the effectiveness and immediate local impact that gender-based research has had on the lives of millions of poor and illiterate women in Egypt? What are the priorities that should be given within the field of gender studies in order to redefine the relationship between men and women? And, of course, the thorny subject of foreign funding for NGOs working in the field and the extent to which such funding influences their agendas as well as issues of development in general.

Huda Elsadda is uniquely qualified to wrestle with and respond to these questions. She entered the field of gender studies through the translation of a collection of short stories that focus on gender issues, was co-editor of the feminist journal *Hajar*, participated in a project to draft a new marriage contract in 1987 that was halted because "it incorporated western values and concepts";[31] she is a founding member of the Women and Memory Forum and she is a professor in the Department of English at Cairo University. More recently, Elsadda has joined the National Council for Women and the National Council for Human Rights, and was one of the authors of the UNDP Arab Human Development Report, 2003.

As Elsadda responds to the questions of her interviewers, she also *writes in* some of the blind spots of the field as it seeks to translate itself within the Egyptian context. Through her answers Elsadda *writes in* the problems of translating the concept of gender to a larger audience, the limited and often absent venues of conversation within the field and outside it (specifically with regard to institutional entities like the school and the university), the internal hierarchy within the field that opposes those who act (and are therefore grassroots-oriented) to those who talk (and are therefore removed from the immediate realities of the under privileged).

One of the immediate symptomatic problems of the field of gender studies that strikes the reader of this telling and dense interview is the fact that none of the interviewers uses the same terminology to translate "gender". There is a whole array of translations that range from *al bu'd al-junusi* (the gender dimension) to *dirasat al-naw'* (studies of kind), to *al-tashakkul al-thaqafi wa l-ijitim'i li l-jins* (the cultural and social construction of sex), to an outright refusal to translate the concept of "gender" since it is perceived as a western introduction for which there is no Arabic translation. This reality points not so much to the plurality of translations but rather to the difficulty of conversation within the field given the diverse understandings of "gender" and gender-related issues as made evident by the very nature of the interviewers' questions.

Another general trait that characterizes the interviewers' questions is the extent to which gender and gender-related issues are perceived as marginal, certainly not a priority when compared to other more central questions such as human rights, democracy, nationalism, poverty. It becomes evident from reading some of the questions that gender studies and those involved in it inspire negative feelings that range from suspicion to outright antagonism. Interestingly, the very same feelings are reciprocated by the interviewee in her responses to those questions. For example, one of the interviewers, whose work is more grassroots-oriented than research-oriented, asks Elsadda an implicitly critical question, in a not so innocent accusatory tone:

> How can you disseminate ideas about women's rights and the constructed representation of women to others who do not share your beliefs? Or, is it no concern to you to try to win over some opponents? ... What are some of the steps that you and the Women and Memory Forum have taken to widen the scope of your work in order to attract a wider audience other than those already interested in the issues you discuss?[32]

Elsadda retorts by dismantling the hidden agenda behind the question and by exposing, from her point of view, the antagonistic position of her interviewer:

> Initially, I did not understand the meaning behind the first question because on the surface it seems like a logical question to ask ... but I stopped for a moment to think about the signification of the very phrasing and formulation of the question and discovered that it carried, in its folds, a high degree of unjustified prejudice that surfaces every time we speak about women. The picture became clearer when I read the second half of the question that has to do with the relationship between the elite and ordinary people.... One of the prevailing problems that women activists have to confront is accusations of elitism and their separation from the reality of the majority of illiterate women and hence the difficulty of communicating with them at the cultural level.... This way of discussing the problems becomes a strategy of attack to destroy what we disagree with or what we oppose.[33]

Given these reciprocal suspicions as to the motives of both sides, my question is the following: are these problems of communication/conversation between Elsadda and her interviewers solely due to the refusal of some to engage with the translation of gender? Or is it not perhaps equally the inability of gender studies proponents to strategically and actively translate themselves convincingly, to an increasingly suspicious interlocutor?

A reading of Elsadda's answers to other questions confirms that activists in the field of gender studies are indeed implicated in this lack of conversation. For example, when asked about the relationship between the Women and Memory Forum and other organizations and NGOs in the field of women/gender studies, Elsadda responds:

Everyone complains about the lack of co-ordination and insufficient channels between these centres. Consequently there is a real need to create such connections.... Co-ordination between groups will happen gradually as they become stronger and more secure. But if co-ordination is imposed it will not achieve the desired results. On the contrary, it may lead to disunity or centralization of power both of which can be problematic.[34]

The lack of sufficient channels of constructive conversation between various groups involved in gender/women's issues is therefore a reality. Why have the activists in the field not found ways to co-ordinate? Is it simply a difference in focus (cultural research versus social activism)? Is it due to ideological differences (liberal versus Islamic)? Or is it due to individual organization visibility and funding? The answer one suspects is all of the above. There is no question that the field of gender studies is polarized into those who speak and those who act, the "intellectuals" and "the activists" without the necessary co-ordination between both. This is made clear from the repeated issue of "priorities" within the field which surfaces more than once during the course of Elsadda's interview where, interestingly, it is the social scientists and the social activists who keep putting it back on the table. Does the work of the Women and Memory Forum touch the lives of millions of illiterate women? How can the work of the Women and Memory Forum transform realities on the ground? Does not the excavation of women's past lead to a glorification of that past? To these questions Elsadda responds by repeated attempts at de-polarizing the field:

I am convinced that all research in the sciences, the humanities or the social sciences that responds to real needs and that attempts to answer genuine questions that have come out from a particular social and historical reality will strengthen, directly or indirectly, the movement for social change.
(...)
Research in history is an exploration of the many layers of consciousness; the sources and reasons of prejudices, representations of ourselves and others, and the relationship between knowledge and power. These issues are important for understanding our present. For us, studying history is our gateway for tackling women's issues. And, one of our main goals is to demonstrate the link between research and social science.[35]

The polarization between the humanities and social sciences in the field of gender studies is not the only one: the secular and Islamic dichotomy is yet another. Some of the accusations levelled against the "secularists" are tackled by Heba Raouf Ezzat, one of the leading Islamists in the field of women's studies, whose article "Women and *Ijtihad*: Toward a New Islamic Discourse" appears alongside Elsadda's interview, in the same issue of *Alif*. In her article, Ezzat complains that "[the secularists'] major concepts go back to Western schools – Marxist or Liberal – without the crystallization of an independent Arab discourse", and criticizes their "failure to point out the dilemmas and problematics of Western feminist discourse (particularly in the questions of social morals and the family)". She argues that secularists are "weak in terms of self-criticism and consideration of their own positions, while outspoken when attacking the Islamicists"; and that they have an "exaggerated concentration on the legal instrument in instituting change" and "neglect ... channels of cultural and moral change". Finally, Ezzat deplores the secularists' "[focus] on addressing the state to undertake changes rather than address the needs of social units ... and the threats of globalism to national culture and traditions".[36]

The very same level of critique articulated by Heba Raouf Ezzat in her article finds its echo in Elsadda's interview through the questions posed by Hasan Hanafi, the prominent Islamist philosopher, well known as a proponent of enlightened Islam, for his work on the relationship between Islamic and western philosophy, as well as his engagement with issues of human rights and democracy:

> Can we impose Western concepts like "gender" on a different social reality like that of the Arab world which has its specific understanding of the status of women or the personal status law? Indeed, the very word has no Arabic translation.[37]

And again:

> Till when will the West continue to implant concepts like "civil society", "gender", "clash of civilizations", "end of history", while our role remains limited to the margin and to singing someone else's tune? Is it not possible to create culture-specific concepts that represent different realities and historical moments?[38]
> (...)
> How can we study a secondary concept like "gender" when the principal one – citizenship that involves both men and women as citizens – is absent?[39]

Elsadda's responses to Hanafi's questions in particular, despite their studied fullness and documentation, expose some of the blind spots of the "secularists'" discursive strategies within the field of gender studies who seem to be besieged in what resembles a war zone minefield. Indeed, one could characterize some of Elsadda's remarks as counter-attacks rather than calculated and strategic arguments that would enable conversation and translation. For example, after a lengthy and salutary explication of what the term "gender" *really* signifies, Elsadda concludes her reply to Hanafi's assertion that the concept of "gender" is a western one that has no translation into Arabic by implicating her interviewer in the problem. If Hanafi's implicit critique is that secularists parrot the West, Elsadda's riposte is that he, given the nature and tone of his questions, represents a nationalist current that is at once politically brow beaten, uncreative and ultimately sexist and self-interestedly obstructionist:

120 *Remaking culture*

> We must also ask ourselves why it is that new concepts and theories originate in the West and not in the Arab world during the twentieth century. We do not find fault with assimilating and using concepts like democracy, or citizenship, when both have not developed out of the realities of Arab research. Why do we translate or Arabize many concepts that we get used to and defend but always stumble in translation when the issue has to do with women. If we say *naw'* (kind, species) you refuse to understand it; if we say *jindar* (gender) you resent it because it doesn't have an Arabic root (democracy doesn't have an Arabic root either).[40]

As for Hanafi's proclamation that gender is a "secondary" concept, Elsadda retorts that his argument is politically self-serving:

> The word "secondary" conjures up the logic of priorities which is one that is used to consecrate the interests of a certain group that seeks to impose its agenda on a whole society in order to convince the latter that the group's own priorities are indeed everyone else's.[41]
> (...)
> In addition, the concept of "secondary" assumes that the movement of women's rights is against men, or the interests of men, and is therefore a movement that will weaken solidarities and fragment energies. This is a fallacy. Indeed it is an oppressive approach that seeks to exploit women and curtail their rights.... The women's movement is a liberating one for both men and women. It is a movement against oppression in all of its guises and practices. It is a movement against implicit and explicit oppression at the most private and the most public levels: the family, institutions, culture and ultimately language.[42]

It is obvious from this rather heated debate between Hanafi and Elsadda that the contest over the use of language and the problems of translating gender lie at the very heart of the field of gender studies in Egypt. It remains unfortunate that this contest finds no resolution in the interview not only because the critics of gender studies are monolingual but more seriously because the proponents of gender studies seem, through their discursive strategies, to adopt an equally monolingual position.

Last, but nowhere near least, comes the question of foreign funding which, even before the notorious Saad Eddin Ibrahim case in 2000 (he was tried and acquitted on charges of receiving foreign funds without permission from the state, among others) was used to stigmatize and discredit civil society activists and non-governmental organizations funded by various international organizations. Indeed, in the context of national and nationalist debates, the issue of foreign funding continues to be used as proof of clientelism to the West and the lack of a national vision and identity that is a threat to national sovereignty. Hasan Hanafi's question to Elsadda with regard to foreign funding is loaded with such accusations and is phrased in the following terms:

Translating gender 121

> How do you explain the willingness of the West to fund any project having to do with "globalization", "civil society", "gender", "governance"? Are these concepts value-free or are they not rather concepts antagonistic to the nation-state, national sovereignty, and nationalism.[43]

Despite its apparent eloquence, Elsadda's response is as clichéd as her interviewer's incriminating question. She begins by acknowledging that the issue of foreign funding is indeed a "sensitive" one that cannot be discussed in isolation from a whole society in crisis, for "foreign funding is the problem of an impoverished society that is in search of possible solutions for its crisis". Elsadda then moves from the defensive position to that of attack, using the very same grounds Hanafi had prepared for his own critique.

> We cannot reduce the problem of foreign funding to that of funds coming from the West while ignoring other sources of funding from many other Arab or Asian countries.... I am not so naive as to disregard or deny the problems and challenges that accompany donor funds and their agendas. However ... I am suspicious of the motives of those who use the issue of foreign funding as a political weapon.... Foreign funding is transformed from a societal problem to a means of settling accounts and questioning the importance or legitimacy of that about which we disagree or that we wish to destroy.... In addition, the real danger is the use of the question of foreign funding as a means to mandate or support the power of one group over all others. If the state is critical of foreign funding for NGOs while its own institutions rely on the same sources of funding we must question whose interest that serves. If a political party criticizes funding for a particular project while maintaining close ties with undisclosed sources of funding we must also question the motives behind that.... Ultimately, serious work will always impose itself. The other important element is that of transparency and openness about orientations, objectives, and strategies of work.[44]

As is clear from Elsadda's response, the confrontation between her and Hanafi leaves us at a dead end where the basic argument becomes: if we, the secularists (here represented by Elsadda herself) receive funds, then so do the Islamists (that Hanafi represents) and, so, we're all in the same boat. Moreover, the showdown between her and some of her interviewers is disappointing since she becomes entangled in the very same accusatory logic and "under the belt" strategies she exposes and denounces. What remains lacking in Elsadda's strategy, as I have stated earlier, is the ability to transcend these pitfalls in order to translate gender in a truly enabling and productive way that would ensure "meaning construction" and agency for the translator of gender.

Finally, I wish to recognize my own implication in translating gender. I have translated Elsadda's interview selectively, focusing almost exclusively on the blind spots and the problems of translating gender without paying due attention to the strength and breadth of many of her answers specifically as she historicizes for the women's movement both in the West and in the Arab region, her explication of the concept of gender and its centrality to any liberating discourse and practice, the importance of excavating women's histories, her critique of a fossilized understanding and approach to the East/West construct and her many well-documented, well-constructed answers. However, my strategy, from the start, has not been self-congratulating. Rather, it has been one that attempts to respond to the critique levelled (by Heba Raouf Ezzat in her article, for example) against the "secularists" of whom I am one, as being incapable of self-criticism.

If I have attempted to translate gender in these rather critical terms it is not to leave the reader with the feeling that we are on the threshold of the untranslatable. Rather, it is to share with her both the frustrations and the aspirations of the translator when she situates herself between two texts. For, as translation theorists are quick to remind us, "translation projects a utopian community that is not yet realized".[45] But, I would add, it is one that certainly merits envisioning through a new ethics of translating gender both locally and globally.

7 Where have all the families gone?
Egyptian literary texts of the 1990s

This chapter will examine the representation of the Egyptian family in the avant-garde literary works of the 1990s in contrast to that which permeated earlier literary texts since the mid twentieth century. I will argue that many literary works of the 1990s announce the death of the family as a literary icon that represents the Egyptian national imaginary. These avant-garde literary representations of the family seem to question and contest an official national imaginary that makes the family the central national icon. Whereas dominant cultural representations continue to reinforce traditional values of the family and moralize its reality, even when critical of the economic and social conditions that surround it, the avant-garde literary imaginary of the 1990s is accused of "immorality", if not nihilism, in its attempts to unsettle the very same icon.[1]

Understanding the 1990s

To say that the literary text of the 1990s in Egypt announces the death of the family as social or literary icon is to imply that the family had a previous life within the literary text. The statement assumes that certain factors have, directly or indirectly, led to the metaphoric death of the icon within the literary text. In order to understand the nature and reasons for this death, it is necessary to identify this previous life within the literary imaginary and to locate the moments that led to the transformation of its representation.

The work of Egyptian Nobel laureate Naguib Mahfouz offers an ideal case study of the family as a central literary, social and political icon. Mahfouz's chefs d'oeuvre, *Al-Thulathiyya* (1956–57; *The Trilogy*), is the family or national saga par excellence.[2] In three long volumes, the reader follows national developments as they unfold within Ahmad Abd al-Gawwad's extended family over more than one generation spanning the historic interwar period in Egypt. The representation of the family in *Al-Thulathiyya* reproduces traditional gender and power relations that characterize the rising Egyptian middle class. Ahmad Abd al-Gawwad, the patriarch, is fearless but feared by all. Relationships within the household, although not always harmonious, are well structured and well aligned to realistic norms of the period. And most important of all, the family's history is one and the same as that of the nation: it is the theatre for conflicting ideologies, the arena for the elaboration of national sentiments and confrontation with the British colonizer.[3] Mahfouz's text presents a family icon that is in perfect harmony with a dominant national imaginary. Even when Mahfouz moves away from social realism to the symbolic mode of *Awlad haratina* (1959; English translation *Children of Our Alley*, 1996), his banned novel that parodies the lives of the prophets, he still uses the family as the central icon of the text.[4] Gabalawi, the godlike patriarch, is distant but all-powerful; his erring son Arafa is punished at the end. It is important to note that these Mahfouzian texts were written during a transitional, revolutionary moment in the national imaginary. It is therefore not surprising to see that the dominant, patriarchal figures in both the realistic *Al-Thulathiyya* and the symbolic *Awlad haratina* die at the end, making room for a new generation in both texts.[5]

The family as icon for a national imaginary is not only a male writer's strategy. Latifa al-Zayyat's classic *Al-Bab al-maftuh* (1960; English translation *The Open Door*, 2000) resorts to the same symbolism even as it represents a "new woman's" awakening. *Al-Bab al-maftuh* is the feminist counterpart to Mahfouz's *Al-Thulathiyya*, albeit a decade later, encompassing the critical years of 1946–56. The national resistance to the British occupier is parallel to the female protagonist's resistance to patriarchy. Her maturity into a free woman is identical to that of the nation. It is through the familial confrontations that occur within this middle-class household that an entire national history is articulated. The battle within is the battle without.[6] Despite the fact that *Al-Bab al-maftuh* introduces the female protagonist's contestation of patriarchal power, it does not totally subvert the family icon, ending with two "modem" family prospects.[7]

Nor is the family icon a traditionalist's representation of society. Sonallah Ibrahim's *Dhat* (1992) is an example of the early beginnings of the disintegration of the family icon from one of Egypt's most radical and avant-garde writers of the 1960s.[8] This unconventional, audacious text looks at the deformation (physical, economic, ideological, and social) of Dhat, the female protagonist, in Egypt during the 1980s. In this celebration of the mediocre, the author intertwines the satiric narrative chapters of Dhat's deteriorating, post-*infitah* life within the family with ten chapters of carefully selected newspaper clippings from the Egyptian press of the 1980s.[9] The complementary relationship between the narrative chapters and the newspaper clippings drives the point home: the national is the familial and vice versa. Even though the novel ends with Dhat alone, crying on the toilet seat, her defeat at the end is one that must be read within the family or national context: it is the defeat of the wife, the mother, the working woman, the individual and, finally, the citizen.

Indeed, the post-*infitah* period in Egypt that is so thoroughly depicted in *Dhat* becomes the turning point in the history of the national imaginary. In his examination of the negative political, economic, cultural and psychological transformations of Egyptian reality since the Sadat era, Sabry Hafez argues that these radical changes have engendered and necessitated a transformation in the emerging literary discourse. One of the more salient points that he raises regarding such transformations is the individual's disillusionment with the validity of all grand narratives.[10] May Telmissany, one of the noted writers of the 1990s, foregrounds this disillusionment in an article appropriately titled "Writing on the Margin of History", in which she outlines some of the important characteristics of her literary generation:

> The title "Writing on the Margin of History" sums up what characterizes this generation with regard to its concern with the margin above all else and with the marginal character above anyone else.
> (…)
> The self becomes the core of literary expression that reflects the writer's dilemma and existential anxiety in confronting the world given the absence of a collective movement that may diffuse such anxiety.[11]

The writers of the 1990s are heir to *Dhat*'s total defeat of the post-*infitah* period during the 1980s; a generation that has been disempowered both personally and collectively; a generation that has come to know "the impossibility of becoming what you want", as Hafez succinctly put it.[12] It is perhaps their awareness of this dismal reality, at both a personal and a national level, that prompts them to write what they want. The result is a literary imaginary that portrays a radically different picture from the dominant national one, especially where the family is concerned.

But to say that the family or national icon has completely disappeared from the Egyptian literary scene as a whole is to misrepresent the actual total make-up of the contemporary Egyptian literary imaginary. The picture painted in this chapter predominantly represents the avant-garde literary corpus of the 1990s where almost all the first novels of this generation contest the dominant national imaginary. Other more senior contemporaries who were themselves part of the avant-garde movement of the 1960s and 1970s share the disillusionment of the younger literati. However, their more recent works, unlike the unsettling narratives of the young writers of the 1990s, seem to reproduce the familiar family or national icon. They are either nostalgic of a lost paradise, as is the case with Mahmud al-Wardani's *Al-Rawd al-atir* (*Perfumed Gardens*) and Ibrahim Abdel Meguid's *La ahad yanam fi l-Iskandariyya* (*No One Sleeps in Alexandria*) and its sequel *Tuyur al-anbar* (*Birds of Amber*),[13] or they are in search of a paradise to be regained, as in Bahaa Taher's idealist, almost Sufi novel, *Nuqtat nur* (*A Spot of Light*)[14] and Edwar al-Kharrat's epic narrative on the Coptic community in the Saʿid (Upper Egypt), *Sukhur al-samaʿ* (*The Rocks of Heaven*).[15]

Not surprisingly, one of the significant elements that bind many of the writers of the 1990s is their collective distance from state-controlled publishing houses. Several rising names such as Miral al-Tahawy, Somaya Ramadan, May Telmissany, Nora Amin, Mustafa Zikri, Adil Ismat, Husni Hasan, Ibrahim Farghali and others have all opted for private publishing where they actually pay, out of their own pockets, for the costly but professional, publication of their works. These writers have come to be known as the Sharqiyyat generation, in reference to the name of the private publishing house that published their work. As for the writers of the 1990s who continue to publish through state-controlled outlets, they are expected to conform to the boundaries of the dominant national imaginary. Those who do not, and they are many, risk being caught and ostracized. This was the case, for example, with Samir Gharib Ali's highly controversial first novel *Al-Saqqar* (*The Hawker*, 1996), which was accused of blasphemy.[16] It was also the case with the crisis surrounding the three Egyptian novels, two of which are by writers of the 1990s generation, Mahmud Hamid[17] and Yasir Sha'ban,[18] where the Minister of Culture Faruq Husni labelled their works "pornographic" and, tellingly enough, accused them of "violation of societal values".[19]

It is interesting to note that the generation of the 1990s displays, for the first time in modern Egyptian letters, gender equality in literary production. The work by women writers of this generation, matches, if not surpasses, both quantitatively and qualitatively, that of their male counterparts. This has earned the women "special" attention from literary critics who celebrated their work, as well as "special" attention from state-owned literary journals (for example, *Ibda'* and *Akhbar al-Adab*) that stigmatized their work with the derogatory label "*kitabat al-banat*" (girls' writing). However, *kitabat al-banat*, rather than be constrained to a "woman's world" in the traditional sense, explored the same ensemble of themes and issues raised by the "boys". This new phenomenon has confirmed, yet again, gender equality within the 1990s generation at the level of both unconventional content and experimental form, not to mention the speedy and envied access of the "girls" to an international translation market.[20]

Gone are the monumental works that explored the family or national icon over hundreds of pages that diligently chronicled the structure of family relations in all its manifestations and detail. In came the slim novels of the writers of the 1990s, none of which exceeded 150 pages, and which focused primarily on the individual, whether male or female. This collapse in size mirrors the collapse of the icon itself. The busy world that sustained the lengthy pages of family sagas gave way to the empty and constrained existence of the lonely and anguished individual. The continuity and logic that governed the family or national icon are replaced by the ruptures and disjunctures of the literary text itself. The omniscient and godlike narrators that controlled and oversaw the world of the family or nation are dethroned by schizophrenic, first-person narrators, whose vision is focused on their split selves. Rather than contemplate the possible unity between the personal and the collective, the writers of the 1990s are intent on representing the antagonism between them.

When accorded a presence at all in the literary works of the 1990s, the family becomes a relic of the past represented through old memories and old photographs fit only to be packed in suitcases for departure (Mona Prince, *Thalath haqa'ib li l-safar*, 1998).[21] In one instance, the family is responsible for the protagonist's parenthetical "madness" (Somaya Ramadan, *Awraq al-narjis*, 2001)[22] and in another it is responsible for the metaphoric death of the son (Adil Ismat, *Hajis mawt*, 1995).[23] The individual protagonists who have come to occupy the space of the family or national icon are at once disquieting and unsettling. Their relationship with the outside world is violent and nightmarish (Mustafa Zikri, *Ma ya'rifuhu Amin*, 1997)[24] permeated with fear, loneliness and anxiety. The total disorientation and alienation of these central characters becomes a shocking but candid comment on the reality that surrounds them whether that reality is familial or national.

The death of the family or nation icon in the works of the writers of the 1990s ushers us into a world beyond our expectations. Rather than announce the birth of the individual, these works race ahead to announce her or his death. Most of the writers of the 1990s seem to share this dominant icon (the imminent death of the individual) despite their radically different social and cultural orientations.[25] The only way we can comprehend and come to terms with this gap in the literary imaginary is by reading the Egyptian post-*infitah* reality outside the literary text where the birth of the individual is equally absent. Suddenly it becomes evident that there too lies a gap: the collapse of the family or national icon in reality announces not the birth but the untimely death of the individual. In this bleak world that confirms "the impossibility of becoming what one wants" it is the very act of writing that becomes the only remaining possibility for salvation. But even then, such an initiative threatens to become a new death – a frightful but brilliantly depicted possibility in Adil Ismat's *Hajis mawt* where the dead narrator, attempting to write about his metaphoric death, can produce only blank pages which the author has paid for out of his own pocket.

Reading the 1990s

Mona Prince's first novel *Thalath haqa'ib li l-safar* (*Three Suitcases for Departure*) opens with a scene of departure from the family home. The young protagonist, Munira, is in her room sitting on the floor, surrounded by books, clothes and photo albums, preparing for her departure from Cairo to India because she is "slowly suffocating" and badly "needs air".[26] Munira has designated three suitcases to take on this trip. The text itself is divided into three sections, each allocated to the items Munira packs in the three suitcases. In the smallest one she places photographs of herself during different stages of her life. As she packs, she lingers over two photos in particular: one taken with a group of university friends and another, in black and white, of her family, taken at a wedding with her uncles, aunts, grandmothers, parents and grandchildren. As she stops to point at the different people in the two photos, she recounts her interlaced memories of childhood, adolescence and university years. Similarly, she packs or discards a number of dresses associated with different love affairs in her life.

Whereas the first photo makes her realize that the friends have all gone, and that "no one remains",[27] with the second one she suddenly confronts the fact that her family has diminished, by at least half.[28] Her memories of family members are predominantly connected to their deaths, all at critical moments in the nation's history. Her eldest uncle died while she was in the Gulf with her parents, her paternal grandmother died during the Central Police riots in Cairo in the 1980s, her youngest uncle of cancer as the Iraqi army marched into Kuwait, and her maternal grandmother subsequently died of grief over the loss of her two sons. As the text unfolds, the reader discovers that Munira is packing the remains of a self unrealized: unrealized as a daughter, unrealized as an individual, unrealized as a lover, and, finally, unrealized as a citizen. The book ends with the question: "Will going away be of help? Will I find there what I have lost here? Will I accomplish there what I couldn't here? Will I free myself of...?"[29]

Munira's sense of loss and defeat is double for it is reflected not only in family relations but also in her relation to the national imaginary itself. The recurring deaths in the family are parallel, throughout the text, to different eclipses of the nation, culminating in the bombing of Iraq during the Gulf War and the total collapse of the remains of the national dream. The official discourse on the Iraqi calamity is at odds with the actual reality: as the Arab nation witnesses its own defeat, Egypt continues to broadcast the revolutionary nationalist songs of the 1960s, "*Watani habibi, al-watan al-akbar*" (My beloved nation, the greatest nation). The glories of the lyrics are juxtaposed against the Egyptian nation's actual disgrace, its unity against its disintegration, its triumphs against its defeat and its liberation against its occupation.

It is the glaring contrast between discourse and reality that brings about the end of Munira's short-lived attempt at political participation. When she listens to *Watani habibi* in the aftermath of the Gulf War she says to herself: "It was no longer possible to listen to that dream song.... What nation were they talking about? What victories and glories?"[30] Almost instantly, her attempt to become part of a lingering national imaginary is thwarted:

> The dream.... It was every past generation's dream till the beginning of the 1970s.... Then it became the remains of a dream for our generation until this moment.... We grew up with it ... and here it is, completely erased before our very eyes. It became one of the legacies of an ancient past and bygone time.... Muddled dreams.
> (...)
> It was as if I had spent my life worshipping and supplicating a sacred God only to discover that there was no God at all; just an illusion of my dreams that I had imagined and to which I had given form only to be let down.[31]

Munira's relationship with men epitomizes her marginal and commodified position vis-à-vis the national patriarchy. Her relationship with her father "was never satisfactory", or almost non-existent, for he believed that "a man works outside the house and a woman inside it. And since [she] was inside the house, [her] mother shouldered [her] responsibility...."[32] The absent father remains uninformed about, and uninterested in, Munira's emotional and political maturation, for his general policy is "keep to yourself".[33] Further, Munira's short-lived affair with Abd al-Rahman, the substitute, father-like, leftist intellectual, encapsulates the impotency of the national dream. Abd al-Rahman's sense of defeat and frustration after the bombing of Iraq are displaced upon Munira, whose own body becomes the site of national violation:

Where have all the families gone? 129

> Suddenly, he stood up and raised me from the floor. I held on to him. We went to bed.... He embraced me without looking into my supplicating eyes that urged him "try ... try ... try." But he couldn't. We remained silent.[34]

And then later:

> He grabbed my arm and pushed me into his room. He hurled the weight of his excited, hot body upon my own still one. I felt I hated him. I couldn't stand him. I don't know whether I was suddenly overcome by these feelings or whether they had been accumulating within me only to reveal themselves at this moment. I felt faint. I pushed him away from me and rushed to the bathroom. I bent over the sink and started to vomit and cry.[35]

Munira is caught between prostituted national values and regressive familial ones. Her participation in the student demonstrations against the Gulf War teaches her a lesson on both fronts. She is suspended for a month from the university because, from the administration's point of view, she and her friends "impeded the work-day and destroyed the plants that the university had just bought for £E500". The demonstrating students are accused of "grand treason for which they deserved execution not just suspension".[36] At home, her family's reaction is equally disillusioning: "Why create problems for yourself and for us? ... You are going to ruin your future. You'll get yourself into trouble for no good reason. You won't accomplish anything. You're wasting your time for nothing."[37] When she complains to Abd al-Rahman, her crumbling idol, he sides with the patriarchal position against her: "They're right. Do as they tell you."[38]

Later, Munira compares her generation's retreating situation to that of Latifa al-Zayyat, one of the leading figures of the student movement in the 1940s whose novel *Al-Bab al-maftuh* had become a landmark for later generations: "Latifa al-Zayyat led the student movement during the 1940s and today we speak about veiling women and sending them back to the home."[39] She decries the defeatism of her colleagues who have either abandoned themselves to drinking and drugs, beards and mosques or money and marriage. The national dream is reduced to roundtable discussions on "Cultural Dependency and the Role of Arab Intellectuals",[40] in which Munira refuses to participate. Her compromised battle on the national level is parallel to her ongoing battle on the familial one. In response to Munira's relentless violation of accepted boundaries, her mother would always say: "It was a dismal day the day I had you." Munira's exasperated response would always be: "It was actually a dismal day the day you met my father to begin with. It's your fault, not mine."[41] Through the constant shift in narrative point of view, from the first-person narrator in the past to the third-person narrator in the present, Munira's alienation from both icons, the familial and the national, is sharpened and intensified.

As the text interlaces the collapse of the family or nation icon, the narrative becomes an inversion of Latifa al-Zayyat's *Al-Bab al-maftuh*. Layla's frustrations in al-Zayyat's text of the 1960s lead her to personal and national

130 *Remaking culture*

accomplishments, while Munira's failed battles leave her only with unanswered questions: "Will I accomplish there what I couldn't here?" Whereas in *Al-Bab al-maftuh* Layla's rebirth is encapsulated in the symbol of the open door, in *Thalath haqa'ib li l-safar*, Munira's symbolic death is rendered through her return to the deceased grandmother's "big house" that has become "ruins inhabited by ghosts".[42] If al-Zayyat's text ends with the reintegration of Layla within a new family and national imaginary, Mona Prince's text ends with Munira's prospective departure after her father's long-overdue embrace which "had it happened years ago might have changed things now".[43]

The fresh yet painful candour we encounter in *Thalath haqa'ib li l-safar* is further explored in Somaya Ramadan's long-awaited, remarkable first novel, *Awraq al-narjis* (*Leaves of Narcissus*), for which she was awarded the AUC Naguib Mahfouz medal and prize in 2001. Even though Ramadan is a more senior writer, with a long academic history and two collections of short stories to her name, it is only in the 1990s that she undertakes the writing of a pseudo-autobiographical narrative that has won her instant acclaim. In an interview conducted with her after the publication of the novel, Ramadan explains the contextual relationship between the decade of the 1990s and her belated first novel:

> The time had come when I could write about myself. The 1990s provided the time and the place for people to write about their individual selves. So I became more confident that what I had written would not be strange or improper. Maybe if I had published it earlier it would have gone by unnoticed. There is always a point of congruence between the writer, the [historical] moment and the content [of the work].[44]

Somaya Ramadan's moving depiction of her protagonist's parenthetical madness in *Awarq al-narjis* confirms and expands the frightening rupture between the individual and the collective already encountered in Mona Prince's *Thalath haqa'ib li l-safar*. Indeed, *Awraq al-narjis* revolves around Kimi, the narrator whose life unfolds before the reader in a series of dislocated, dialogical sequences, written in densely rhythmic language that places this mature work within the category of the prose poem. At the heart of these sequences, is the ever-lingering question "How is it possible for one to understand?" This is the question that Kimi re-asks as she repeatedly attempts to write her "papers", making the question a central, anguished one for herself and for her reader. In *Awraq al-narjis* life, its meaning and its representation are no longer linear, causal or logical as so many earlier texts had depicted them. Rather all has become "parallel, parallel", as the narrator of this labyrinthine text continues to remind us throughout. Just as Kimi writes and rewrites moments of herself in order "to understand", so too does the reader read and reread in a parallel, frustrating attempt. Just as the beginnings of the text are multiple, so too are its levels of reading. This multiplicity is accentuated in the narrative through the key word that bears the title of the first chapter, punctuates the entire text and

Where have all the families gone? 131

finally appears as the very last word at the end: "perhaps" (*rubbama*). The repetition of the word "perhaps" intensifies the quest for understanding (of the self and of the world) and provides the narrative with its spiral, open-ended, quality. "Perhaps" becomes the key and ultimate answer in the text. The narrative therefore remains suspended from beginning to end, incomplete, on the threshold of knowledge or ignorance, sanity or madness, life or death, all of which remain "parallel, parallel".

The text opens with the disturbing statement: "The moment before surrender is the most difficult."[45] The narrator, who throughout the text alternates between the first-person and the third-person points of view, proceeds to unravel this central story of resistance and surrender:

> No sooner does the pill enter my mouth than I spit it out. It is a small pill, with it you will go into deep sleep. This is all that is required. My friends require it, my siblings, and my mother. My closest of kin conspire kindly. After that you will go into deep sleep. Then, negotiations begin. I exhaust them.... They all become the angels of death. They unite in a block while I resist alone. My whole body is prepared. My mind is alert, ablaze with clarity, consuming its neurons like lightning inside every corner of the brain where truth appears bright and clear and where memory today is iron-sharp. They cannot kill you. Otherwise, they will become murderers. They just want to make sure that you will carry out the sentence yourself. A small pink pill after which you will sleep for ever and your suffering will end.[46]

From the start, we are immersed in a warlike situation where the narrator is resisting alone the "kind" conspiracy of the world against her, a world united like the "teeth of a comb", constituted by the "wise" members of her family and her closest friends. When she finally swallows the small pink pill her body is flooded with signs of very slow death. In preparation for that death, she recites her own *shahada* as "they" had taught her:

> A strong muffled convulsion begins to overtake me from the tip of my toes ending in the strongest, slowest and most blissful orgasm that I have ever known. Followed by another and another; wave after wave with the same strength and the same slowness. When the contracting, relaxing waves subside, and numbness permeates my head I become certain that I have died. I recite the *shahada* in a clear loud voice as they had taught me. The kingdom of the Lord is forthcoming, and there is no God but Allah, and the wise ones around me smile. Now I have their blessings and they have mine. The peace of surrender prevails.
>
> By God I swear: I have done everything I can. I have resisted with all my will power and have held on until the very last moment, even as I watched my brain take flight, and I did not give up. If I have not understood, it is not because I was lazy but because goodness is beyond my comprehension.[47]

132 *Remaking culture*

Even though *Awraq al-narjis* begins with "the moment before surrender", the reader quickly understands that this is but one of the possible beginnings to Kimi's parallel episodes of resistance. In one of those possible beginnings, Kimi, like Scheherazade, tells another version of her own story:

> Once upon a time there was an intelligent, sharp, clean girl, innocent to the point of naivety at times. She had read many books. But we spared her experience so we did not allow her to suffer. We provided everything for her. And when she wanted to continue her education, we sent her to a respectable university in a conservative Catholic country. We constantly monitored her good behaviour through an honourable Arab professor who chose for her a field of specialization, at a University that he often visited. He read everything she wrote himself. He guided, advised and protected her. A conscientious girl, obedient and respectable. She never once upset anyone. She went to the library and came back to her room to read. She finished her studies within due time and returned home. We are very proud of her and expect a lot from her.[48]

Kimi writes this perfect fairy tale as imagined and told from the point of view of the "kind" conspirators, the members of her family. This account is juxtaposed against her own nightmarish version of the same fairy tale. When she returns to Egypt her family chooses to block out the episode of her "madness" in Dublin in order to preserve their fairy tale at her expense:

> That is how I came to eat regularly and sleep regularly. That is all that is required; only that, not the freedom of remembering or intuitive expression and speech; only that, not the oral tale. No one asks. No one shows the slightest sign of curiosity. What happened? How did it happen? How did you not sense the danger? Why did your letters not reveal any disruption? How did you conceal the pain from your voice on the telephone? No one asked. So I did not answer. And I had to pretend. Here like there.[49]

The juxtaposition of the two passages on the same page bespeaks an unbridgeable gulf between Kimi and her immediate world, what was expected of her and what she has become. Her sense of loneliness and isolation is reflected on many levels throughout the narrative: "I did not notice them as they constructed this huge, thick bell jar around me.... What had I done for them to isolate me so?"[50] As a child, Kimi makes a constant effort to remain within the boundaries that are set for her; however her fear of failure continues to haunt her.

> Judgement is on the Day of Judgement, as in the religion lesson. On the Day of Judgement people are made to walk on a tight hair. Those who are good fall into paradise, those who are bad fall into hell. My only concern was not to fall. And judgement was a daily thing.[51]

Kimi's daily trip to school as a child encapsulates this lifetime experience. She walks to school carefully balancing her feet on the edge of the sidewalk by way of "perfecting self-discipline" and remains engulfed with the fear of falling from "the straight path".[52] On her way home she falters and can no longer walk on the edge: "I realize that it is fear of error. The possibilities of error are endless, infinitely endless. No one notices and no one remembers but I."[53] She is taught "precision, order, cleanliness, and self-discipline".[54] At home voices must not be raised. Quiet is of absolute importance.[55] As a teenager she is reprimanded:

> You spoke, you watched; you laughed louder than you should. You were too informal when you shouldn't have been, you did not keep your legs tightly held, you ate with gluttony, you gave your opinion in matters that do not concern you, you butted in on a conversation, you are conceited, you are aloof.[56]

And more importantly, the repeated advice or premonition from Amna, her nanny: "Don't look at your face in the mirror; those who look at themselves in the mirror for too long go mad."[57] Eventually, Amna's advice becomes one of the recurring leitmotifs in Kimi's story of madness or awareness.

In Dublin, where Kimi spends four years studying, she secludes herself in her room at the hostel, she speaks to no one and no one speaks to her. She writes but no one reads her. She comes to be known as "the strange woman" and is likened to Sylvia Plath by the Dublin dorm residents. On her wall is a map of exile. Not of her own homeland, Egypt, but rather of her "imagined homeland" and refuge: posters of James Joyce, Samuel Beckett, a confused Chinese woman at a crossroads, an old man looking out desperately at sea.[58] To these landmarks of her imaginary homeland she adds Salvadore Dali's *Metamorphosis of Narcissus*, the image responsible for her own metamorphosis. Dali's poster on Kimi's wall becomes her looking glass: the dismembered human figure, the glasslike lake and the narcissus flower itself all send her on her own Narcissus journey and her first moment of awareness or madness, resistance or escape through writing, culminating in *Leaves of Narcissus* (*Awraq al-narjis*): "This was the moment when the minute crystal threads that constituted the bell jar began to slip.... Wake up. Come out from under that bell jar. Write me. Only you can. Only you can save me."[59] Flashbacks of Kimi's relationship with her mother equally reinforce her sense of loneliness and alienation. She describes her mother sitting in the winter morning sun on the balcony with her sewing box, dressed in a sweater and skirt, panty hose and a pair of white *"pantoufles"* cutting small things with "absolute precision": "I sit watching her on the opposite chair. And when I speak to her she does not reply. Between us stands an erect wall of cut glass that allows only images, and not voices, to glide through. I remain silent and watch."[60] The rift between the mother and the daughter takes on dramatic proportions when the mother fails or refuses to see the reality of Kimi's breakdown:

Why do you insist on nullifying me? Why don't you ask me whether I want to go to the beach with them?

Because every time you go you come back and spend days staring at the ceiling.

I scream at her but my tongue rebels against shaping the air into letters. Nothing but a long, angry, shackled wail emerges from my throat. My mother weeps.[61]

The absent mother is juxtaposed against Dada Amna's very strong presence. Whereas the mother's voice is seldom heard, "Amna's is clear and strong".[62] Kimi completely identifies with her nanny, Amna. Indeed, Kimi's mother describes Amna as being "stupid", the same adjective used by Miss Diana, the arithmetic teacher, to describe Kimi herself. Amna is also seen as "stubborn, like a mule", not so different from Kimi, whose head is pounded by Miss Diana on the glass of the dining table, splitting it in two. Amna is Kimi's alter ego: she is the illiterate, peasant woman whose oral, popular mythology is braided into Kimi's Greek and western myths and stories that resonate throughout the narrative. Towards the end of the text, the scent of oranges that accompanied the mother's presence is displaced on to Amna: "My mother, my mother is the scent of oranges. How has Amna come to possess my mother's scent?"[63] The climax of Kimi's identification with Amna occurs when she wrestles against her "satanic" self that refuses to accept the peaceful death of the small pink pill. Rather than command the death of the self, the "I" (*ana*) Kimi inserts an "m" into the word *ana* thereby commanding the death of Amna within her:

Die *ana*!
Die *ana*!
Or am I saying:
Die Amna![64]

However, Kimi survives this imposed death through her repeated attempts at writing. It is in the process of writing and rewriting that she kills all the "kind" others, only to discover that writing "is never complete" for "how can anything be complete except if it dies?"[65] Writing therefore becomes her way of "becoming what she wants", her way of defying non-meaning, and her hope to start life anew:

Many pages were torn over three days, pages that were no good. A Lie! It's just that I didn't know that they were any good. The thing was, they were written in English.[66]

Even if I knew how to write, my language remains unreadable. All languages are foreign and that of my kin is fit only for oral tales. All of my tales are foreign. If I could tell, who would listen.... All the stories have been written, all the tales told. There is no truth except in silence.[67]

Yes, I killed everyone. I muted the nine-year-old Amna by giving her a voice. I strangled her....[68]

> I killed them, all of them, in three days. I wrote them and then I shredded them when their breath overtook the air in the room and swallowed it leaving me without any breathing space.[69]
>
> And before all else I cut Kimi into fourteen pieces. I threw her mutilated body into the wastebasket.[70]

Reading *Awraq al-narjis* is the process of collecting Kimi's mutilated body, the attempt to paste together the various shredded pieces of the story that has been written and rewritten. One of the recurrent leitmotifs in Ramadan's text is the image of Kimi's mother's pair of scissors that has lost the middle screw which allows the hands of the scissors to create new life and to generate new meaning. The lost screw has rendered things "parallel, parallel". "Today, nothing happens in my father's house", says Kimi, a situation that is mirrored outside that house: "Mr. President, Mr. President, Mr. President, and flowers in a tall crystal vase, two arm-chairs, and a table. And nothing happens, not in our house or in anyone else's … parallel, parallel, parallel."[71]

But despite all this, Kimi resists and writes with the conviction that "Poets write from the vantage point of the little screw that allows the hands of the scissors to create meaning."[72] Finally, it is important to note that the diminutive name of the protagonist Kimi is very close to the word "Kimit" that denotes Egypt (the black earth) in ancient Egyptian. It may therefore be said that Kimi's search for meaning on a personal level, through writing, is also a search for a collective one, "perhaps".

If *Awraq al-narjis* can be read as resurrection through writing, then Adil Ismat's *Hajis mawt* (Fear of Death) is a text that opens up no space beyond death, even in writing. *Hajis mawt* is the story of a "dead man" who desperately tries to retrieve himself from his condition through writing but: "the novel does not advance" for "how can a dead man write a novel?"[73] Apart from brief interventions by Basima, the mother, the entire narrative of *Hajis mawt* is the text of this nameless narrator's papers or memoirs described in Basima's prologue as "satanic".[74] The text is a palimpsest divided, as it is, into two large sections: "First Writing" and "Second Writing", where the elliptical story told in the first section is retold and rewritten in the second.

The very first line of *Hajis mawt* initiates us into the death of the family icon. The narrative begins with the death of the father, the patriarch, and the symbol of order:

> constant order like that of the days: the order of changing bed sheets on Fridays, the order of prayer-times on velvet rugs, and the resounding voice of the father with the grammatical rules of classical Arabic in different corners of the house.[75]

The image of the dying family becomes a microcosm for a dying national imaginary. The "good house" that produced "good men" is slowly emptied of its occupants. No one remains but Basima, the mother and one of her sons. All the other children have chosen to leave, having been "breast-fed on exile".[76] Only the nameless "dead" narrator remains: a skinny medical doctor who had been imprisoned because of his political activism as a university student during the late 1970s. In Basima's eyes, he had become the "poison" that she served to her husband on his plate causing his untimely death.[77] The death of the patriarch that is announced at the very beginning triggers the symbolic one of the only remaining son and comes to inhabit the entire narrative:

> During the first years of Medical School I met new friends and I joined the student movement. Revolution was within our hands and we could see its light shining on our fingertips.
> (…)
> After I came out of prison and graduated, my brother's emigration, my father's death, and the emptiness of the world around me, all constituted the dead skin behind which I thought I hid comfortably. I thought life would be better this way and that I can live like this forever. But then this man came and began to crawl out, taking us unaware. He inhabited the apartment on the second floor. He died there, leaving holes in my dead skin, and drove home the conclusion that I could not reach while I was in prison: I am a group of creatures interchanging roles.[78]

From then on, the metaphor of death reigns over the text, over the family, the nation and the individual. The narrator's decision to move into the other apartment marks the rupture between him and his past life: "the father, the mother, God, the nation, marriage, love, virtue, everything".[79] It becomes the means by which he blocks "the well inside which stood [his] wife" who had not believed his "desire to enter his room and die".[80] In the first segment of this anti-narrative, entitled "First Writing", the metaphoric death of the nameless protagonist is depicted in nightmarish, surreal terms. He is at once the narrator and the dead man whose body is being invaded by screaming creatures:

> Their whispers approached the liver. When they started to touch its smooth walls my attention collapsed. When they entered inside it, they emitted shrill screams like sheets of light to confront the darkness that descended upon them. One of them looked around in fear of the screams. He listened to the live space and seemed to know his path as he exited from the liver on his way to inhabit near my brain. I followed his footsteps and asked myself: "where did he come from?" I try to listen to his voice in my entrails. I test the simple idea of his presence. He spoke confidently as if he guessed my thoughts. He said: "Are you afraid?" When I examined the matter, I discovered that he was right.[81]

The voice that emerges from among the screaming creatures to ask the question "Are you afraid?" is the narrator's alter ego that continues to haunt him as another voice, throughout the narrative, forcing him to re-examine, reread and rewrite every minute of his story. The narrator's voluntary withdrawal from life, in general, and family, in particular, is associated with an all-encompassing fear: fear of his wife's anger, fear of his father's intimidating gaze, fear of his grandfather's pointed shoe, like a flash of fire, on his back, fear of not doing his work properly.[82] In his attempt to overcome his fear, he urges his alter ego to rip up his brain, for he wishes to have no memory. His memory is constituted by failure: individual and collective, personal and national. He was detained for political activism as a student, spent three years of unemployment after his graduation from medical school, and baked in the sizzling heat of the Red Sea where he tried to find a job in a restaurant. Finally, there is the arrival on the scene of his wife with "the glittering rings, seven years in the Gulf, the brand new car",[83] who finds him "without anything" and gives him a hand. However, this "rescue" becomes his death: "What does this woman want? How could I have lived with this face, swollen with jaundiced family evenings, calculations of our weekly budget, the neighbours' gossip and soap operas?"[84] Juxtaposed against this metaphoric death that permeates the body of the narrator is his mental awareness and his fixed attention to "complete his story". He writes, reads, and rewrites his papers, constantly distancing himself from himself thereby producing a self-reflexive, anti-narrative:

> This man, in winter clothes, sitting on the brown velvet couch flooded with a faded yellow light and the smell of dust and books, has a story. But he is hiding it. Hiding his story is itself a story. And his conflict with hiding his story is a story. This man is a net of stories. But he doesn't know how to write a story.[85]

Like Kimi in *Awraq al-narjis*, the protagonist in *Hajis mawt* comes to discover that he is "a group of creatures interchanging role". He is at once dead and alive, the narrator and the reader, the teller and the told. Like Kimi, he tries to struggle against his "dead" satanic self:

> I will throw out this dead man's papers. I will go to work tomorrow. I will sleep all afternoon, and in the evening I will go to the syndicate club to play another game [of chess] with Khalid. Late at night, I will answer my brother's letter and I will think about emigrating.[86]

But again, like Kimi, the protagonist of *Hajis mawt* discovers that the only way to overcome this meaningless existence is not to throw away the "dead man's papers" but rather to "organize the dead man's papers and make them into a book".[87]

The second section of this anti-narrative, titled "Second Writing" becomes a renewed attempt, through writing, for the protagonist to rid himself (again like Kimi) of all *his* kind conspirators and "their breath that permeates his innermost dreams".[88] However, unlike Kimi in *Awraq al-narjis*, whose leaves of Narcissus become her salvation and hope for a new life, the dead man of *Hajis mawt* catches himself buried in lies. When he attempts to write, he finds himself submerged, yet again, in dead images and metaphors of house and family:

> Here I am hiding myself once more. I surround myself with a man, a home, a balcony, a summer day, and a wife, despite the fact that I really think of myself as an empty straw man with nothing but dust in his throat. I am taken by these guises and can no longer describe my state. Writing weighs upon me and I can no longer continue. The poetic images sitting on the surface of my copybook like pimples, transform everything into a field of rotting onions.[89]

The protagonist's inability to transcend this "dead" language explains the large blank spaces that dominate "Second Writing" and that are meant to indicate the impossibility of writing itself. Hence, a double death: not Kimi's awareness of writing "from the vantage point of the little screw that allows the hands of the scissors to create meaning", to start life anew but rather the mad recognition that:

> You are but a stone, a shadow of something you don't even know. Why did you have to go beyond what you are? Just a stone, a shrivelled branch, a page in an old book, a frame for a dead man's photograph.[90]

Adil Ismat's "dead man" in *Hajis mawt* ultimately fails to be "normal", i.e. to go to work, to gain a living in the city or even to return to his village to help his devastated, dying mother. He tries to seek salvation in writing but even there he discovers that he is shrouded in lies, and that language itself, with its metaphors and images, is incapable of articulating his anguished soul. The text that he "completes" is reflective of this state: it is elliptical, repetitive and laden with blank spaces that language has failed to occupy. It remains to be said however, that the long, blank spaces have been printed at the author's own expense.

In Mustafa Zikri's short narrative *Ma ya'rifuhu Amin* (*What Amin Knows*), we sink further into the abyss of the "misfit" where the whole idea of knowledge and certainty are put into question. The text begins with Amin, the protagonist, seated in a comfortable armchair, in his tidy bedroom, alone, about to watch the evening TV film: *The Misfits*, starring Marilyn Monroe and Clark Gable. Amin's life, or rather existence, is recounted through a camera eye that captures the details of every movement he makes inside and outside his apartment, the space that represents the only safe and orderly place in the world that surrounds him.

The text fully exploits the contrast between an inner, private, controllable space and a public, vicious, surreal one. Amin, who is around forty, lives alone in a well-furnished, tidy apartment in one of the suburbs of Cairo. There is no mention of family, nor is there a mention of individual history. There is no imaginary beyond that of the moment, encapsulated in Amin's unrealized obsession, throughout the narrative, to watch or avoid watching *The Misfits*. For at least fifteen pages of the book, the camera eye follows Amin around his apartment as he seemingly prepares for his viewing of *The Misfits*: from the bedroom to the kitchen, to the living room, to the study, to the bathroom, and ultimately to the street where he continues to glimpse scenes of the film in a supermarket, in a bar and in a hotel, without ever returning to his bedroom to watch it. *The Misfits* follows Amin around town, an unrelenting reminder of his own position.

Amin's existence within his apartment is dominated by constant fear that someone will come in from the outside. He searches behind doors, closes shutters, verifies the various locks, and ends up panic-stricken in front of his suddenly unlocked apartment door, when he mistakes his own hand, clutching his screaming mouth, for the hand of someone else! Outside Amin's self-sufficient world in the apartment there exists another violent one. Every time he ventures outside he finds himself entangled in a threatening situation over which he has no control and of which he has no understanding.

When he leaves his apartment to fetch his regular, mostly uneaten, dinner, he is harassed by three neighbourhood gang youths, Nunna, Adil Rita and Busy, who seem to have developed the habit of tormenting him. They end up throwing Amin into the pond at the Japanese garden with his nightgown and his dinner bag as Farid, the owner of the supermarket, watches with indifference the violence against Amin while enjoying *The Misfits* on TV. At home, with tons of stale food piled up on his table, Amin eats his dinner "hysterically" and "very quickly" as he listens to the sound of the film coming from the bedroom. Later on at the bar, Amin finds himself drawn into a one-sided conversation with an old acquaintance whose appearance threatens to revive an undesirable relationship with the outside world. To escape this threatening human encounter, Amin takes a taxi to a downtown hotel. But that episode proves to be an even more horrifying experience: he sees or imagines himself to have seen the dead girl that the taxi driver had been talking to him about sitting in the front seat. He dashes out of the taxi, leaving his change behind.

A series of nightmarish scenes ensue: Amin is mocked and ridiculed by two young couples in a car; he then follows a young man holding an artificial leg in his hand through the dark street leading to the hotel to avoid a barking dog. In the hotel lobby where Amin collapses with fatigue and anxiety he finds himself alone, face to face, with *The Misfits* still showing on TV. In the hotel lobby, two children spray Amin with water. An old man with the same artificial limb that Amin had seen with the young man appears in the lobby. The text abruptly ends with the children yelling: "Grandpa, Grandpa, look, the man has wet himself."[91]

All of these absurd episodes are seen through a camera eye that follows Amin in his cracked eyeglasses that keep falling and through which he himself experiences cracked visions of the world. What Amin knows (*ma yaʻrifuhu Amin*) is constituted through this cracked vision. True, the reader laughs at Amin the misfit, but one also feels sympathy and an eerie sense of identification with his total alienation and complete disorientation, especially in his failure to relate to a nightmarish and aggressive outside world that he confronts totally on his own.

140 *Remaking culture*

Beyond family and nation?

All four works examined in this chapter focus, to a great extent, on their protagonists' rooms, their internal, private, spaces. In *Thalath haqa'ib li l-safar*, the entire narrative is generated as Munira sits in her room packing. In *Awraq al-narjis*, Kimi's life unfolds between her room in her father's house and her room in Dublin. Similarly, in *Hajis mawt*, the dead man from the start confines himself to a room from which he does not emerge. *Ma ya'rifuhu Amin* further complicates and questions the idea of a safe private space, for the room that Amin leaves to descend into the street proves not to be a refuge from a world that can only create misfits. The use of the spatial element in these texts sharply contrasts with earlier works from the 1960s onward where the street and the public space are an integral part of the growth and maturity of the protagonists.

The protagonists of all four of these texts of the 1990s, like many other contemporary examples, cut loose from conventional icons of family and nation. All four confront "the impossibility of becoming what one wants". Their salutary response to such a trying confrontation is to bravely write that impossibility, even if it means blank spaces on the printed page. The courage these writers demonstrate resides in writing against the grain, against dominant discourses and practices that continue to prize an empty and constraining national imaginary at the expense of a thwarted individual.

In his work on the Egyptian literary field since 1967, Richard Jacquemond evokes the relevant question of whether the collective characteristics of the literary avant-garde of the 1990s are indeed intrinsic to this particular generation. Jacquemond's reading of the literary avant-garde works of the 1960s, such as Sonallah Ibrahim's *Tilka l-ra'iha* and Bahaa Taher's *Al-Khutuba*, leads him to suggest that the general contestatory tendencies that mark the works of the 1990s may have to do with these writers' relatively young biological and/or professional age. Once established and recognized, will the writers of the 1990s not return to the family or national icon, he asks?[92] My answer to this question is no. Their journey, like Amin's in Mustafa Zikri's *Ma ya'rifuhu Amin*, is one of no return, for there is, perhaps, nothing left to return to.

Indeed, more recent Egyptian literary texts of the turn of the century confirm that the literary avant-garde has taken a decidedly new leap in its relationship with dominant national icons like the family. In its spring issue of 2006, the literary journal *Banipal* ran a special feature on new writing in Egypt providing several examples of translated excerpts from younger Egyptian authors such as Ahmed Alaidy, Mansura Izz al-Din, Wa'il Abd al-Hafiz, Safa' al-Naggar, Wa'il al-Ashri, Haytham al-Wardani, among many others including poets as well, all of whose works bear testimony to the new directions these writers have taken at the level of literary genre and structure, literary icons and literary language.[93] In her introduction to the *Banipal* special feature on new Egyptian writing critic Marie-Thérèse Abdel-Messih confirms my argument in this chapter through her description of this younger literary avant-garde in the following terms:

Where have all the families gone? 141

> Since the early nineties there has been increasing attention given to the location of the writer; and the "political" dimension of narrative – though with no agreement on its definition. Eventually "political" came to signify the subversion of all fixed meanings arising out of state policies and social mores. In this writing there is always a conflict between self and community, spontaneity and social order; and little interest in formality or historical symbolism and reference.
> (…)
> It deals with what has been for long deliberately or unconsciously suppressed; touches on the existential dilemma, conflicting choices, or conflicting love affairs and subverts media representations of heroism or romance.
> (…)
> Narrative has become a covert political activity. By revealing the masks that shield the self – as well as the single party state – the new writing debunks the heroic unified self, the totalitarian idea of the nation, and the single voice.[94]

Perhaps the most radical example of all these developments has been Ahmed Alaidy's notorious *An takun Abbas al-Abd* (2003, English translation: *Being Abbas El Abd*, 2006), which has rightly been described as "the millennial generation's most celebrated literary achievement".[95] Like Sonallah Ibrahim's *Tilka l-ra'iha* of the 1960s that severed ties with dominant literary aesthetics of its time,[96] *An takun Abbas al-Abd* is a rebellious child of its own time, by the most junior member of the Egyptian literary field who describes himself as part of the "autistic generation" in reference to "the nerdy tendency to turn in on himself, feeling the brunt of an existential communication block that deprives him of social sustenance".[97] Not surprisingly it was indeed Sonallah Ibrahim who recognized this experimental text for the milestone that it has become and recommended its preview publication on the pages of *Akhbar al-Adab* in 2003 one week before it appeared on the market through Merit publishing house after having been rejected for publication before.

An takun Abbas al-Abd amplifies and complicates the many anxieties in the narratives of Alaidy's peers whose works I have analysed in this chapter.[98] Munira's sense of alienation and isolation in *Thalath haqa'ib li l-safar*, Kimi's "madness" in *Awaraq al-narjis*, the narrator's deadening fears in *Hajis mawt* and Amin's misfit existence in *Ma ya'rifuhu Amin* converge in Alaidy's narrator who represents the author's own triangle of angst: hallucination, schizophrenia and phobia.[99] *An takun Abbas al-Abd* is at once a hilarious but also tortuous account (for both the narrator and the reader) of the life of a schizoid that revolves around his colliding selves: the narrator, a disturbed and introvert video rental attendant, his uncle, an experimental psychiatrist (who used to put him in the refrigerator as a child) and his nihilistic, streetwise friend Abbas al-Abd, a cosmetics salesman who sets him up on a blind date with two girls with the same name (Hind) on two separate floors of the same coffee shop in one of Cairo's new shopping malls. With its carefully conceived structure, the text unfolds through fragments that reflect the narrator's own fragmented being and life. One of the text's reviewers likened it to "a Cubist painting that precariously juxtaposes motifs, anecdotes, critiques, encounters and conversations that reflect one man's mental chaos, for it transpires that all three characters are but projections of the same diseased psyche".[100] A disturbingly candid reflection of Egypt's young generation at the turn of the century, *An takun Abbas al-Abd* echoes the intensity of Chuck Palahniuk's *Fight Club* (1999) and the hip sensibility of Douglas Coupland's *Generation X* (1991) while invoking a mind-boggling range of references to global consumer culture from the media, film industry, communication technology (computer, internet, mobile phone, mp3s) as well as Cairo's underworld of microbus culture, pharmaceutical abuse, prostitution, experimental psychiatry, all audaciously rendered in an irreverently hybridized everyday street Arabic that breaks down the barriers between the written and the spoken.[101]

When compared to the four narratives analysed in this chapter *An takun Abbas al-Abd* becomes a text in which the nation itself with all of its official icons has ceased to exist. In one of the many conversations between the narrator and his friend or alter ego, Abbas al-Abd, the latter knowingly advises the narrator saying:

> You want us to progress?
> > So burn your history books and forget your precious dead civilization.
> > Stop trying to squeeze the juice from the past.
> > Destroy your pharaonic history.
> (…)
> We will only succeed when we turn our museums into public lavatories.
> (…)
> Remember you're on your own now.
> > On your own, imbecile![102]

And indeed, the text is fully inhabited by the fragments of this self on its own.

Furthermore, rather than be inhibited by writing and language like Kimi in *Awraq al-narjis* and the dead protagonist of *Hajis mawt* who ends up with blank pages in his narrative, the narrator of *An takun Abbas al-Abd* uninhibitedly confronts his readers on the very first page head-on, announcing: "An Introduction You Can Suck or Shove". Later, the narrator blatantly dismisses any of the readers' conventional expectations of the text:

> IF THIS WERE A NOVEL, IT WOULD NOW BE TIME FOR YOU TO STOP and have a sandwich.
> > Unfortunately, however, it isn't.
> > This is not a novel.[103]

Having defiantly declared this to his readers, the narrator cuts loose from all the conventional expectations of a novel at the generic, structural, representational,

Where have all the families gone? 143

and linguistic levels and transforms the feelings of impasse, death and fear that haunt the earlier examples provided in this chapter into new daring and risky possibilities. For example, the text begins with Hind, one of the girls at the narrator's blind date, writing her mobile phone number on the insides of the doors of the toilets at Geneina Mall with waterproof lipstick, then passing a Kleenex soaked in soda water over it "cos that way, cupcake, it can't be wiped off!"[104] The number Hind writes "at the eye level of a person sitting on the toilet seat" (010 6 40 90 30) all over Cairo's shopping malls (Arkadia Mall, Ramses Hilton Mall, The World Trade Center) with two words above it, "CALL ME", is actually the author's own mobile number. The text ends with an almost identical sequence only Hind is replaced by Abdullah (one of the vying selves of the narrator), who writes the same number in the same malls with a waterproof Parker pen, then passes a Kleenex soaked in soda water over it "cos that way, Neddy, it can't be wiped off".[105] This simple request (CALL ME) attached to the mobile phone number that is repeated several times at the beginning and end of the text is not only the characters' answer to their sense of alienation and isolation but it also becomes, at least until he changes the number, an answer to the sense of isolation or "autism" of Alaidy himself, who has received hundreds of phone calls from readers who actually dialled the number printed in the text.

The first edition of *An takum Abbas El Abd* sold out within a month and a half and has been pirated and sold at the Azbakiyya bookstalls between its subsequent reprints thus establishing itself as "the Arab world's answer to a millennial cult classic".[106] Indeed, Abbas al-Abd himself prophetically explains the success of the text within the text itself elucidating the decided rupture with dominant national icons that this younger generation has made:

Egypt had its Generation of the Defeat.
    We're the generation that came after it. The "I've-got-nothing-left-to-lose generation".[107]

It is precisely this generation of urban, savvy and streetwise "I've-got-nothing-left-to-lose" youth that has carried contemporary Egyptian avant-garde fiction beyond family and nation, opening up new literary imaginings and linguistic possibilities that promise uncharted referential, technical and aesthetic territories, thereby sealing the death of the family as a literary icon that represents the Egyptian national imaginary.

8 From the *hara* to the *imara*
Emerging urban metaphors in the literary production on contemporary Cairo[1]

Given the dominance of the realist tradition in Egyptian literature, it is no surprise that Cairo, whether it is the historic city or the modern metropolis, should be the main metaphor for much of the literary production during the twentieth century. Urban space, for the writers of the city, has been a major architect of its social, economic and political fabric. At one level, the city of Cairo emerges as an actor with real agency that embodies and structures social power as well as political, economic and symbolic processes. Cairo is not simply a physical presence which writers reproduce. Rather, the city is a construct that continues to be reinvented by these writers, each according to his or her experiential eye and personal encounter with it. As the writers come to represent the city in literature, they, in turn, become architects of the history of Cairo, whose literary works reconstruct and remap the city.[2] Cairo becomes a protagonist whose existence is indispensable for the existence of the narratives themselves, not to speak of our own reading and decoding of these narratives.

Consider, for example, Naguib Mahfouz's metaphoric use of the *hara* (alley) in old Cairo, specifically in the Gammaliyya neighbourhood, in many of his literary works in order to represent Egyptian society at different historical junctures and the various transformations that beset it. Mahfouz, himself a product of the historic *hara* in Gammaliyya, becomes its literary architect par excellence. Gradually, however, as the urban space expands, and as the *hara* loses many of its distinctive social and economic fabric through the exodus of its population to the modern metropolis, writers of the city, including Naguib Mahfouz himself, will migrate to other locations, mapping out many of Cairo's new boundaries and their accompanying social changes and economic developments. Hence, the city becomes a text that is constantly rewritten, a space that is continuously reconstructed or deconstructed through its ever-shifting, ever-changing signs. Indeed, as the cultural critic Franco Moretti aptly put it when describing his original work on a literary atlas of the European novel:

> Behind these words, lies a very simple idea: that geography is not an inert container, is not a box where cultural history "happens", but an active force, that pervades the literary field and shapes its depth. Making the connection between geography and literature explicit, then – mapping it: because a map

From the hara *to the* imara 145

is precisely that, a connection made visible – will allow us to see some significant relationships that have so far escaped us.[3]

Indeed, during the twentieth century, specifically since the 1960s, Cairo witnessed an accelerated pattern of physical expansion beyond its historic Islamic neighbourhoods and its modern colonial ones. As the renowned historian of the city of Cairo, André Raymond, has noted:

> Cairo's impetuous growth in the past half-century complicates any image one might try to form of it. The traditional city of the late Ottoman era and the two side-by-side cities of the colonial era have been absorbed into a whole so diverse as to prevent any simple conclusions. The faces of the city blur; its centers are many and mobile. But this "fragmented" Cairo can still be reconstituted into more or less coherent wholes, each clearly revealing deep social differences.[4]

Many factors have converged to produce this image of "fragmented" Cairo. The socialist, centrally planned and public-sector-dominated state economy of the Nasser regime of the 1960s was abandoned during the Sadat period (1971–81) for an "open door" one that encouraged the private sector and Arab and international investment. This, together with rural–urban migration, has led to the appearance of informal and illegal housing during the 1980s, as well as the "ruralization of urban areas", the deterioration in living conditions and infrastructure in the old city, and class inequalities and urban problems both social and economic.[5] The state's laissez-faire policies, not only within the economic field but also in the field of urban planning, have resulted in the uncomfortable coexistence of skyscrapers and multi-million-dollar commercial centres side by side with shantytowns and informal settlements. The mega-city of Cairo has also experienced new patterns of geographic, economic and social mobility: the influx of an immigrant rural population, the rise of professional and labour migration to the Gulf, new internal migration to the factories in satellite cities or coastal tourist developments, the emergence of new patterns of investment and consumption, the disintegration of the "traditional" social fabric and the emergence of new urban affiliations. The fragmentation of old familiar spaces and the encroachment of new unfamiliar ones led to a heightened sense of mobility and anonymity as well as an imminent sense of alienation and isolation. As the city transformed itself, so did the metaphors that came to represent it in literary texts. Gradually, the historic *hara*, which dominated the representation not only of Cairo but also of Egypt in general, faded out and was displaced by new metaphors that are more representative of the new realities of both the city and the country at large.

One such emerging urban metaphor that has captured the literary imaginary, specifically since the latter half of the twentieth century, is that of the *imara* (apartment building), in all of its manifestations, in the different suburbs of the mega metropolis of Cairo. As the city expanded beyond control, and beyond recognition, it came to be represented by the self-contained, well-defined unit of the *imara* that, alone, in the midst of the increasing chaotic, haphazardness of the city, was able to arrest and encapsulate its fragmentation. If Mahfouz's *hara* represented a set of economically and socially structured relations (for better or for worse), the *imara*, by contrast, reflects the deconstruction of these relations at the economic and social levels. Whereas the *hara* represented the well-ordered urban fabric of the old city, the *imara* has come to embody the contradictions of the global face of the mega-metropolis.

This chapter looks at four Egyptian contemporary novels that offer complementary representations of the *imara* as an emerging urban metaphor. A close reading of these texts will help us trace many of the changes in Cairo's urban fabric during the second half of the twentieth century. By examining four Egyptian novels of the 1990s – Sonallah Ibrahim's *Dhat*,[6] Hamdi Abu Golayyel's *Lusus mutaqaʻidun (Thieves in Retirement)*,[7] Alaa Al-Aswany's *Imarat Yaʻqubyan (Yacoubian Building)*[8] and Mohamed Tawfik's *Tifl shaqi ismuhu Antar (A Naughty Boy Called Antar)*[9] – I will map out some of the new spatial and social forms of polarization within the mega-city. Between them, the four novels take us on a tour of *Cairo from Edge to Edge*, edges that are substantially different from those that delimited the city in Sonallah Ibrahim's descriptive essay of it some years ago.[10] Each *imara* in these texts is telling not only of one face of the expanding city but also of how local and global flows in Cairo are translated by different groups of urban actors into practices which transform the physical as well as social and cultural spaces of the city.[11] Moreover, each of these literary representations of the *imara*, whether on the northern edges of the neighbourhood of Heliopolis or in the densely populated, informal settlement of Manshiyyat Nasir on the outskirts of the southern industrial district of Helwan, in the heart of faded colonial downtown Cairo or the Maadi Nile Corniche to the south, attests to new patterns of inclusion and exclusion, new forms of identity and belonging within the borderless boundaries of the expanding mega-city. Moreover, at the architectural level, and depending where the *imara* is situated in the larger metropolis, the four examples in the novels provide a spectrum of the different styles and modes of building that coexist in the mega city: from the Bauhaus-style apartment block in *Dhat*, and the colonial art deco style of the Yacoubian Building to Mohamed Tawfik's postmodern skyscraper, and Hamdi Abu Golayyel's mudbrick house of the urban poor.

Not only does the metaphor of the *imara* in the four novels represent transformations of and in the metropolis but it also corresponds to the space that each of these writers occupies within it. In the grand Egyptian realist literary tradition, all four writers depict their own familiar urban spaces and contexts. In the process, they reconstruct them from their respective political and ideological positions as literary architects of the city. In *Dhat*, the transformations that beset Sonallah Ibrahim's "modern" *imara* of the 1960s, on the edge of Heliopolis, are not unlike the one where he lives, in that same neighbourhood; Hamdi Abu Golayyel, author of *Lusus mutaqaʻidun*, offers us a unique experience of the informal settlement of Manshiyyat Nasir on the margin of the mega-city where he resides; Alaa al-Aswany's fictional rendition of the real Yacoubian Building is based on his own experience of downtown Cairo; and Mohamed Tawfik's skyscraper on the Maadi Nile Corniche, which, through his pre-diplomatic career as engineer, he was involved in constructing, is one of the latest representations of the globalized metropolis and its most recent patterns of capital flow and symbols of power.

The four writers also offer us an interesting historical cross-section of the actors within the literary field in the city. Sonallah Ibrahim (b. 1937), the most autonomous of all four as a literary producer, is one of the established writers of the 1960s; detained from 1959 to 1965 under Nasser for his communist political activism.[12] Hamdi Abu Golayyel (b. 1968) is the youngest of the four writers and the most representative of many of the mega-city's more recent, migrant, young literati: he is an immigrant to Cairo from an impoverished Bedouin background in the Fayyoum region and worked as a construction worker in the city until he was integrated in one of the literary institutions of the Ministry of Culture alongside his career in journalism.[13] Alaa al-Aswany (b. 1957) is the son of a noted Egyptian author (Abbas al-Aswany) and is a practising professional dentist whose first office was in the Yacoubian Building that offers the setting for his novel.[14] And finally, Mohamed Tawfik (b. 1956) is an Egyptian diplomat with degrees in civil engineering from Cairo University, international law from the University of Paris and international relations from the International Institute of Public Administration in Paris.[15] Four different profiles indeed that, together, represent the broad spectrum of class affiliation (with Abu Gollayel from the lower middle and Mohamed Tawfik from the upper middle flanking Ibrahim and al-Aswany from the wider middle class) as well as generational breadth and attest to the changing structure and boundaries of the literary field itself, ones that mirror the expanding mega-city and its ability to produce such diverse literary architects who cohabit in the same literary and geographic space.

Taken together, the four novels also map out the developments that have taken place over the past 15 years in the very representation of the city through the novel as a literary genre. Both *Dhat* and *Lusus mutaqaʿidun* are unique examples of satire and black humour. *Imarat Yaʿqubyan* is a more sober realistic text reminiscent of the popular Arabic classics of the 1940s and 1950s.[16] And finally, *Tifl shaqi ismuhu Antar* is the city thriller, par excellence; a genre that has not received proper attention or study in modern Arabic literature.[17] But, despite these differences in modes of writing, all four authors are united by the fact that they continue to work within the general tradition of literati who consider themselves the conscience of the nation, responsible for articulating its collective disillusionments and for voicing its silenced realities.[18] It is therefore no surprise that all four novels have received wide acclaim upon their publication both nationally and internationally: all have gone into more than one reprint, with *Imarat Yaʿqubyan* topping the list with unprecedented numbers of reprints and sales in the original Arabic as well as its English, French, Italian and other translations; all have been enthusiastically reviewed and have acceded to an international readership through translation and on the internet; and finally

148 *Remaking culture*

Imarat Ya'qubyan has been made by Marwan Hamid in 2006 into a film that is one of the largest productions ever in the Egyptian film industry and has been acclaimed both nationally and internationally.

The noted success of these four novels reconfirms the important role that writers play, vis-à-vis the collectivity, as underground historians of the city whose narratives participate in the construction of an imagined community and a national imaginary.[19] Moreover, as Franco Moretti has argued in *Atlas of the European Novel*, these works provide us with literary maps of the city not as metaphors but as analytical tools that dissect the text in an unusual way:

> First, they highlight the *ortgebunden*, place-bound nature of literary forms: each of them with its peculiar geometry, its boundaries, its special taboos and favorite routes. And then, maps bring to light the internal logic of narrative: the semiotic domain around which a plot coalesces and self-organizes. Literary form appears thus as the result of two conflicting, and equally significant forces: one working from the outside, and one from the inside. It is the usual, and at the bottom the only real issue of literary history: society, rhetoric, and their interaction.[20]

Such a relationship between literature and geography, writers and the space that they and their narratives occupy has been succinctly articulated by Gamal al-Ghitani, one of Egypt's major writers and literary architects of the city, in the following terms:

> Fundamentally, writing is linked to a specific place, the history and past of this place, and the spirit of this place. To be interested in time, and the passage of time, is to be interested in a specific place as well. For space and time are indissolubly tied. Place contains time. That is why remembering a certain event, at a certain date, cannot but evoke the place, the space in which we were at that given moment.
> (...)
> It is for this reason that the relationship between a writer and a place is very important, because place implies time, history, society and human relations.[21]

Once upon a *hara*

One of Naguib Mahfouz's most detailed descriptions of the *hara* occurs on the opening pages of his 1947 novel *Zuqaq al-midaqq* (*Midaq Alley* 1966). In less than one page, Mahfouz captures the *hara*'s architectural, historical and social characteristics, all at once:

> Many things combine to show that Midaq Alley is one of the gems of times gone by and that it once shone forth like a flashing star in the history of Cairo. Which Cairo do I mean? That of the Fatimids, the Mamelukes or the

From the hara *to the* imara   149

Sultans? Only God and the archeologists know the answer to that, but in any case the alley is certainly an ancient relic and a precious one....
(...)
Although Midaq Alley lives in almost complete isolation from all surrounding activity, it clamors with a distinctive and personal life of its own.
(...)
The sun began to set and Midaq Alley was veiled in the brown hues of the glow. The darkness was all the greater because it was enclosed like a trap between three walls.... One of its sides consisted of a shop, a café and a bakery, the other of another shop and an office. It ends abruptly, just as its ancient glory did, with two adjoining houses, each of three storeys.[22]

Mahfouz's *hara* is predominantly depicted as a self-contained world: it has been there since time immemorial; only "God and the archeologists" can date its history. The *hara*'s residents seem to be as historic as the alley itself. Their lives, fortunes, and misfortunes have been shaped by their presence within it. True they venture out into what the narrator describes as the "surrounding activity" of other neighbourhoods like Ghouriyya, Hilmiyya, Abbasiyya, but they all return to the *hara* at the end of the day. Despite Hamida's escape from Midaq Alley in search of a better, less confining life, in the modern neighbourhoods of colonial Cairo where she ends up prostituting herself to British soldiers, the alley, though momentarily rocked by the event and its fatal consequences for Abbas, Hamida's betrayed fiancé, eventually "returned to its usual state of indifference and forgetfulness", as the narrator states on the very final pages of the text.[23]

This isolated, indifferent setting eventually gives way in Mahfouz's later works like *The Trilogy* (1952–56) and *Children of Our Alley* (1959), to the *Harafish* (1977) and *Stories of Our Alley* (1975) as the bustle of the metropolis lures more and more of the *hara*'s real and fictional inhabitants. Not just characters but also authors migrate from the *hara* and join Hamida's journey venturing out into the city's modern neighbourhoods.

Indeed, in *Najib Mahfudh yatadhakkar* (*Naguib Mahfouz Remembers*) we, as readers, are invited on a walking tour of Old Cairo with Naguib Mahfouz himself and Gamal al-Ghitani, both sons of the Gammaliyya neighbourhood in the old city, to witness the changes that have beset the *hara*. As they stroll together, they identify for us familiar alleys, drinking fountains, mosques, coffee shops and mansions and reminisce about their respective encounters with these places. As they speak about such landmarks we come to realize how much Gammaliyya has changed, and by implication, of course, the larger metropolis:

The *hara* in which Mahfouz lived during the 1920s is different from the one in which I have lived in the mid-1970s. During Mahfouz's time, Old Cairo was the centre for middle-class merchants and high-ranking civil servants. The alleys of Gammaliyya were of a strange social fabric. In the same *hara* one would find a palace with entertainment gardens, an average-size house

that belonged to a merchant's family, a huge quarter inhabited by tens of poor families, all next to each other, sharing the same space. There are remnants of this paradigm in Darb al-Tablawi in Kasr al-Shawq, where I used to live. The famous palace of the Musafir Khana, the private guest-house of the Muhammad Ali dynasty, where Khedive Ismail was born, still exists today. However, it is now a museum and a workshop for artists.
(...)
Today some alleys have been transformed into social trashcans (...) how saddened I am today when I see them flooded with sewage water....[24]

Rather than being the microcosm of the entire city, the *hara* becomes the margin to the centre, a dwelling place for the predominantly poor and underprivileged. The historic heart of the city has visibly declined; its residents have moved elsewhere in search of more favourable conditions, and what survives has been transformed into a reservation for tourists where monuments and relics of the past are now the focus of the state's Islamic heritage industry and touristic globalization projects.[25]

The march of demolition and construction

Published in 1992, Sonallah Ibrahim's *Dhat* inaugurates the era of the *imara* metaphor in the final decade of twentieth-century Egyptian literature.[26] The title of the novel is the name of the woman protagonist in the text that, in Arabic, means "self". As we read the narrative we discover that *Dhat* (self) is not just an individual story but rather a collective one that represents the transformation that Egypt undergoes during the 1970s from being a socialist, state-dominated economy, to becoming an "open door", private sector oriented, and foreign-investment-friendly one.[27] Indeed, through Dhat's *imara*, her apartment and those of her neighbours, Ibrahim chronicles how new capital flow transforms the urban space at the material and social levels and how it impacts new modes of consumption and social behaviour.

Dhat's story is that of the unmaking of the Egyptian middle class and its aspirations for economic welfare and social equality under the reign of a centralized state economy. It begins during the 1960s with her marriage to the university dropout Abd al-Maguid "Oov Koors" (Of Course), as the omniscient narrator labels him because of his constant use of the English expression that during the socialist 1960s was the mark of his privileged cultural status but becomes, during the 1970s an obstacle to his integration in the new "open door" economy with its new Islamic social markers. The novel begins with a slim Dhat in a miniskirt and ends with her in new attire: the long shapeless Islamic dress that covers her now overweight body and the head cover with the dainty *iqal* (headband) which she takes up to ensure her acceptance at work. The physical changes that Dhat herself undergoes during the 1970s and 1980s are parallel to those that occur to her *imara* and its occupants. Indeed, Dhat (self) is reshaped by the very space that she inhabits and ends up participating in the "march of [its] demolition and construction".[28]

Dhat's and Abd al-Maguid's choice of their apartment building in the 1960s encapsulates a collective middle-class dream of modernity, homogeneity and social equity, all symbolized by the very architecture of their modern, Bauhaus-style *imara* in a newly constructed neighbourhood on the limits of the 1960s modern city. Dhat's and Abd al-Maguid's *imara* is situated on the edge of Heliopolis, equidistant from his parents' house in Abbasiyya and her parents' house in Zaytoun (both declining bourgeois neighbourhoods), in a side street not far from the tram line, which was still the pride of the district for its cleanliness and punctuality. The apartment, as the narrator tells us, was located in a recently built, clean *imara* where many tenants were newly married like Dhat and Abd al-Maguid Oov Koors and "the doors of the future were wide open before them".[29] Soon enough, however, this collective dream of a rosy future is slowly demolished:

> their street which had been so peaceful and shaded when they moved into it, had filled with small stores and car mechanics' workshops and was covered in sewage and rubbish ... The walls of the building itself had turned black, the windows in the back stairwell all smashed ... local rubbish piled up in buckets left in front of apartment doors, which allowed the [street] cats to hold riotous carnivals that went on all night. The contents of the buckets spilled onto the floor (over a wider area than when the rubbish collector emptied them), and residents would be compelled, when going up and down, to tiptoe cautiously through the mess with the bottoms of their trousers and skirts hitched up.[30]

Inside the *imara* itself begins the "march of demolition and construction", as the narrator satirically calls it. This process is the mark of the "open door" policies, one that encapsulates the same "march" in many of Cairo's middle- and upper-middle-class apartment buildings that since the 1970s witnessed collective illegal and unregulated redesigning of spaces of residence by adding more levels, tearing down walls, creating new rooms, adding on balconies, opening new windows, closing off others etc. These illegal accommodations cut across the social ladder and are not just limited to dwellings of the urban poor.[31] The march of demolition and construction in *Dhat* is enabled by the changing fortunes of the residents who, as a consequence of the new-found economic and social mobility of the 1970s, were transformed both on the economic and social levels – locally (through a market economy), regionally (specifically through the influx of petro-dollars from the Egyptian labour force in the Gulf) and globally (through international investments). The material and social changes that beset Dhat's *imara* symbolize the transformation of the larger urban space that is Cairo. In Dhat's building the march of demolition and construction is shared by all the residents whose changed destinies and trajectories during the 1970s become the hallmark for an entire city. As the narrator in *Dhat* deftly sums it up, it all began with:

> The Ministry of Agriculture man when his fortunes began to take a turn for the better after competition flared between the foreign insecticide companies that supplied the ministry The banner then passed on to the

schoolteacher who had worked in Kuwait, then to Hagg Fahmy, the butcher who had just joined the residents of the building more recently, and in the latest way i.e. buying rather than renting, until eventually it was picked up by the armed forces: the police officer after his return from a security mission in Oman, and the army officer after he took part in a training mission in the United States.[32]

All the residents of the *imara* take turns in painting walls, pulling down doors, changing old tile into imported ceramic, renovating the "combinations" in their bathrooms, installing stainless steel pipes, etc. All of them kept successfully to the marching timetable except for Dhat who held Abd al-Maguid, her university-dropout husband, responsible for their underdeveloped situation. When Dhat fails to keep up with the march, she begins to have dreams: she received "nocturnal visits" from both Gamal Abdel Nasser (the symbol of socialist Egypt) and Anwar El Sadat (the symbol of the open door economy). In Dhat's dreams, "Gamal Abdel Nasser would regularly turn away from her all of a sudden and charge into the kitchen, pick up a hammer, and lay into the walls and cupboards, then move onto the bathroom"[33] while behind him Anwar El Sadat, with great care and attention, was fixing up colourful high-quality ceramic tiles.[34] After Dhat succeeds in catching up with the march of demolition and construction, through the modest renovation of her bathroom and kitchen "Gamal Abdel Nasser stopped coming with his hammer of demolition, but Anwar El Sadat continued nocturnal visits with the popular ceramic tiles in his right hand".[35]

The march of demolition and construction in Dhat's *imara* is accompanied by new patterns of consumption and new modes of economic and social behavior. For example, her neighbours begin to acquire "sumptuous blouses and shirts, and chamois and leather jackets, and modern skirts and expensive shoes and contact lenses and Cartier spectacles" and "the miserable Ideal washing machine" is replaced with "a full automatic Westinghouse".[36] Similarly, the neighbourly family evening visits, filled with conversations about Egypt's military victory in October 1973, are replaced, with video machines and pornographic films that the male neighbours watch without their wives after midnight, leading to what the narrator, in a clear sexual reference, sarcastically labels "the technique of withdrawal and self reliance".[37]

Ibrahim's *Dhat* is a celebration of the mediocre, written in a highly layered satiric style that recalls, at every instant, the ironic distance its author has adopted vis-à-vis the characters, events and space they inhabit. At the same time *Dhat* (self) represents a pathetic version of Ibrahim's own frustrations and disillusionments, ones that he is able to objectify by displacing them, at one level in the text, on the *imara*, the space that Dhat (self) inhabits.

Journey to the underworld

Lusus mutaqaʿidun (*Thieves in Retirement*) by Hamdi Abu Golayyel takes us to another edge of the cityscape, namely Manshiyyat Nasir, itself on the edge of industrial Helwan. Manshiyyat Nasir is one of Cairo's 111 *ashwa'iyyat*, i.e. informal housing communities that, together, house over six million people, if not more.[38] As explained by Eric Denis, the terms *ashwa'i*/*ashwa'iyyat* refer not only to the physical space but also, and in a stigmatizing way, to the very people who inhabit that space:

> [T]he word *'ashwa'iyat*, which derives from the Arabic root that signifies chance, appeared at the beginning of the 1990s to designate slums, shantytowns, and the self-made satellite cities of the poor, i.e. illegal and/or illegitimate quarters. By the end of the 1990s, the term came to describe not just spaces but peoples, encompassing a near majority of the city as risky, "hazardous", errant figures. The figure of the errant is that which most frightens this urban society.[39]

The novel uses black humour to historicize for the initial emergence of Manshiyyat Nasir during the 1960s in a satiric manner that implicates the short comings and short-circuited socialist dreams of the Nasser era:

> The Leader – Gamal Abd al-Nasir – paid a surprise visit to one of the factories his Revolution had established in Helwan. He found that an enormous number of workers were spending all night in the factory. Delighted with their extraordinary self-sacrifice in the cause of labor, he went up to one of them and pumped his hand with obvious enthusiasm. "Good going, keep it up, hero!"
>
> The man tried to plant a kiss on his palm. "God protect you, Pasha.... Abdel Halim Abdel Halim here."
>
> "So you're working two shifts, then?"
>
> Trying to respond as he thought the Leader would want, the man said, "God's truth, Pasha, just one shift. Your honor."
>
> "Then why aren't you going home?"
>
> "Where'm I gonna go, Pasha?" – addling the Leader, who had supposed the workers were sleeping in the factory because they were so keen to keep on working, night and day. Surely not because they couldn't find a place to live. For the sake of safe-guarding his Revolution, the Leader waved toward a vacant stretch that happened to be within eyesight.
>
> "Let them live there!" And the workers rushed forward in a perfect likeness of Revolutionary zeal, toward the empty zone. It was a mere matter of days before Manshiyat Gamal Abd al-Nasir – Nasser's Newtown – entered the world.[40]

Hence, Nasser's fictive haphazard gesture in the novel is translated into a real haphazard reality where today more than one million of Cairo's poor live in highly inadequate structural and infrastructural conditions. Workers, immigrants, dislocated individuals: a pot-pourri of the truly disadvantaged. In *Lusus mutaqa'idun*, Abu Golayyel provides a literary map of Manshiyyat Nasir that is

Plate 8.1 Heliopolis main street, courtesy of Randa Shaath.

Plate 8.2 Heliopolis: Man in balcony, courtesy of Randa Shaath.

Plate 8.3 Heliopolis Laundry, courtesy of Randa Shaath.

Plate 8.4 The train, courtesy of Jean-Pierre Ribière.

Plate 8.5 Along Tariq el Nasr Road facing Manshiyyat Nasir, courtesy of Jean-Pierre Ribière.

Plate 8.6 Cairo Rooftops I, courtesy of Randa Shaath.

Plate 8.7 Cairo Rooftops II, courtesy of Randa Shaath.

Plate 8.8 Wash in Nile, courtesy of Randa Shaath.

closer to a collective grave whose boundaries are each more deadly than the other: a "mongrel place" that is "part village and part unplanned city fringe, destination of squatters and incomers" whose eastern rim, "is hemmed in by high-tension wires that stretch all the way up the Nile to Aswan", its western boundary is determined by "the filtration area into which all of Cairo's sewage lines pour". It is basically one modest street that provides "the battlefield for a permanent war between the sewage administration and the bureau of roadworks".[41]

The "hazardous" people of Manshiyyat Nasir (to use Eric Denis's description), the "Saidis, those southerners who are constitutionally suspicious when it comes to sons of the north, perhaps in fear of them" (to use Abu Golayyel's rendition), have a definite class identity "thanks to the wave of Gamal Abd al-Nasir's hand". They are all immigrants from various villages in Egypt's governorates and their nostalgia for their hometowns is described with warm sympathy:

> Although they have rebelled against the tin shacks they threw up immediately after the historic hand flick – rebelled and moved into real houses – they remain loyal to their villages, those faraway farming villages that they never, ever visit, yet the memories of which give them a sense of security and protect them from the betrayals of time and the bosses at the factory.[42]

Lusus mutaqaʿidun revolves around the lives of the residents of one building or rather one house (*bayt*) owned by Abu Gamal, the very same man who, in the novel, had shaken hands with President Gamal Abdel Nasser in the 1960s. He has now been laid off from the Helwan factory and spends his day on a chair in front of the entrance to his property. Abu Gamal's house is a five-storey one with balconies, a green façade, decorated with square designs in a deeper shade of green. The strategic entrance, where Abu Gamal sits, is sprinkled with water and against the wall of the house rests a chair comfortable enough for "a fairly commanding backside". On top of the main entrance hangs the head of a wild animal with an imposing jaw and angular fangs.[43] Descriptions of Abu Gamal's house set it apart from Sonallah Ibrahim's *imara* on the edge of Heliopolis: here there are no apartments; rather they are called *matrah* (rooms), all of which are in close proximity given the very narrow and crumbling stairway and the doors that are left ajar by the neighbours thus creating a sense of imminent licentious community. Eventually, the tenants, the owner's sons and their wives are all brought together through drugs, violence and mind-boggling, promiscuous sex.

Abu Gamal's history is encapsulated in the fact that he was the first factory worker to be hired thanks to the nationalization laws of the 1960s and he was the first to be fired thanks to the privatization ones of the 1970s. Having been dropped by the state, Abu Gamal's life project is to search for "some sort of approbation, for respect befitting his head of gray hair".[44] However, in this underworld of the urban poor, his traditional patriarchal power, ironically symbolized by the head of the wild animal with an imposing jaw and angular fangs hung on the entrance of his house, is subverted and the very structure of traditional hierarchical power relations within the family is undercut. His four sons, who all live in the house he built, treat him with disdain, if not with violence. Indeed one of the earliest scenes in the text is a ferocious physical fight between Abu Gamal and his eldest son, Gamal, who beats up his father in the stairway calling him "a son of a bitch" because he failed to kill one of his other sons who is openly homosexual, or as the narrator calls him "a fag".[45]

Abu Gamal's four sons are unemployed, and between them they manifest the urban poor's informal, and illegal, venues of survival. Gamal, the eldest, is the handsome playboy and drug dealer whose business thrives under the complicit eyes of the police officers and the legal establishment. Sayf is the homosexual who is temporarily put away in a madhouse by his elder brother Gamal because his behaviour and demeanour have brought shame on the family honour. Amir is a drug addict, a failed mechanic and a chronic thief who steals only from his family and the tenants. The fourth brother, Salah, is a former basketball player whose yearly two-week vacation in Alexandria allows his brother Amir to clean out and sell all the appliances in his apartment during his absence.

Abu Gamal has also taken in tenants in his house, but, unlike the disparate upwardly mobile middle-class residents in Sonallah Ibrahim's *Dhat*, his tenants are united by one element that constitutes Abu Gamal's only stipulation to rent: kinship. Not that they are Abu Gamal's blood relatives, but they are his *baladiyyat*, i.e. from the same region. For, like him, the tenants are all immigrants from Upper Egypt. As Catherine Miller has shown in her study of "Upper Egyptian Regionally Based Communities in Cairo", living among kin is a social ideal for it provides a sense of comfort and security as well as a degree of social cohesion despite migration and displacement.[46] Abu Gamal takes in Sheikh Hasan, a repentant runaway from Suhag who had slept with his mother-in-law, Ustaz Ramadan, a primary school teacher and failed traditional poet, the *ductura* (i.e. medical professional) from Qina in the basement who abandoned nursing for house cleaning and prostitution both in the workplace and at home, with Abu Gamal's knowledge and paid blessing. We are also introduced to Adil the subservient Copt from Suhag who ran away from his village's wrath after he accidentally killed a Muslim sheikh and who shuddered incessantly at the derogatory label "*Koftis*" (for Copt) that Abu Gamal bestowed upon him. And finally, there is our narrator from the south (Al-Saʿid), who, like the author himself, is a construction worker who has participated in constructing many of Cairo's high-rises. He ends up electrocuting and killing Amir, Abu Gamal's son, for attempted theft of his scantily furnished room.

This underworld in Abu Gamal's house, however, also bustles with frustrated and unrecognized creativity: Gamal the eldest son is a writer whose texts are quoted by the narrator in the novel; Sayf loves to sing and act; Amir is a poet, and Ustaz Ramadan the primary teacher seeks an audience for his unfashionable traditional verse in his primary school students. Most importantly of course, there is our narrator, whose trajectory is tailored to match that of the author, Hamdi Abu Golayyel. It is the narrator's bitterly humorous testimony (i.e. the

160 *Remaking culture*

novel itself) that ultimately places the human intimacies of this underworld of the urban poor on the map of the mega-city beyond the impersonal statistics and figures. A literary architecture of the poor, by the poor.

The post-colonial Yacoubian building

From this edge of Cairo we move back to the heart of the once-fashionable colonial centre of the city in Alaa al-Aswany's bestselling novel *Imarat Ya'qubian*. Unlike the first two texts, where we discover the *imara* metaphor gradually as we begin reading, Alaa al-Aswany's novel affixes the metaphor to its title. The name of the building conjures up downtown colonial Cairo in the early twentieth century and evokes a history of the city's elite foreign minorities and their sumptuous ways of life. Unlike the earlier examples, al-Aswany's building is a real one whose name and location are familiar to many Cairo residents. It was built in 1934 by an Armenian millionaire and still carries his name. In its golden years, the building was occupied by Armenian, Italian and Greek residents as well as prominent Egyptian figures. However, in post-revolutionary Egypt its more recent lodgers (a mixed bag of relics from the past, middle-class professionals and downtrodden low-income individuals and families) have indeed come to resemble many of al-Aswany's characters – so much so that they are now suing the author for libel.[47] The history of the transformations that beset the Yacoubian Building from colonial to post-colonial times in Egypt, as depicted by the omniscient narrator, encapsulates not just the history of twentieth-century Cairo but also that of modern Egypt at large. Conversely, the changes in the urban space that the author inhabits are directly responsible for his first novel:

> A single episode inspired the idea behind the novel. El Aswany was walking in Garden City when he saw an old building being demolished to make way for a garage. The building was being torn down in longitudinal sections, making its many separate rooms visible. Those rooms had life. There was someone studying, someone who was in love with the girl next door, a newlyweds first apartment, recalls El Aswany. It had people who lived and people who died. The idea stayed with him for eight years until he finally sat down and began writing the novel in 1998.[48]

Through the changing catalogue of residents of the Yacoubian Building, and their use of the urban space, al-Aswany traces the political, ethnic, economic and social changes that have occurred in the city over more than five decades. First readers learn about the history of the building, its architecture and its residents during the first half of the twentieth century:

> In 1934, Hagop Yacoubian, the millionaire and then doyen of the Armenian community in Egypt, decided to construct an apartment block that would bear his name. He chose for it the best site on Suleiman Basha and engaged a well-known Italian engineering firm to build it, and the firm came up with

a beautiful design – ten lofty stories in the high classical European style, the balconies decorated with Greek faces carved in stone, the columns, steps, and corridors all of natural marble, and the latest model elevator by Schindler.[49]

The cream of society of those days, "ministers, big land-owning *bashas*, foreign manufacturers, and two Jewish millionaires" lived in "luxurious apartments, of eight or ten rooms on two levels joined by an internal stairway".[50] The garage of the Yacoubian Building housed the wealthy residents' luxury cars (Rolls Royce, Buick and Chevrolet) while the front of the building was a large showroom for the silver products made in Yacoubian's factories.[51] Each apartment came with a two by two metre iron room on the rooftop that had a variety of service uses: storing foodstuffs, overnight kennelling for dogs and, during pre-washing-machine days, washing laundry by professional washerwomen.

With the 1952 revolution, and the exodus of the foreign and Jewish communities, every apartment that was vacated in the Yacoubian Building was taken over by officers from the armed forces whose wives began using the iron rooftop rooms for housing their servants and raising rabbits, duck and chickens. With the "open door" policies of the 1970s these occupants left the downtown building for the new upper-middle-class neighbourhoods of Muhandisin and Nasr City, selling or renting their apartments, or using them as offices and clinics for their newly graduated sons. Similarly, the servants of the rooftop rooms ceded their rooms for money to new migrant, working-class residents employed in the city. The final outcome, as the narrator tells us, "was the growth of a new community on the roof that was entirely independent of the rest of the building".[52]

Unlike the first two novels, whose worlds remain geographically, economically and socially apart, with Dhat's *imara* marching up and Abu Gamal's house sinking further down, al-Aswany's building brings together the opposites and looks at the intersection of the fates of his privileged and disadvantaged characters that cohabit the same space. On the one hand there are the rich, in all their manifestations: the old aristocracy, the colonial bourgeoisie and the nouveau rich. On the other hand there are the poor, again in all their manifestations. Together, they inhabit the Yacoubian Building differently: the rich live in its stately, spacious but rather dilapidated apartments; and the poor occupy its rooftop where they have transformed the servants' and storage rooms, originally meant to service the apartments, into their homes and workshops after fierce financial competition accompanied by violence, in some instances, to secure the space.

Even though the worlds, histories and fantasies of the haves and have-nots in the Yacoubian Building are different, their lives come to intersect on the basis of one principle: exploitation, specifically that of the bodies of the poor by the rich. Zaki Bey, son of Disuqi Basha, the "folkloric" francophone old flirt, ends up exploiting young Busayna, a rooftop resident, who has to give up college in order to support her family. Busayna is initially in love with Taha al-Shazli, the young hard-working, and god-fearing son of the *bawwab* (doorman and guard) of the building who is her neighbour on the rooftop. This love story is crushed like Taha's dream of becoming a police officer since his aspirations of social mobility (the Police Academy being an elite institution) are obstructed by his social reality: he is the son of the *bawwab*. Taha persists in his dream of upward mobility by joining the university where he is recruited by a militant Islamic group. He is arrested after a demonstration and ends up tortured and violated in prison. After his release he volunteers to be part of a suicide mission against the state where he ends up killing the same police officer who had tortured him in prison before dying himself in the shootout. Then there is Hatim Rashid, the homosexual editor of the French magazine *Le Caire*, who engages in a same-sex relationship with Abd Rabu, a poor Central Security Forces recruit from Upper Egypt whose sense of guilt and violated self-dignity lead him to murder Hatim. We are also introduced to Hagg Azzam, who was once a shoeshine boy and has now become a rich drug dealer and member of parliament. He takes as second wife the young and poor Alexandrian widow Suʿad Gabir, who marries him in order to secure a better life for her own son from her first husband only to discover that Azzam has stipulated in the secret marriage contract that she not bear him any children.

Furthermore, the already rich exploit those who are richer, and the already poor those who are poorer. In the former case, Kamal al-Fuli, a ruling party bigwig, demands £E1 million to get Hagg Azzam the Kasr al-Nil seat in Parliament. As for the poor, they too have their own thugs: Hamid Hawwas who reports his neighbours to the authorities and the scheming tailor Malak who manoeuvres to illegally set up and expand his shop in the rooftop rooms.

Alaa al-Aswany's *Imarat Yaʿqubyan* is a ruthless attack on the Egyptian state that, as Joseph Massad has pointed out, aims to show the decadence, degeneracy and misery to which Egyptian society succumbed as a result of the post-colonial state.[53] As the author himself put it:

> We are talking about a system that needs to be changed completely.... It has reached a point where we have reached zero. The zero we received in the Mondial [Egypt's bid for the World Cup] is a fair result, very fair, not only in the Mondial, but in everything. That zero really should not be given to the Egyptians, it should be given to the Egyptian government. The Egyptian government should get a zero in all fields, not only in soccer, but in health and education, in democracy, and in everything really.
>
> Egypt deserves better than this.[54]

Murder on the Nile

Finally, with Mohamed Tawfik's *Tifl shaqi ismuhu Antar* (*Naughty Boy Called Antar*), all these contradictions are further accentuated and drawn to phantasmagoric conclusions. Indeed, this text brings to dramatic narrative closure the logical end of the colliding realities of the urban rich and the urban poor through a brilliant symbolic moment that opens the text and comes to encapsulate the whole Egyptian situation. The novel is set inside one of the luxury towers that have been planted, like an alien body, on the agricultural land that still surrounds them on the Maadi Nile Corniche.[55] Interestingly, Tawfik was actually one of the engineers working on the real construction site of that very same tower during the 1970s. The relationship that he establishes between the structure of the building and that of the novel, the architecture of the tower and that of the text, collapses the boundaries of the real and the imagined architecture of the city. Responding to an interview by email, Tawfik wrote:

> It is amazing how your simple question has brought into focus the mental foundations for the idea of Borg El-Saada in [*Tifl shaqi ismuhu Antar*], details of which I had not been fully conscious. Naturally, I was aware that I spent a few years (in the late 1970s and early 1980s) building a tower facing the Nile in Maadi, so I had a clear visual image of both the surroundings and vistas as well as the floor plans of apartments, elevators, entrance ... etc. Also, that the tower was being built for a wealthy sheikh from the Gulf. But other important elements had somehow slipped through the cracks of consciousness, such as the hours I spent – during night shifts – wondering how one person could make use of a forty-storey tower, which people he would surround himself with, what kinds of decadent relationships would evolve (I now think of Kaseb Bey's enormous bed strategically placed in his reception area) and the lavish lifestyles such a tower with a swimming pool in the fortieth floor would witness (the tower was reduced to only twenty storey in the novel to avoid too many characters and the undue complication of plot lines). And more generally, the sense of wonderment that you inevitably feel as your building grows taller by the week and the reality that the steel and concrete you are methodically putting together will one day become a living hub, home to hundreds of people and millions of experiences, loves fulfilled, dreams lost. In fact, grasping the sheer size and capacity of a tower, I, only now, trace to those days.[56]

Tifl shaqi actually takes us inside the apartments of Borg al-saʿada (The tower of happiness), a tower as luxurious as the Manhattan skyscrapers,[57] and exposes the "lavish lifestyles" of its residents and "their decadent relationships" through the unresolved murder of the young and beautiful actress Ahlam, whose name significantly means "dreams" in Arabic. On 2 August 1999 at exactly 3:15 p.m. Sergeant Ashmuni, who spends his day on the highway divider trying to remain alive as he regulates the fast-moving traffic on the Corniche (the boulevard along the Nile), is awakened from his stupor by a falling armchair that hits the ground causing a noisy traffic accident. Before Ashmuni has time to react, the sky falls on top of his head: he looks up, in the glaring sun to find that plates, glasses, vases, forks and knives are falling like rain from an apartment on the thirteenth floor of the tower, followed by pillows, napkins, books, papers and finally a piano that lands on Shakir Basha's silver Mercedes that was parked in

164   Remaking culture

front of the tower, transforming it into *kufta* (a popular finger-length grilled minced meat delight; here the word is used figuratively to signify squashing flat, or deforming beyond recognition).[58]

This ominous moment on the very first pages of the novel drives home all that we come to discover inside the tower through the lives of the residents. At the heart of this city thriller lies the dead body of actress Ahlam al-Shawarbi, found strangled and completely naked inside one of the tower's elevators. Sergeant Ashmuni, who had found the body, is interrogated by the police inside the apartment on the thirteenth floor where he witnesses an apocalyptic scene of destruction. In the midst of it all sits a lonely vase with one white rose, the reincarnated spirit of Ahlam herself.

This luxury tower on the Corniche houses the transnational mega-capital of the city and encapsulates the global, geo-political and multicultural dynamics of the "critical cosmopolitan".[59] It is owned by Sheikh Wahdan from the Gulf who seldom comes to Cairo but whose property is administered by Kasib Bey, his Egyptian representative: a sleazy, *nouveau riche*, overweight character, with a hair wig who is decked in gold chains and bracelets. As we escort the characters up and down the tower's elevators and become privy to their illicit relationships, we meet many of the residents: Abd al-Tawwab Mabruk Basha (also known to his close friends as Tutu Basha), a wealthy contractor who had been subletting his now destroyed apartment on the thirteenth floor to the rich and powerful film producer Shukri Shakir. The latter is the man who had launched Ahlam's acting career and was now after her younger sister Didi. Abd al-Malak is the unemployed Ph.D. in genetic engineering from Georgetown University; he turns into a psychic in order to earn a living and sells his new-found powers to the insomniac Tutu Basha since Ahlam's murder. We also meet Farah, Abd al-Malak's college-day sweetheart, now transformed into a Barbie doll and having an affair with Shukri Shakir in one of his apartments in the tower. Then there is Gawdat Hanim, a bourgeois lady who serves as informer to the journalist Islah al-Mohandis who is covering Ahlam's murder. The skyscraper is also home to Lula Hamdi, the well-known belly dancer, owner of two flats in the luxury tower, who once said that if she piled up all her money and stood on top of the pile she would be able to see Timbuktu. Madame Esmeralda is the society lady from Chile who had invited Ahlam to a party, along with Shukri Shakir, on the night of her murder and then left the country immediately after. As for Ductur Mahgub, Antar's father, he is a rather homely academic type whose economic status is remarkably lower than that of his neighbours. And, of course, there is Antar, the little naughty boy, who roams the tower, enters apartments, overhears conversations, mischievously unsettling and exposing the decadent occupants of the tower and their relationships. In one of the symbolic leitmotifs of the novel that punctuates many of the chapters, Antar steals Sergeant Ashmuni's cap and usurps his place in commanding the mad Cairo traffic like Ashmuni has never done before. And finally, we also meet Ahlam herself, whose point of view we discover through her diary entries, found by Islah al-Mohandis, the reporter, next to the lonely vase with the white rose.

Even though the police have amassed enough clues to solve the riddle of Ahlam's murder, with most of the evidence pointing to the powerful film producer Shukri Shakir, the case is closed and Islah al-Mohandis's investigative reporting is abruptly interrupted by the editor of the newspaper where she works. However, Ahlam (dreams) comes back to haunt them all, through Antar, who becomes her medium, denouncing everyone and repeating in her voice: "You are all guilty. And you know it."[60]

The intricate literary detail, structure and architecture of *Tifl shaqi ismuhu Antar* is all the more intriguing when we discover that it was entirely written in Geneva (1998–2002) during Mohamed Tawfik's lunch hours between meetings at the United Nations where he served as a diplomat.[61] It is as if the sheer size, complexity and magnitude of both the physical tower and the fictional one required this kind of distance. This is perhaps the ultimate transnational rendition of the *imara* as urban metaphor where actual global structures and dynamics require equally global literary distance and space for the "critical cosmopolitan" to so vividly materialize.

The Tower of Babel

One of the fascinating dimensions of reading these four novels against each other is the emergence of a complex map of urban language(s) in the texts. Even though the four *imaras* are all situated in the mega-city of Cairo, the linguistic lexicon and symbolic signs, depending on where the *imara* is located, become important distinguishing markers that immediately identify the colliding economic, social and cultural spaces that its occupants inhabit. *Dhat*'s urban space is filled with anglicizations such as Abdel al-Maguid "Oov koors", the social marker of the 1960s, and various names of imported commodities and new everyday household words of the 1970s *infitah* period (dressing, heavy duty, ceramic, etc.). The novel also reproduces the contradictions of the emerging Islamization or globalization of culture: when Dhat calls to register her son in one of the budding Islamic schools of the 1970s, the voice that greets her on the other end of the line answers, to her utter surprise: "*assalamu alaykum wa rahmatu l-lahi wa barakatu* the Islamic University" instead of the so-far customary "*alo*" (for hello); Dhat is then put on hold to the theme song from the American 1970s film *Love Story*![62] The language of the urban poor is radically different from that which we encounter in Dhat's building: the character dialogue in *Lusus mutaqa'idun* is written in the most popular level of Egyptian Arabic while Abu Gamal's family uses the most open insults all the time and the text does not shy away from reproducing all of them: son of a bitch, pimp, fag etc. Indeed, there are moments in the text where certain expressions would require "translation" for a middle-class Cairene: for example, Abu Gamal incites his son Amir against Hamdi the "bango" (weed) dealer saying "*ghuzzu*" which literally means "prick him", but in Abu Gamal's lexicon means "get him", "beat him up".[63] By contrast, the world of the Yacoubian Building immerses us in other colliding languages: the words of the songs of French singer Edith Piaf who is Zaki Bey's favourite are pitted against Taha Shazli's militant Islamic lexicon of *jihad* (holy war) and the *shahada* (matyrdom). Finally, Mohamed Tawfik's *Tifl shaqi* confronts the cacophony of the local and the global, the language of the poor and that of the mega-rich: the jinn and the internet, Sergeant Ashmuni's subservient "*ya basha*" and "*ya hanim*" that he uses to address all the other characters in the text and Shakir Bey's "*marsidis bodra*" (name given to one of the models of Mercedes-Benz that signifies that its price has been bought from drug dealing, "*bodra*").

Given this Tower of Babel, it is no surprise that the four novels end in similarly disconcerting ways: Dhat's heroic attempts to resist the tide of "demolition and construction" are completely crushed, and we leave her sitting alone on her toilet seat crying; in *Lusus mutaqa'idun*, Amir dies an absurd death after his attempted theft of the narrator's impoverished room; in *Imarat Ya'qubyan* young Busayna is married off to the old and lecherous Zaki Bey; and finally in *Tifl shaqi ismuhu Antar*, Ahlam's unresolved murder is drowned in a phantasmagoric cacophony of New Year Eve's celebrations in the luxury tower. A dismal map of Cairo indeed!

In *Cairo Cosmopolitan*, the Cairo School for Urban Studies whose work has greatly informed this chapter provided a fresh interdisciplinary approach to the study of ambivalent and contradictory forces at work in contemporary Cairo, thereby deconstructing modernist dichotomies of the local and the global, the traditional and the modern. As Diane Singerman and Paul Amar put it in their introduction to *Cairo Cosmopolitan*, the contributors' case studies are predominantly anchored in the "practical wisdom" of the diverse voices of Cairenes that are at once "contextual, grounded in experience, and inextricably linked to the world and its concrete relations of power". It is through this grounding in the voices of Cairenes that their contributions compellingly dismantle the "obscuring legends or meta-narratives" around Cairo, the "City Victorious", the legacy of post-orientalist studies that have consistently depicted the city either as a bomb or as a tomb.[64]

In the same spirit, this chapter provides a literary intervention that complements and dialogues with the findings of the Cairo School for Urban Studies, exploring the same contradictions and challenges in Cairenes' lives through the works of creative writers, themselves citizens of the globalized city. Indeed, reading the literary works of Sonallah Ibrahim, Hamdi Abu Gollayel, Alaa al-Aswany and Mohamed Tawfik amply demonstrates, as Diane Singerman and Paul Amar have aptly stated, Cairenes' remarkable ability to negotiate their political, economic and social worlds. At the same time, all four writers, each in his own way, map out the obstacles that the citizens of Cairo face as they "move within, through, and against dominant state institutions and spatial and economic structures, articulating forms of subjectivity and agency, but under conditions not of their own choosing, and within relations of power that can radically dehumanize and militarize daily existence".[65] The ultimate picture, whether it be through the contributions in *Cairo Cosmopolitan* or through my own literary map of Cairo, is far from utopia.

Fifty years ago Naguib Mahfouz's narrator had bewailed that Midaq Alley always "returned to its usual state of indifference and forgetfulness".[66] Despite the displacement of the *hara* by the *imara*, the endings of the four novels, written half a century later, seem to echo the same indifference and forgetfulness. However, one could turn to Mahfouz's *Midaq Alley* for consolation and repeat Sheikh Darwish's very last lines in the text:

> Oh people of the House! I will be patient so long as I live, for do not all things have an end? Oh yes, everything comes to its *nihaya*.
> And the word for this in English is "end" and it is spelled END.[67]

Part III
The bounds of change
State, street and self-censorship

9 Taking the soap out of the opera
The case of Hagg Mitwalli's Family

Once again, as is the case every year, Egyptian television greeted us during the 2001 Ramadan season with an awesome mass of TV serials exclusively fashioned for the holy month of Ramadan. The Arab viewer, who would have just broken his or her fast with the typically heavy Ramadan meal, *iftar*, could slip into a state of drowsiness and sprawl lazily in front of the small screen. Watching television – after almost half-a-century-long experience of special programming, produced specifically for these post-*iftar* hours during Ramadan – is an activity that hinders the already arduous process of digestion (of both the heavy *iftar* meal and the even heavier dose of Ramadan serials) with an intensity that almost brings the process to a halt.

It has become safe to say that, in general, the typical Arab viewer has a special appetite for Ramadan serial television programming. These serials dominate the small screen because they are aired at prime time, in the time bracket when the entire family gathers around the television screen at the end of their meal, a captive audience that rarely has occasion to reunite in its entirety during the year, as the father may be out, or the mother busy with the children etc. The shows summon the family to gather around them, in its smaller single unit or in the context of larger, extended family gatherings. The unravelling of events governs the process of digestion, only to be interrupted by, or concluded with, heated discussions, accompanied by tea and Ramadan's traditional sweets. The debate spills on to the streets and overruns public spaces, hovering over that viewer who thought he or she could flee the family setting and rebel against its authority and dominion. The debate travels across continents and the well-guarded national borders that the Arab viewer finds increasingly difficult to cross, particularly after "9/11". Indeed, there is no escaping Egyptian TV serials during Ramadan. Even those like me, who do not watch TV, are entrapped, after constantly scheming to avoid the lure of the small screen, and bound by a commitment to write this chapter on Ramadan television serials.

In this chapter I will focus specifically on the notorious TV drama *A'ilat al-Hagg Mitwalli* (Hagg Mitwalli's Family), which was aired during the 2001 Ramadan season locally, in Egypt, and simultaneously on 21 satellite TV channels in the region thus becoming a regional household favourite that millions of Arab viewers followed and that triggered a spectacular amount of debate and critique, ultimately causing the intervention of the National Council for Women (NCW) that is presided over by Egypt's first lady. Both the debate surrounding the serial and the ensuing intervention by NCW transformed the show and the main protagonist (Hagg Mitwalli), played by the Egyptian superstar Nur al-Sharif (particularly famous region-wide for his nationalistic, historical and political roles), into a threatening, transnational phenomenon that impacted – from the point of view of the "modernist" authorities and proponents of modernist discourse, specifically where gender issues are concerned, the very image of a modern Egyptian state within a global context.

Families, imagined and real

Ramadan serials are created with the understanding that their target market is a family audience, one which crosses the class divide and encompasses the poor and the wealthy, the rural and the urban. Since the keepers of the Egyptian state-run media industry are fully aware of the power of this Ramadan siege, and of its commercial and economic returns, they have not spared any effort to invest in the most qualified, available talent in terms of script-writing, direction, performance and set design, to pleasantly surprise their restfully reclined spectator.

The producers, particularly at the level of script-writing, have thus directed their focus towards the social themes deemed best suited, from their point of view, for the collective viewership – all the children of the nation – a viewership that is expected to engage with the shows despite differences in age, gender, class and creed. Every year, Egyptian families spend long hours watching a bouquet of Ramadan TV serials that are meant to foster a sense of collective belonging and a common national imaginary: some are historical dramas like the highly popular 1988–92 instalments of *Layali al-Hilmiyya* (*Hilmiyya Nights*) named after the once posh Hilmiyya neighbourhood in Cairo; others provide readings and critiques of current societal transformations (for example, the rise of Islamic fundamentalism) such as the 1994 *Al-A'ila* (*The Family*), others like the 2000 Ramadan serial on Egypt's diva Umm Kulthum are mythmakers that transform some of the country's cultural figures into national icons, still others like the 2000 serial *Awan al-ward* (*Time of Roses*) tackle issues of national unity and community between Muslims and Copts. Every year all these serials generate a tremendous amount of national debate, controversy and conversation in the national public sphere. For, as James Lull has already argued:

> Television does not give families something to talk about, it directs their attention toward particular topics and, because families like to gather in front of the screen, the viewing situation is a convenient social setting in which to talk and otherwise communicate.[1]

Since Ramadan TV serials regularly represent images of social life, including those of families and family relationships, they are themselves "an agent of socialization to role differentiated behavior in families".[2] Hence the general concern on both the producing and consuming ends about how such family structures and relationships are represented and the impact such representations might have on different members of the family even if such "social uses of television" are not identical for different social groups.[3]

Depending on the issues raised and the pertinent problems addressed on the small-screen, Egyptian Ramadan TV serials (and TV drama in general) always ultimately cause schisms, conflicts, even litigation, with some of the audiences for and others against certain modes and forms of representation in the shows.[4] However, despite the multiple levels of reception of Ramadan serials and all the ink that is spilt over them, they invariably unite Egyptians in an imagined community albeit with a dominant centre, Cairo, where all these TV dramas are produced, and marginalized peripheries where they are consumed. Even when readings of the same visual text differ among various social groups, they still bring together the nation in a collective, multi-layered conversation focused on a set of issues which audiences take to heart and debate heatedly long after the Ramadan nights are over. Every year, one or more of the serials programmed for Ramadan succeed in grabbing public attention, and in the rewriting of this collective social text, a ritualized confirmation to viewers and commentators alike of their belonging to the same imagined nation and imagined community or collectivity that is bound by the least common denominator of meanings and signs in the past and present, regardless of how conflicting the readings and commentaries of that one serial appear to be. For as viewers make their own interpretations of shows they also construct subsequent communications activities: TV talk that reinscribes them in a larger imagined community.

From the moment of its inception in the 1960s, the Egyptian state-run TV industry, like many other instances around the globe, has been keenly aware of the national role of the small screen as a tool for influencing audiences and shaping their collective consciousness. Since the Nasser period, as many scholars have already argued, TV has been used as "an instrument of national development and political mobilization" expected to provide "guidance and education of all Egyptians".[5] Indeed, the small screen has been used as "an important means for disseminating modernist ideology in Egypt"[6] and is "the main instrument for transmission of ... public narratives of the state and the urban middle classes".[7]

However, as Lila Abu-Lughod has argued in her analysis of Egyptian TV serials of the 1980s, this general didactic tendency is far more complex and complicated than what first meets the eye. One fundamental problem is the "social location" of the producers of media on the one hand and its consumers on the other. While many of the influential writers and producers in the Egyptian state-run TV industry "have a certain independence from the government that is reflected in the social criticism characteristic of their productions, they nevertheless participate in a shared discourse about nationhood and citizenship".[8] Even when a television serial ventures into lashing out a critique of the reality of economic and social disparity, or changes in moral values deemed to threaten – from the point of view of the state and its institutions – the construction and well-being of the imagined and the real family, the critique itself stems from a constructive or corrective drive, aimed, in its entirety, at disseminating values intended to protect the collective communal image. Hence, the position of TV drama producers invariably translates into a "general attitude of knowing what is good for 'society' (seen as an object to be manipulated by one's expertise)".[9] However, such intentions do not always necessarily coincide with the levels of audience reception of the "message" and "meaning" of the shows. For example, in *Dramas of Nationhood: The Politics of Television in Egypt*, Abu-Lughod confronts the feminist ideology embedded in one Egyptian TV serial written by a Cairene progressive feminist script-writer with how differently its "progressive" message is received and read by illiterate village women in Upper Egypt. Abu-Lughod's reading of these Upper Egyptian women's reception of the show makes us rethink monolithic ideas about TV audience(s), intended message, meaning and influence. Indeed, it becomes evident that "the same cultural texts have different imports in different contexts",[10] and that TV audiences are not like sponges that suck up intended messages and meanings but that they are active participants in the production of meaning(s) according to these audiences' specific social, economic and religious values, contexts and locations. However, as Larry Strelitz justifiably reminds us, in his deconstruction of the myth of global media homogenization, even if the meaning of particular media or cultural products resides not in the form but primarily at the point of their consumption in a particular context, "the power audiences have to use media messages as they will should not blind us to the fact that meanings generated and circulated by particular media can, and do, in specific contexts, help sustain relationships of domination and subordination".[11] Indeed, as Farha Ghannam rightly points out in her analysis of globalization and the production of locality in Cairo, where she argues for broadening the concept of globalization to account for the multiplicity of flows that shape cultural identities and practices, "social imagination" in Cairo is shaped, not primarily by American movies and TV programmes but rather and more strongly perhaps by "Indian films, Lebanese singers, Brazilian soccer players and Algerian *rai* music" and last, but definitely not least, by "oil-producing countries in particular [that] have a major role in stimulating desires and fulfilling dreams".[12]

From the Atlantic to the Gulf and beyond

The position of Egypt as a primary producer and exporter of TV serials in the Arab world, specifically in the market of the Ramadan season, is an undisputed fact.[13] This continues to be true despite the major shift from national to transnational satellite TV in the Arab region. For decades, Egypt and the Egyptian vernacular have dominated the Arab TV screen as they have even earlier through Egypt's pioneering film industry and its long-standing production and dissemination of song, drama and literature. Primarily, of course, these Egyptian TV serials are conceived for national consumption and are therefore predominantly focused on local and national issues. They equally reflect the Egyptian state's cultural institutional position with regard to many such timely issues. However, the hegemony of Egyptian TV serials also meant that the nationalist and modernist ideology of the Egyptian state could be disseminated throughout the region albeit at times requiring some navigation in order to meet or bypass red lines and possible censorship from its more conservative Arab clientele specifically in the Gulf region. Up until the late 1980s other Arab audiences could "watch" the representations of Egypt's local social, economic and historic transformations without necessarily partaking in debates that erupted in Egypt in the aftermath of such representations on the small screen since many of the problems were indeed Egyptian-specific.

With the advent of the 1990s and the spectacular boom of satellite TV in the Arab world that started after the Gulf War in 1991 and the initial launching of the Saudi MBC in London (1992) and the Qatari Al-Jazeera (1996), Egypt's uncontested leadership in the regional media market has undergone several transformations.[14] Today, Arab audiences whose TV lives up until the late 1980s depended solely on their respective states' cultural politics have the freedom to select from dozens of satellite channels that have succeeded in defying national and cultural boundaries. Indeed, on one level, the new reality of satellite TV in the Arab region has effectively made real an Arab unity that has remained a discursive weapon/illusion over the past 50 years:

> Satellite television has created a sense of belonging to, and participation in, a kind of virtual Arab metropolis. It has begun to make real a dream that 50 years of politicians' speeches and gestures have failed to achieve: Arab unity.[15]

This new-found virtual Arab unity has also meant the displacement of the cultural centre of the Arab world: Cairo. The spectacular emergence of the once marginal and marginalized Gulf countries on to the global transnational media map has brought with it a new Arab cultural scene that competes not just at the economic but also on the aesthetic and ideological levels with the "centre" and heart of the Arab world that once upon a time in the 1960s dictated its own version of mediatic modernist/nationalist modes of representation:

> The days of the insurrectionary Voice of the Arabs [Sawt al-ʿarab] broadcast from revolutionary Cairo are gone. In the Arab world today, where nearly 70 million out of three hundred million are illiterate, TV is indispensable. It is the primary means of entertainment and news for the average Arab citizen. The Arab consumer can choose from more than 140 channels, of which Egypt produces more than 27.[16]

The recent virtual Arab unity has actually led to what has come to be known as a "pan-Arab market" that traverses national differences between Arab countries at multiple levels. As Jon Alterman has argued in "Transnational Media and Social Change in the Arab World":

Whereas national differences could be maintained in the twentieth century because geography and governmental efforts combined to create distinct markets for information, new technologies make it cheaper, faster, and easier for information to transcend those obstacles to create something much more closely resembling a single market. In that market, the imperative is to create products that enlarge and unite the market rather than those that fracture it.[17]

Such a new pan-Arab unified market, as Alterman further points out, has had contradictory effects on Arab audiences. On the one hand, it has empowered Arab audiences, allowing them to expand the bounds of dialogue and debate across the Arab region and beyond in ways simply unimaginable only a decade ago. On the other hand, this newfound dialogue "has also had the effect ... of solidifying an 'Arab consensus,' which can become its own form of restraint".[18] Suddenly Arabs became more aware of their "Arabness" and Islam emerged as a unifying element among these diverse audiences living in considerably different national contexts.[19] Furthermore, not only has this new transnational media significantly allowed for the reintegration of migrant Arab communities into Arab life and society[20] but it has also opened up the Arab region to the entire world, making its language, politics and culture an integral part of a global media viewership and market that has produced a "virtual" disempowerment of Arab states whose national cultural politics had been thus far staunchly guarded with varying degrees of red lines and censorship.

At the same time, the proliferation of Arab satellite TV has also meant that Egypt, which had for decades secured the lead role specifically where cultural production is concerned, was no longer the only player in the field. Suddenly the cultural heart of the Arab world found itself competing with a host of other new trends in transnational media: from regional news, religious programming and political commentary to variety and talk shows, video clips and TV dramas. Indeed, in recent years Syria has emerged as a strong competitor in the field of TV serials courting the important Gulf market with "Bedouin" soap operas that "[are] accepted by the Gulfis as distant cousins from across the *badiya* [desert] in a way the 'Pharaonic' Egyptians [are] not".[21] Moreover, whereas Egyptian TV dramas are produced in the Egyptian vernacular (except for the historical Islamic serials), the Syrians have adopted a level of pan-Arab language that is more representative of a wider Arab collectivity.[22]

Not only was Egypt losing ground in its hegemony over mediatic representations in the region but it was equally being subjected to new regional values and representations that had never been on its nationalist modernist agenda. Given this new global transnational context, Egypt has had to negotiate new strategies to maintain its "cultural sovereignty" and its "cultural hegemony" simultaneously in order to have an edge in the transnational market and its new demands. As Abdallah Schleifer has explained in an early reading of pan-Arab broadcasting:

The Egyptian communication philosophy is also influenced, implicitly if not explicitly, by a conservative Islamic ethic. There is no soft porn or even partial nudity or obscene language on Egyptian TV, but it is an Islamic ethic that is broadly or liberally interpreted to allow belly dancing, Broadway-style chorus girl routines, miniskirts and bathing suits, movies with night-club scenes that involve alcoholic consumption, and films, both Western and Egyptian, in which only the final sequences of seduction scenes must be cut.

Basically, this philosophy, as articulated frequently by Egypt's [former] Minister of Information Safwat al-Sherif can be called the "cultural sovereignty theory". This means that instead of attempting to bar or heavily restrict and censor foreign TV programming, Egypt should concentrate upon upgrading and expanding its own television product, be it news or entertainment, so that it can ensure its cultural sovereignty in a globally competitive situation. This philosophy is particularly attractive to Egypt since it alone among the Arab states has the depth of talent for such an undertaking – actors, singers, dancers, musicians, comedians, journalists, producers, directors and even Quran reciters – and, courtesy of its earlier domination of the once-powerful Arab film industry, a colloquial version of Arabic that is fairly universally understood throughout the Arab world.[23]

As Arab satellite stations have widened the scope of their broadcasts to include a worldwide audience, Egyptian producers, and more specifically the producers of specialized TV programming for the month of Ramadan, have had to take note of such transformations in the profiling of their transnational audiences and market. Given the new global economy in which these producers are operating, they can no longer fashion TV serials exclusively with the Egyptian family in mind. Rather they have to make allowances for the wider Arab "satellite broadcast" family audience, whose values and beliefs with regard to important social issues like sex, marriage, love and family, of course, may be substantially different, if not conflicting with Egypt's 1960s modernist nationalist agenda. These new marketing imaginaries and strategies are perfectly understandable for, as George Gerbner, the American media theorist, has argued: "Competition for the largest possible audience at the least cost means striving for the broadest and most conventional appeals, blurring sharp conflicts ... and presenting divergent or deviant images as mostly to be shunned, feared, or suppressed."[24] Hence, Egyptian TV drama producers have had to adjust, to a certain extent, their considerations as to what might be this "satellite" family's values and expectations of such serials. They have also had to contend with the limitations that such expectations have brought to the marketing and the distribution of TV serials throughout the Arab region. In other words, the "globalization" of Ramadan serial television production has brought forth a new set of contentions and contradictions to their authors, who are subsumed in the drive to please all while trying to sail safely through the multiple boundaries of censorship in their native country as well as fellow Arab countries. Notably, in this new transnational game, the authority of the Egyptian state has been impacted in its attempts to produce an image consistent with its representation of the imagined nation, community and collectivity. The ultimate result has predominantly been the production of contradictory and competing discourses and images that aim at hitting two birds with one stone, so to speak – at attracting and/or alienating the right and the left, the Islamists and the seculars, the traditionalists and the modernists, so as to impose a sense of authority – set by the state – that is designed to maintain the "cultural sovereignty" and "cultural hegemony" strategies.

Conversely and quite ironically for that matter, in this transnational satellite era, the sway and control that Egypt had held over its own national audiences has also been considerably unsettled. Indeed, satellite TV broadcasting has provided the Egyptian producer of TV serial drama with a new realm of freedom and independence from dominant official representations (not necessarily positive or progressive) as well as a new market that does not share the same Egyptian nationalist taboos and red lines. As Ursula Lindsey has shown in her review of recent controversial Ramadan TV serials in the Arab world, pan-Arab censorship and "red lines" are not always in line with state television guidelines. This basically means that what may be considered a controversial production by one country may be permitted and well received by another. Indeed, Lindsey gives the example of the Egyptian Ramadan serial *Bint min Shubra*, which dealt with the sensitive and always problematic representation of Coptic–Muslim relations. The serial was banned by Egyptian censors and blocked from being aired by Egyptian state TV. However, it was broadcast on several private satellite stations whose audiences found nothing wrong with its content.[25]

Hagg Mitwalli and his family

It is against this pan-Arab satellite backdrop that Egyptian TV aired the serial entitled *A'ilat al-Hagg Mitwalli* (*Hagg Mitwalli's Family*) during Ramadan 2001: written by the veteran script-writer Mustafa Muharram and directed by Muhammad al-Nuqali, it flared an uproar never witnessed before. Hagg Mitwalli and his family invaded the lives of Egyptian families and their Arab "satellite" kin, overshadowing anything and everything else broadcast on the small screen during this prime-time bracket, including the bombing of Afghanistan and daily Israeli invasions into Palestinian cities. Not that debate surrounding TV programming is a novel affair. In fact, in past years, many serials have generated intense, national debates during and after their broadcast.[26] However, in the case of *Hagg Mitwalli* the nature, scope and levels of the debate opened up issues of modernity and its representation, and the Egyptian state's cultural politics in an era of a globalized media market.

The story-controversy of *Hagg Mitwalli* is, briefly, that of the economic and social rise of Mitwalli Saʿid, a self-made man, who began his life as an apprentice working for Muʿallim Salama, the wealthy textile merchant. Mitwalli (actor Nur al-Sharif) rose to achieve the height of wealth and power after the death of his master. In many ways, Hagg Mitwalli's saga is the counterpart to the all-

American Horatio Alger myth *à l'arabe*: his profile redefines the possibilities of ascent through honest hard work rather than through privilege, connections or class; he makes his fortune as a textile merchant gradually and legally by being a good and fair polygamous husband; he is sympathetic to the underprivileged, having been one himself; he is good-natured, generous, funny, clever, romantic, a lover of life, money and women and a lovable man. Most important of all, Hagg Mitwalli is a god-fearing man and a good Muslim who abides by Islamic teachings: he is shrewd but just, ambitious but not deviant, adventurous but faithful to the values of both his religion and his class. Indeed, the very name of the serial carries with it many of these positive significations: the title "hagg" attached to Mitwalli's name bestows upon him both religious and social respect which he, in turn, extends to his family members. Mitwalli's climb up the social ladder begins with his marriage to his late master's wealthy widow, Zibida (actress Fadya Abd al-Ghani) who dies soon enough leaving him a baby son, Sa'id. The situation therefore calls for remarriage: the young and virile Mitwalli finds Amina (actress Mona Zaki), a good-natured, kind-hearted, modest woman who shoulders the responsibility of mothering his baby son and eventually becomes the caring matriarch of Hagg Mitwalli's subsequent empire of women.

As the events of the serial unfold, a parallel relationship is constructed between material and sexual exploits: Mitwalli's continued accumulation of material wealth and possessions is matched by the increase in his sexual desire and need for more well-connected and/or wealthy women. Soon enough, Mitwalli meets another wealthy widow, Ni'ma (actress Ghada Abd al-Raziq), whose late husband like Mitwalli was a rich textile merchant. His marriage to her consolidates his expanding textile empire and his parallel dream of a domestic one which he pursues by taking a third wife, Madiha (actress Somaya al-Khashshab), an accountant whose professional knowhow he can rely on. Unlike Amina and Ni'ima, Madiha represents Mitwalli's rise not on the economic ladder but on the social one: she is a young, educated, middle-class university graduate who opts for marrying Mitwalli despite not only difference in age, class and education but also her knowledge of his two other marriages and Mitwalli's stipulation that she cohabit with his two wives in the same building that he owns. Madiha eventually becomes a good investment for Mitwalli, for he uses her university training to service his business by making her manage his accounts and taxes through a private office that he sets up for her. To keep the wealth in this ever-expanding empire, Mitwalli's son is married off to his second wife Ni'ma's daughter even though the young man is in love with another more compatible young woman. Finally, Mitwalli realizes his legitimate empire of four wives (accorded by Islam under very specific stipulations) by marrying another young, this time bourgeois woman, Ulfat (actress Munia), who is yet another step up the social ladder. With her bourgeois lifestyle and never-ending demands for gifts and money she is the black sheep for the other three wives who by now have become like sisters united in their love for Mitwalli and their content, submissive, wealthy, healthy and egalitarian domestic haven that he provides. The fourth wife, Ulfat, marries Mitwalli for his economic not his

180 *The bounds of change*

social stature, basically to secure a fortune and sustain her parasitical bankrupt and drinking bourgeois parents. She becomes the only wife who attempts to transform him into something more conversant with her own decadent values and mores. She changes his wardrobe, takes him dancing and drinking (which, like a good Muslim, he devoutly refuses), and calls him "Meeto" because it is more *chic* and hip when compared to Mitwalli, the marker of a popular, possibly lower-class origin. Towards the end, Mitwalli collapses with a heart attack, unable to gratify his four demanding wives who keep him to a rigorous schedule of sexual performance divided more or less equally around the week between them. But, thanks to the loving care of his first three wives who constitute a homogeneous entity of solidarity he recovers and ousts his fourth greedy, exploitative and parasitical bourgeois wife from his paradise on earth. The serial concludes with Mitwalli surrounded by the remaining women of his harem with their and his progeny.

Despite the comic, phantasmagoric, stereotypical and blatantly farcical if not surreal plot line and character rendition, Hagg Mitwalli's family still embedded a number of timely contentious social issues, such as the rise to prominence of a new class of parvenus and *nouveaux riches*, this time rendered positively through the representation of Mitwalli's career, the dilemma of a growing number of ageing middle-class unmarried women captured through the third wife, Madiha, and the more central issues of polygamy, gender relations, and family values and structure. Despite the deliberate absence of an analytic dimension to these social manifestations in this comedy/fantasy, the serial was undoubtedly held together by the stellar performance of its cast, with the great artist Nur al-Sharif – popular far and wide across the Arab world – at its helm. The calibre of the actors' delivery explains the unprecedented success of the serial even with audiences who were opposed to its overtly conservative discourse.

While a framework of light-hearted sarcasm overshadowed the complexity, reality and gravity of the issues touched upon by the serial, it none the less marked a contrast with the more familiar, long-established pattern in which television serials approached such issues, namely the absence of clear value judgements, resolutions or moral indictments of those problematic social manifestations represented in the serial. For instance, Mustafa Muharram, the author of the text, chose not to indict the framework in which Hagg Mitwalli and his totally subordinate family evolved. Moreover, the polygamous and authoritarian Hagg Mitwalli was presented in affectionate and endearing terms. Similarly, Hagg Mitwalli's empire of women and wealth was rendered positively, representing Mitwalli's wives as friends and sisters united in the preservation of their own harem. Furthermore, Hagg Mitwalli remains a triumphant patriarch till the end, surrounded throughout by his cast of submissive, obedient and grateful women, all happy to be commanded and dominated by him in one episode after another for the entire month of Ramadan. Except for one episode, to which I shall return shortly.

Hagg Mitwalli and his family swept audiences in Egypt and elsewhere off their feet. People had memorized Amina's (Hagg Mitwalli's second wife) catch lines that had become like leitmotifs in the nightly episodes of the serial: "Three for one is more than enough", "Four for one is sacrilege" (*talata ala wahid yadub*; *arbaʻa ala wahid haram*), the cast was hosted *ad nauseam* on endless national and satellite programmes, and Arab audiences all over the region partook in a transnational conversation about the polygamous Hagg Mitwalli and his wives and the extent to which the serial reflected and/or influenced several social realities (gender relations, polygamy, social mobility, wealth, power and class) not just in Egypt but in the Arab world at large. This lively and multi-layered debate of Arab transnational social and cultural significance, as I will attempt to show shortly, prompted the rather naive, quite ineffective and presumptuously condescending and authoritarian intervention of the National Council for Women that dictated a change in the ending of the notoriously popular episodes of Hagg Mitwalli and his family.

Contextualizing "Meeto"

In order to understand the various contradictory reactions to *Hagg Mitwalli* it is important to place the entire serial within its immediate context. At the global level, we must remember that this Ramadan favourite was being broadcast immediately after "9/11" during December/January 2001 when Islam and Islamic culture were both an easy target for misrepresentation if not demonization. The main protagonist in the attack against the World Trade Center was an Egyptian (Muhammad Ata), a fact that impacted negatively on the Egyptian state's self-propagated image of modernism and secularism, the hallmarks of integration into a global community and global market. In addition, the "war against terrorism" had started with the bombing of Afghanistan and the ongoing Osama ben Laden/Qaʻida saga whose discourses and images, broadcast globally, further fuelled the war against the Islamic "other" and helped propagate ideas about the "clash of civilizations".

Conversely, despite the general Arab understanding of the tragic events of "9/11" and the sympathetic official and unofficial discourses that followed the disaster, there was still a sense of euphoria in the dominated Islamic world that emanated from a collective feeling of subservience and submission to American imperialism and its politics and practices in the region specifically with regard to Iraq and Palestine. The bombing of Afghanistan and the imminent American invasion of Iraq along with daily Israeli incursions into Palestinian territories regularly sanctioned by the US all led to an increased phobia towards things American and an equally exaggerated pride in things Islamic: a politics of difference in which markers of Arab and Islamic cultural identity became overvalorized, an unsurprising reaction to the US-led "war against terrorism" and an understandable self-reassertion in the face of American hegemony.

Moreover, the Egyptian local context also provided an interesting episode to which the story of Hagg Mitwalli was being compared and against which it was being read. During the broadcast of the serial, parallels were being drawn between the story of the polygamous Hagg Mitwalli that unfolded on the small screen and that of Hagg Midhat al-Siwirki, whose story was unfolding concurrently during the autumn of 2001 in the pages of the press. Al-Siwirki is the owner of an "Islamic" popular bargain clothing store chain – Al-Tawhid wa l-Nur – a self-made man in his mid-fifties who was charged, tried and imprisoned for marrying more than four wives simultaneously when Islamic law allows him only four concurrently. Hagg al-Siwirki's accumulation of wives was driven by exploitation: he married and took advantage of impoverished young women, who eventually turned on him and reported him to the authorities. Al-Siwirki's story ended with a seven-year jail sentence for breaching the laws of polygamy and for marrying a minor. The Siwirki story was used by the Egyptian press and media to slash at "Islamists" and to show how quick "Islamic" wealth can be both lawless and abusive. Al-Siwirki was an example of "bad" Islam, certainly not one to be tolerated by the modern Egyptian state.

For those who had been following the Siwirki saga, Hagg Mitwalli's TV drama seemed identical. Both were self-made men, both were in the textile industry, both rose to unimaginable heights of wealth and power and both were polygamous! Nevertheless, a notable difference separated Hagg Mitwalli from Hagg al-Suwirki: while the latter's multiple marriages were driven by his sexual obsessions and fantasies, the smart-talking Hagg Mitwalli's accumulation of wives was driven by material and economic calculations. Miwalli married his four wives with designs to accrue more wealth and power and to improve his social standing and his connections within the public sphere. While the real Hagg al-Siwirki drama concluded with a jail sentence, the fictive *Hagg Mitwalli* serial ended with his personage – a progenitor and the absolute ruler – sitting cross-legged atop a small empire comprised of women and money where all are obedient and content and all live happily ever after.

Another important subtext to *Hagg Mitwalli* was the extent to which this polygamous man's life was modelled on that of the popular image of the Prophet Muhammad himself. Mitwalli, like the Prophet Muhammad, was a merchant whose fortunes were made through properly administering his first wife's fortunes in the market. And again, like Muhammad, Mitwalli was fair to his multiple wives, distributing his attention, love and sexual energy equally between them. So, in many ways, Mitwalli, was represented as a model to be desired and followed by devout, god-fearing, and, yes, polygamous but fair Muslim men. This was an example of "good" Islam unlike the case of Hagg al-Siwirki that was being played out in real life.

All these contextual elements combined brought forth many intriguing reactions to this TV blockbuster, ones that confounded the national and the transnational as well as the popular and the official readings of the serial. While at the broader popular level it seemed from audience reactions in the Arab world that the *Hagg Mitwalli* serial was received for what it was – i.e. as a polysemic, heteroglossic text of family entertainment that successfully mixed comedy and vaudeville traditions with recognizable elements from social reality, cultural identity and family life, albeit an exaggerated, almost farcical representation of that reality – other more monolithic, ideologically charged readings, specifically within Egypt, treated the "text" of *Hagg Mitwalli* as threatening, condemning "the reality" it represented as backward, misogynist and antagonistic to modernist discourses.

At the popular level, the image of Hagg Mitwalli, especially in the Gulf, seemed like a familiar one. For example, men interviewed in Saudi Arabia openly acknowledged their polygamous marriages, citing the licence given them by Islamic law so long as they can be fair to their multiple wives. Indeed, some said that wealthy men *should* marry more than one woman in order to help curb the problem of ageing unmarried young women. Some young women who were interviewed in Egypt and elsewhere also agreed that polygamy need not be an evil if the husband treated his wives equally, and expressed their willingness to become second wives if these exceptional material conditions were fulfilled.[27] As for the Iraqis who watched the serial and spent their Ramadan in anticipation of an American attack at any moment, Hagg Mitwalli was regarded as a genial entrepreneur and became a hit in the slumping textile market where Iraqi merchants honoured him by lending his name and the names of his wives to a variety of traditional cloth. For Hagg Mitwalli, merchants had chosen a particularly flashy pink cloth to celebrate his "youthfulness" and sold a metre for 3,500 Iraqi dinars, the equivalent of half a month's salary for a middle-class Iraqi employee.[28] At the other end of the Arab world, specifically in Tunisia, where polygamy has been banned by the state, male audiences dispossessed of their traditional Islamic rights found in Hagg Mitwalli the dream of a lost Eden, regarding him with the envious eyes of those deprived from God's paradise on earth.[29]

At the other end of the spectrum of reactions, particularly with regard to the various venues in the media, there was concern over the "message" that Hagg Mitwalli was propagating and that risked contaminating family life at large. From the first instance of the serials' broadcast, the principal preoccupation of Egyptian and Arab satellite TV stations, in addition to other debate forums such as Egyptian sporting clubs, syndicates and radio stations, was to host the serial's superstar Nur al-Sharif, and interrogate him unrelentingly on his views with regard to polygamy, with the intention of extracting from him a definitive, crystal-clear, absolute rejection of that social phenomenon, all the while getting him to reiterate his tremendous love for his real wife, Pussy (whom he has recently divorced after one of the longest and most successful relationships within the Egyptian star world).

Moreover, both the national and regional press carried numerous articles denouncing polygamy and accusing the serial of wanting to reinstate the "era of the harem". For example, the weekly *Ruz al-Yusuf* ran a whole debate forum and several articles focusing on polygamy and the representation of women on the small screen. The tone was predominantly incriminating, accusing the "highly seductive" Hagg Mitwalli and his family (which "captured the hearts and minds" of Egyptians for 33 episodes more successfully than the US army in Iraq) of providing human experiences that appear to be a model to be emulated.[30] Equally enraged was the prominent feminist Nawal Saadawi, who said she had watched a few episodes and was scandalized at the "glamorous image" that was accorded to the polygamous "Meeto", citing her own knowledge as a psychiatrist of many women in Egypt who "suffered psychological problems linked to the fear that their husbands might take a second wife".[31] Likewise, Nariman al-Daramali, a female MP, demanded that soap operas "be vetted by the National Council for Women before they were shown on television". She was joined by other female MPs who requested an explanation from [former] Minister of Information, Safwat al-Sharif.[32]

Furthermore, many views focused on the dangers of the serial in relationship with the economic situation in Egypt arguing that the serial "was an insult to young people suffering from an economic recession who could not afford to get married at all".[33] On another scale, many saw the image of "Meeto" as a model that emerged because of the absence of social justice, the breakdown of the middle class and the excessive accumulation of wealth in the hands of the few abetted by the government.[34] Yet others saw in Hagg Mitwalli's control over his wives, progeny and the textile market a representation of the new world order – the embodiment of the decadence of American hegemony that acts with power, control and injustice, all masked under a guise of spreading justice and prosperity.[35]

Obviously, the social text of Hagg Mitwalli and his family was both intricate and diverse, and so were the social readings and uses to which it was put. However, the range of social issues that the serial approached was, in reality, nothing new for its audience. The question of polygamy in particular has been exhausted by the media and has generated a tremendous amount of relentless debate, as has the question of the retreat of moral values in the face of materialism. Indeed, as a character, Hagg Mitwalli is not far from that of Ahmad Abd al-Gawwad, the ruthless patriarch in Naguib Mahfouz's *Thulathiyya* (*The Trilogy*), another household favourite which generations of Egyptians were raised on during the second half of the twentieth century. Likewise, the popular Egyptian comic film of the 1960s *Az-Zawga at-talattashar* (*Wife Number Thirteen*), starring Rushdi Abaza and Shadia and directed by Mahmud Abd al-Aziz, also portrayed a polygamous, dubious and whimsical husband who had married 12 wives and was now seducing a thirteenth. However, Mahfouz's *Thulathiyya* ends with the death of the domineering patriarch with his conservative traditional values, leaving the path open for his young modern and nationalist son. Similarly in the film *Az-Zawga at-talattashar* Rushdi Abaza (the polygamous husband) finally repents after being redressed by the thirteenth wife (Shadia) with whom he falls in love leaving his other twelve wives behind. The film ends with the victory of monogamy and the triumph of the ideal modern couple. But in contrast to these works of the modernist 1950s and 1960s the *Hagg Mitwalli* serial of the turn of the twenty-first century ended with the patriarch squatting cross-legged on his throne in his harem, dominating his son and thwarting all of the latter's attempts to escape or overturn the father's authority and conservative values.

"Meeto" between the national and the global

The victory of the traditional over the modern at the end of the serial after at least a century-long battle fought by Egypt's official "modernist" discourses and narratives against more traditional and conservative social values became simply unacceptable, causing an instructive tension between Egypt's national or global image and the regional media market. Concerned entities in the Egyptian state rushed to convene with the producers of *Hagg Mitwalli* with the aim of inducing changes in the script and introducing the moral directive so blatantly absent from the narrative, as well as infusing the text with the ever-familiar tone of the unilateral, unified "message". The National Council for Women issued a statement condemning the serial because it did harm to the image of Egyptian women and accused it of going against the cultural politics of the Ministry of Information that have been approved by the state:

> Supposedly everything that the television broadcasts reflects the essence of the [state's] policies.... All TV drama [this season] not just one serial represented an image of the Egyptian family completely at odds with these values.
> (...)
> The *Hagg Mitwalli* serial in particular has triggered a huge debate. I feel it needs close reading and analysis. Not only does it represent images of women but also the image of the Egyptian family, of the relationship between father and children, the value of education and the extent to which Egyptian families believe in it. What does it mean for a father [i.e. Hagg Mitwalli in the serial] to say: "I am better than a doctor or an engineer"?[36]

Not only were modernist values "endangered" by the serial but so was the very image of Islam at a time when Islam was already being targeted.[37] The National Council for Women therefore called for a general meeting with Egypt's cultural producers – intellectuals, journalists and media specialists – to "produce jointly a formula that reflects harmony among state institutions".[38] Hence, despite the multiple popular readings of the text of *Hagg Mitwalli*, the National Council for Women still sought to impose a monolithic, literalist one that was not only paternalistic and condescending towards a highly diverse viewership but that was equally oblivious of the regional media market in which it was intervening. Indeed, Dr Farkhunda Hasan, Secretary General of the National Council for Women, deemed that the most dangerous thing about the serial was its enormous success on all levels: outstanding acting, sense of humour, excellent directing and a beautiful script. Even though Hasan confessed that she had followed the entire serial during Ramadan, she still condemned the production: "It is as if we are presenting poison in honey", she said, expressing her wish that the ending of the serial be changed to make Hagg Mitwalli repent for his polygamous marriage.[39]

186 *The bounds of change*

Subsequent to the intervention of the National Council for Women the Egyptian press reported that influential figures in the TV industry have had to "succumb" to the enraged public opinion and tried to "rescue" the remainder of the episodes. The National Council for Women's didactic attitude was reiterated by the President of the Television Broadcasting Production Sector:

> When we saw the kind of confusion that the serial created in people's minds we sought to correct the situation.... We sat together [with Mustafa Muharram] and thought about the ending of the serial and we came up with the final "preaching scene" that brings Mitwalli and his son Sa'id together where the father advises his son not to repeat his own experience with four wives.[40]

The veteran script writer Mustafa Muharram was made to change the ending of the serial by adding a passage in the second-to-last episode, where Hagg Mitwalli presents a contrived confession explaining away his polygamy and claiming it was the result of deprivation from contact with women in his early years because he was so poor! The dialogue with his son Sa'id revealed the precariousness of the official discourse that forced its way into the text:

MITWALLI: By the way my son, one wife, good and loyal, who loves you, is more priceless than many wives.
SA'ID: Do you mean to say that you regret your many marriages?
MITWALLI: Of course Sa'id! I wish everyone could hear me and understand that one wife, good and loyal, is more priceless than many wives, and I don't want anyone to do what I have done. Actually, one is hardly able to cope with one ... imagine having to cope with four![41]

In order to ascertain that the "message" was clear, Mustafa Muharram said he made sure that Nur al-Sharif (Hagg Mitwalli) repeated the same sentence "one wife, good and loyal, is more priceless than many wives" more than once lest the viewers should assume that the serial was an open invitation to engage in polygamy![42]

In reality, this intervention on behalf of the National Council for Women, mandated to "enlighten" the nation, confirms the state's persistent infantilization of the audience; an audience that it perceives as being in continuous need for protection from the multitude of readings and potential interpretations of a given text. Indeed, the contrived changed ending of the serial exposed how lightly the viewership that watched a whole month of *Hagg Mitwalli* was taken.[43]

Ironically, despite the National Council for Women's heavy-handed didactic intervention, the last image of *Hagg Mitwalli* on the TV screen depicted a harmonious existence between the *hagg* and his three wives, after expelling the fourth, bourgeois opportunist wife from his paradise. The image of the Eden that Mitwalli built survived as the last frame of the serial on the screen even after his forcibly induced repentance. It is this image that sealed the representation of the

Egyptian family and the Arab "satellite" one, not the one mandated by the National Council for Women's Secretary General! A dubious ending indeed that not only left "Meeto" in mid-air between the national and the global but also revealed the crisis and transparency of Egyptian official modernist discourse within a global context and a global market.

10 The new kid on the block
Bahibb issima and the emergence of the Coptic community in the Egyptian public sphere

The release of the controversial Egyptian film *Bahibb issima* (*I Love Cinema*), directed by Usama Fawzi and written by Hani Fawzi (two young and already distinguished Coptic filmmakers), in summer 2004 triggered a heated debate of national proportion. Not only has the film propelled the Egyptian Coptic community into the very heart of the public sphere but it has also confirmed the Coptic community as a new player in the cultural politics in Egypt, a challenging new force for the Egyptian state to contend with in the latter's balancing act of secularism and religious nationalism.[1]

Bahibb issima is definitely the most radical example of the Coptic community's engagement in and with the public sphere. Not only is it a revelatory realistic representation of the Coptic community by members of the community itself but, perhaps more importantly, it is one that actively participates in the elaboration of a national, not Coptic, metaphor that unsettles oppressive patriarchal power, in all of its manifestations, and upholds freedom of expression at the religious, political and artistic levels. Because of its unprecedented audacity – social, religious and political – *Bahibb issima* was subject to official state censorship as well as "street censorship" by non-state actors and finally ended up in the Egyptian courts for "contempt of religion".[2]

The crisis surrounding *Bahibb issima* may be viewed as the culmination of a complex situation that had been developing over more than a decade during which the Egyptian state was compelled, by various internal and external factors, to step up its efforts to contain further exposure with regard to the Coptic question both locally and globally and to engage in manufacturing a new image of national unity.[3] The irony remains, however, that it is precisely the state's anxious intervention to control the *kind* of image produced of the Copts that enabled the Coptic community to become a real and active participant in the cultural public sphere.

(Mis)managing the Coptic question

Many elements have converged to reorient and redefine not only the relationship between the Egyptian state and the Coptic community since the 1990s but also the space that the Coptic community has traditionally occupied in the Egyptian public sphere. The nationalist banner "*yahya l-hilal ma'a l-salib*" (Long live the crescent alongside the cross) that continues to be produced at an official level with every national or religious crisis is one that conceals a history of discrimination and marginalization, if not alienation, of the Coptic community, not only in its relationship to the Muslim majority but, more crucially in its relationship to its own self-perception and representation within Egyptian society as a whole.[4] It is true that the Copts supported the nationalist uprising of 1919, and were among the founders of the Wafd Party (the nationalist party against the British occupation) from the 1920s to the 1950s, but it is equally true that they were viewed, because of their elite's western education and hence the positions they occupied, as pro-British, pro-western and therefore suspect, if not separatist.[5] It is also true that the Arab–Israeli conflict has been crucial in cementing the national imaginings of the Coptic and Muslim communities, but it is equally true that the Copts are generally viewed (from the point of view of the Muslim majority, and from within the Coptic community itself) as second-class citizens.[6]

This ambiguity and duality explains not only the place that the Egyptian state accorded the Copts, the largest religious minority in the country, during the twentieth century but also the place that the Copts have accorded themselves. On the one hand, the Egyptian state has continued to seek an official national representation of the Coptic community by appointing one or two Copts to ministerial and parliamentary positions, and by seeking the official representation of the Coptic Orthodox Church as part of a national or nationalist and secular public discourse. On the other hand, the state has actively sought to underrepresent (if not misrepresent) the Coptic community in the public sphere whether that be in public service, educational curricula or the cultural field in general, leading to grave misconceptions within the majority Muslim community in its relationship with the Coptic one.[7] This misrepresentation of the Coptic community has understandably translated into two important reactions: a predominantly disgruntled Coptic diaspora that exposes, at the international level, the discriminatory practices of the Egyptian state with its transparent secular discourse, and a predominantly, equally disgruntled, visibly less docile, and dominated Coptic minority within Egypt.

The Sadat era witnessed the rise of Islamic extremism (as well as Coptic fundamentalism, as a consequence) that eventually led to unprecedented, bloody clashes during the 1980s and 1990s between Muslims and Copts, with the latter paying the highest toll in lives and persecution.[8] The state's repeated and scandalous mishandling of these crises has totally exposed the dangers of the Egyptian state's practices toward the Coptic community. Furthermore, the regime's inadequate responses to sectarian violence called into question the long-standing and now flimsy official banner of national unity "*yahya l-hilal ma'a l-salib*", and opened up to public scrutiny the Egyptian state's practices toward its largest religious minority as it attempted to cultivate a dual image of secularism (for global consumption) and religious nationalism (for the local one). All this coincided with the birth of the human rights movement in Egypt that started in 1982 and took 15 years to be recognized by the Egyptian state. It also coincided with the

190 *The bounds of change*

Egyptian state's increasingly compromising economic and political dependence on the blessings of the United States, whose religious right in Congress, key supporter of the Bush administration, has increased attention to Christians abroad.

With the convergence of these diverse, but interrelated, elements, the Coptic question became a thorny issue for the Egyptian regime both internally and externally, and a cause for the state to rally most of the Coptic and Muslim secular and religious elites behind an official national or nationalist discourse. In its attempt to safeguard its secular image, the state resorted to two simultaneous strategies: one of denial, the other of reconciliation. An example of the denial mode was the 1994 international conference on Minorities in the Middle East that was supposed to be hosted by Saad Eddin Ibrahim's Cairo-based Ibn Khaldun Center for Development Studies, which was forced to hold its meetings in Cyprus after being denied permission by the Egyptian authorities to host the event in Cairo. This decision was based on the state's refusal, along with most of the dominated Muslim and Coptic cultural and religious nationalist elites, to publicly acknowledge the minority status of the Copts, insisting that they were part of a homogeneous Egyptian nation.[9] Likewise, when the members of the US Congressional Commission on International Religious Freedom arrived in Cairo in March 2001 to investigate religious discrimination against the Copts, in the aftermath of the notorious Kosheh incidents,[10] they were received by President Hosni Mubarak, the head of the Coptic Church and the Sheikh of Al-Azhar in an official show of unshaken national unity.[11] The US congressional committee was otherwise boycotted by both Coptic and Muslim intellectuals, including Egyptian human rights activists committed to the Coptic question, all of whom felt that the commission represented direct US intervention in national affairs.[12] This official or nationalist denial phase was accompanied by the Egyptian state's rather transparent effort to doctor its global image and to appease the outraged Coptic community at home and abroad. The state moved to implementing various symbolic, conciliatory measures toward the Copts: in 2000 an effort was made to remedy the representation of Coptic history in educational curricula, in 2002 the Copts were granted, for the first time in history, a national holiday for Coptic Christmas, and the Egyptian state-run TV broadcast Coptic Christmas celebrations live.

National unity, official style

Besides these symbolic measures, the Egyptian state sought to remedy the historic and glaring underrepresentation or misrepresentation of the Coptic community in the Egyptian media. Indeed, the history of the film industry in Egypt is telling of both the position of the Copts as a minority within the larger context of Egyptian society and the various stereotypes that are attached to this community as well. It is true that some of these cinematic representations reflected the cosmopolitan social fabric during the first half of the twentieth century with a spectrum that included many minorities in Egypt; however, they were also examples of where such minorities were positioned vis-à-vis the dominant Muslim majority.[13] In early representations of the Copts, and others that were to follow throughout the second half of the twentieth century in theatre, cinema and TV, the dominant mode was stereotypical, comic, predominantly lacking at the realistic level. Indeed, the very first Egyptian film, *Barsum Affandi yabhath an wadhifa* (*Barsoum Effendi Looks for a Job*), produced in 1923 and directed by Muhammad Bayumi, was a comedy that featured a Copt in the lead role and was intended as a series that was never completed. It is also worth noting that, whether such representations were made by Muslims or by Copts, they almost always resorted to the same familiar roles which included the exploitative calculating clerk, or the liberal or loose Coptic woman, or in sharp contrast, simply the good, devout cross-bearing Copt. For example, in Hilmi Rafla's 1949 *Fatima wa Marika wa Rachel* (*Fatma, Marika and Rachèle*) a Muslim young man tries to seduce three young women – a Muslim, a Copt and a Jew respectively – by pretending that he belongs to the same faith as each woman and reproduces (in the case of his relationship with the Coptic and Jewish girls) various stereotypical markers of that faith to win over the girl's family. He ends up marrying the Muslim girl Fatima because she is morally superior to the Copt and the Jew. Another example is the representation of the Coptic head of the estate (*al-nazir*) and his daughter in Henri Barakat's 1965 adaptation of *Al-Haram* (*The Sin*), based on Yusuf Idris's 1959 novel, where he is depicted as greedy and his family as "other" in its mores and lifestyle from the Muslim peasants and workers on the estate. The persistence of stereotyping the Copts as greedy and exploitative of under-privileged Muslims can be seen also in Marwan Hamid's internationally acclaimed film *Imarat Ya'qubyan* (*Yacoubian Building*, 2006) based on Alaa al-Aswany's bestselling novel with the same title.[14] Other superficial and stereotypical representations of the Coptic creed and religious practices abound in some of the more recent TV serials where Copts are clearly marked as "other" by wearing crosses, by using certain religious idioms or with pictures of the Virgin Mary and Christ clearly adorning their living rooms. Despite these clichéd representations however, the message in many of these media representations is often one of national unity. Such noted representations have included *Hasan wa Murqus wa Kuhin* (*Hasan and Murqus and Cohen*) by Fu'ad al-Gazayirli in 1954, based on a Naguib al-Rihani play with the same title: a stereotypical representation of the kind but impulsive Muslim, the cunning and elusive Copt and the sly and Machiavellian Jew who, despite their differences, are business partners, united in their interests, and represent national unity against all odds. A later example of more romanticized and idyllic national unity can be seen in the television series *Khalti Safiya wa l-dayr* (*Aunt Safiya and the Monastery*), a 1996 adaptation of Bahaa Taher's 1990 novel with the same title that depicts positive and respectful relationships between Muslim villagers in a small village in Upper Egypt and Coptic monks in a nearby monastery.[15] A more light-hearted version of this same romanticized national unity is depicted in Nadir Galal's 1994 film *Al-Irhabi* (*The Terrorist*), where Muslim and Copt watch and support the same national soccer team together. Interestingly such representations of national unity have often notably coincided with religious communal unrest.[16] These dominant formulaic modes of minority representation in the media abound and have been thoroughly internalized by Muslims and Copts alike, leading to the absence of realistic dramatic representations of the Coptic community on the screen whether in cinema, or, eventually, in the popular Egyptian TV serials. Furthermore, as noted earlier, the fact that, on the one hand, the Copts have historically refused to claim the status of minority, cementing themselves in a national identity discourse, while on the other seeking to forge a separate space for themselves that is exclusive of the dominant Muslim other, has had lasting effects on their willingness to openly represent their own community. As Viola Shafik has noted, some of Egypt's most distinguished filmmakers are Christian (for example, Henri Barakat, Youssef Chahine, Yousry Nasrallah, Khairy Beshara and Dawud Abd El-Sayyed); however, allusions to Christianity are almost absent in their works. She argues that such absence may be attributed to several reasons: their own level of integration in the dominant Islamic culture and their contempt for all forms of religious fundamentalism both Muslim and Christian, as well as their fear of being labelled confessionalist or separatist.[17] Whatever the reasons, the ultimate result is the lack of public representation of the Coptic community from within the community itself.

With the escalation of repeated confrontations between the Coptic and Muslim communities in the 1980s and 1990s, specifically in the aftermath of the Kosheh violence, and all the local and global repercussions of these bloody events, the Egyptian state made a decision to take Coptic representation, on the screen, into its own hands. In the grand tradition of didacticism that dominates the state-run TV serial productions, the controversial Ramadan serial *Awan al-ward* (*Time of Roses*), written by Wahid Hamid, one of Egypt's most acclaimed script-writers and directed by the Coptic filmmaker Samir Sayf was broadcast in December 2000 on the eve of the release of the Kosheh victims from prison.[18] *Awan al-ward* was intended as a lesson in "moderate" religious values for both Muslims and Copts, rendered through dialogues about premarital sex, together with low-cut and sexy actress outfits that scandalized the Muslims during the holy month of Ramadan. As for the theme of national unity, it was symbolically represented through the unacceptable marriage (from a religious, Coptic point of view) between a Coptic woman and a Muslim man. This rendition of "national unity" where Copts and Muslims literally became "bedfellows" outraged many in the Coptic community and caused at least four Copts to file lawsuits against the Minister of Information to stop broadcasting the series. As Lila Abu-Lughod has argued, the case of *Awan al-ward* demonstrates that "Television's enthusiasm for circumscribing religious sensibilities" "ends up revealing and exacerbating social cleavages, thus seemingly undermining the government's and some secular intellectuals' intentions of creating national community".[19] Indeed, never before had any other Ramadan TV series generated such controversy and debate or garnered such national and international attention. Ultimately, the legal pressures, from the Coptic community in particular, led to a change in the script during the final episodes of *Awan al-ward* where the Coptic woman was made to recognize, at the end, that her marriage to a Muslim was a mistake.[20] So much for national unity official style.

Rather than serve, as a didactic lesson on peaceful and harmonious coexistence between Copts and Muslims, *Awan al-ward* became a lesson for the Egyptian state itself in its new representational strategies of national unity, one that will inform and shape its involvement in other episodes. Likewise, the legal pressures exercised by the Coptic community in this instance heralded the Coptic community's new-found active involvement with regard to its representation within the Egyptian public sphere.

As can be seen from the case of *Awan al-ward* and other TV serials that dealt with Muslim or Copt relation and representations, the state's determination to control the *kind* of image that is produced of the Copts in order to avoid "sectarian strife" and promote "national unity" did not achieve its desired effects.[21] Indeed, the state's active and frantic involvement in representing the Copts, and its attempts at reviving the lost paradise of national unity and the golden age of Egyptian liberalism, have all been at the expense of more recent realistic endeavours to deal with these taboo topic. One such example is that of *Film hindi (Indian Film)*, which was written by Hani Fawzi in 1994, directed by Munir Radi and belatedly produced in 2003 by the state-owned Media Production City (MPC), the biggest information and media complex ever built in Egypt. The final production, however, bore little resemblance to Hani Fawzi's original script.

The title of Hani Fawzi's film, *Film hindi (Indian Film)*, is actually a take-off on Bollywood films of the 1960s that were so popular among the middle- and lower-class movie audiences in Egypt. The expression "Film hindi" has passed into colloquial Egyptian Arabic to refer to the melodramatic, the tear-jerker and the excessive. Hence the very title tells us from the start that the film is intended to be a parody, a satire. However, this initial intention in the script is lost in the final heavily censored production. *Film hindi* is a simple story about two friends from Shubra (one of the more popular areas in greater Cairo that has a sizeable middle-class Coptic community and a concentration of churches, the same neighbourhood where Hani Fawzi, himself a Protestant, grew up). In the film, Sayyid, an outgoing Muslim barber who dreams of becoming a *rai* singer, and Atif, a nerdy, sexually frustrated Coptic satellite dish installer, are friends. Sayyid is engaged to Aida while Atif is in love with Mary and they are both looking for apartments to get married. They end up falling in love with the same dream flat. Because they are friends, each is willing, in an act of mutual sacrifice, to give it up for the other. However, their respective sweethearts' fight over the flat not only causes its loss but also brings their respective relationships to a close. However, despite their unrealized dreams at both the professional and emotional levels, at the end of the film Sayyid's and Atif's friendship is preserved against all odds thereby confirming the contrived allusions in the film to national unity, the legacy of the 1919 revolution. Even though the script was written in 1994, *Film hindi* was released only in 2003 and, despite the long and problematic wait, received lukewarm reviews. A particularly scathing one appeared in *Al-Ahram Weekly* where the film was deemed naive, simplistic and nostalgic of the officially trumpeted "national unity" between Muslims and Copts. Both the script-writer and the director, Munir Radi, were blamed for a crude and hysterical reproduction of traditional religious, gender and national stereotypes in a film that was produced by the state-owned Media Production City (MPC).[22] Many of the weaknesses of the film listed in the review were true. However, the question remained: how did a film that was initially described by the Censor as a "time bomb", and whose production was delayed precisely because of that, become so compliant and so complicit?

The answer is simply that the screenplay and the film as a whole were not what the filmmakers set out to make! *Film hindi* was released nine years after it was originally written. During that time it was transformed, through the labyrinths of state intervention, from a realistic representation of Egyptian religious diversity, with all this might entail of both conflict and harmony, to an ideological statement on national unity where Muslims and Copts happily share the same paradise. Entire scenes and dialogues were cut because, from the point of view of the authorities, they may have caused "national strife".[23] The authorities' apprehensive position and the length of time required to refashion the film led to a change of director, a change of actors and a change of producer, which squarely landed the film in the lap of the Egyptian state through the MPC production.[24]

National unity: unofficial style

Despite the massacre of *Film hindi*, or perhaps because of it, Hani Fawzi, proceeded to write and complete his film script for *Bahibb issima* (*I Love Cinema*) in 1996, i.e. two years after he had finished writing *Film hindi* and was still negotiating the final details of its production. Unlike *Film hindi*, the script for *Bahibb issima* was initially approved; however, it eventually encountered several sites of discontent and resistance before its final controversial release in June 2004 and its subsequent trial for "contempt of religion".

Once more the title of the film is significant. Rather than call it "bahibb *issinima*" which would be the standard way of referring to cinema in spoken Egyptian dialect, Hani Fawzi chooses the more popular, lower-class deformation of the English word, "*issima*", thereby expanding and extending the love of cinema to a much wider range of social classes and grounding his film in the heart of the Egyptian middle class. Based largely on autobiographical elements, *Bahibb issima* focuses, in an unprecedented way, on the daily life of a Coptic middle-class family in Shubra from the point of view of Na'im, the youngest child in the family, who, like one of his young uncles, loves cinema but is deprived of it because of his father's fundamentalist religious views. The story is framed by the voice of adult Na'im who recalls memories of his childhood.[25] At another level, this audacious film may be read as Hani Fawzi's riposte to the massacre of his first script of *Film hindi*, for, like young Na'im in *Bahibb issima*, the adult scriptwriter, Hani Fawzi loves cinema but is deprived of it by the "fundamentalist" views of the Egyptian censor who made sure that the film would not cause "national strife". Both the child, Na'im, and his author, Fawzi, rebel against the oppressive forces that deprive them of cinema. In *Bahibb issima* the mischievous little boy, Na'im, literally pisses in more than one scene on all voices of censorship and authority. In writing the script for this film, Hani Fawzi does the same, and echoes his young hero's proclamation in the film: "All my life I have hated doctors. Not just doctors, but all those who want to control us and to control our lives with the pretext that they know what is best for us."[26] Hani Fawzi's rebellious and uncompromising vision is brilliantly translated on the screen by the young and already prominent director Usama Fawzi, whose earlier controversial, avant-garde films *Afarit al-asfalt* (*Asphalt Devils*, 1996) and *Gannat al-shayatin* (*Devil's Paradise*, 1999) won national and international acclaim and awards at several festivals at home and abroad.

Bahibb issima opens with a highly dramatic scene in which Adli (Mahmud Himida), the fundamentalist Coptic father who incriminates all forms of art, threatens little Na'im (six years old, Yusuf Usman) with hell for his love of cinema. This initial patriarchal image that condemns the freedom of the artistic imaginary is juxtaposed against Na'im's imaginings of cinema, in an equally dramatic and phantasmagoric scene, when the child imagines cinema as the gateway to heaven where he enters and is greeted by many loving angels. Similarly, the father's cowardly relationship to God, which is based exclusively on fear, is juxtaposed against his child's subversion of that constraining relationship, symbolically rendered through Na'im's deliberate public pissing in different authoritarian contexts: at home, in his doctor's clinic and in the church. Not only does Adli oppress his little son but he does the same to his wife Ni'mat (Layla Ilwi) whose self-realization is crushed on multiple levels. She is crushed as a wife, as a painter and as headmistress of a primary school: her paintings of nude women are hung backwards on the wall and painted over with natural scenes because, according to her husband's beliefs, they are *haram*, i.e. against religion. She is crushed again as a wife whose physical and emotional desires are thwarted by a fundamentalist orthodox husband who imposes a relationship of chastity within the marriage, leading Ni'mat to "fall" for an extramarital relationship.

As the film progresses, we begin to make links between Adli's oppression of his family in the private realm and his own oppression in the public one. Set in 1966, during Nasser's increasingly paranoid repressive era, and on the eve of the Arab defeat of 1967, *Bahibb issima* translates private oppression into a national one. Adli is denounced to the state authorities as "a communist" by his superior for daring to expose the corruption that he witnesses in the school where he is a social worker. Adli's torture at the hands of the state becomes *the* moment of revelation and reversal in his life. It all culminates in one of the film's most powerful, moving and loaded scenes: Adli's monologue with God where he tells Him, in his drunken stupor: "I do not love you. I want to love you, not fear you." Adli's discovery of his heart condition finally brings about a total transformation

Plate 10.1 Naʿim at barred window, *Bahibb issima*, courtesy of Arab Production and Distribution Company.

Plate 10.2 Adli praying, *Bahibb issima*, courtesy of Arab Production and Distribution Company.

Plate 10.3 Angels greet Naʿim at cinema, *Bahibb issima*, courtesy of Arab Production and Distribution Company.

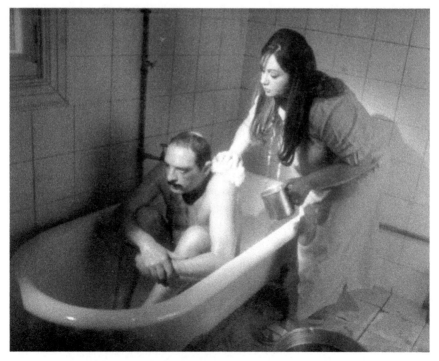

Plate 10.4 Adli bruised after State Security handling, *Bahibb issima*, courtesy of Arab Production and Distribution Company.

Plate 10.5 Family fight in church during wedding, *Bahibb issima*, courtesy of Arab Production and Distribution Company.

Plate 10.6 Naʿim and Adli play at the beach, *Bahibb issima*, courtesy of Arab Production and Distribution Company.

Plate 10.7 Adli having a stroke while cycling with Naʿim, *Bahibb issima*, courtesy of Arab Production and Distribution Company.

in his relationship with his family: he buys a TV set and takes Naʿim to the cinema; he makes love to his wife and dismisses her attempt to confess her betrayal. Adli finally dies, in another highly charged scene: he is hit by a stroke as he is peddling his son Naʿim on a bicycle at the seashore with the sun setting on the horizon on the very day that President Nasser delivered his abdication speech (simultaneously played on the soundtrack) after the Egyptian defeat against Israel in June 1967.

The makers of *Bahibb issima* have described their film as one that is against all forms of oppression where "cinema" in the title is synonymous to "freedom". Such a declaration represented, from the outset, an open invitation to read the life of the Coptic family on the screen as a metaphor for all Egyptians, both Copts and Muslims, not only during the 1960s (when the film is set) but also in present-day Egypt. Moreover, the tyranny that Adli exercises over his young son, Naʿim, who loves cinema but is denied it because it is *haram*, i.e. prohibited by religion, is the same tyranny that the Nasser regime exercised over him; the censorship the young child faces at home is simply a reflection of wider forms of institutional oppression: religious, political, social and cultural.

200 *The bounds of change*

Containing representation

A higher committee for censorship had approved the script for *Bahibb issima* and the censor (as is routinely practised) had signed and approved every scene that was shot before the negatives were sent for development abroad. However, given the unprecedented realistic representation in *Bahibb issima* of the Coptic community, one that sought to liberate the Copts from stereotypical roles and render them human, national subjects, with emotions, faults, contradictions, as well as physical, social, political and metaphysical aspirations, the film was submitted, yet again, to another censorship committee before its commercial release. As has been the case in many other potentially explosive episodes in the cultural field, state-employed cultural actors within the field are always reluctant to bear the brunt of the responsibility. Setting up committees in moments of crises has routinely become a strategic way to diffuse such responsibility and to remap the limits of representation within the context of the official discourse on "freedom of thought and expression".[27]

The representation of the Coptic community on the censorship committee that viewed the film was deliberately constrained: there was one Copt out of twelve members. However, this one Coptic member objected to several scenes in the film. Tellingly, her objections alone were enough to launch the chain of subsequent censorship committees that were to view *Bahibb issima*. These subsequent committees had a double unstated mission: either to isolate the objecting Coptic member of the second committee or to confirm her objections via new members who are invited to serve on these never-ending committees. The very constitution of these committees is also noteworthy for they represent the hierarchy among various actors within the cultural sphere ranging from civil servants in the office of the Egyptian Censor to prominent intellectuals from both the Muslim and Coptic communities, and finally the upper echelon of representatives from the ministry of culture, not to mention the possible inclusion of religious authorities, Muslim or Copt, depending on the case. Ultimately, the objective is to arrive at a consensus that would help minimize the risks taken by the state even if at the detriment of the cultural product it claims to "protect".

Given that the Coptic objections to *Bahibb issima* represented a minority view within the second censorship committee, a third committee was formed with predominantly Coptic intellectuals,[28] who, despite their general enthusiasm about the film, noted that it would cause controversy and recommended that another committee be formed! At the top of this pyramid of censorship committees came one that was headed by the Secretary General of the Higher Council for Culture, Dr Gabir Asfur, who is also the General Director of the Office of the Censor, a Professor of Arabic Literature at Cairo University and a distinguished literary critic: a series of official or public functions that may at first seem contradictory but which are also meant to bestow cultural legitimacy on some of the key actors in the state's cultural apparatus. In this final stage, and because of the pressures that were being exerted by the Church through the media, an invitation was extended to a number of Coptic priests to serve on this high-ranking censorship committee. The inclusion of religious Coptic authorities seems to have been prompted by the initial Coptic censor's negative report that had allegedly been leaked to the Coptic Church, thus putting the Censor's office on the spot.[29]

It is important to note that the pressures exerted by the Coptic religious authorities and the acquiescence of the state cultural apparatus to their demands were not surprising. On the one hand, the Coptic authorities were actually reproducing a pattern that had repeated itself over the years with regard to the intervention of Muslim religious authorities and groups in cultural affairs.[30] The most recent examples of such interventions and potential threats during the same year had been the banning of Nawal al-Saadawi's *The Fall of the Imam* and the state's decision to grant Al-Azhar's Islamic Research Academy (IRA) search and seizure powers over illegitimate and unlicensed copies of the Qur'an and *hadith* (the Prophet Muhammad's collected sayings) which intellectuals and human rights' activists feared might tempt Al-Azhar to extend its newly acquired powers to creative and artistic works.[31] On the other hand, the state's acquiescing position vis-à-vis interventions from religious authorities in general, and its systematic strategy to seek their deliberation over cultural production, ultimately reconfirmed the state's moral authority over its citizens and neutralized the religious groups' claim to that same authority. This strategy on the part of the state has not necessarily always worked, for sometimes consulting religious authorities has backfired and rather than containing the situation has rendered it more volatile.[32]

Not surprisingly, the makers of *Bahibb issima* (the producer, the director and the scriptwriter) refused the arbitration of the Coptic religious authorities, correctly arguing that the film had already been approved by the censor as attested by the fact that the negatives were signed and approved and being developed abroad. They were supported in their endeavour to block the intervention of the Church by a massive sympathetic press campaign that warned against setting a precedent in the handling of this case and reminded readers of earlier examples of Muslim religious authorities and groups' interventions in the cultural field. In a strategic move to contain the onslaught on the film, and contest the legitimacy of both the state cultural apparatus (represented by the various censorship committees) and the Coptic religious authorities, the producer of *Bahibb issima* (Arab Production and Distribution Company) organized a preemptive private screening of the film for journalists, intellectuals, filmmakers and critics, during which a questionnaire was circulated about the audience's reaction to the film and whether or not certain scenes should be censored. This strategy proved highly successful because it displaced the debate from the closed arena of the authorities, both political and religious, and opened it up to a cultural or national debate. By so doing, the makers of *Bahibb issima* effectively hijacked both the state's and the Coptic priests' "moral authority" over the film and placed it with the public that on such occasions is never heard but is always spoken for. The comments from the viewers, who represented a mix of specialized and non-specialized individuals, were overwhelmingly supportive of the film: "a daring and unique film. I recommend that it be shown in full" (Mustafa Darwish, film critic and former censor); "Magnificent" (Ali Idris, film director); "Unprecedented in the history of Egyptian cinema" (Samir Farid, film critic) as well as many other profusely enthusiastic comments by professionals and young students, both Copts and Muslims.[33]

Not only did the public debate over *Bahibb issima* redefine the parameters of the debate by including "the public" but it effectively embarrassed many high-ranking state-employed cultural players who found themselves caught between their cultural and political roles. For example, the Chief Censor, Madkur Thabit, himself a filmmaker and academic, who, in his official capacity as censor, had set up all these censoring committees, confessed, after one private showing of *Bahibb issima*, that he had been moved to tears. Indeed, Thabit's public reaction on that occasion is a testimony on the compromised position of many noted Egyptian intellectuals within the state apparatus:

> I was so moved by the film, that I wept, because I found myself split in two. The first half is the professor in the Academy of Arts, the filmmaker and artist within me, all of which drive me to support the freedom of artistic endeavours. In addition, I consider Usama Fawzi a son and a student for he is one of the most talented film directors. My other half is the censor, facing pressures and demands to cut.[34]

Moreover, the effectiveness of the public debate spearheaded by the makers of *Bahibb issima* was further confirmed when the fourth censorship committee, headed by the Secretary General of the Higher Council for Culture, met on 7 June, without extending an invitation to the Coptic religious authorities as had been repeatedly announced and denounced in the press.

At the same time, the debate surrounding *Bahibb issima* gave the state cultural apparatus occasion to enforce its moral authority over all citizens (both Muslim and Copt) and to contain the Coptic religious authority's power within the cultural sphere. For deliberations on the film were made by the final censorship committee *without* the presence of the Coptic priests. The committee's verdict, two days before the release of the film, was the following: remove the word "religion" from Layla Ilwi's pronouncement in the film "Damn this world and religion" (*mal'un abu l-dunya ala l-din*), cut the kissing scene in the church tower and shorten the rowdy family fight inside the church. In addition, the committee recommended that *Bahibb issima* should be shown to adult audiences only. This last decision prompted Yusuf Usman, the ten-year-old child who played the part of Na'im in the film, with mesmerizing brilliance, to ask the logical question that seems to have perhaps escaped this final round of censoring committees: "How can a film in which the lead part is played by a child be released for adult audiences only?"[35] Ironically, little Yusuf, who is a Muslim was removed, by his mother, from his primary "Islamic" school where the headmaster persecuted him precisely because he was acting in a film! Cinema, as the Muslim headmaster told the mother, in an ironic parody of the father in *Bahibb issima*, is *haram*.[36]

The new kid on the block 203

Bahibb issima was released on schedule, on 9 June, in some forty cinemas, where it was shown for a short two-week period, to gradually decreasing audiences. Several factors combined to further contain the film's commercial success. In order to limit the confrontation with both the angry faction of the Coptic community and the state, the producer of *Bahibb issima* – Arab Production Company – labelled it a "festival" film, not a commercial one, thereby condemning it to a highly disadvantageous release-time bracket. This strategy impacted on the visibility of the film in the cultural sphere and buried the prospects of the commercial success that both the director and script-writer expected. In addition, the month of June is final exam period for most students so the "adult audiences" to which *Bahibb issima* was restricted were grounded with their children at home. Furthermore, after the negative publicity and literalist reading that the film received in some of the press, *Bahibb issima* was definitely not deemed a specimen of "clean cinema" (*sinima nadhifa*) with which it was competing for the beginning of the summer season when younger audiences are on vacation and can go more often to the cinemas.[37]

Religious authorities, state secularism and the public sphere

More importantly, perhaps, than all of these containment strategies exercised by various state actors and market factors, *Bahibb issima* was subject to an unprecedented public boycott orchestrated by members of the Coptic religious authority and the objecting faction within the Coptic community, a campaign that spilled over into the Muslim conservative one. To begin with, in this particular instance, the Coptic religious authorities felt betrayed and marginalized. Historically, they had been systematically called upon by the state as part of a national or secular discourse. In return, the Coptic religious authorities had, on several other occasions, successfully embarrassed the state, without head-on confrontation, into various symbolic concessions. However, this time the Coptic priests were disinvited from the last censorship committee that viewed *Bahibb issima*, thereby depriving them of partaking of the "moral" authority usurped by the state. Their riposte was therefore in the making, modelled to a great extent on the relationship between the state and the Muslim religious authorities.

First, the Coptic priests went to press as representatives of the Coptic Church and the mobilized and outraged majority of the Coptic community. Like their Muslim counterparts, who have a longer history in cultural intervention, the Coptic priests used a literal and fragmentary reading of *Bahibb issima* to incriminate it.[38] Their arguments against the film included the following: the film misrepresents the reality of the Coptic community and its values in so far as the main character Adli (a devout member of the Coptic Orthodox Church) is married to Niʿmat (a Protestant), a highly unrepresentative example of marriage in the Coptic community; the film represents the Copts as fanatic; the film misrepresents the principle of chastity within a Coptic marriage; the film advocates sinful relationships; the film misrepresents basic Christian teachings about sin and repentance; the film offers a highly negative and vulgar image of the Coptic extended family; the film misrepresents the Coptic religious authorities and the Church itself through scenes that violate the sanctity of the holy place; the film misrepresents Christ and ultimately, God himself and our relationship with Him.[39] A hefty list of accusations never before levelled by the veteran Muslim authorities against any work they attempted to sack! To top it all, the film is made by a "self-hating" Copt who converted to Islam to marry a Muslim woman. Not only does the director, Usama Fawzi, the "convert" who continues to identify himself as part of the Coptic community, misrepresent the Coptic faith and traditions but he does so at the expense of causing internal division within the larger Christian community in Egypt by using a Protestant church (not a Coptic one) as a site for shooting some of the most objectionable scenes in the film (the kissing scene in the church tower and the family fight during a church wedding).

Ironically, the Coptic attackers of the film then used the "national unity" banner to mobilize their "Muslim brothers" through a set of magical rhetorical questions that struck a very sensitive chord: "Is this how our Muslim brothers perceive us?" "Would our Muslim brothers accept the same misrepresentation of the Muslim faith and community?" And finally, the not so subtle harping on the abhorred topic of "sectarian strife": "What is the reason behind the production of this film?"[40]

The next strategic move involved the mobilization of the Coptic masses against the film. This was initially conducted in church and through the internet. Copts were called upon to boycott the film and cripple it financially. This was a successful boycott campaign that left the cinemas showing the film practically empty.[41] At a later stage, the boycott campaign spilled into the street: there were demonstrations by Copts and some Muslims in solidarity against the film even though the demonstrators, as is always the case, had not seen it, neither had the priests who campaigned against it!

The Coptic religious authorities further escalated the confrontation with both the state and the filmmakers by using another unprecedented manoeuvre: a statement was issued through the Holy Council of the Coptic Orthodox Church by the little known (at least outside the Coptic community) Committee on Church Artistic Works with the provocative title: "An Egyptian View of *Bahibb issima*". The statement basically incriminated, first and foremost, the Censor, i.e. the state, for having approved a film that misrepresents the Coptic community and faith, thereby holding it responsible for sowing the seeds of "sectarian strife".[42] This particular move held mimetic resonance for it was reminiscent of other occasional statements issued by the Muslim religious authorities during previous confrontations with the state in the cultural sphere. Furthermore, this new strategy on the part of the attackers of *Bahibb issima* shifted the battle from being one against the makers of the film alone to becoming one against the state and its apparatus that allowed the film in the first place.

In another duplication of Muslim religious authorities' contestation of the cultural sphere, forty Coptic priests together with Christian and Muslim lawyers (who were equally outraged at the scenes in the church) wrote a statement to the

General Public Prosecutor on 5 July 2004 protesting against the release of *Bahibb issima* and demanding that legal action be taken against both the director and the producer.[43] The alliance between Coptic and Muslim religious and legal authorities with regard to things cultural is not unprecedented. For example, the same combined pressure was exercised in 1994 when Muslim religious authorities (the Islamic Research Academy of Al-Azhar), opposed to the human representation of prophets in artistic works, called upon the Copts to support a case against the Christian film director Youssef Chahine for his representation of the prophet Joseph in his film *Al-Muhajir* (*The Immigrant*, 1994). In the Chahine instance, the State bowed to the pressure and, as usual, to outdo Al-Azhar, which has consistently sought to extend its purview over cultural matters, ruled, at the level of the Court of First Instance, that the film never be exported or shown to the public again.[44]

Ultimately, the Coptic attackers took *Bahibb issima* to court with the grave charge of "contempt of religion". The significance of the court case is that it extends the accusation beyond the film's producer, actors, director and scriptwriter, to include no less than the Minister of Culture (for having allowed the film through the Censor that falls under his purview), the Censor himself, and the Minister of Interior (for not having stopped the film as the plaintiffs had demanded in their statement to the Public Prosecutor). This escalation represented an open confrontation with some of the Egyptian state's most powerful men. Given the state's unquestionable experience in dominating both the cultural and the religious fields it also meant that the attackers were now in no position to win. Eventually, the case against the film was dropped once the final censoring committee of the Ministry of Culture ruled that it be shown to adult audiences only.

A close look at the scenario of the long-winded censorship procedures undertaken in the case of *Bahibb issima* is proof enough of the Egyptian state's ability to manipulate and control both the secular and the religious wings of the public sphere. First, the Censor did not make an immediate, unilateral decision to release the film. Rather, a series of advisory committees was set up with the membership of prominent Coptic public figures whose testimonies have been used, throughout the crisis, to counter and deflate the outraged faction of the Coptic community. Second, the state has excelled in the role of guardian of public morality in numerous other crises with regard to the Muslim community. It has also succeeded in containing and neutralizing the repeated attempts by Al-Azhar to exercise that role. In the case of *Bahibb issima*, the state was simply repeating the same strategies with regard to the recent emerging voice of the Coptic religious community: the Censor did not release *Bahibb issima* without stipulating cuts and stigmatizing the film as an "adult audiences only" production. The state was also able to use dissenting voices within the Christian religious community at large to counter the disgruntled Coptic priests.[45] Despite the damage that the Censor has caused the film, the state still won the battle at the end of the day and was congratulated on its defence of artistic freedom! The censorship committee that actually censored the film was depicted as a "secular" committee that "will not succumb to any blackmail" and the Secretary General of the Higher Council for Culture who headed that censorship committee was described as "the man who allowed explosive films".[46] Ultimately, the state itself, with its cultural apparatus, was trumpeted as an enlightened one that had challenged and defeated the forces of obscurantism.[47]

We love cinema

Despite the ferocious confrontation between the attackers of *Bahibb issima* and the state that ultimately led to the substantial containment of the film on the political, religious, artistic and economic levels, one must still acknowledge the active role that has been played by the filmmakers themselves in defining the parameters of the debate surrounding their film. It was evident from the outset that, given their respective histories and cinematographic experiences, both Hani Fawzi, the script-writer, and Usama Fawzi, the director, thoroughly understood the local and global context in which they were making the film. It is true that the film represents a Coptic family, and it is equally true that it is pseudo-autobiographical; however, it is also true that *Bahibb issima* aspires to a national not a sectarian or historically bound representation. By setting the film in the 1960s and focusing it on an oppressive Coptic father, the film was able to neutralize the state by not representing it in the present, thereby winning its silence, if not its support. In addition, the film's attack on Coptic fundamentalism and its ridicule of religious authorities (in one scene a Protestant pastor is beaten during a rowdy family fight in a church wedding celebration) was complementary to a larger catalogue of attacks on Muslim fundamentalism in the public sphere (TV serials, films and plays) that have consistently received the blessing of the state. Furthermore, the filmmakers knew that they could count on the support of the secular cultural players, both Muslim and Copt, who, over the past decade, have conducted endless battles against both the religious and political authorities to safeguard the receding space accorded them within the public sphere.[48]

Finally, these young filmmakers could count on the new global rules governing the visual sphere, ones that are above and beyond the immediate control of the Egyptian state. The negatives for *Bahibb issima*, like many other films in the industry today, were developed abroad. Copies of the negatives were outside Egypt as the crisis surrounding the film developed. Creating a scandal for the Egyptian state was definitely a card to be played in the case of severe censorship, especially since the director, Usama Fawzi, repeatedly announced that he would not accept the massacre of his film. In this particular instance, the state had limited leverage, especially since *Bahibb issima* was made by two Copts, about the Coptic community whose situation in Egypt was already under global scrutiny. Last but not least, *Bahibb issima* was after all a post "9/11" film that came to light at the same time as the ongoing US plan for the "Larger Middle East", "democratization", "reform" and "good governance" in the Arab world. Given the Egyptian state's keen interest in promoting itself as one that is conducting its own democratic reforms, it would have been unbecoming to allow for heavy-handed censorship of the film.

But the real victory in the crisis surrounding *Bahibb issima* does not lie with any of these actors whether it be the state, the religious authorities or even the filmmakers themselves. Rather it lies with the film's audiences, Coptic and Muslim alike, for whom this magnificently conceived film has placed the question of representation squarely on the table. Within certain segments of the Coptic community that saw the film, there was an undeniable malaise at confronting the comic, at times farcical, representation of the community, so much so that some Coptic viewers confessed that they felt more comfortable with the stereotypical representation of the Copt in the history of the industry. However, this malaise has been attributed to the almost total absence of realistic Coptic representations in the visual sphere for close to a century during which, images of the Muslim majority, in all of its manifestations, have dominated. Interestingly, the same malaise characterized the reaction of some Muslim viewers who had grown accustomed to the image of the Copt as a villain or a saint, but not as an ordinary, realistic, lower-middle-class person who is actually just like them! At the same time, *Bahibb issima* provided a kind of looking glass for the Muslim community who, in watching the representation of its "fundamentalist other" could not but draw parallels with regard to its own situation. Conversely, other factions within the Coptic community welcomed the realistic and non-stereotypical representation of the Copt in the public sphere and considered that the film heralds a new era for the representation of the Coptic community. This new realistic image of the Copt has actually created a national conversation between Copts and Muslims, with the latter suddenly realizing how little they know about the Coptic faith, traditions and values. Suddenly a whole community was brought out into the public sphere in a manner unprecedented in Egyptian society. Another important triumph for *Bahibb issima* is that, in many instances, it was indeed understood as a film not about them (the Copts) but about all Egyptians, both Muslim and Copt, who identified totally with the freedom loving, mischievous child Na'im in his small, daily battles against the father simply because he loves cinema. Finally, and within the context of Egyptian cinema that for almost a century has participated in elaborating Egyptian national imaginings, *Bahibb issima* will be remembered as the first Egyptian film to forge these national narratives and imaginings through the life of a Coptic family that assumes the breadth and depth of a national metaphor in the public sphere.

11 *Found in Cairo*
The limits of representation in the visual field

This chapter will read the work of Huda Lutfi, one of Egypt's leading avant-garde artists, focusing specifically on her widely reviewed and controversial exhibit *Found in Cairo* (Townhouse Gallery, Cairo, May 2003) as a way to enter the field of contemporary visual practices in Egypt and to explore the cultural politics that govern this increasingly vibrant and transnational sphere. Lutfi, who is at once a cultural historian and a self-taught artist, formally entered the field of visual arts in Egypt during the early 1990s just as major changes were occurring within it, the most important of which is the visible expansion of an international, private curator market in Egypt that is perceived as a threat to the national state-run visual field.

At the heart of the contest within the visual field lie questions of representation, authenticity, identity, modernity. Who will represent Egypt? And how will Egypt be represented? The historical development of modern art in Egypt is entangled in the history of colonialism and the subsequent visual construction of the modern nation. It is therefore no surprise that the state has taken it upon itself to become the patron of modern visual production on both the academic and curatorial levels. Such patronage has meant the institutionalization, surveillance and control of the visual field in order to instil and produce a national image of "modern Egypt": at once modern but authentic, secular but traditional.[1]

The advent on the scene during the 1990s of international gallerists and curators as new players in the production and consumption of an "Egyptian" image has allowed a younger generation of artists to seek more independence vis-à-vis the state-run institutions and has offered them the "illusion" of autonomy within a field that continues to be defined not only by the state but by dominant conservative aesthetic values that can ultimately reinforce old boundaries on these new artists.

It is within this general context that I wish to read Huda Lutfi's work in the visual field. Lutfi's position is doubly complicated by the fact that she is perceived, owing to her academic career, as an "intruder" on the field. Ironically, it is precisely her academic training and professional career that have afforded her an experimental and contestatory leverage not necessarily available to other, more institutionally bound actors. Lutfi's *Found in Cairo* and the crises that surrounded it are a testament to the complex and unpredictable dynamics that govern the visual field in Egypt. For the question that arises is: who has the power to interpret the visual and its symbolic meaning? What role do societal values play in determining the boundaries and limits of the artist's work? And what are the visible and invisible strategies practised by the state in order to enforce these boundaries? As Peter van der Veer rightly argued, the state is not always visible; it also has its secret and hidden practices: "The modern state does not only show, it also hides. Spectators see only part of reality and may say later that they did not know what happened, although it happened under their very eyes."[2] Finally, as I will argue, the entire *Found in Cairo* crisis becomes not only a test of the artist's autonomy in face of street, state, and self-censorship but an instructive moment of the politics of artistic representation and reception in Egypt today.

The state and the cultural field

The modern culture industry in Egypt has historically been produced and administered by the state. The making of a modern nation state in the aftermath of the initial western colonial encounter – the French expedition to Egypt – involved the creation of a national imaginary, the construction of a national identity and the protection of national sovereignty, all of which were primary concerns for the nineteenth-century reformists. To this end, the Egyptian state, since the rule of Muhammad Ali (1805–49), has instated various institutions responsible for the production and dissemination of modern cultural products in the cultural sphere. Initially this enterprise manifested itself in the establishment of a printing press, Arabic newspapers and literary translations but also the establishment of a school of translation and a modern infrastructure for secular education. Gradually the modern institutionalized culture industry expanded to other fields of cultural production including the establishment of the School of Fine Arts in 1908. Despite the fact that these modern institutions and cultural products were initially set up according to the western colonial model, they were permeated from the start with a serious effort to forge a national Egyptian image and culture. This effort can be clearly seen in the pioneering translation or Egyptianization projects in the fields of literature, drama, music, painting and architecture meant to render the cultural field at once a modern and an authentic Egyptian one.

The change of political regime in Egypt in 1952 was a continuation, and systemization of the role of the state in the production and dissemination of the expanding Egyptian culture industry. The new socialist regime created a Ministry of Culture, a Ministry of Information, and a Ministry of Tourism, all concerned with defining, producing and regulating national culture at home and abroad. The culture industry was reoriented from a pro-western, elitist, exclusive field to a more indigenous, populist, developmentalist one. The Nasserite regime's strategic alliance with the Soviet Union allowed for the dissemination of new models of cultural production, the impact and stamp of which can be readily seen in the various realms of the cultural sphere of the 1960s.

210 *The bounds of change*

With the advent of the 1970s the historic role of the Egyptian state in administering and controlling the culture industry began to recede with the late President Sadat's (1971–80) economic open-door policies (*infitah*), his decision to sever ties with the Soviets, court the United States, sign a peace treaty with Israel, promote "village ethics", accord more space to Islamist movements, close down the Ministry of Culture in 1980, "cleanse" the university from oppositional voices and finally, in a desperate move to contain the increasingly volatile situation he created, crack down on all voices of dissent. These major shifts in political, economic, social and cultural policies, over less than a decade, produced a series of new realities on the ground: an accelerated immersion in a global capitalist market, the deregulation of a socialist economy, the collapse of the state cultural apparatus, the increasing visibility and influence of Islamic fundamentalism, the exodus of many members of the cultural field (professors, journalists, critics, writers, artists, painters) and the advent of foreign investors in several domains.

The Mubarak regime of the 1980s is heir to this contradictory set of realities that actually culminated in the assassination of President Sadat. In its attempt to restore its control over the cultural sphere, as a way of countering the rising Islamist wave and recapturing a modern secular image, the Egyptian state reinstated the Ministry of Culture that had, during the Nasser period proved to be one of the strongholds of its control over a national, modern and authentic Egyptian cultural sphere. This renewed attempt at the control of the national cultural sphere also seemed like a needed compensation for the loss of control over the political and economic fields that were now increasingly dominated by international global forces. Hence, even though the Egyptian state adopted new economic and political policies, it resorted, in the cultural field, to familiar, old ones. Rather than rethink the Nasserite defunct cultural machinery, the Mubarak regime revived the very same institutions that had practically collapsed under Sadat. This perhaps indicates not only the political field's designs for the cultural one but also the importance and centrality of state control over the local cultural field in global contexts.

However, during the 1980s and 1990s in particular, it became increasingly clear that the cultural field was not insular to the general global flux of capital, privatization, "democratization", and civil society movements. Hence we witness the emergence of a small but influential private publishing business, a private film industry, culturally oriented NGOs, a private curator market and private galleries, all of which are areas that were predominantly controlled by the state and of which it had now, partially, conceded patronage but not ultimate control.

At the same time, the Egyptian state was engaged in re-establishing itself as the moral and religious authority in face of the increasingly influential Islamist groups, discourses and practices, at home and abroad, as well as the surging power of "street censorship" and its moral or religious authority that became the hallmark of the Islamization from below of Egyptian society.[3] As Richard Jacquemond has pointed out, "street censorship" is actually a term used by the cultural milieu itself to designate "third parties who seek for themselves the authority of censors, at the margin of, or outside, a legal system to which they oppose superior, moral, or religious norms".[4] These self-proclaimed censors have included journalists, independent religious figures, academics, MPs, librarians, employees in publishing houses and print-shops, as well as student parents.[5] Hence, in order to preserve its moral or national sovereignty in face of this volatile wave of "street censorship", the state needed to maintain "moral" surveillance over the cultural field despite its discourse about "freedom of thought and expression" intended mainly for global consumption. This new situation can be readily proved by examining the many erratic and mostly unpredictable censorship cases that have occurred during the last decade with regard to books, publications, newspapers, plays, films, all deemed threatening to the nation, the nation's youth, national ethics and national unity.[6]

The visual field in context

Any discussion of the relationship between the state and the visual field in Egypt during the 1990s necessarily needs to be placed in the larger context summarized above. The general strategies that the state has adopted within the cultural field at large certainly apply to the visual one as well. Researchers working on the art world in Egypt have argued that the appointment in 1987 of the artist Faruq Husni as Minister of Culture has given the visual field a second lease on life in the aftermath of the Sadat era that witnessed the exodus of many artists, the closure of state-run cultural journals and the rising Islamist wave that also infiltrated existing art institutions, all of which had left the field practically lifeless. For example, Jessica Winegar has argued that Husni, himself an abstract painter, rejuvenated the visual field by pumping substantial funds to support biennials, competitions, awards, stipends and new exhibition halls. He groomed a young generation of artists and succeeded in reviving a local public and private art market and was determined to make Egyptian art internationally known.[7]

While all of these assertions are true, it is also important to remember that the artist Faruq Husni is a minister, an employee of the Egyptian state. As I have pointed out in the Prologue to this book, Faruq Husni thoroughly understands his double task: his carefully chosen title – the artist or minister – is proof of his double role as both artist and "commissar" and embodies the relationship between the cultural and political fields.[8] Many of Husni's comments during various censorship crises in the cultural field point to the ministerial rather than the artistic role he plays. For example, in May 2000, when the Haydar Haydar affair exploded in Cairo because of a newspaper article in the Islamist paper *Al-Shaʻb*, where Faruq Husni, in his capacity as Minister of Culture, was personally implicated, the minister withdrew the Egyptian edition of the Syrian "blasphemous" novel *Walima li-aʻshab al-bahr*, appointed a committee to investigate the charges against it (even though they were based on a literalist and out-of-context reading), and finally called for the intervention of none other than Sheikh

Al-Azhar himself who, in turn, confirmed the minister's implication. Again in January 2001, when the minister faced a crisis in Parliament mounted by a Muslim Brother MP over three novels that the parliamentarian argued were "explicitly indecent material amounting to pornography", Husni asked his legal adviser to conduct an "interrogation" of those responsible and ultimately dismissed them, arguing that his responsibility was to "defend society from cheap writing" and to "protect [its] values from pornographic works".[9]

Hence, while it is true that the margin of "freedom" seems to have expanded, it is equally true that the surveillance of such freedom, the regulation of how and where it is exercised, is an integral part of the minister's business, not the artist's. Indeed, the minister is aided in his role as "commissar" by the state apparatus as well as by different levels of "street censors" ranging from malicious individual interventions and conservative public servant objections to opposition newspaper articles and scandalizing parliamentary confrontations, which together help him, especially in times of crises, to realign and ensure the "moral" and national sovereignty of the state that he represents and serves.

Behind the façade of state prizes, awards, stipends and costly public events in the fields of literature, theatre, music, dance, film and visual arts lurks the ghost of censorship, at all levels including self-censorship, that ensures the political field's domination and control over the cultural one. It is therefore not surprising to have witnessed the young Egyptian avant-garde literati feverishly applaud novelist Sonallah Ibrahim's public refusal of the Ministry of Culture's £E100,000 Arabic Novel Award in October 2003 because, as Ibrahim said in his concluding statement, "it is awarded by a government that ... lacks the credibility of bestowing it". When during his refusal speech Ibrahim turned his criticism to cultural policies declaring: "We have no theatre, no cinema, no research, no education. We only have festivals and conferences and a boxful of lies", the auditorium went wild with applause.[10] This overwhelmingly approving reaction to Ibrahim's outspoken critique from a packed auditorium in the elegant Small Hall of the Opera House, with the artist/minister presiding, and a festive dinner for all, is proof of the transparency of the minister's *double casquette* and the cultural players' understanding of the self-serving nature of state-cultural politics.

Furthermore, within the visual field itself artists have been critical of the constraints placed on their own medium specifically at the institutional level (for example the continuing ban of nude models in the School of Fine Arts and the exclusion of nude paintings by some of Egypt's leading artists from the Museum of Modern Art).[11] Many complained of the lack of systematic support for the art movement and the extent to which it remained dependent on occasional resounding festivities.[12] They have also deplored the complete absence of a movement of art history and criticism that would accompany the production of art in Egypt "to identify its strong and weak elements or to record its development and the questions it raises in any serious way".[13] Recent scandals surrounding the sales of forged paintings by renowned Egyptian painters at astronomical prices to Egyptian and Arab tycoons in the business world have exposed the extent of deregulations and negligence of which the field suffers, raising doubts as to the authenticity of works on display in Egyptian museums.[14] In the aftermath of these scandals, Muhammad Abla, one of the prominent independent contemporary painters, commented sarcastically:

> I cannot deny my happiness, as an artist, that this [scandal] should make the news. For the whole idea of fake and forged works means that there is a budding market and that the Egyptian artist has a price and is worth talking about even if only in courtroom hallways.[15]

It only makes sense then that many younger, avant-garde cultural players – writers, filmmakers, playwrights and performing artists – have chosen to distance themselves from state-run cultural institutions, preferring the risk and the cost of aligning themselves to the private sector. For example, increasing numbers of young avant-garde writers publish at their own expense with private publishers. Despite this economic burden, they are able to ensure a better level of production, expand their margin of freedom, obtain more effective distribution and find their way, much more easily, to an international market through translation. The more experimental visual artists have gone down the same lane, for more or less the same reasons, with the added advantage that they, unlike the literati, can seek and obtain substantial international funding. In both instances, however, and in other fields of the performing arts as well, the politics of the international market are marked by unequal exchange, the dictates of a capitalist market, and the hegemony of the "Other's" desires of the representation of Egypt and what might be "Egyptian". Whether it be translation, production or curatorial politics, there is no doubt that the global market, given the dependent position of the cultural field in Egypt, has an important role in fashioning and determining what is "authentic", modern and avant-garde Egyptian cultural production.

Despite these unequal terms of exchange, however, there is no denying that the emergence of an alternative cultural scape, whether or not showcased on the global market, has allowed cultural players more freedom, more visibility, more mobility and more experimentation with their context and media as *Egyptian* artists. In many instances this new reality has not received the state's blessings since it challenges and unsettles the latter's historic role as producer and patron of the cultural industry. So, occasionally, the Ministry of Culture has sought to marginalize or intimidate those cultural players who question its historic role. For example, the "deviant" Sonallah Ibrahim, one of the Arab world's foremost writers, who publicly refused the Ministry of Culture's Arab Novel Award, was not included on the list of writers who represented Egypt at the Frankfurt Book Fair that hosted the Arab countries in 2004. It is interesting to note that some younger writers, who were included, chose to refuse the invitation and issued statements against the political and institutional representation of the Egyptian delegation to Frankfurt.[16] Parallel situations have occurred in the visual field where alternative public exhibit events, like the Nitaq I (2000) and Nitaq II (2002), organized by a group of private curators and galleries, in conjunction with several foreign cultural centres and the participation of established and young artists, have angered the ministry and collided with state-run Biennials. Other examples include threats by the ministry to ostracize artists exhibiting at the American University in Cairo in the aftermath of the US invasion of Iraq, and ministerial objections to an alternative delegation of Egyptian artists who shared the representation of Egypt with its own at the 1999 Venice Biennial.

With regard to the visual field in particular, there is no doubt that the increasing number of private galleries and curators in Cairo over the past decade, offering both symbolic and economic recognition, has allowed young avant-garde artists and some established independent ones an alternative space for cultural production. This private cultural scape may have been initiated in the 1990s by some of Cairo's downtown foreign gallerists and curators at the Mashrabiyya, Espace Karim Francis and Townhouse galleries. However, this alternative cultural scape has now taken on a life of its own, with new Egyptian players on the scene like Al-Warsha Theatre Company, Saqiyat al-Sawi Cultural Center, Studio Imad al-Din for the Performing Arts, Al-Mawrid al-Arabi for young Arab artists, the Contemporary Image Collective group, among others. One must note the collaborative work that exists within this expanding space between many of these entities both foreign and Egyptian that has definitely enhanced and enriched the culture industry in Egypt. However, it is also a space that has perhaps given all those involved in it a certain illusion of autonomy vis-à-vis the state, and the local and global contexts in which they operate.

The historian, the artist and the city

Huda Lutfi, a medieval Islamic cultural historian at the American University in Cairo since 1983, entered the visual field in Egypt at the beginning of the 1990s, just as all these changes were beginning to occur within it. Even though Lutfi was never formally trained as a painter, her interest in art manifested itself early on through her meditative practice of Arabic calligraphy, her readings in art history, her fascination with local and international art movements that she followed through exhibitions and museums, and her attraction to the beauty and charm of old objects. Lutfi's artistic beginnings were, from the start, closely linked to her academic career as a historian, and much, if not all, of her work can be considered a translation of her interests and research in the professional world into images and symbols in the artistic one. Her academic work on Sufism, *mulids* (celebrations of the birthdays of venerated religious figures), medieval Coptic and Islamic festivals, dreams, women and gender permeates her paintings and is transformed, on the canvas, into magical signs and imagery, scripts and geometric figures, icons and numerals, snakes and scorpions, Coptic dolls and androgynous figures, dancing bodies in still harmony and inward-looking portraits, all of which attest to the process of historical layering that she has thoroughly assimilated: ancient Egyptian, Far Eastern, Islamic, Coptic, Mediterranean, and Western art and history. In addition, Lutfi's interest in architecture and design found expression in the two homes that she built in the 1980s in Tunis, an oasis village in Fayyoum. In her own words, the construction of these mud-brick houses and their murals was inspired by "Nubian, rural Egyptian, African and Arabic floral, geometric, calligraphic and architectural decorative motifs". She used "natural dyes, mud, broken pieces of glazed pottery and stained glass".[17]

Furthermore, as Lutfi has indicated, her graduate student years in the West have had a lasting impact on her cultural identity:

> I found out that even though I was missing Egypt, I was enjoying the taste of another culture, and appreciated many aspects of it. I was gradually coming to terms with my anti-colonial and nationalistic feelings. I am less conflicted about my cultural identity. Being culturally attached prevents one from appreciating or experiencing the beauty and richness of other cultures. And it was through art that I got to understand this.... Yes the West has colonized the East, but its part of our experience, like any negative or positive experience, one must not get stuck on it.[18]

This cultural hybridity has allowed Lutfi to travel within the many artistic and cultural traditions that she explored. She traces her genealogy to modern Egyptian and western artists alike: Iffat Nagui's and Abd al-Hadi al-Gazzar's magical imagery and bruteness; Mahmud Sa'id's and Kamal Khalifa's women at once masculine and sensuous, figurative and abstract, quiet but flowing with energy; Anna Boughigian's strong ability to capture everyday movement, Picasso's confidence and humour, Basquiat's and Allouise's playfulness and spontaneity.[19] Lutfi's experience with Cairo's street children and Sudanese refugee children in Cairo has impacted the level of playfulness and simplicity in her own work:

> I was learning from them a tremendous lot, even though initially they did not know how to use paint. What I appreciate most is their spontaneity in the use of lines and colors.... The children use very bright colors whereas I often use more sober colors.... Watching how some of them strike lines without much concern with symmetry is quite edifying for me, because it exposes the inhibitions that we do not question in painting.[20]

Moreover, Lutfi's immersion in the historical has fashioned the archival dimension of her artistic production. All of her exhibits have invoked this relationship: *Women and Memory* (1996), *Magic and the Image* (1996), *Conjuring the Past* (1997), *The Old in the New* (2001), *Imagining the Book* (2002), *Dawn Portraits* (2002), *Calligraphic Abstractions* (2003) and *Found in Cairo* (2003) to mention some of the most prominent. In all of these exhibits the archival dimension is very strong and is rendered through collages, old and modern images and figures from Egyptian and other histories, juxtaposed against each other. Such layering and manipulation of icons are steeped in the artist's fascination with change over time and her cultural play with objects to reinvent their very reason for existence: "I was playing the game of bricolage", she says, referring to the experimental aspect of her work that involves "cut[ting] and past[ing] seemingly unrelated images, piec[ing] them together, and observ[ing] the metamorphosis that happens".[21] Furthermore, several common patterns re-emerge in many of these exhibits: an inward, psychological experience, a spiritual and Sufi depth, a fascination with the power of repetition, a very strong relationship to script and writing, and the eternal search for continuity between the present and the past.

Script and calligraphy in particular have a very special place and signification in Lutfi's work. Over the years she has moved from deciphering medieval documents as a historian to abstracting the calligraphic icon as an artist. This process has simultaneously involved discipline and play, constraint and freedom, technique and meditation, imitative repetition and creative subversion, in order to render the magical and mystical, the material and the spiritual. Lutfi's use of script is not simply decorative; rather it is consistently contextual and is an integral part of reading her artistic world. Mystical texts, Sufi poetry, or her own stylized etchings and experimental abstracted icons, are part and parcel of our encounter with her paintings that become elevated to a level of private language, at once revealing and concealing:

> I was joining words, did away with dots.... This was very convenient because sometimes I feel that I don't want everyone to see through me. You couldn't really read it and it doesn't follow any rule.... I don't follow the correct proportions or measurements between letters, I don't do that at all. I break it into pieces: so a word can be broken and continued on the next line, I forget diacritical marks, etc.[22]

On one occasion, when responding to a question with regard to the use of script in her art, Lutfi described herself as being "bookish", and talked at length about her relationship to books, medieval documents and writing, in general.[23] However, she is also thoroughly a city girl: her choice to live in bustling downtown Cairo is perhaps one dimension of her keen attachment to the city, its everyday movement, its shops, its artisans, its objects, its junk and its treasures. She walks to AUC's downtown campus and knows every carpenter workshop, antique shop and junk stand along the way. She is part of Cairo's downtown art and intellectual scene, moving, with great ease, in what novelist Sonallah Ibrahim once described as the "triangle of horror", i.e. downtown Cairo's gossipy intellectual den that stretches between the Cairo Atelier, the Greek Club, the Riche Café and Zahrat al-Bustan coffee shop, but also includes, in close proximity, the Townhouse, Espace Karim Francis and Mashrabiyya galleries. When she teaches her class on Sufism at the university, she escorts her students to historic parts of Cairo to attend *mulids*, *hadras* (Sufi rituals), Sufi gatherings and religious festivals, acquainting them with the living aspects of Egyptian and Islamic cultural history. This fascination with the city, with its present and past treasures, with its bustle and its quiet, has led Lutfi to some of Cairo's main "repositories": from Suq al-Imam in Cairo's City of the Dead, where the poor and marginal stall holders, who sell discarded objects, " have a place in the traffic, and commerce of life",[24] to the downtown Azbakiyya bookstalls, which represent Cairo's cosmopolitan and global culture, where Lutfi spent two years collecting objects that would become part of her recent exhibit *Found in Cairo* (Townhouse Gallery, 2003).

The artistic life of things

Through *Found in Cairo*, Lutfi reinvents the city. By using bricolage as her point of departure she endows old objects with new signification:

> All the while I was thinking how do I want Cairo to look like? Choosing the found object as my documentary material, the image that I constructed was a mixture of fantasy and documentation. My imagined city was going to be cosmopolitan, multi-cultural, for the objects I found came from different and distant places of the world.[25]

The exhibit occupied two of the three floors in the recently renovated downtown apartment building that houses the Townhouse Gallery: a floor for the transient, worldly life and a floor for the steadfast, mystical one, with a stairway between them that allowed visitors at the exhibit to move freely from one level to the other, thereby enacting, by their very presence, the unspoken philosophy behind Lutfi's work. During the exhibit, the artist conducted several walking tours with commentary, where she escorted her audience from each displayed artistic piece to the other, first on the lower floor, reconstructing the histories of her images, installations and objects from the city, and the relationship between this bustle of transformed pieces and the quiet, stillness and resoluteness of the larger installations on the upper floor.[26]

Between them, the two floors of the exhibit translated most of Lutfi's artistic preoccupations and spiritual aspirations. The lower floor comprised several photo collages and icons of the women she loves such as Umm Kulthum, Marilyn Monroe, the *Mona Lisa*, Naʿima Akif, Freda Kahlo, the artist's mother, all juxtaposed against each other in different postures and contexts: dancing, elevated on a pedestal, denuded, veiled or shrouded in mummy-like gauze. Their togetherness transgresses time, boundaries, culture and history and bespeaks the artist's freedom in appropriating icons and images, her humorous playfulness with cultural identity, and her acute sense of the body in its journey of decay and eternal life. The many other pieces on the lower floor were composite in origin and busy with signification: headless dolls, standing inside an old paper box protesting against the war with raised broken arms, a bodiless head stuck on an old piece of wood transformed into a calendar, chair legs transformed into a circle of sombre human faces, an armless metal toy soldier seated on the front of a restored toy carriage. The lower floor was that of contradictions but also of conversations, of the unexpected and the shocking but also of the humorous and the endearing; a festive entry into Lutfi's personal world recreated from the city's archival memory – Suq al-Imam, Azbakiyya bookstalls and downtown artisan and antique shops.

218 *The bounds of change*

The journey to the upper floor transported the visitors to a quieter, more elevated, level of being. The bustle of the city is left behind and the visitor is invited to enter the private, intimate realm of the artist's imagined consciousness. This is the encounter with the spiritual aspect of the city and Sufi Cairo, inspired by the artist's own interaction with it. Script, both stylized and etched, is a dominant component of the installations: masks of the artist's head fitted on three mannequins whose bare bodies are covered with script, a row of small wood and glass boxes along a wall, with mummy-like figurines eternalizing some of the artist's cherished people, including her parents; a dark, roomful of carefully aligned, steadfast rows of shoe moulds covered with stylized Sufi, Arabic script, like a prayer rug, facing a mirror that endlessly multiplies them; and finally the dark room, with blue phosphorescent light that hovers over a circle of plain white shoe moulds, placed in a circle, elevated from the ground. Here, the text and script have a meditative function, through repetition, in most of the installations, until we reach the plain white floating shoe moulds, the ultimate stage of clarity, serenity and quiet.

The rules of art

Given Huda Lutfi's profile and artistic history, it is not a coincidence that she should exhibit at the Townhouse Gallery in particular and to take up residence in one of its artist studios. Lutfi's initial artistic moment coincided with the establishment of this avant-garde space that played a leading role in the new cultural scape in downtown Cairo with the launch of the Nitaq I festival in the year 2000. The owner, William Wells, a determined, entrepreneurial Canadian curator with

Plate 11.1 Shoe moulds I, courtesy of Huda Lutfi, artist.

Plate 11.2 Shoe moulds II, courtesy of Huda Lutfi, artist.

Plate 11.3 Shoe moulds III, courtesy of Huda Lutfi, artist.

Plate 11.4 Shoe moulds IV, courtesy of Huda Lutfi, artist.

Plate 11.5 Shoe moulds V, courtesy of Huda Lutfi, artist.

long experience in the art world in the US and England, has succeeded over the past decade in expanding the scope and space of this gallery so that it has become a veritable alternative cultural centre. Besides the spacious exhibition spaces, there are new annexes, artist studios, a bookstore and gift shop, and an art library. The Townhouse regularly hosts a comprehensive cultural programme that includes, besides the regular artist exhibitions, film showings, performing arts events, workshops, lectures, roundtable discussion, artist talks, and writers' talks. Right around the corner from the Townhouse is the state-run Cairo Atelier, the 1950s hub of Cairo's now predominantly institutional cultural elite that basically offers the same functions. A comparative study of the two spaces, the physical premises, the budgets, the administration, the audience and the form and context of the cultural activities they host will shed light on the growing gap between the public (state-run) and the private artistic initiatives. Not only is the latter unquestionably more effective in responding to the challenge of constructing a comprehensive cultural scape in the ailing heart of the city, but it is also more successful in responding to a younger generation of producers and consumers alike. It is true that other attempts have been made by the Mashrabiyya Gallery, for example however, they remain seasonal, erratic, limited and confined by the very space of the gallery itself. The sheer physical size of the Townhouse has also allowed it to simultaneously host installation art, video art, and experimental visual and performing arts projects that have attracted some of the more promising young artists in search of more freedom and profit, away from the constraining, hierarchical, institutional prerogatives of state-run institutions.

It is not surprising, therefore, that the Townhouse, with its foreign owner, should be at the centre of controversy and the battle over "national culture" and its representation. Not only is this space perceived as a "parasite" by other national artistic institutions but it is equally envied by other downtown, gallerists, both Egyptian and foreign, who feel that its expansion may be pulling the rug from under their feet as well.[27] Given the modest size of both the local and global markets for Egyptian art, the Townhouse is seen by both, state and private actors in the field, as unashamedly eating a lot of the cake alone. Accusations of sabotage and misrepresentation of the Egyptian "national" art world have been unrelenting.[28] But so have strategies of state-orchestrated intimidations that have ranged from accusations of exploitation and corruption of the national young crop to insinuations of entrepreneurial and colonial foul play,[29] which have occasionally justified surprise raids and searches of the Townhouse premises by security forces, not to mention occasional censorship episodes of exhibiting artists' work. The Ministry of Culture's antagonistic position toward the private sector in the art world is unambiguous and was articulated by the Minister of Culture himself on the pages of *Al-Qahira*, the weekly newspaper owned by the Ministry of Culture, which is used to announce ministerial policies vis-à-vis the cultural field: "if there is anything around these galleries that is being hidden behind a curtain, then there are authorities that are taking care of it".[30] Evidently, the comments of the artist/minister reinforce the domination of the political field of the cultural one so that the cultural players remain in the "barn", to use the minister's own description of the process.

The drama perhaps is that artists working predominantly in the private art world tend to forget the rules of the game that ultimately circumscribe and define their "illusions" of freedom and their "autonomous" artistic production. The crises that surrounded Huda Lutfi's *Found in Cairo* are a case in point. Lutfi's choice of the image to publicize the exhibit, on both the poster and the invitation card, threatened to cause the cancellation of the entire event. Both the poster and card bore the image of the shoe moulds adorned with her stylized and repeated Sufi inscription, which read as follows: *"Ana jalis man dhakarani, wa man dhakarani, ana jalisuhu"* (I am in the company of the one who mentions me. The one who mentions me is in my company). Lutfi was told by the police officer who summoned her that an unknown "informer", whose identity has never been revealed, went to the police station and proclaimed that the poster was "blasphemous" because it reproduced, on *shoes*, a sacred saying (*hadith*) of the Prophet Muhammad. As is the case in all of these censorship crises in the cultural field at large, the poster was taken completely out of the symbolic context in which the image was conceived by the artist. It was read literally – as shoes, not as hand-painted and "cleansed" (to use the artist's description of scraping and painting) wooden shoe moulds; as a reproduction of a *hadith*, not as an artistic Sufi inscription inspired by Sufi poetry; as sacrilegious to Islam, not as a symbolic rendition of a state of human consciousness – and was immediately incriminated.

Given the general and rather transparent rules of the politico-cultural game, one has to ask why Lutfi chose this particular image from among the other installations of the exhibit. I wish to argue that Lutfi's marginal yet privileged position vis-à-vis the politics of the visual field have caused this crisis. Lutfi is an outsider to the institutional mandates in the Egyptian art world: she has come to this rather densely populated, yet economically and symbolically sparse, artistic space as a professional in a foreign private institution, namely the American University in Cairo. Even though Lutfi's artistic work has been both symbolically and economically profitable to her, she continues to have the privilege, unavailable to most of her peers in the art world, of having another primary, breadwinning profession. This unusual and enviable position has led her to refuse to see, or, perhaps, to actively test, the boundaries. However, this slippage or strategy on the artist's part has also meant that Lutfi was subjecting herself to the literalist and mutilated readings that characterize censorship crises in the cultural field at large, ones that can have serious repercussions on many cultural players, for they crystallize the risks involved, and reconfigure the artist's future strategies.

On the eve of the opening of *Found in Cairo*, Lutfi was summoned to the police station where a "friendly" interrogation took place. There she attempted to situate the image on the "blasphemous" poster in the larger context of her exhibit arguing that the image was not of *shoes* but rather of *shoe moulds* that she had cleansed and hand-painted with a Sufi inscription, not one of the prophet's sayings. She also explained that script, in general, was part of her professional and artistic worlds, revealing, at the same time, that she is a professor of history at the American University. According to Lutfi, the authorities were both courteous and accommodating. They explained to her that their duty was "to protect her" from the "street" that does not understand the symbolism involved in her work, and stipulated that all posters be removed, and all invitation cards be seized, immediately before the opening of *Found in Cairo*. The opening of the exhibit, however, took place as scheduled, with the actual "blasphemous" installation of Sufi shoe moulds untouched:

> What [the officer] seemed to be concerned about was the safety of the public space from contamination, from images that may be offensive, and hence cause trouble on the street. The gallery's enclosed walls were perceived more as a private space protected from the potential reaction of the man on the street.[31]

The "friendly" summons of the artist at the police station had immediate and effective results that reinstated the boundaries imposed by the political field on the visual one. The exhibit was contained from the public eye (it was publicized only by word of mouth and through a mailing list on the net), the transgressing artist was reminded of the boundaries she bystepped, the Townhouse Gallery received yet another message from the watchful authorities, state sovereignty and morality were reinstated and aligned to that of the "street", and the state's domination of the public sphere was reconfirmed. Not visibly, but invisibly; not in public, but in private, through a quasi-secret intimidating meeting with the artist of which there is no written record. At the same time, by dismissing charges against the artist, and allowing the exhibit to take place, the authorities became the artist's "protectors" and patrons of the "freedom" they granted her. In addition, the incident was whispered widely to other potential, less privileged, transgressors who, having learned a lesson by example, were more likely to appreciate "the dangers of working"[32] with the private sector that is responsible for this illusionary freedom. As in most cases of state intimidation of the cultural players, there is no written record of this incident and the "informer's" identity was never discovered or revealed.

Unfortunately, the above scenario was repeated, with far more damaging repercussions for the artist, in December 2004, almost a year and a half later, when Lutfi accepted an invitation to exhibit her *Found in Cairo* installations in Bahrain. The invitation coincided with internal unrest between the Coptic and Muslim communities and authorities, in the aftermath of the alleged conversion to Islam of the wife of a Coptic priest in order to marry a Muslim man.[33] Lutfi herself has rendered a detailed account of this episode which I will quote at length:

> In the summer of 2004, Bayan Kanoo, the owner of a gallery in Bahrain invited me to have a retrospective show during the month of January 2005. She insisted that I include the installation of inscribed shoe moulds in the show. I admit that I felt uneasy about this, what if similar reactions occur in

Bahrain? But in the end I submitted to the temptation. Once again the reaction came from Egypt, when the pieces for the exhibit were being shipped from Cairo to Bahrain, traversing the local to the global. The site was Cairo international airport, Department of Artistic Items, where the airport police authorities inspect all items exported to the outside world. I receive a phone call from the representative of the shipping agency informing me that the airport police officials found a problem with the inscribed shoe moulds, and that they have decided to detain the shipping official who was responsible for shipping the pieces until further notice. More phone calls from the shipping agent followed informing me that those officials are suspecting a case of blasphemy, and that the inscribed shoe moulds were being subjected to the inspection of a religious expert.

The suspect nature of the installation piece was further heightened in the eyes of the Muslim airport officials by the fact that the shipping agents involved were Coptic. In their panic, the case was immediately interpreted as a Coptic conspiracy. As it happened, Egyptians had been witnessing another case of communal conflict between the Coptic and Muslim community. Much to the rage of the Coptic community, the wife of a Coptic priest converted to Islam in order to marry a Muslim. The Egyptian media made a sensational story of the conversion case and accusations between the two communities were being hurled back and forth. The shipping agents involved were thus summoned by the office of the prosecutor for more interrogation, where they denied any sort of conspiratorial accusations: they did not know the artist, they did not know what the inscribed text signified, that they were simply doing their work The following day an official was sent to the Townhouse gallery to conduct more investigations, one repeated question was asked of the staff and employees working in the gallery: What religious denomination do you belong to? In the meantime, I was asked to go and meet an official at the Ministry of Interior; a meeting negotiated through the security office of the American University in Cairo. The young interrogator who interviewed me proudly hung his certificates of specialization from the American Federal Bureau of Investigation. The meeting was short and cordial, and I explained at length that no subversive intentions were meant by the piece. A more lengthy and arduous session however followed the next day in the office of the deputy prosecutor in the Heliopolis courthouse. During the meeting my lawyer and the assistant curator of the Townhouse gallery were also present. The official accusation was read out to me: exploitation of the Islamic religion in my artwork; conspiracy with the Coptic community to disparage the Islamic religion; threatening the national security of the Egyptian nation. It was explained to me that the religious expert who was asked to investigate the case judged the inscribed text as a Prophetic hadith, and therefore inscribing such a text on "shoes" was perceived as a serious religious offence. Once again I was confronted with a literalist interpretation of the work, and it took three hours to explain to my interrogator that these moulds were not shoes, that they stood for the human figure in meditation, and that my intentions were far from disparaging Islam. Whether out of conviction or political strategy, the state official decided not to press charges, and I was acquitted. However, the state officials involved in the case refused the release of the incriminated piece, and it still remains somewhere in the dark storage houses of Cairo airport.[34]

Lutfi's testimony raises several important issues with regard to the risks involved in challenging the boundaries of power for she confesses that she was "tempted" by the invitation despite the fact that – given her earlier experience with state officials – she felt "uneasy" about including the shoe mould installation in the shipment to Bahrain. Nevertheless, she takes the risk which in this second confrontational instance seems to have shifted from being that between the private and the public, i.e. the Townhouse Gallery and the Egyptian street, to becoming that between the local and the global, i.e. Cairo airport and Bahrain.

The state's response to both episodes is equally instructive as examples of dealing with a local crisis (in the first instance of censorship) and with a global one (in the second instance). Whereas in the first reaction the interrogating officers represented themselves as the "protectors" of the artist against the street, in the second round of interrogations the artist was actually confronted with a formal and alarming set of accusations – exploitation of the Islamic religion in her artwork; conspiracy with the Coptic community to disparage the Islamic religion; threatening the national security of the Egyptian nation – together more serious, in their legal and political implications, than the set of accusations levelled against the pro-democracy activist Saad Eddin Ibrahim (who was tried and acquitted on charges of receiving foreign funds, smearing the image of Egypt abroad and forgery, among others),[35] or the feminist Nawal al-Saadawi (who was also accused of "contempt of religion", but later acquitted).[36] Whereas in the "local" crisis the Sufi shoe mould installation was allowed to be exhibited within the private space of the Townhouse Gallery, in the "global" one the installation was confiscated and remains in the custody of state authorities.

However, the "global" nature of the second confrontation with the artist also dictated new constraints on the state authorities. On the one hand, their power over street morality was being compromised and on the other their secular and democratic credibility was now at stake. The response was tailored to respond to both: on the "local" level the artist was accused of conspiring against the nation, national unity and national values; on the "global" level the entire shipment, except for the Sufi shoe mould installation, was released and the exhibit proceeded on time in Bahrain with the artist present. The renewed literalist onslaught on artistic representation also served a double purpose: the acquittal of the artist allowed the state to continue to present itself as the protector of the cultural sphere and patron of artistic production but the simultaneous confiscation of the Sufi shoe moulds installation was the symbolic act of reinscribing the boundaries of representation within the visual field, albeit literalist or out of context. Indeed, the first instance of state intimidation in the *Found in Cairo* crisis seemed to be an act of retaliatory containment mainly directed against the

Townhouse Gallery and its "contaminating" foreign owner, since no charges were pressed against the artist herself. However, in this second instance, where Lutfi was interrogated, formally charged and ultimately censored, without recourse to retrieving her work from the authorities, the intimidation was definitely directed against her, as artist.

Even though this potentially life-threatening episode found its way to "resolution" (the case was closed and charges against her were dropped), mainly because of Lutfi's position both socially and professionally and the informal institutional support she received through the security officer at the American University, the "incriminating installation" was never returned to her. More seriously, however, to date, she has no official written record from the state of the incident, or the charges or the "arduous" interrogation. The only record lies with the state itself: the written interrogation and the "incriminating" installation both of which continue to hang over the artist's head despite the fact that the case has been "closed".

Silence is silver

In "The Shifting Limits of the Sayable in Egyptian Fiction", Richard Jacquemond argues that the two-player game between the Egyptian state and the writers that characterized both the Nasser and Sadat eras "has been replaced, under Mubarak, by a game whose rules are indeed more flexible, but also more blurred".[37] These blurred rules, as mentioned earlier in this chapter, become even fuzzier because of the interference of "street censorship" and self-proclaimed third-party interventions. Even though Jacquemond's article deals exclusively with instances of street censorship with regard to literary texts, it is obvious from Lutfi's *Found in Cairo* crises that the same kind of street censorship applies to the visual field. In fact, one can argue that street censorship is potentially more threatening to the visual arts, for the written word continues to be less accessible and less visible. Moreover, since the visual arts use a symbolic medium that is not immediately decipherable by the general public, the problem becomes not that of interpretation (as with language) but that of literalist equation between the artistic object and its literal, not symbolic, signification. In speaking about her Sufi shoe mould installation, Lutfi describes her representational intentions in the following terms:

> As a bricoleur the challenge here was greater; the question that kept coming to my mind, how is it possible for me to visually convey the intangible state of silence, of meditation, the turning away from the noise and from objects to quietness.
> (…)
> Like the poet who chooses an economy of language to convey her/his image, the visual artist resorts to an economy of signs, thus a part or a fragment is used to symbolically stand for the whole. And so it was that these found shoe moulds were meant to represent human figures in a state of con-

templation and remembrance (*dhikr*) repeating endlessly the meditative Sufi adage: I am in the company of the one who remembers me and the one who remembers me is in my company (*ana jalis man dhakarani, wa man dhakarani ana jalisuhu*) in order to reach that state of being leading to silence.[38]

However, the installation of the Sufi shoe moulds became "blasphemous" in the literalist reading of both the anonymous "informer" and the airport officials; it became a *hadith* by the Prophet Muhammad that was reproduced on "shoes".

Moreover, besides the self-proclaimed censors that Jacquemond enumerates (journalists, independent ulamas, lawyers, MP's, librarians, publishing houses' employees, students' parents etc.) and of which the anonymous informer and the airport officials in the *Found in Cairo* crises are two more examples, there is a fourth, well-meaning peer group, that, acting out of genuine, but short-sighted, concern, found itself implicated in street censorship as well. Even though Lutfi did receive support from many fellow artists, she was blamed, by many parties involved in the *Found in Cairo* crises, including her closest friends and admirers of her work, for this grave oversight of the limits of representation. This "friendly" censorship that was perfectly aware of the symbolic and contextual signification of the installation, and its importance to crystallizing some of the artist's substantive symbolic and conceptual developments, suddenly aligned itself with state- and street-enforced boundaries and limits of visual representation. The state's more visible intimidating power represented by its interrogating police officers was complemented by more invisible incriminating elements that ultimately lead to the artist's self-interrogation:

> As a humanist, cultural historian and bricoleur, I have always admired the ideal of the artist who tests the limits of tolerance in his/her culture; the romantic notion of the artist, whose work situates him/her "on the very edges of what can be said at a particular place and time…" Was I testing the limits of tolerance, the limits of the sayable? Was I doing this consciously or unconsciously? I really cannot say, perhaps I was carried away by a sense of elusive autonomy as an artist and scholar independent of state patronage and its institutional affiliation. Seduced by the experimental play of bricolage, its potential freedom of play to re-assemble and re-invent images, the bricoleur slipped! I came to learn the hard way that bricolaging is not an innocent or hermetic act, that the mixing or juxtaposing of specific cultural objects may evoke strong cultural anxieties; that I have underestimated the political and ideological significance of representation.[39]

Furthermore, as a social scientist, Lutfi grapples with the relationship between representation and cultural values and the complementary relationship between cultural restraints and cultural mobility that is achieved through a continuous process of experimentation and improvisation. However, despite this "rational quest", as an artist, the more pressing question for her remains how to safeguard her own free spirit, that of "the bricoleur, whose ideal is to experiment, re-invent new meanings and juxtapositions, and whose bricks are drawn from different cultural icons and historical moments".[40] What are the strategies available to the artist in confronting the duplicitous visible and invisible boundaries of state, street and ultimately self-censorship? The answer that Lutfi provides is an instructive one. In May 2005 Lutfi was invited to exhibit her Sufi shoe mould installation at the Falaki Gallery at the American University in Cairo. Instead of duplicating the confiscated installation, Lutfi exhibited fifty pairs of silver-painted shoe moulds that had undergone the same process of "cleansing" but without inscribing on them the Sufi/*hadith* text. In parallel, she mounted two of these silver shoe moulds on a wooden pedestal with the inscribed Arabic text that read "Silence is silver" (*al-Sukut min fadda*), a playful and provocative rendition of the Arabic proverb *idha kan al-kalam min dhahab fa l-sukut min fadda* (If words are of gold, then silence is silver). This symbolic insinuating gesture became the artist's creative response to the real silence imposed upon her.

12 Literature and literalism
The *Al-Khubz al-hafi* crisis reconsidered

In December 1998 I found myself at the heart of a major crisis surrounding my teaching of the Moroccan writer Mohamed Choukri's controversial autobiographical text *Al Khubz al-hafi* (*For Bread Alone*) in one of my literature classes at the American University in Cairo. The crisis that began on campus as part of a debate over academic freedom and freedom of expression soon took on national, regional and international proportions when the parents of two students sent an unsigned letter to the AUC administration calling for my dismissal and threatening to take me and the university to court.

This chapter is a personal testimony on the *Al-Khubz al-hafi* crisis that lasted for almost six months.[1] It is also an attempt to produce a participant objectification of the academic field inspired by Pierre Bourdieu's work in *Homo Academicus* where he uses his own position within the academy in order to read the academic field, arguing that a key pole of academic power stems from the attainment of positions which govern the reproduction of the corps, i.e. the same structure of relationships of power, within the academy.[2] According to Bourdieu, the academic field, like all other fields of power is organized around positions of dominance and subordination in which different actors within the field are located depending on their respective symbolic capital. In academia these positions are represented by faculty holding "orthodox" institutionally approved intellectual viewpoints (who are in dominant positions that preserve the corps) and faculty who hold uninstitutional, "heretical" views (who are in subordinate positions that cause structural dissonance within the general structure of the corps).[3] The academy therefore is a site of struggle over symbolic capital between actors in various positions of dominance and subordination. The *Al-Khubz al-hafi* crisis offers an example of these struggles that within the academy get played out on two levels: the struggles over the forms of knowledge within an academic discipline (in this case the "canon" of Arabic literature) as well as the knowledge produced by the agents or actors within that same discipline about these forms of knowledge. For, as the *Al-Khubz al-hafi* crisis unfolded, it exposed internal battles at once over representations of the Arab literary "canon" as well as the boundaries and limits of Arab literary expression within the literary field itself.

Furthermore, through my reconstruction of the circumstances and debates that surrounded the crisis I will raise a number of central issues in the Egyptian

230 *The bounds of change*

cultural field: the place of literature in society, the relationship between society and the academy, the place of liberal education in a society that constrains freedom of expression, the relationship between power and knowledge, and finally the notion of citizenship in a society that insists on treating its youth like children. The *Al-Khubz al-hafi* crisis is also an important and instructive example of the increasing encroachment of third party actors within the academy, i.e. third-party interventions by self-proclaimed censors who, in this instance, were represented by students' parents and journalists. Finally, the *Al-Khubz al-hafi* crisis provided a crucial lesson in strategies of resistance and collective transnational solidarities that, given the scope of the chapter, remain hopelessly underrepresented.

By way of introduction: the Rodinson affair

On 13 May 1998, two weeks before final exams at the American University in Cairo, *Al-Ahram* daily newspaper, *the* mouthpiece for the Egyptian state, published an article by the prominent columnist Salah Muntasir entitled "A Book that Must Be Stopped" (*Kitab yajib waqfuhu*) in which he demanded the state's immediate intervention to ban Maxime Rodinson's biography of the Prophet Muhammad, an established classic since its publication in French in 1961 and a reference that had been in circulation, in libraries and in the possession of Egyptian students and intellectuals since then. Rodinson's *Muhammad* had been assigned, as secondary material, to students in the Survey of Arab History course at the AUC where it was being taught that same semester by a French part-time faculty member. In his article, Muntasir cited specific passages from the text, taken out of their general context, on the basis of which he was convinced that both the book and its author denigrated not only Islam and Muslims worldwide but, more seriously perhaps, the Prophet Muhammad's life history itself.[4] The article showed no knowledge of the distinguished status of the book, or its history within its field of study, nor, for that matter, its eminent author who is well known in the Arab region for his sympathetic political views towards the Arabs and the Palestinians in particular expressed in many of his other works on the region.[5]

According to the AUC administration, on the same day President Mubarak gave a direct order, through the Minister of Higher Education, to withdraw from use Rodinson's *Muhammad*, which had been in circulation in the university since 1971.[6] It is important to note that the President's personal intervention came at a sensitive and challenging moment in the confrontation between the state and liberal intellectuals on the one hand and radical Islamists on the other that culminated in several grave outcomes: the assassination of the liberal intellectual Farag Fuda by Islamic fundamentalists in 1992, the stabbing of the Egyptian Nobel laureate Naguib Mahfouz by two radical Islamists in 1994 and the forced exile of the well-known scholar of Islamic studies Nasr Hamid Abu Zayd in 1996 after having been accused of apostasy. In the case of the Rodinson affair, the combination of a Jewish author, an American institution and a French instructor could have made for an even more lethal episode specifically with regard to the role of the state as guardian of moral, ethical and religious values. Hence, the rush, at the highest level of the Egyptian state, to ban the book and to intervene directly in academic curricula was, first and foremost, a political move to assert the state's authority over and domination of the cultural, educational and religious fields.

Some members of the university administration found it imperative that AUC be accorded an opportunity to present the context in which the book appeared in the course; however, given the level of the Egyptian state's intervention, the university "had no other recourse but to obey this directive".[7] Rather than the University defending the book the author, and the instructor, the next day *Al-Ahram* newspaper carried on its front page an official apology from the American University and its interim President deeming the Rodinson affair an "individual mistake", and vowing to preserve Egypt's values and religious beliefs. The AUC public apology and the labelling of the incident by its administration as an "individual mistake" resulted in a long and vicious press campaign against the French instructor who, despite the solidarity of many of his colleagues and students, found himself eventually outside the university (as a part-time instructor whose services were no longer needed) and ultimately outside the country.

Given the swift and visionless manner with which the AUC administration sought to resolve the crisis, the Rodinson affair was to have a long-lasting impact on the university and the parameters in which it operates. On one level, the intervention of the national press (on behalf of the student's parent who instigated the complaint) meant that the university was called upon to transform specialized academic knowledge into decontextualized public opinion issues, thereby collapsing the distance between free academic learning and the dominant mores and values of the society at large. Moreover, Muntasir, who attacked *Muhammad* and demanded that it be "stopped", relied in his attack on passages taken out of context, thus legitimating the incrimination of intellectual works without any contextual reading or analysis. This set the precedent of seeking to resolve an academic problem outside the academy when the latter enables students and parents alike to discuss academic issues at various levels of the institution's hierarchy (instructors, chairs, deans, administration). Indeed, both the complaining parents and the national press were not seeking any kind of open intellectual debate or discussion surrounding the academic context of Rodinson's *Muhammad*. Rather they meant to create a scandal and to publicly pressure, embarrass and incriminate the whole (American) institution.

The fact that AUC bowed to this kind of blackmail was itself a self-deprecating move given its fragile position as an American institution in a host country where its presence, operation and motives have always been suspect and subject to both scrutiny and critique.[8] Instead of defending academic freedom and the right of its faculty to equip their students with critical and analytical skills, the AUC's acquiescence to the state's unpredictable "red lines" and its strategy of blaming the victim (the French instructor) by labelling the incident an

232   *The bounds of change*

"individual mistake" set another dangerous precedent whereby academic faculty found themselves targeted and defenceless for doing their job within a liberal institution. Despite the mobilization of many AUC faculty who rallied around their French colleague and the intervention of several noted public figures and journalists in defence of freedom of the academy, what ultimately remained of the incident was the new limits that AUC as a liberal institution was now willing to set itself in order to avoid any future confrontation both with the Egyptian state and with society at large.

Teaching *Al-Khubz al-hafi* in Cairo

The Rodinson affair at AUC coincided with my sabbatical year. I was therefore not directly involved in the developments of the crisis even though I followed the press and various positions articulated on campus. Many among the faculty were outraged at AUC's unjustified public apology and acquiescence to the Presidential directive. From a distance, however, I felt that, if there was an "individual mistake" to be concerned about, it was certainly not that committed by our French colleague but rather that committed by the AUC interim administration that, because of its insufficiently informed position, I believed, rushed into a hasty political decision without calculating the academic repercussions. Naively, perhaps, and given the general and heartening solidarity with our French colleague, I felt reassured that despite the state's intervention, and the AUC administration's uncalculated (from my perspective) apology, all would be well with AUC and that the Rodinson affair alerted the academic community to the dangers of compromising on liberal education.

The academic year of 1998–99 brought with it a new AUC administration and much concern about actual and potential censorship and self-censorship.[9] It also began with mobilization among the faculty, who, given the university's compromised position at the end of the previous academic year, drafted a statement calling on the administration to defend its faculty and their academic freedom. I had been approached by some of the faculty members who had drafted the statement to read it at a general faculty meeting during December 1998 because I was both tenured and Egyptian and had agreed to do so. However, the situation at AUC was about to take a new turn in which the role intended for me by my colleagues who selected me was to be drastically changed.

As usual, I was teaching a section of the Introduction to Modern Arabic Literature course which I teach every semester, sometimes in Arabic and sometimes in English. As usual also I had changed my reading list slightly in order to reflect the wide spectrum of literary works from the Arab region. For the autumn semester 1998–99 I had included *Al-Khubz al-hafi* (1982; English translation, *For Bread Alone*, 1972), the autobiographical narrative of the Moroccan writer Mohamed Choukri,[10] a work I had taught before in a different class and that had been taught by another colleague in the university in one of her courses.[11] Several considerations motivated the reinclusion of *Al-Khubz al-hafi* on my rotating reading list. Firstly, *Al-Khubz al-hafi* has a very special status in the modern Arab literary repertoire, for its author Mohamed Choukri had been illiterate until the age of twenty when he made a decision to become literate and subsequently write his "novelistic" autobiographical text that has since been highly acclaimed by some of the Arab world's leading literary critics, has been translated into at least twelve languages and is studied worldwide in academic institutions.[12] Indeed, *Al-Khubz al-hafi* is not only a unique example of audacious writing from the underworld about the underworld but also one that unsettles notions of conventional literary representation and aesthetics. Secondly, as a text from the underworld, *Al-Khubz al-hafi* lays bare the cruel and shocking reality of the street that is consistently and comfortably ignored, marginalized or silenced.[13] Indeed, the elite institution of the American University in Cairo is located in the heart of downtown Cairo where street misery is rampant and surrounds its privileged students – the future key players in their country – throughout the day as they make their way from one campus building to the other. We all walk past these wretched of the earth: street children and homeless creatures sprawled on the pavements in tattered clothes barely covering their emaciated bodies. Mohamed Choukri's *Al-Khubz al-hafi* articulates with eloquence and humanity the reality of these wretched of the earth; a voice from within that voiceless underworld albeit from another Arab metropolis (Tangiers). True, *Al-Khubz al-hafi* is a controversial work because of its bare and open representation of a street child's subhuman life; however, so are many other Arab literary works including those of Naguib Mahfouz, Yusuf Idris, Sonallah Ibrahim, Tayeb Saleh, Hanan al-Sheikh, Ahdaf Souief and Ahlam Mosteghanemi, to mention only a few of the well-known Arab authors whose works I regularly teach. Indeed, controversy is the hallmark of great literary works throughout human history, and part of the very nature not only of courses on literature but of liberal education itself is to engage students and invite them to think critically and analytically about controversial issues.

In my Introduction to Modern Arabic Literature class that I was teaching in Arabic during the autumn semester 1998, *Al-Khubz al-hafi* was the text before the last on my reading list. There were many reasons for introducing it that late during the semester. Primarily, the course is meant to provide the students with the political, historical and literary contexts of literary works and their aesthetic modes and conventions during the nineteenth and twentieth centuries: hence the positioning of Choukri's narrative, a relatively more recent text, towards the end of the reading list. Secondly, reading *Al-Khubz al-hafi* can be a rather daunting experience for ill-prepared readers whose moral, social and aesthetic values have never been called into question or unsettled. It was therefore important for students to be equipped with the proper analytical and interpretative skills in order to avoid the all-too-easy pitfall of value and moral judgement. Thirdly, one of the central axes of the course is to explore developments that have taken place in the relationship between literature and reality as well as writers and society focusing specifically on modern Arab writers. In this respect, *Al-Khubz al-hafi*, like many other milestones in modern Arabic literature – for example Sonallah

Ibrahim's *Tilka l-ra'iha* (1966; English translation, *The Smell of It*, 1971), which was initially banned and accused of vulgarity during the 1960s – is certainly a significant text that has revolutionized the relationship between the writer, the world and the text.[14]

Al-Khubz al-hafi on trial

On Thursday 17 December, at approximately 12:15 p.m., as I was teaching my Modern Arabic Literature class a messenger appeared at the door to deliver a message asking me to contact the administration urgently. Since the class hour had already started, I put the memo slip aside, with the thought that I would finish what I had been saying, and then dismiss the class. However, within less than ten minutes another, out-of-breath messenger, arrived in the classroom. With the door of the room ajar, and in the presence of some 30 students, the messenger proceeded to reiterate the content of the written memo slip with some added details: "they are all waiting for you!" When I asked who "they" referred to, she let me know that the pronoun referred to three of the highest officials at AUC. Needless to say, given the messenger's panic-stricken voice, the students' obvious bafflement and my own rising misgivings, I abruptly stopped the lecture, and proceeded to the main campus, with a thousand possible scenarios for this unprecedented event in my years of professional academic life.

Once I arrived in the designated office, I found myself indeed surrounded by the three high officials and another gentleman, to whom I was not immediately introduced, but was later informed is the AUC clinic physician. Before us, on a table, lay a copy of one of the works I was teaching, that semester, in Introduction to Modern Arabic Literature course, in bound, photocopied form, namely *Al-Khubz al-hafi* by the Moroccan writer Mohamed Choukri. I was told that we had an urgent and serious matter to attend to, that we were fortunate that the AUC physician was bringing the matter to our attention before it was leaked to the press, and that every effort must be made to resolve this crisis immediately. The AUC physician then explained to me that "two or three parents" had contacted him with complaints concerning the reading material that lay before us, on the table. According to them, this material constituted a work of "pornography" (two or three passages from the text had been handpicked, photocopied and translated into English for the benefit of the administrators and lay, next to the text, on the table). The AUC physician added that the unidentified parents were certain that I was teaching a banned book, and were threatening to go to press, citing the passages that had been photocopied. Another scandal for the American university and one of its instructors!

It became obvious to me then and there that I was witnessing a replay of the scenario of the Rodinson affair, only this time *I* was expected to play the role that had been allotted to my French colleague who had left the university in silence. It was equally unsettling to see the same incriminating tactics being used: a series of passages that had been translated and taken out of context that were meant to prove that Choukri's work was "pornographic". Moreover, it was obvious from the general attitude in the room that none of my "interrogators" had bothered to read the text itself, or to inform themselves about the status of the work and its significance in the modern Arab literary repertoire. In addition, as was the case in the Rodinson affair, this meeting with AUC high officials with a non-academic third party (the AUC physician as representative of the anonymous parents) was in itself a violation of due process and academic procedures that should have been followed.[15] It was also evident that, this time around, the complaining parents had decided to give the university a golden opportunity – through the intervention of their "friend" the AUC physician who was supposed to contain the crisis – an opportunity that was not accorded to the previous administration during the Rodinson affair where the complaining parents had gone directly to the press. Given the precedent, the new AUC administration immediately seized this golden opportunity before the whole episode was turned, once more, into a public opinion scandal especially since the *Al-Khubz al-hafi* crisis coincided with the much-resented US/UK bombardment of Iraq in December 1998.

After the preliminary accusations I received, initially from the physician to whom no one introduced me until the end of the meeting, I was given the chance to respond. I explained to my audience that Mohamed Choukri's novelistic autobiography (*sira riwa'iyya*), as the subtitle of the text indicated, occupies a unique position in modern Arabic letters. Since its publication, first in English translation, by the well-known American writer Paul Bowles, in 1972, then in French in 1980, by Taher Ben Jelloun, the distinguished Moroccan francophone writer, and finally in Arabic, in 1982, this work has risen to regional and international acclaim. I also added that *Al-Khubz al-hafi* has been translated into several other European languages, and represents one of the most widely read books in modern Arabic literature, both in Arabic and in translation.

I informed my audience that this work has been taught before in our university, both in the Department of Arabic Studies (in more than one of my courses) and in the Department of English and Comparative Literature. It was not a banned book. Indeed, it was available in downtown Cairo bookstores, and when used in translation, in other AUC courses, was available at our own bookstore.[16] Further, I explained that *Al-Khubz al-hafi* was certainly not a work of "pornography" but, a very moving and candid tale of an illiterate Moroccan child of the underclass who acceded to literacy, at the age of 20, and was able to weave the appalling conditions of his life history into a mesmerizing text that is taught in universities all over the world, both at the undergraduate and graduate levels. I cited several names of distinguished Arab critics who have written academic studies on this work in which they analyse the literary aesthetics of the text, its structure, its language, etc.[17] Among the many facts I forgot to mention, as I strove to rescue this literary text, was that Mohamed Choukri himself had been interviewed by AUC's *Alif: Journal of Comparative Poetics*, an interview that was later translated into English, and selected for an anthology of *Ailf* articles entitled *The View from Within: Writers and Critics on Contemporary Arabic Literature*, published by AUC Press in 1994. Ferial Ghazoul and Barbara

Harlow, the editors of the volume, described the contents of the volume in the following terms: "articles that were selected for this anthology were not only deemed the best but also those that together constituted a representative sample of the current intellectual and literary debates of the Arab world".[18] As to the explicit sexual language in Choukri's text, I assured my audience that I could probably be invited back to similar meetings on a weekly basis given the unconventional and contestatory nature of many modern Arabic works, both prose and poetry, citing a long list of distinguished names. I reminded my audience that the photocopied passages were handpicked, and taken out of context, and that if the same were to be done to any of the writers I had mentioned, they could all become either pornographic or blasphemous![19]

After having listened to this rather long but necessary defence, one of the high officials asked me to suggest a way out of the crisis. Since I had already read and discussed the text with my class, I simply could not think of a way out. So I asked him for his suggestions. I was utterly shocked to hear two of the officials present and the AUC physician express the following: one of them and the physician started by suggesting that I should apologize to my class for having assigned this reading material, all three agreed that I was harassing my students by exposing them to such a text, and finally, as I showed reluctance to comply with the apology scenario, the AUC physician suggested that I should inform my students that I would remove the Choukri text from the semester's reading list.[20]

It was the third official's protest against the suggested apology, and her articulate defence of the nature of literary texts in general, that allowed me to collect my thoughts and enter into negotiations over what I would be willing to do, to overcome this crisis. We finally arrived at a consensus that the class was better left undisturbed. However, the highest attending official asked the AUC physician to relay to the parents that the administration had taken the necessary measures to contain the crisis, and that the teacher (myself) has agreed not to teach this book again (a statement I did not make), and that this official and I would be happy to meet with the parents (a suggestion I welcomed).

Despite the rather conciliatory ending of this first meeting, I was both surprised and enraged to learn (through the Chair of my department) a couple of days later that this same highest official had circulated an internal memorandum by email to the HUSS (Humanities and Social Sciences) Council stating that I had agreed not to teach *Al-Khubz al-hafi* again.[21] This unfounded declaration was a turning point in what the administration and I had thought was the end of the crisis. I spent several anguished days during which I oscillated between the comfort of a chapter considered closed and the unbearable feeling of being at once professionally and ethically compromised. It was a decisive moment in my career as a teacher and an educator not only with regard to my commitment to the principles of liberal education and academic freedom but more importantly perhaps my obligation towards my students and their own commitment to critical thinking and freedom of thought and expression. Moreover, I was gravely troubled by the lack of due process throughout the entire crisis and the fact that everything had happened behind the closed doors of the administration without any consideration for academic procedures or the academic community at AUC. All these crucial elements, not to mention the fact that I am a tenured member of the faculty, determined my subsequent response to the high official's declaration that I had agreed not to teach *Al-Khubz al-hafi* in the future.

On 28 December 1998, during a general faculty meeting, I broke the silence that had surrounded *Al-Khubz al-hafi* and publicly briefed my colleagues on what had taken place between me and the administration ten days earlier. That same afternoon I sent an open letter to all AUC faculty via email detailing what had happened (from my point of view) during my meeting with the administration.[22] My intention was to involve the AUC community in an open debate over academic freedom and the responsibility of the academic institution in defending the rights of its faculty as they exercise their profession. This was particularly pressing since only a few months had passed since the Rodinson affair which had ended without any resolution to many crucial issues pertaining to academic freedom. Naively perhaps, I imagined that the whole debate is an academic one and that it concerned the members of our academic community. Initially, the conversation surrounding the crisis and my open letter were indeed internal, generating many sympathetic responses from among several of my colleagues who were concerned about the way in which the crisis was handled within a liberal academic institution.

However, the text of my open letter to all AUC faculty was leaked to the complaining parents, who must have considered this internal response to the meeting with the administration an escalation of the crisis that they had hoped could be regulated on their own terms, behind closed doors. In addition, in the aftermath of my letter to the faculty, the administration had sought to appease the academic community by declaring its commitment to academic freedom, and to defending its faculty, as well as its willingness to establish clear procedures for handling complaints.[23] The administration's renewed commitment to the principles of liberal education was received by the academic community as a salutary move that the previous administration had not considered in the context of the Rodinson affair. Indeed, in a second open letter to all AUC faculty I responded to the administration's memo with a conciliatory short reply with which I sought to close the immediate crisis and to work collectively with other colleagues and the administration towards a more rigorous commitment to the principles of liberal education.[24] However, the administration's renewed commitment to the philosophy of liberal education and its informal apology to me seem to have been interpreted as a sign of weakness by the complaining parents, who perhaps expected a replay of the Rodinson affair scenario that ended with the banning of *Muhammad* and the departure of our French colleague.[25]

Al-Khubz al-hafi incriminated

On 3 January 1999, I received an email from the administration informing me that we were not "quite out of the woods". In a meeting with two top AUC

238 *The bounds of change*

officials the next day, I was given a copy of an unsigned letter written by "some parents" that had been received by the Affirmative Action Office at the university threatening to sue the university if it did not take action against me.[26] The letter had obviously been written in Arabic and had been translated literally into English. Surprisingly, even though unsigned, the letter had been accepted and forwarded to the AUC administration by the Affirmative Action Office in violation of university regulations which stipulated that anonymous complaints were not acceptable. To this day, I have no knowledge of who submitted this document, who translated it or how it made its way up to the highest AUC officials. What I have in my possession is the text of the translated unsigned letter that I was given by the administration on 4 January.[27] It is this text that was eventually leaked to the press, presumably by the complaining parents, thereby transforming the *Al-Khubz al-hafi* crisis from an academic one into a public opinion scandal. In fact, over the span of six months, the text of this unsigned letter was to provide the basis for the press campaign against the book, its author and myself. Subsequently, once the *Al-Khubz al-hafi* crisis occupied the public sphere, it triggered a long and heated debate in which the national, regional and global press and intellectual communities participated. Eventually the crisis escalated further when the Egyptian Minister of Higher Education was questioned about it in an urgent meeting of the Egyptian Parliament's Committee for Education and Academic Research that demanded disciplinary action against me.[28] Interestingly, however, the Minister of Higher Education declared that no such disciplinary action would be taken against me, claiming that the AUC had set up a committee to review books taught in its curriculum (this had actually been suggested but vehemently resisted by AUC faculty) and had provided assurance (based on his communication with the AUC administration) that *Al-Khubz al-hafi* would not be taught again. Other press articles reported that I had threatened to sue the university and the AUC administration for violating my academic freedom, a threat I had not entertained throughout the crisis even though several colleagues and supporters had suggested litigation as a possible and rightful resort in case of further escalation.[29]

Just as the parents' unsigned letter was leaked to the Egyptian press so did the text of my all AUC faculty letter circulate on the internet between colleagues in Egypt, the US and elsewhere. The first assaulting article against me appeared on 7 January 1999 in *Al-Wafd*.

The text of the article openly referred to the parents' unsigned letter that was obviously leaked to the reporter along with my open letter to the AUC faculty:

> The grave blow that descended upon the parents was that the university administration refused to intervene when they submitted a complaint, arguing that instructors are "free" to teach their courses however they wish. The teacher insisted that the students discuss the content of the novel. Imagine, with me, an 18-year-old girl, standing in front of her male classmates, to comment on an autobiography whose author describes how his father had intercourse with his mother and his homosexual adventures.[30]

Literature and literalism 239

This first assault prompted a reply by the Chair of my department (Arabic Studies) about which I was not consulted, nor was the department sitting as a whole and to which the administration was allegedly opposed.[31] The Chair of Arabic Studies signed his response to *Al-Wafd* in his capacity as Chair of the Department of Arabic Studies. In so doing, he presented his position not as that of an individual colleague but as the official spokesman for members of the department. The letter that was sent to *Al-Wafd* depicted my teaching of *Al-Khubz al-hafi* as a "solitary, individual case" in "some 30 years" of the Department's history.[32] This response effectively focused press criticism against me as an individual. In addition, it instructively adopted the same institutional position that characterized the case of the Rodinson book where the crisis was described as an "individual mistake". Hence in both cases, rather than defending its faculty from what are straightforward attacks on basic principles of liberal education, the institution accorded legitimacy to the attacks and left its faculty exposed as defenceless, "individual" targets. Indeed, up until that juncture during the crisis no public institutional statement had been issued to the effect that, in the first instance, *Al-Khubz al-hafi* was in legal circulation in Egypt (and was obtainable from state-run bookstores) and that my decision to assign it to my class was entirely consonant with the principles of liberal education that govern AUC's educational philosophy.[33] Rather than pacify the press, the Chair's response in *Al-Wafd* was followed by a long and hostile article on 14 January in the same paper that was to mark the beginning of an avalanche of attacking and supporting articles.[34]

After the 14 January article in *Al-Wafd* I received a concerned phone-call from a prominent member of the administration who suggested that for my personal security it might be in my interest to consider going on leave from the university until the storm blew over. Not only did I refuse this suggestion but I consulted with senior colleagues who had supported me through these difficult weeks and was given assurances that they would publicly oppose any such action against my will.[35] It is crucial to note that from the very beginning of the crisis I had received unwavering support and selfless solidarity from many colleagues in the university whose generosity, energy, advice and commitment helped me sail through very troubled water.[36]

Global battle for academic freedom

The support I received internally at AUC was further strengthened when in the aftermath of the press campaign concerned friends and colleagues in Egypt, the Arab World, the US and elsewhere spearheaded a counter-campaign in the national, regional and international press and over the internet in defence of academic freedom. In Egypt, the novelist Gamal al-Ghitani, editor-in-chief of *Akhbar al-Adab*, was the first to denounce the press campaign against *Al-Khubz al-hafi*, citing examples of transgressive classics in the Arab literary repertoire: from pre-Islamic poetry to the Abbasid poet Abu Nuwas and the *Thousand and One Nights* and describing the campaign as both "ignorant and backward".[37]

240 *The bounds of change*

Later, in an interview about freedom of expression, the Nobel laureate Naguib Mahfouz expressed his surprise at, and opposition to, the parents' intervention in university curricula, refusing the premise that a book taught to "mature people in the university" can "corrupt" them.[38] In Morocco, the literary critic and novelist Muhammad Barrada spearheaded another supporting campaign that culminated in a statement by the Moroccan Writers' Union denouncing "narrow minded censorship" against *Al-Khubz al-hafi* and expressing their "utmost" solidarity with me.[39] The late Mohamed Choukri himself intervened in the crisis by sending a letter to the AUC administration stating that the crisis surrounding my teaching of *Al-Khubz al-hafi* was in "violation of both the principles of freedom of thought and expression guaranteed by the American constitution and of academic freedom inside and outside the United States" and describing the text of *Al-Khubz al-hafi* as "a testimony on Arab and human reality that is not meant to incite students toward delinquent behaviour as alleged by the ill-intentioned".[40] In Lebanon, the novelist Hassan Daoud wrote a column in the regional *Al-Hayat* during the early stages of the crisis detailing what had happened to me and bewailing the AUC administration's reaction to attacks against its faculty that "debased the university to the level of a neighbourhood school where pupils are taught only what their parents understand and want".[41] It is beyond the scope of this chapter to include all the articles that have appeared in the press. I have cited only the earliest examples and suffice us to say that the debate that started in early January 1999 continued well into June involving some of the Arab world's most prominent intellectuals. I will return to some of the most noted interventions shortly.

Concurrently, an international academic solidarity campaign was promptly launched by Magda al-Nowaihi, Professor of Arabic Literature at Columbia University, and Muhammad Siddiq, Professor of Arabic literature at the University of California Berkeley, in defence of academic freedom and liberal education. My dear friend and colleague the late Magda al-Nowaihi happened to be in Cairo as the *Al-Khubz al-hafi* crisis was beginning to unfold.[42] She was genuinely concerned for me and, before she left Cairo for New York, made me promise that I would keep her informed of how the situation developed. At the same time, I received a heartening message of solidarity from my colleague Muhammad Siddiq, who offered to host me at Berkeley should the need arise. As the crisis escalated and spilled over into the Egyptian press it became apparent to me that I would be incapable of weathering the storm on my own. I turned to both Magda and Muhammad for help. Together, they took the initiative to draft and post a letter on the internet against censorship and in defence of academic freedom, calling on colleagues to support me during this crisis and to defend the Arab literary imaginary.[43] I will for ever remain indebted to Magda's and Muhammad's resolute intervention, sustained energy and inspiring commitment that was to provide the seed for the spectacular international support I received. Sympathizers were asked to write individual letters to the AUC administration with copies sent directly to me. I still have in my possession some three hundred letters. I have also been forwarded many of the AUC administration's responses

Literature and literalism 241

to these letters by the authors themselves. The magnificent communal avalanche-like impact of this campaign went far beyond anything I could have possibly imagined. Letters came from colleagues, students, former teachers, former students, public figures and entire institutions and departments of Arabic Studies in the US, France and Spain.

Beyond this international communal support, I received daily sustenance and courage from Magda al-Nowaihi, with whom I was in contact on a daily basis. Magda was just beginning a study leave. She was busy writing and trying to make the most of the year before coming up for tenure despite the relentless cancer attacks that had besieged the beginning of her illustrious years at Columbia. It was a decisive moment in her career. Rather than focus on her research, she put herself in the eye of my storm and shielded me valiantly to safety. Magda gave me her study leave, with grace, with certainty and with courage. For six months, the span of the *Al-Khubz al-hafi* crisis, we were on email daily. We shared memorable moments of fear, of anxiety, of anger but also of laughter and of mischief. We were able suddenly to live the many dimensions of our long-distance relationship in a uniquely intense and intimate way: as girlfriends, as colleagues, as women, as mothers and as terrible children who were perhaps playing with fire. Magda managed the *Al-Khubz al-hafi* crisis: she responded to queries, replied to email messages, contacted various scholarly organizations and spoke to many members of the press community. Her letter of support for me during the crisis was deemed by the AUC administration itself "extremely thoughtful", "the most eloquent by far", of the many, many letters of support that were copied to me.[44] Despite the fact that the *Al-Khubz al-hafi* crisis was draining for both of us, it was also a most rewarding experience of friendship and of solidarity.

But beyond Magda al-Nowaihi's own pivotal role in the *Al-Khubz al-hafi* crisis, she was also instrumental in bringing the entire case to the attention of the late Edward Said, her colleague at Columbia University and a dear friend of my own.[45] Said's response was at once swift, powerful and discreet. On 28 January 1999 *Al-Ahram Weekly* carried an article by Said entitled "Literature and Literalism" in which he defended literary representation and the literary endeavour against dogmatism inside and outside the academy:

> there can be no civilized society in which the life of the mind is ruled dogmatically by laws of what is forbidden and what cannot be read. This is especially urgent in the case of universities where it is precisely the role (and the rule) of academic training to teach the young that the mind has capacities for investigation, criticism and inquiry that it would be a crime to stifle, abridge or forbid.[46]

Indeed, not only was Said's intervention a defence of academic freedom and freedom of thought and expression but it was equally a defence of the autonomy of the work of art and the necessary rupture between art and morality reminding us that modern ideologies of art from romanticism onward maintained that "[a]rt was supposed to be different from life, it was intended to subvert ordinary reality; it was created in order to be extreme, not to be 'normal'."⁴⁷

Ironically, the same issue of *Al-Ahram Weekly* that carried Said's defence of freedom of thought and expression also carried an interview with the AUC President in which he was questioned on the *Al-Khubz al-hafi* crisis and where his responses stood in stark "entrepreneurial" contradiction to Said's humanist position:

> I am sympathetic with the parents who are paying these huge fees, and then the child (*sic!*) comes home in tears and says "I have been given this book to read". You have to respond to this – you have to be sensitive ... [*Al-Khubz al-hafi*] has sexually explicit passages that are very offensive. I was offended when I read them. I couldn't read them aloud. The other one [Rodinson's *Muhammad*] was controversial.... But we are talking about two out of thousands of books. So, I don't think we have been significantly affected by the censor.⁴⁸

Later during the year, and upon the recommendation of an AUC faculty committee, Edward Said was awarded an honorary doctorate from AUC in June 1999. At the commencement ceremony Said delivered a speech that crowned the *Al-Khubz al-hafi* solidarity campaign in the presence of the graduating class, their parents, distinguished guests and dignitaries, the faculty, administration and the board of trustees of the AUC. In his speech, Said again defended liberal education and argued that if the academy were to play its role in the development of knowledge its inhabitants must be guided by the spirit of the traveller, not the sultan: "Most of all, and most unlike the sultan who must guard only one place and defend its frontiers, the traveler *crosses over*, traverses territory, abandons fixed positions, all the time."⁴⁹ On the global collective academic level, the solidarity campaign culminated in MESA's (the Middle East Studies Association that counts close to three thousand academic members worldwide) intervention through a letter sent by its Committee on Academic Freedom in the Middle East and North Africa (CAFMENA) to the AUC President with a copy to me.⁵⁰ This was followed by the CAFMENA letter to President Husni Mubarak calling on him to defend freedom of expression:

> Governments and universities share an obligation to society to work together in promoting tolerance and a diversity of viewpoints. The government of Egypt recently issued a commemorative stamp to celebrate the 50th anniversary of the Universal Declaration of Human Rights. We ask you to make operational the commitment contained in the preamble to the Declaration, in which member states pledge themselves that "every organ of society, keeping this Declaration constantly in mind, shall strive by teaching and education to promote respect for these rights and freedoms".
>
> This cannot occur when educators and students are denied the right to receive and impart information, and when the government capitulates to

intolerant elements in society and itself participates in silencing competing ideas. We ask you to take steps now to end official and state-sanctioned book-banning in Egypt, and thereby to affirm publicly your government's commitment to the rights of free expression and the free flow of ideas that are fundamental to a civilized society.[51]

To teach or not to teach: the battle within AUC

As friends and sympathizers at home and abroad made the *Al-Khubz al-hafi* battle their own, the faculty and the students at AUC remained divided during the crisis. Among the faculty who participated in the debate on the pages of *Caravan*, the weekly student paper, there were those who defended academic freedom and liberal education[52] and those who argued that literary works should respect the feelings and values of a given society and its culture, concluding, as had the AUC administration, that whatever cannot be read aloud should not be taught within the classroom.[53] Various versions of these two positions were also articulated during university senate and general faculty meetings. Student letters and articles in *Caravan* further echoed these two positions.[54]

I too was invited to participate in this debate by the AUC students' Philosophy Club on 3 March 1999. Rather than give a lecture or testimony I chose to use a literary text that I regularly teach in my introductory classes as a parable not just for the whole *Al-Khubz al-hafi* controversy but as a literary outcry from a courageous and committed Arab writer against various forms of oppressive institutional and societal structures and practices as well as a defence of freedom of (literary) expression. I retold the story of "The Monkey Trainer" by the contemporary Egyptian woman writer Salwa Bakr, where I read the rebellion of Ma'tuq, the monkey, against his trainer as analogous to the position I inhabited throughout the crisis with Mohamed Choukri's book.[55] The story is about a monkey trainer who tries to teach three monkeys tricks in order to exploit them and force them into a servitude that violates their very essence as monkeys. He does so initially by bringing a goat in front of them and asking it to perform the tricks he will later ask the monkeys to execute. When the goat fails, the monkey trainer beats it repeatedly and then ruthlessly kills it in front of the monkeys. The example of the goat leads two of the monkeys to submit to the trainer's order out of fear for their lives. But the third monkey (whose name is significantly Ma'tuq or "freed slave") takes the risk of disobeying the trainer and attacks him with his sharp claws. Ma'tuq is therefore deemed untrainable and is returned to the rockery at the zoo where the last image in the story is of Ma'tuq lecturing the young monkeys in the rockery on "the splendour and beauty of the forest, which they had never seen, having been born in a world full of rocks".[56] My intervention with and through a literary text was a deliberate riposte to all those who supported the censorship of literary texts and was actually very well received especially by the students.[57]

Since the *Al-Khubz al-hafi* crisis had already become part of the public sphere, the debate on campus in which the AUC faculty participated spilled over into the national and international arena. More than one AUC faculty member contributed to the public debate through interventions that mirrored the polarization of the faculty positions on campus with regard to teaching Choukri's autobiography.[58] Those positions were succinctly read and analysed by Richard Jacquemond in "The Shifting Limits of the Sayable in Egyptian Fiction".[59] Jacquemond basically made a distinction between the faculty who argued that the teacher must respect "the students' sensibilities", and those who defended or attacked *Al-Khubz al-hafi* on the basis of what he described as "a realist–reformist paradigm". In the former case, Jacquemond qualified the argument as:

> the democratic version of an argument which was usually presented in a more elitist way: students are deemed minors ready to fall under all kinds of bad influences.... One only has to replace the students by "the masses" – those eternal minors – to find oneself back to the elitist mentality that dominates the Egyptian cultural field as a whole. Because literary writing is only accessible to a small elite, it has the right to transgress, up to a certain limit, the norms set for the society as a whole. As soon as it gets read beyond those "happy few", reserve and censorship are *de rigueur*.[60]

As for those who inserted the *Al-Khubz al-hafi* crisis within the realist–reformist paradigm, Jacquemond rightly focused on the two most significant and diametrically opposed interventions: one by Ferial Ghazoul, Professor of English and Comparative Literature, defending *Al-Khubz al-hafi*, and the other by Galal Amin, Professor of Economics, attacking it as a work that violates not only our own societal and religious values but also those of any other society or religion.[61]

In her article "When the Subaltern Speaks", Ghazoul described *Al-Khubz al-hafi* as "a modern classic of subaltern autobiography", inserting it in a line of literary milestones that include St Augustine's *Confessions* and James Joyce's *A Portrait of the Artist as a Young Man*. Furthermore, Ghazoul established a parallel between Choukri's new-born literary and political consciousness in *Al-Khubz al-hafi* through the power of the revolutionary poetry of Abu al-Qasim al-Shabbi, to which he was introduced while in prison, and the new-born consciousness and "coming of age" of his country that declared its independence in 1956. For Ghazoul, *Al-Khubz al-hafi* is not a *succès de scandale* (except for a voyeuristic reader, as she argued in another intervention)[62] but rather, as she concludes in "When the Subaltern Speaks", Choukri's autobiography is:

> a tale of the subterranean in the city, a tale of utter dispossession and degraded childhood, and yet it is an inspiring narrative because it tells us that one can pull oneself from the gutters, and furthermore, how literacy and literature do uplift and upgrade.[63]

At the other end of the realist–reformist paradigm lay Galal Amin's attack on *Al-Khubz al-hafi* that triggered another debate led by the writer and journalist

Muhammad Salmawi, columnist in *Al-Ahram* and editor-in-chief of the French-language weekly newspaper, *Ahram Hebdo*, who in a series of articles in *Al-Ahram* critiqued Amin's moralist and moralizing position as one that trespassed academic fields of specialization and presented itself not as a point of view but as a definitive prescription for acceptable literary texts.[64] The very title of Amin's intervention – "Fasl al-maqal fima bayn *al-khubz al-hafi* wa *mawsim al-hijrah* min infisal" (A Definitive Demonstration of the Difference between *Al-Khubz al-hafi* and *Season of Migration to the North*) – already announced both an authoritarian and patronizing position vis-à-vis a whole academic field of study, namely Arabic literature and literary studies. Indeed, Amin's article incriminated Choukri's autobiography not on a literary but on a moralistic level and called for an all-out ban against it since, as he authoritatively declared, it violated the values of any society and any religion! According to Amin:

> A novel can be humanistic while describing theft, debauchery, drunkenness or drug addiction, but of course under certain conditions. The most important of them is that the hero, the narrator of the story, from whose perspective we see events and through whose eyes we judge them, must be fundamentally noble (…), intrinsically clean, however dirty the actions he is led to commit, despite his own will…. As a matter of fact, there is not, in the one hundred and fifty pages that constitute the novel [*Al-Khubz al-hafi*], the faintest indication that the hero is intrinsically clean … [He] appears to be a rogue, devoid of any positive attribute…. So what is to be expected from the reader except indifference and disgust?
>
> Indeed, you leave the novel in anger not because of the social circumstances that have led all these wretched characters to their fate but in anger against the hero and ultimately the author himself.[65]

Galal Amin's intervention in the *Al-Khubz al-hafi* crisis was particularly significant for several reasons. First, as Richard Jacquemond pointed out, not only is Amin a senior faculty member at AUC but he is "an intellectual in the grand Egyptian tradition, that is to say someone who intervenes regularly into public debates of all sorts, including literary ones".[66] This fact is indeed what allowed for the definitive, authoritarian, moralistic and archaic tone announced by the very title of his intervention that actually imitates the rhymed prose of premodern Arabic. Moreover, Amin's position is representative of the elitist "happy few" who seek to protect all those masses – the eternal minors, as Jacquemond called them – from a work that only he has the right and freedom to read and pass moral judgement on while forbidding it to all others who haven't read it! Finally, unlike Ghazoul's compelling interpretation of *Al-Khubz al-hafi*, Amin's unwaveringly damning judgement of Choukri's autobiography leaves us with Edward Said's crucial question "who is going to control the controller?" worrisomely unanswered. Indeed, in his early contribution to the debate surrounding the *Al-Khubz al-hafi* crisis Edward Said, one of the leading cultural

246   *The bounds of change*

and literary figures of the twentieth century, had warned against this "intellectual barbarism" as he called it:

> The whole point of educating university students in the liberal arts generally, and literature specifically, is to train them to read not just pious books about good behaviour, but all books, particularly those that are morally and intellectually challenging. What would become of literature if it was to be subjected to rules formulated by a committee of experts as to what can and cannot be read? This is more like the Spanish Inquisition than it is the curricular practice of a modern institution of learning.[67]

Terms of incrimination

In late 2002, almost three years after the *Al-Khubz al-hafi* crisis had subsided, Samah Idriss, editor of the distinguished Lebanese cultural and literary journal *Al-Adab*, invited me to write a testimony on the entire episode for the *Al-Adab* issue dedicated to censorship in Egypt. Ironically when the issue was published, it was censored in Egypt![68] Hence my testimony remained, by and large, unread within the Egyptian context. When I accepted Samah Idriss's invitation, I felt it was my duty to inform the AUC administration of the matter since I had decided to make the anonymous parents' letter against me during the *Al-Khubz al-hafi* crisis the focus of my analysis and my reading of the various levels of the crisis. I therefore scheduled a meeting with the one of the members of the administration, who, upon learning of my intention, reminded me that the letter was submitted by only two parents, i.e. it did not represent the view of the majority, and accordingly, warned me against making general statements based on this anonymous "minority" letter.

However, it was precisely this anonymous letter, written by only two parents, as the AUC administrator had said, that served as the incriminating document against me at the level of the Egyptian public sphere at large. It was used by several newspapers practically on a daily basis during the crisis. Indeed, several press articles had adopted verbatim the discourse and details in the parents' letter, thereby transforming it from a private anonymous discourse to a public collective one that ultimately raised a host of highly significant questions and issues. Among such crucial issues were the boundaries of specialized fields of knowledge and study, the location of literary production within society at large, the position of the academy and the concept of liberal education in a society where freedom of expression was becoming increasingly constrained, the relationship between power and knowledge and the tactics of surveillance and punishment that target creative expression, the whole notion of citizenship and the indispensable role played by the academy in elaborating its very foundations in a society that insists on treating its youth like children. Because of these vital issues raised in the anonymous, but public, parents' letter, I was convinced that this document lay at the very heart of the *Al-Khubz al-hafi* crisis. Hence my decision to read it closely in my testimony for *Al-Adab* more than three years after the end of the crisis.

It is important to note that the polarization of the AUC community at large

Literature and literalism 247

during the *Al-Khubz al-hafi* crisis was also reproduced within my own department, where I was accused by some senior colleagues of sexual harassment of my students.[69] This accusation, along with the letter of the Chair of Arabic Studies on 11 January 1999 in *Al-Wafd* describing my teaching of *Al-Khubz al-hafi* as a "solitary, individual case" in "some thirty years" of the Department's history, placed me in the heart of another battle with other, more senior colleagues or guardians of Arabic literature and culture within my own department. I came to realize that this crisis was not just about the complaining parents but rather that it was equally about power struggles and contests of knowledge within the academy itself and specifically within my own field of specialization, namely Arabic literature. Suddenly, given what had happened in my own department, I began to see that the *Al-Khubz al-hafi* crisis was not unlike Nasr Hamid Abu Zayd's in his own department at Cairo University where he was accused by one of the colleagues on his promotion committee of "clear affronts to the Islamic faith".[70] Subsequently, Abu Zayd was declared an apostate (*murtadd*) by an Egyptian court that annulled his marriage and ruled his divorce from his Muslim wife, a sentence that ultimately forced the uncomplying couple into exile. Given the sexual harassment accusations leveled against me within my department, I warned the administration against a repeat of the Abu Zayd scenario and demanded, and was granted, assurances of legal protection, should the need arise.

Indeed, when I was given a copy of the complaining parents' unsigned letter by the AUC administration, I was surprised to see that it contained entire sentences that reproduced, verbatim, the same struggles and battles that were already taking place within the Department of Arabic Studies.[71] It was then that I realized that the anonymous parents and some of my colleagues had united in their patriarchal interests and power against me and against an "other" vision of contemporary Arabic literature and culture. Suddenly, the unsigned parents' letter acquired a new signification since it actually articulated questions concerning the very essence of literature and the literary canon, ones that have yet to be settled within the Arab cultural field itself. For example, commenting on the reading list in my course which included works by leading writers such as Tayeb Saleh, Hanan al-Sheikh, Sulayman Fayyad and others, whose works use sexual politics at the symbolic level to gauge the complex relationship between the "East" and the "West", the self and the other, and the search for identity in a colonial or postcolonial context, all of which are questions that permeate modern Arabic literature, the parents stated that:

> Most of the books in the list are sexually oriented (we do not know why?). These books are talking about, Lesbians, Sexual betrayal and so on....
>
> But the disaster came when our children came to us shocked and astonished of the content of a story written by a Moroccan writer that the teacher is admiring very much (Mohammed Shookry). This story is far from the principles of Arabic literature, he is talking about his dirty life that is of no interest to any body.
>
> (...)

> Our children asked us if this is Arabic literature, we explained to them that we are as shocked as they are and we clarified to them that there are many Arabic writers such as Naguib Mahfouz, El Hakim, Anis Mansour (Ihsan Abdel Koudouss If she wants to be liberal) that are pioneers in the Arabic literature.[72]

In the anonymous parents' letter, literary works on my syllabus suddenly become ones that "would make [their] children sexually professional", and, in the case of Mohamed Choukri's *Al-Khubz al-hafi* in particular, "enough to corrupt a whole generation".[73] Not only do the parents deal with these literary texts at a *literalist* level but they reproduce Salah Muntasir's strategy in the Rodinson affair when he called for banning *Mohammad* on the basis of specific passages taken out of context. In fact, in their letter to the AUC administrators, the parents ask them to read specific passages, citing their page numbers. In addition, the anonymous parents further establish themselves as an authority on what should and should not be taught within a specialized academic discipline thus collapsing the distance between the academy and society at large, a distance that Edward Said had insisted upon in his 1999 AUC commencement address.[74] Indeed, the anonymous parents' letter was an attempt to dominate the academy and to ordain its mission aligning it to the values and mores of their own privileged class:

> Most of the sophisticated and highly educated persons are sending their children to AUC to get the best of the liberal education.
> (...)
> Please do tell this teacher on our behalf that the students of the American University in Cairo comes from good respectable, religious families (whether Moslem or Christians)....[75]

More seriously constraining, classist and exclusive is the extent to which the "sophisticated" and "highly educated" parents define, from their privileged vantage point, the very nature and face of Egyptian (and Arab) reality at large:

> [the teacher] thinks what she is teaching our children is a normal thing that happens in the Egyptian streets (This is what she told the students in class). I think it only happens in the street where she lives and between the people she is surrounded by.

Hence for these privileged parents, an entire underworld of wretched human beings, many of whom actually cohabit the same AUC downtown campus space with their privileged "children" (who actually work with these street children on a volunteer basis through many AUC student clubs and student organizations), simply does not exist. Theirs, as they rightly pointed out in the letter, is a "good respectable" reality very much like the reality of some of my colleagues in the department who deemed my teaching of *Al-Khubz al-hafi* a "solitary, individual

Literature and literalism 249

case" in "some thirty years" of the department's history. Indeed, the parents (who are not academics) volunteer in their letter an alternative "good respectable" reading list for my course. Tellingly, in their letter they consider the teaching of *Al-Khubz al-hafi* in English translation acceptable, once again echoing my own colleagues' position concerning the teaching of *For Bread Alone* (the English translation of *Al-Khubz al-hafi*) in another class at AUC:

> We knew that this same book is translated into English and is given in a seminar course to graduating seniors, no problem because the English language used was much more polite and the students are more matured and may be can accept such a thing in English, but I think that if the story was given in Arabic to more matured person they would have protested.[76]

Like some of my colleagues in the department, not only are the anonymous parents guardians of "good respectable" Arab literary texts but they are also the custodians of Arabic language itself and the limits of literary expression within it. For Arabic, from their perspective, is a "good respectable" language that should not be used to represent Mohamed Choukri's "dirty life that is of no interest to any body". Such a puritanical position on Arabic language, whether that of the parents or that of some of my colleagues, actually amputates a rich and seminal body of transgressive Arabic literary texts, both classical and modern, whose history attests to century-long heated battles over the limits and boundaries of creative expression.

Furthermore, it is instructive to note that, throughout the parents' letter, the AUC students – who are young adults – are referred to as "children" who need to be "protected" from the "harassment" of their teachers. This patriarchal and patronizing position vis-à-vis both the students and the academy itself is radically at odds with the whole notion of citizenship that perhaps constitutes the fundamental role of the university.[77] The sad irony, of course, was that the AUC President, to whom the anonymous parents appealed in their letter as a "father", in effect abandoned his position as the highest responsible officer in a liberal university and echoed the same paternalistic attitude towards the students.

Equally striking in the anonymous letter was the extent to which the parents threatened to deploy a host of surveillance and punitive strategies against the university should it fail to comply with their demands. First they called upon the surveillance powers of the patriarchs of Arab literature and culture: "the [male] heads of departments", who would be aided in their job as custodians of Arab culture by an arsenal of punitive laws which the parents did not fail to cite in their letter.[78] All this to "protect" the "innocence" of the AUC "children". Indeed, at the heart of the anonymous parents' concerns was their conviction that teaching *Al-Khubz al-hafi* was "enough to corrupt a whole generation". Behind this stated fear lies perhaps another, unstated one: that teaching *Al-Khubz al-hafi* may indeed constitute a radical change in one's awareness and understanding of the world. In fact, when asked about the importance of the text in Morocco on an Egyptian television programme dedicated to Mohamed

250 *The bounds of change*

Choukri's autobiography, the Moroccan writer and literary critic Saʻid Jilani described *Al-Khubz al-hafi* as a "revolution, especially for Moroccan youth".[79] Daunting as it is, this unassuming text can indeed be threatening, for, like all great literature, it seeks to create a new consciousness and a different relationship between reality and literary representation. Hence, the "sophisticated" parents had every right to fear Al-*Khubz al-hafi* for it unsettled *their* vision of reality and is indeed enough to "corrupt" (radicalize) a whole generation.

Finally, the anonymous parents' letter remains an important document that attests to the increasing commodification of education in Egypt where those who hold economic sway can dictate the kind of knowledge offered within institutions of learning. The very fact that this anonymous letter found its way to the AUC top administrators in violation of university affirmative action regulations is further indication of the extent to which the academy itself is implicated in this process of commodification.

Epilogue

After *Al-Khubz al-hafi* crisis ended Magda al-Nowaihi and I organized a panel at MESA 2000 on Censorship and the Arab Literary Imaginary with the participation of Richard Jacquemond (University of Aix-Marseille, France), Magda and myself, chaired by Shahab Ahmed who was then at the Society of Fellows at Harvard University after having been my colleague in the Department of Arabic Studies for two years. None of us on the panel spoke about the *Al-Khubz al-hafi* crisis. We had all lived it together very intimately throughout. It had become just one instance of the many other battles that needed to be fought. And Magda was ready for them all, having fought yet another of her own battles against chemotherapy just before the scheduled panel.

Magda was diagnosed with cancer in 1995 just as she was launching her brilliant career at Columbia and savouring the gratifying taste of her maturing family. She stood tall among us as we bent over in fear for her life. The world flocked to her side when she underwent her arduous bone marrow transplant in Los Angeles. Her friends literally arrived from the four corners of the earth to be with her. I called her then, from Cairo, with a trembling voice to ask about her. Her voice came back steady and strong. "I am well", she said. "I just worry about them", referring to the anxiety of the friends who surrounded her. To our immeasurable joy, Magda transformed this moment of potential death into a new life and emerged from this ordeal triumphant and radiant. But the cancer attacks were ruthless and Magda was destined for more battles.

After our panel on Censorship and the Arab Literary Imaginary at MESA 2000 Magda walked out of a full auditorium and said, "This is a book." She sat us down to coffee and commitments: list of contributors, areas to be covered, joint editorial work. When she volunteered to co-edit the volume despite her already very frail health I could not but grab the partnership. The fusion that was generated between us during the *Al-Khubz al-hafi* crisis was meant to continue. And so we began.... However, the work remained unfinished. This time Magda's health had to take precedence. But, to our enormous grief Magda passed away on 2 June 2002 after a long and courageous battle, leaving us devastated by her untimely death. I packed our call for contributions for the book and the abstracts we had already received. But I knew, deep in my heart, that Magda would not have wished it to be so.

In my tribute to her I had promised Magda that I would complete our unfinished work, but various circumstances have not allowed me to pursue it in the collective form we had originally intended for it. However, now that these pieces that I have mostly written after her death have been brought together in this volume, I can see that I have indeed been working, alone rather than collectively with other colleagues, and without being conscious of it, towards producing a very similar project to what Magda and I had planned. I would therefore like to think of this work as a fulfilment of my promise to her.

Appendices

Appendix I

Gamal al-Ghitani, "Sharaf Sonʿallah" (Sonallah's Sharaf/Honour), *Akhbar al-Adab*, 5 January 1997. My translation.

The appearance of *Tilka-l-ra'iha* and its immediate banning during the 1960s was certainly eventful on all levels. It marked the beginning of a new trend in the development of the Arabic novel that is deservedly led today by Sonallah Ibrahim; a trend that assimilates modern narrative techniques and a new neutral language devoid of ornamentation or excess. It was clear then that the writer was challenging both unwritten and uncharted prohibitions that had settled within the writers themselves, in what may be referred to as conventions (*ʿurf*). Even though the issues raised by *Tilka-l-ra'iha* may now be considered quite modest in comparison to the writings, in recent years, of the younger generation that continue to challenge prohibitions and dominant positions, still by all measures of its time *Tilka-l-ra'iha* was certainly a mark of considerable creative courage.

Thirty years is the distance that separates the appearance of *Tilka-l-ra'iha* and the publication, on the pages of *Akhbar al-Adab*, of the first chapters of Sonallah's latest novel, *Sharaf* which he has just completed three weeks ago. Thirty years filled with the publication of important works that are today considered milestones in the history of the Arabic novel: *Najmat Aghustus*, *Bayrut Bayrut* and *Dhat*.

The two most important features that characterize Sonallah's career can be summed up in two words: dedication and asceticism. Sonallah's dedication to literature is unparalleled: he has devoted his entire life to literature, abandoning every other work or job that he had occupied. He has lived at a minimal level of subsistence that would ensure persistence, without the ambitions that have contained or constrained numerous forms of expression and ultimately destroyed great talents, transforming some of our generation into traffickers and mercenaries. He applied himself to reading and writing in his small apartment, on the sixth floor in Heliopolis, keeping himself abreast of international cultural developments through his command of the English language, living with his small family in isolation, rarely appearing in the cultural events that crowd Cairo.

Despite this, however, Sonallah is forever sought out by every Arab writer, every Arabist who arrives in Egypt. He receives many invitations to world-famous universities and international conferences, some of which he accepts without ever seeking to promote his image, or boast about himself and the recognition he received, to the exhausted, worn-out reader, even though Sonallah is well deserving of recognition. He has never once appeared on Egyptian television, I think he has never sought to. However, I believe that this failing on the part of the media is an error that should be corrected.

Twice we travelled together: once to Algeria in 1987 and once to Tunisia in 1994 to a conference sponsored by the UNESCO during which I witnessed confrontations between the representatives of the UNESCO who wanted to impose an Israeli writer within a conference on Arabic literature, and between the late Emile Habibi whose loud positions in recent years have been quite disturbing for his admirers and Adonis who has an eye on the Nobel Prize. Sonallah's position was clear and firm, unblemished by any considerations that seek to court a prize, or an authority in France, or a ministry in the United States, or a university in England. Sonallah defended the values of Arab culture and the principles of national identity to which adhering has become a matter of sarcasm for some. Sonallah has a vision and a position that rejects the status quo in pursuit of a better future, and in this he is passionate.

Sharaf is perhaps his chef d'oeuvre, where he represents a whole age towards which he feels total estrangement; an estrangement that he audaciously and astutely expresses artistically and creatively. He does so with techniques which characterize his work alone, especially the documentary level which he transforms into pure creative energy, replete with black humour.

This novel will cause numerous debates and contradictory reactions, but I must say that it is the essence of an age and the vision of a great creative writer who moulded it powerfully. It is perhaps a hot beginning for 1997, one that confirms the firm stability of beautiful creative values in face of mushrooming phenomena in our literary life that warn of alarming corruption and the widespread fickle and facile values of traffickers (*tuggar shanta*). The same values we have come to know in the market and business world are creeping into our literary and cultural life, but here is not the place to elaborate on this. Hence the appearance of a new literary work by an established writer like Sonallah can only bring forth optimism and confidence and an inspiration for creativity.

Unfortunately, I have never been very close to Sonallah; we seldom meet, we call each other up sometimes. During my travels with him I have learned to appreciate his simplicity in everything and his contentment with what is on hand, and what is possible, be that with regard to food or accommodation; I have learned to appreciate his humour and sarcasm despite his visible depression and his hidden grief.

Sonallah's literary experience is naturally different from my own in both its orientations and its techniques, for this is the essence of creative work. He remains one of the few for whom I consider the appearance of a new work an event that merits attention and contemplation. What characterizes my relationship with Sonallah is the great respect that I have towards such a great writer whose work we are proud to present on the pages of *Akhbar al-Adab*. It is indeed an auspicious beginning for the new year.

Appendix II

Receipts for the purchase of *Al-Khubz al-hafi* from Roz al-Yusuf and Dar Saki, Cairo International Book Fair, January 1999.

Appendix III

My email letter to all AUC faculty.

MEMORANDUM
Sunday, 27 December, 1998.
To: All AUC Faculty
From: Samia Mehrez
Subject: Meeting with AUC Administration: Briefing and Questions

On Thursday, 17 December, at approximately 12:15 p.m., as I was teaching my ARBS 208 class (Modern Arabic Literature) in Rm. 203 at the Jamil Center, and just before the riot police started clamping down on AUC students who were protesting against the US/UK bombing of Iraq, a messenger from the administration's office appeared at the door to deliver the following message: "Please contact the administration *urgently* before your class at Ext. 5161." Since the class hour had already started, I put the memo slip aside, with the thought that I would finish what I had been saying, and then dismiss the class. However, within less than ten minutes another, out-of-breath messenger, arrived in the classroom. With the door of the room ajar, and in the presence of some 30 students, the messenger proceeded to reiterate the content of the written memo slip with some added details: "they are all waiting for you!" When I asked who "they" referred to, she let me know that the pronoun referred to the three highest AUC administrators. Needless to say, given the messenger's panic-stricken voice, the students' obvious bafflement, and my own rising misgivings, I abruptly stopped the lecture, and proceeded to the main campus, with a thousand possible scenarios for this unprecedented event in my 14 years of professional, academic life.

Once in the administration's offices, I found myself indeed surrounded by the three AUC administrators and another gentleman, to whom I was not immediately introduced, but was later informed is Dr X, the AUC clinic physician. Before us, on a table, lay a copy of one of the works I am teaching, this semester, in ARBS 208, in bound, photocopied form, namely *Al-Khubz al-hafi* by the Moroccan writer Mohamed Choukri (English trans.: *For Bread Alone*; French trans.: *Le pain nu*). I was told that we had an urgent and serious matter to attend to, that we were fortunate that Dr X was bringing the matter to our attention before it was leaked to the press, and that every effort must be made to resolve this crisis immediately. Dr X then explained to me that "two or three parents" had contacted him with complaints concerning the reading material that lay before us, on the table. According to them, this material constituted a work of pornography (two or three passages from the text had been handpicked, photocopied, and translated into English for the benefit of the administrators and lay, next to the text, on the table). Dr X added that the unidentified parents were certain that I was teaching a banned book, and were threatening to go to press, citing the passages that had been photocopied. Another scandal for the American university and one of its instructors!

I was then given the chance to respond. I explained to my audience that Mohamed Choukri's novelistic autobiography (*sira riwa'iyya*), as the subtitle of the text indicates, occupies a unique position in modern Arabic letters. Since its publication, first in English translation, by the well known American writer, Paul Bowles in 1971, then in French, by Taher Ben Jelloun, the distinguished Moroccan francophone writer, and winner of the 1987 *Goncourt* Prize (the French equivalent of the Booker Prize) and finally in Arabic, some ten years later, this work has risen to international acclaim. I also added that *Al-Khubz al-hafi* has been translated into several other European languages, and represents one of the most widely read books in modern Arabic literature, both in Arabic, and in translation.

I informed my audience that this work has been taught before in our university, both in the Department of Arabic Studies (in more than one of my courses), and in the Department of English and Comparative Literature. It is not a banned book. Indeed, it is available in downtown Cairo bookstores, and when used in translation, in other AUC courses, is available at our own bookstore. The fact that my students were using photocopies of the original Arabic text pointed, not to the legal status of the book, but to the small, and unreliable supplies in downtown Cairo.

I explained that *Al-Khubz al-hafi* was certainly not a work of pornography but, a very moving and candid tale of an illiterate Moroccan child of the underclass who accedes to literacy, at age 20, and is able to weave the appalling conditions of his life history into a mesmerizing text that is taught in universities all over the world, both at the undergraduate and graduate levels. I cited several names of distinguished Arab critics who have written, not reviews, but academic studies on this work in which they analyze the literary aesthetics of the text, its structure, its language, etc. (for example: Sabri Hafez, Professor of Arabic Literature at SOAS, England; Mohammad Barrada: Professor of Arabic Literature at Mohammed V University, Morocco). Among the many facts I forgot to mention, as I strove to rescue this literary text, is that Mohamed Choukri himself has been interviewed by AUC's *Alif: Journal of Comparative Poetics*, an interview that was later translated into English, and selected for an anthology of *Alif* articles entitled *The View from Within: Writers and Critics on Contemporary Arabic Literature*, published by AUC Press in 1994. Ferial Ghazoul and Barbara Harlow, the editors of the volume, describe its contents in the following terms: "articles that were selected for this anthology were not only deemed the best but also those that together constituted a representative sample of the current intellectual and literary debates of the Arab World."

As to the explicit sexual language in Choukri's text, I assured the administrators that I could probably be invited back to their offices on a weekly basis given the unconventional and contestatory nature of many modern Arabic works, both prose and poetry. I cited a long list, beginning with Naguib Mahfouz himself, and including distinguished writers like Yusuf Idris, Sonallah Ibrahim, Tayeb Saleh, Abdel Hakim Qasim, Hanan al-Sheikh, Ahdaf Soueif, Elias Khoury, Ahlam Mosteghanemi, Miral al-Tahawy, etc. I reminded my audience that the photocopied passages were handpicked, and taken out of context, and that if the same were to be done to any of the writers I had mentioned, they could all become either pornographic or blasphemous!

After having listened to this rather long but necessary defence, one administrator asked me to suggest a way out of the crisis. Since I had already read and discussed the text with my class, I simply could not think of a way out. So I asked the administrator for his suggestions.

I was utterly shocked to hear two of the administrators and Dr X express the following: one administrator and Dr X started by suggesting that I should apologize to my class for having assigned this reading material, all three agreed that I was harassing my students by exposing them to such a text, and finally, as I showed reluctance to comply with the apology scenario, Dr X suggested that I should inform my students that I will remove the Choukri text from the semester's reading list. It was the third administrator's protest against the suggested apology, and her articulate defence of the nature of literary texts in general, that allowed me to collect my thoughts and enter into negotiation over what I would be willing to do, to overcome this crisis. Since Choukri's text was assigned after the two mid-term examinations in ARBS 208, none of the students have had to write on it, as yet. Their final paper gave them the freedom to choose their own topic (in consultation with the instructor) and to select only two works out of eight, from the semester's reading list to write on this topic. What I would do is not reiterate that Choukri's text had to be one of the selected texts for the final paper (I had previously requested this of my class in order to ascertain that students have indeed read assignments for the latter part of this term. Those include works by Mohamed Choukri and Miral al-Tahawy).

We finally arrived at a consensus that the class was better left undisturbed. However, the administrators asked Dr X to relay to the parents that they had taken the necessary measures to contain the crisis, and that the teacher (myself) has agreed not to teach this book again (a statement I did not make), and that the administrators and I would be happy to meet with the parents (a suggestion I welcomed). After the meeting was adjourned, Dr X suggested we have coffee. We chatted further about the matter, he assured me that he was only trying to protect me, and that I should consider the matter closed. He would ring me that same evening, he said, to brief me on his meeting with the parents.

Dr X did not call me (I do have an answering machine). Saturday morning the Chair of my department rang me at home and asked to be briefed on my meeting with the administration to which he was not invited. Apparently the administrators had not contacted him, before, during or after our meeting. He later told me that it was Dr X who had called him, Friday night, at home to brief him on the Thursday meeting. I admit that I too did not think of calling the chairperson given the highly intimidating politics of the meeting, as far as my position was concerned. The Chair said he would discuss the matter with the Dean on Sunday, after the HUSS (Humanities and Social Science) Council.

On Sunday, after the Chair returned from the HUSS Council, he informed me that the issue was raised and discussed, at length, during the meeting, that the Dean had read the text of an e-mail message sent to her by the top administrator in which he communicated the outcome of Dr X's mediation. According to the Chair, the top administrator's e-mail message announced that the matter was closed, and that the teacher agreed not to teach this book again! However, the Chair informed me that the Dean told the Council that I had not made such a commitment.

Before I proceed to voice my concerns regarding the disturbing politics of this entire episode, I would like to make a series of statements. I am fully aware of the top administrator's critical position as the head of an American institution in Egypt. I am completely sympathetic to the complexity, at times impossibility, of negotiating the university's autonomy within a cultural climate that is increasingly stifling, if not deadening, not just for us, but for the Egyptian intelligentsia at large. I realize that the *Rodinson Affair*, and its continued repercussions are not a happy, or easy beginning for a new administration. All this I understand and admit. However, such *is* the job of the administrators at AUC who are at once bound, in their policies and practices within the academy, by an international academic community, as well as a host culture. Having said this, I wish to raise a series of questions:

260 *Appendices*

1   Why was my chairperson not rushed from his classroom, or his home to attend such a critical meeting, one that lasted for more than an hour, and had obviously been meditated, as can be attested by the photocopied and translated passages from Choukri's text? Why was I, a tenured member of this institution, treated as an isolated, delinquent, irresponsible individual when I serve within an academic structure: the Literature Unit within the Department of Arabic Studies?
2   Why did the administration succumb to the threats of two or three, unidentified parents even after I presented the case quite clearly and elaborately to them? Does not such a position undermine the credibility of the new administration's publicly stated concern for academic freedom, put forth in their first public address to the faculty? Does such a policy not call into question the integrity of the Liberal Arts education that we espouse?
3   Why didn't aides to the top administrator alert him to necessary academic, procedural measures to be taken in this situation? Or is academic terrorism a policy the administration is condoning?
4   How can top administrators of my university suggest that I apologize to my students when I have transgressed no university regulations or norms of academic conduct? Had I agreed to apologize, who would have rescued my credibility as an individual teacher and that of the entire faculty of the American University in Cairo?
5   Why did no one, from the administration, who so energetically went in search of me last Thursday, and who convinced me, through their behavior, of the utmost confidentiality, and volatile nature of the matter, not bother to communicate anything to me themselves since last Thursday? Why was the chairperson of my department, who was not initially party to all this, left with the task of relaying to me the outcome of the lengthy discussion at the HUSS Council?

The above questions are not related to our presence as an American institution in a host culture. These are questions related to the American University, in and of itself, as an accredited, academic, Liberal Arts institution. I therefore request an answer, in writing, from the administration, that would address the above concerns, for my own benefit, as well as that of the entire AUC faculty. Further, I would appreciate my colleagues' comments and input on this matter.

Appendix IV

To: AUC Faculty
From: Administration
Subject: Parental Complaint About Readings in an Undergraduate Course

Academic freedom and security are vital to the success of the University in fulfilling its obligations to its students and to society. It is in this light that the recent memorandum of Dr Samia Mehrez concerning the handling of parental complaints about sexually-explicit passages in a book assigned in our Modern Arabic Literature Course ARBS 208 should be considered. Unfortunately, Dr Mehrez has made several errors and omissions in her account of the meeting in my office on 17 December. It is not the administration's business to select readings in this or any other course, but it is my business to respond promptly to parental complaints, especially when they have the possibility of bringing new cases of censorship to the University. As Dr Mehrez indicates in her memo, I was informed that the book in question was a banned book being used illegally and that the parents were on the way to the newspapers to report this. No doubt it would have been better to postpone a meeting until a later date when the matter could be raised in the Department concerned. However, given the timing and pressure of the incident, I do not believe there was any good alternative to asking her to join the meeting already taking place and give us a correct account of the facts. While with hindsight we certainly should have included the Chair of the Department, this did not occur to any of us, including Professor Mehrez herself, at the time. We understand from her memo that Dr Mehrez felt intimidated by the meeting. It was not our intention to intimidate her but rather to obtain accurate information as quickly as possible. The absence of her Chair did not prevent Dr Mehrez from giving a clear and concise explanation of the book, its importance, why it was chosen, and the difficulty of avoiding sexually explicit passages in many contemporary Arabic novels.

On learning that the book was not banned, was a major work in modern Moroccan writing, and was not obtained illegally, the attention shifted to how to respond to the parents involved. I suggested that she should discuss the book in class, explain that some parents had objected to the book's use, and repeat the reasons for its selection, which had nothing to do with the salacious material contained in a small part of the book. I did *not* say that she should apologize for assigning the book but suggested she might do so for any hurt that had been caused. After some discussion we all agreed, including Dr Mehrez, *not* to recommend an apology or an in-class discussion, both because the book had already been covered in class and because it might imply criticism of the professor, which we wanted to avoid.

What Dr Mehrez has omitted from her account of the meeting was the fact, which she acknowledged at the time, that one or more students had already protested the use of the book and had allegedly been told to "grow up" and accept reality. The student had then gone to her parents who called other parents and eventually approached Dr X, a family friend, about what to do. Dr X agreed to bring the matter to our attention and seek a response. One cannot blame the messenger for delivering an unhappy message.

In the meeting, according to all four other parties present, Dr Mehrez stated that the book was *not* required in the course paper or on the final exam as all students had a choice of using two of the eight books. (She did *not*, as stated in her email, indicate that in fact the book *was* required to be one of the two books used in order to ensure that the students read the last two books in the course).

The others present and I all realized that the University could not withdraw a perfectly legal book from the syllabus of a University course. I suggested as a compromise that we request the instructor not to use the book in future and leave a decision on this to the instructor and the department. Indeed, relying on the judgement of its faculty can be the only policy for a university in selecting and approving what is read in its courses. At no time (including in my later email to the Dean) did I say that Dr Mehrez had agreed to withdraw the book. In her rush to recapitulate a long conversation, Professor Mehrez had missed the point of the conclusion.

This obviously won't be the last time we have to deal with outside complaints. How should we deal with parental concern about books (and other matters) arising in the University? I would welcome Professor Mehrez's willingness to meet with the parents concerned about the book and hope that we will have this opportunity. One suggestion has been to have an established procedure for receiving and responding to attacks and queries of this sort. Another is to restate at the beginning of every year both verbally and in writing the principles of a liberal arts education and ask parents to sign a statement before their child is admitted that they have understood that this includes tolerating unpopular, disturbing, or sometimes unpleasant views and opinions. I do not believe we can ask parents to forgo their rights to protest any aspect of their child's education, but it might help to forewarn them that they may object to some ideas to which their children will be exposed. While it is worth restating these principles, I think we have ultimately to rely on the individual and collective wisdom of our faculty to select and assign works that they believe are appropriate to the subject matter and to the society in which we live and work. This is a difficult balance to achieve but it is also what a liberal education is about.

Following the meeting, I asked the others present to work on a draft statement reiterating the University's policies of liberal education and explaining that we try to teach students to think critically about topics under discussion, including sensitive ones. When our faculty are subjected to criticism such as this it is vital that we defend them. In order to do that, we need to be able to consult them in order to get the facts straight. That was the purpose of the meeting, not academic terrorism, as Dr Mehrez has inaccurately stated. I can understand that she was offended by being called abruptly to consult. Had she accorded us the same courtesy of consulting before acting, however, the final outcome might have been better served.

Appendix V

My reply to the AUC administration's memo, 30 December 1998
To: All Faculty
From: Samia Mehrez
Re: Reply to AUC Administration's Memo to ALL Faculty

I have read the administration's memo to the faculty with care. I was reassured to see the administration's renewed commitment to both "academic freedom and security" and to the "policies of liberal education". I commend the administration for recognizing the need for "an established procedure for receiving and responding to attacks and queries" and hope that the University will move to develop, and implement such a *policy* as soon as possible.

Given this positive response from the administration, I do not deem it constructive to enter into further scenarios of "errors and omissions" concerning the two versions of the *Choukri* incident submitted to the attention of the faculty. I only wish to indicate that had the administration articulated its above commitment to me *during our meeting*, or during the ten days after the incident, I agree that "the final outcome might have been better served".

I would like to seize this opportunity to express my gratitude to all the colleagues who have stood by me during this recent crisis. The integrity they have shown, and the support they have given me (whether oral or written) have certainly been indispensable. I hope we can continue to work together towards a better future for AUC, the institution to which I am indebted for my own education.

Happy New Year to All

Appendix VI

To the Affirmative Office,
The American University in Cairo
Dear Sirs,

We are some parents of the students of the Arabic Literature class, the so called Modern Arabic Literature in Translation (ARBS 208), given by a so-called Samia Mehrez.

We would like to inform you that with great pain and shock we discovered that the respectable teacher is given our children who are minors (age between 16 and 20) pornographic stories that any mature dissent man can never read or allowed any person to read.

At the beginning of the Semester she asked them to buy these books from public bookstores like Madbouli and others but of course some of these books and especially the one called *Al-Khubz al-hafi* was not found.

We the parents did not give any attention to this because many books are sometimes not available, the teacher gave her copy to a store behind the University called Artistic that would photocopy to each student upon request. Most of the books in the list are sexually oriented (we do not know why?) These books are talking about, Lesbians, Sexual betrayal and so on. We said may be this is the liberal education that we hear about at the American University in Cairo.

But the disaster came when our children came to us shocked and astonished of the content of a story written by a Moroccan writer that the teacher is admiring very much (Mohammed Shookry). This story is far from the principles of Arabic literature, he is talking about his dirty life that is of no interest to any body.

The teacher asked some of the students to make oral presentation, some of them were very shy and asked their friends to read what they wrote, another male student apologized to his colleagues and told them he will try to be as polite as possible (imagine the students were shy and the teacher was happy seeing this expression on the faces of our children). Isn't this the sexual harassment that you are asking any person to write to you if he is facing it. What about if children are forced to read such things. *We are sending you herewith the book to read and we hope that you read it carefully, and ask yourself if this is modern literature.* We will make it easier for you and tell you about some pages that you ought to read. The pages (Pages 33, p 35, from pages 42 onwards and so on).

We are all very depressed and astonished of such thing at such a respectable well reputed University. Most of the sophisticated and highly educated persons are sending their children to AUC to get the best of the liberal education. And this is what they get. We knew that this same book is translated into English and is given in a seminar course to graduating seniors, no problem because the English language used was much more polite and the students are more matured and may be can accept such a thing in English, but I think that if the story was given in Arabic to more matured person they would have protested.

The same course is given in Arabic by another teacher but he is dealing with the characteristics of the Arabic literature and he is giving the students materials that would really help them to understand the Arabic literature, and not stories that would make our children sexually professional. In one of the chapters of the book the author is writing about his experiences with prostitutes in a very low abusing language. Is this Arabic Literature? If the teacher would defend herself by saying that it is some of the chapters and not all the book, *we believe that what has been written in some of the chapters is enough to corrupt a whole generation.* You have to know dear sir that our children had a psychic shock when they read the material and this in itself is an issue that if we want to raise and prove it we can sue the teacher, but for the sake of the University that we like very much we will not do so especially that one of the parents told us that he knew that the President of the University was shocked to hear the issue and as a father he promised to stop this teacher, but it seems the teacher is not given attention to any advise and as a corrupted person she thinks what she is teaching our children is a normal thing that happens in the Egyptian streets (This is what she told the students at class). I think it only happens in the street where she lives and between the people she is surrounded by. Please do tell this teacher on our behalf that the students of the American University in Cairo comes from good respectable, religious families (whether Moslem or Christians) because we do think that no religion in the world would allow such materials to be read by minors and teenagers. It is true that the semester is over and although our children had a psychic shock from what they read and were asking if this is *the modern Arabic literature*, we are writing to this office to investigate on the matter in order to protect the new comers from such harassment. Of course we do not want to say our names because we do not want our children to pay for refusing to be polite. May be some teachers who we do not know about are following the same system. We are not saying lies but we are saying facts, you have the book in front of you and you have the list of books that the teacher gives at the beginning of the semester stating that the book is an assigned one, that is they have to read it to be examined on it. If it was a recommended one, we would have asked our children to keep it away, and would have prayed to

God to punish this teacher but because it is an obligatory one we are writing to you because we heard about this new office that is very much concerned about sexual harassment. If you go back to the Caravan of the 20th of December you will find that one of the student wrote about the same class, and she was wondering if this is really a literature course. I think the girl was to shy and she wrote the article in a very polite way. It is very strange that no one gave this article any importance. The name of the article is 'Hurriyya am diktaturiyya' [Freedom or Dictatorship]. Is this the liberal education. We care about the new students in the coming semester if they are left in the hands of such a teacher. *Please do protect our children and the children of the Egyptian and Arab Societies from such persons who are attacking the innocence of our new generations. Make sure that the heads of the departments know the material taught and do not leave the teacher to control and destroy the minds of our children.*

We the parents are asking for whose sake is she teaching these materials and for what purposes is she stimulating our children. May be we are some parents who discovered this scandal and other parents have confidence in the administration of the University and in the conscience of the teachers and do not look on what books the university is forcing the children to read. What if the reputation is spread that the books taught at the American University are of this kind. I am sure that all persons will advise any one who cares about the future and the morale of his children not to let them join the American University in Cairo. *I think this professor is purposely destroying the good reputation of the American University. We were very proud that we have children at AUC and we were defending any one who would take about the disadvantage of the liberal education in our University, now I think that the least that we will do is that we will keep quite*

Our children asked us if this is Arabic literature, we explained to them that we are as shocked as they are and we clarified to them that there are many Arabic writers such as Naguib Mahfouz, El Hakim, Anis Mansour (Ihasan Abdem Koudouss If she wants to be liberal) that are pioneers in the Arabic literature.

We are leaving this matter in your good hands and hope that you do something about this matter and with this teacher, not for our sake because as we told you before the semester is over but for the sake of the coming generations and because it is your duty to protect the students against such actions. If we want we can sue the university and the Arabic department but we are not doing so, only because of the attitude of the President and his concern that we knew some friends of one of the parents.

Please do forgive us that we have written to you but you must know that most of the parents are boiling against the University and we were planning to sue the University for destroying the morale of our children and according to Egyptian law Qanun al-adab raqam 17 [law of public morality no. 17] we can do a lot, but when we knew about this office we thought of leaving the matter to you to take action against the teacher, if you think that we are right. But if you think that the teacher is doing the right thing and we have no reason to be angry, and that this is the liberal education, then we will go to someone who will hear us and I think that being in a culture that respects tradition and religion and morale we will find many responsible persons that will understand our problems and help us willingly, more over we will give a chance to the anti-AUC to play an important role.

Please do read the following pages carefully: 49–57 and 61, 66–67, 80–86, 93, 106, 121, 128, 131–139, 144, 147, 160–162, 167, 189, 215.

Appendix VII

My translation of the letter by the Chair of the Department of Arabic Studies sent to *Al-Wafd*, 11 January 1999.

With reference to Mr Muhammad Mustafa Shirdi's article published in *Al-Wafd*, Thursday 7 January 1999 concerning the teaching of the novel *Al-Khubz al-hafi* at the American University in Cairo I am honored to inform you of the following:

First: The curriculum in which this novel was taught, in one of the sections of this course, is described in the [university] catalogue in the following manner: "Introduction to modern literature including poetry, the novel, the short story and drama with a focus on the literature produced in Egypt". I think that this is a description to which no one can object. *If there has been one individual case that has transgressed this description in one section out of eight for the same course and over nearly thirty years* such a situation can happen in any other university. In fact it has happened quite recently both at Cairo and Mansura Universities. For example, at the former university Abdallah Al-Nadim's book *Al-Masamir*, which included explicit sexual passages, was taught. When the affair was discovered the book was withdrawn. At Mansura University one of the books taught was deemed inflammatory against our great writer Naguib Mahfouz, may God grant him good health. The university [administration] intervened and the book was withdrawn. Hence, such situations are not particular to the American University.

Second: It is not true that the university [administration] did not listen to the parents' complaints concerning the aforementioned novel, nor is it true that it refused to intervene under the pretext that "the professor is free in choosing his material" and can teach it the way he pleases, as was mentioned in the article. *The truth is that the university [administration] did intervene, and that the concerned department held several meetings where it was decided that books taught to new students in any course must be chosen by the instructors from a list of books prepared by the department for this course. This in order to guarantee that what happened will not be repeated.* [My italics]

Third: Most of the students at the American University are Egyptian; so are most of the professors, who are all eager, like Mr. Muhammad Shirdi, to uphold the values and ideals of their society. But we must remember that neither the American University, nor any other university can guarantee that what it offers will please everyone, all the time.

Thank you in advance for your prompt publication of this response.

Y
Chairman, Department of Arabic Studies
American University in Cairo

Appendix VIII

AUC Statement on the *Al-Khubz al-hafi* crisis
3 March 1999

The American University
Statement on Al-Khubz al-hafi

The American University in Cairo confirms the statement of the Minister of Higher Education, the Honorable Moufid Shehab that the issue of the use of a Moroccan novel, *Al-Khubz Al-hafi*, is being dealt with within the University. The novel in question has been sold in English, French and Arabic versions in Egypt since it was first published in 1971. Decisions regarding the curriculum are the prerogative of the faculty. The University relies on the individual and collective wisdom of its faculty to select and assign works that they believe are appropriate to the subject matter and that respect the culture and values of the society in which we work. Following complaints by students and parents about the book, the Department of Arabic Studies decided not to use it in the required introductory Arabic literature course. The faculty is also engaged in a serious and responsible effort to produce an agreed list of readings for core courses. No action will be taken against the professor, who is a tenured member of the Arabic Studies Department. The purpose of tenure is to protect faculty members from threats of intimidation and to ensure stability and continuity without which a university cannot operate. Egypt has a tradition of tolerance and scholarship that accounts for its intellectual leadership in the Arab world and AUC will continue to operate within that context.

Appendix IX

Magda al-Nowaihi's and Muhammad Siddiq's internet letter
(posted on Arabic Info, 25 January 1999)

Dear Colleagues,
Recently, Samia Mehrez, Professor of Modern Arabic Literature at the American University in Cairo came under attack for assigning to her class the fictional autobiography of the Moroccan writer Muhammad Choukri, *Al-Khubz-al-hafi*. This work is probably known to many of you as an important and powerful text that has been translated into many languages (into English by Paul Bowles under the title *For Bread Alone*).

Several students presumably complained to their parents about the "pornographic" content of the novel. The parents brought the matter to the attention of a family friend, who is the university physician and who, in turn, brought it to the attention of the President of AUC, presumably to hush up the matter discreetly and spare AUC adverse publicity.

On 17 December, while teaching her class, Professor Mehrez was whisked to the office of the President for an impromptu meeting with the President, the Provost, the Dean, and the said physician. In this meeting she was informed of the nature of the charge against her and of the desire of the University to hush up the matter by having her withdraw the book and apologize to the class for assigning it. Professor Mehrez, a tenured professor and a highly respected scholar of Modern Arabic Literature, declined to do either but expressed willingness to exclude the novel, which she had already taught, from the examination.

In the wake of this incident a public campaign was launched by some Egyptian newspapers to discredit Professor Mehrez and to embarrass the American University. One immediate consequence has been the removal from the shelves of the AUC Bookstore of works that are deemed by self-appointed custodians of public morality as injurious to good taste. Among these are: Sonallah Ibrahim's *The Smell of It* and Alifa Rifaat's *Distant View of a Minaret*. In addition, the committee for the core curriculum at AUC is now seriously considering removing al-Tayyib Salih's novel *Season of Migration to the North* from its reading list for this coming semester.

Meantime, the campaign against Professor Mehrez has grown steadily more vicious in the last few weeks, as she is being charged now with sexual harassment for assigning "pornographic material" to minors and forcing them to discuss it.

From all appearances, this is not merely a gross violation and infringement of the academic rights of one professor of Arabic literature, grave and unconscionable as that is, but a wholesale attack on the literary imagination and on the very foundations of modern Arabic literature. If it is allowed to go unchecked, this eager censorship will ultimately consign imaginative literature to the role of beautifying and consecrating the ugly reality of violence, oppression, and injustice that prevail, alas, in much of the contemporary Arab world.

We strongly urge all concerned colleagues to write directly to the President of AUC to protest the campaign of terror and intimidation against Professor Mehrez and to support the principles of academic freedom and a liberal arts education on which American universities stand, at home and abroad.

Please email and cc. to Prof. Mehrez at samehrez@hotmail.com.

If you prefer smail, the address is:

American University in Cairo,
113 Kasr El Aini St., Cairo, Egypt

If you need any more information on this matter, please feel free to contact either one of us.

Prof. Magda Al-Nowaihi Prof. Muhammad Siddiq
Columbia University   Univ. of California, Berkeley
605 Kent Hall
New York, NY 10027

Appendix X

Magda al-Nowaihi's support letter
22 January 1999

Dear President X,

I am writing to express my deep concern over the events unfolding around Prof. Samia Mehrez's teaching of Muhammad Choukri's *Al-Khubz al-hafi* at AUC. I write as a professor of Arabic Literature, a former AUCian, and, on a more personal level, as the daughter of a long-time Professor and Chair of the Arabic Studies Department at AUC. I strongly urge the AUC to fully support and protect Prof. Mehrez for the following reasons:

1   Professor Mehrez is without any doubt a first-rate scholar and teacher of modern Arabic Literature, highly respected and admired worldwide. When our students here at Columbia University contemplate doing a semester or year abroad at AUC, or are about to join the CASA program, one of the first pieces of advice I give them is to be sure and get in touch with Prof. Mehrez and to try and take a course with her. The reports from the returning students are always glowing.
2   Choukri's novelistic autobiography is neither an obscure nor a pornographic text, but rather a well-established classic of contemporary Arabic literature, translated into many languages, taught by many universities in classes on Arabic and world literature, and researched and analyzed by various critics of Arabic literature, including myself. It is true that the text includes unsavory details, and this brings me to my next point.
3   It is in the nature of serious literature, Arabic literature being no exception, to deal with sensitive and controversial subjects. Indeed, that is the source of its power. We all know that the Nobel Prize winner Naguib Mahfuz regularly populates his fiction with characters who question the existence of God and the value of religion. And a vast majority of serious Arabic literature deals with human sexuality with brutal honesty. To mention just a couple of examples from works by writers whose stature no one can doubt: Yusuf Idris routinely describes, in quite graphic details, incidents such as that of a child sleeping under his mother's bed and listening to the sounds ensuing from her sexual activities with her customers (liana al-qiyamata la taqum), or a mother and three daughters all knowingly having sexual relations with the mother's husband and their step-father because of the unavailability of another man (Bayt min lahm). Yahya al-Taher Abdallah begins his masterpiece *Al-Tawq wa-al-Iswira* by describing the incestuous desire of a sister for her brother, and her sniffing of his underpants and the sweaty armpits of his undershirts before washing them. He later describes how that incestuous desire gets played out in a sado-masochistic relationship between brother and sister. I can fill pages and pages with more examples of the explicit sexual details of many works of Arabic literature, but the point I want to

make is this: these writers are not including these horrifying sexual details in their works to corrupt their readers or tempt them to do likewise, quite the contrary. They believe, and they ARE right, that literature does not affect positive change in society, does not contribute to the making of moral human beings, by restricting itself to the portrayal of decent, law-abiding citizens doing good deeds. Rather, the role of a writer can be compared to that of a physician. Just as a physician, to heal the human body, needs to expose it and examine it in all its nudity and deal with its guts, blood, urine, etc, a writer must fully expose human society in all its ugliness and oppressiveness in order to move his/her readers enough for them to join the struggle to create a better world. Just as we cannot afford to deny students of medicine the right, in fact the duty, to dissect the human body, we cannot afford to allow students in the humanities to avert their eyes from dissecting human nature and human society in all its aspects and manifestations. The phrase "la-haya'a fi l-din" (there is no shame in religious matters) is routinely applied to the sciences by educators explaining to parents why their daughters, for example, need to touch male genitalia, and must likewise be applied to the study of the humanities.

4 My final point has to do with the AUC as an institution. I have always been extremely proud of my AUC education, and have been brought up on memories of my father's pride in belonging to that institution. I hope I will be able to continue to do so. Above all, what makes AUC occupy an important and special placed in Egypt has been its commitment to academic freedom and the principles of a liberal-arts education, which allows it to train young men and women not just to parrot information but to develop the capacity to analyse, to question, to examine critically – in short, to be thinking human beings. AUC, over the past few months and starting with the incident involving the teaching of Rodinson's book, has begun to renege on this commitment, and that is terrifying. Instead of adopting an apologetic tone and retracting, which will not, I assure you, appease its enemies, and may very well cause it to lose its friends, AUC must emphasize its strengths, of which there are many. It has graduated, both through the college and CASA, a large number of academicians and professionals who have, for one thing, served to improve the view of Egyptians, Arabs, and Muslims in the West. Its students are not, as some critics seem to think, a bunch of kids being brain-washed by Americans evidenced by the recent demonstrations of the students against America's bombing of Iraq. Young men and women come from universities all over Egypt (Tanta, Asyut, etc.) to use the AUC library and bookstore, which they consider havens for seekers of knowledge. Many AUC students volunteer in hospitals, orphanages, schools, etc., and they are fully committed to working with Egypt's poor and oppressed. The ironic part is that it is through their exposure to works like Choukri's that they gain knowledge and understanding of those less privileged then they, and this must be made clear to the public. I

urge you to support Prof. Mehrez and the values on which AUC stands – for her sake, for AUC's sake, for Egypt's sake, and for all our sakes.

Thank you.
Prof. Magda Al-Nowaihi
Columbia University

Appendix XI

Edward Said's AUC commencement address
17 June 1999

In every known society the academy, as Plato called it, was a protected, almost utopian place. Only there could collective learning and the development of knowledge occur and, as in recent years we have discovered, it could occur only if academic freedom from non-academic authority was somehow guaranteed and could prevail. It is an extraordinary thing to discover that the origins of the modern system of knowledge that we call humanism did not originate as Jacob Burckhardt and many others believed it did in Italy during the fifteenth and sixteenth century Renaissance, but rather in the Arab colleges, madrasas, mosques and courts of Iraq, Sicily, Egypt, Andalusia from the eighth century on. And in those places were formed the traditions and the curricula of legal, theological as well as secular learning – the so-called studia adabiya – from which European humanists derived many of their ideas not only about learning itself, but also about the environment of learning where disputation, dissent and argument were the order of the day.

For those of us who are of Arab origin and who in the modern period have got used to the notion that the West gave rise to modes of study, notions of academic discipline, and the whole idea of what in Arabic we call ijtihad, or the central role of individual effort in study and interpretation, it is salutary indeed to realise that our Arab–Islamic culture contributed substantially to what later was to become the whole system of education which today we call modern, liberal and Western.

I have very little patience with ethnocentrism of the kind trumpeted by Samuel Huntington and others like him who claim that all ideas of democracy, freedom and enlightenment are Western ideas, since the facts of history are, as we now know with reference to education, very mixed, very various, very much a matter of the contribution made by all humankind, all peoples, all cultures. There isn't a single source for anything: all peoples share in the making of history, all peoples make history. So let us agree then that whether we look to the time of Ibn Arabi or that of John Dewey we will find serious thinkers suggesting more or less the same thing, that the place of education is a special province within the society, a place where freedom of inquiry and thought occur and are protected and where – it must be said – the social and political context plays an important role by defining the limits and expectations of the learning process.

Yet the status of university or school as well as what goes along with them intellectually as well as socially is special, is different from other sites in society like the government bureaucracy, the workplace, or the home. To say that someone is educated or an educator is to say something having to do with the mind, with intellectual and moral values, with a particular process of inquiry, discussion, and exchange, none of which is as regularly encountered outside as they are inside the academy. The idea is that academies form the mind of the young, just as – to look at things from the point of view of the teacher – to teach is to be engaged in a vocation having principally to do not with financial gain but with the unending search for truth.

These are very high and important matters and they testify to the genuine aura surrounding the academic and intellectual enterprise. There is something hallowed and consecrated about the academy: there is a sense of violated sanctity experienced by us when the university or school is subjected to crude political pressures. Yet, I believe, to be convinced of these genuinely powerful truths is not entirely to be freed of the circumstances – some would call them encumbrances – that impinge on education today, influence our thinking about it, shape our efforts in the academy. The point I want to make is that as we consider these situational or contextual matters, the search for academic freedom becomes more important, more urgent, more requiring of careful and reflective analysis. So whereas it is universally true that contemporary societies treat the academy with seriousness and respect, each community of academics, intellectuals and students must wrestle with the problem of what academic freedom in that society at that time actually is and should be.

The best definition of a university that I know is by John Henry Cardinal Newman who in 1854 came from England to Ireland to establish what has since become University College, Dublin. He said: "A university has this object and this mission; it contemplates neither moral impression nor mechanical production, it professes to exercise the mind neither in art nor in duty, its function is intellectual culture; here it may leave its scholars, and it has done its work when it has done as much as this. It educates the intellect to reason well in all matters, to reach out towards truth and to grasp it." "Knowledge", Newman says in another place, is "something intellectual, something which grasps what it perceives through the senses; something which takes a view of things; which sees more than the senses convey; which reasons upon what it sees, and while it sees; which invests it with an idea." Then he adds: "not to know the relative disposition of things is the state of slaves or children; to have mapped out the universe is the boast, or at least the ambition, of philosophy", which Newman defines as the highest state of knowledge.

These are incomparably eloquent statements, and they can only be a little deflated when we remind ourselves that Newman was speaking to and about British men, not women, and then also about the education of young Catholics not of Egyptians or Arabs. Nonetheless the profound truth in what Newman says is, I believe, designed to undercut any partial, or somehow narrow view of education whose aim might seem only to re-affirm one particularly attractive and dominant identity, religion and authority. Perhaps like many of his Victorian contemporaries Newman was arguing earnestly for a type of education that placed the highest premium on English, European or Christian values in knowledge. But sometimes, even though we may mean to say something, another thought at odds with what we say insinuates itself into our rhetoric, and in effect criticises it. When we read Newman we suddenly realise that although he is obviously extolling what is an overridingly Western conception of the world, with little explicit allowance made for what is African, or Arab, or Latin American, or Indian, we realise that he says that education should map out the universe. Thus letting slip the note that even a British or Western identity wasn't enough, wasn't at bottom or at best what education and freedom were all about.

Certainly it is difficult to find in Newman anything like a licence either for blinkered specialisation or for gentlemanly aestheticism. What he expects of the academy is, he says, "the power of viewing many things at once as one whole, of referring them severally to their true place in the universal system, of understanding their respective values, and determining their mutual dependence." This synthetic wholeness has a special relevance to the fraught political situations of conflict, the unresolved tension and social as well as moral disparities that are constitutive to the world of today's academy.

But what happens when we take Newman's prescriptions about viewing many things as one whole or, referring them to their true place in the universal system, and we transpose these notions to today's world of embattled national identities, cultural conflicts, and power relations? Is there any possibility of bridging the gap between the ivory tower of contemplative rationality ostensibly advocated by Newman and our own urgent need as Arabs for self-realisation and self-assertion with its background in a history of repression and denial? Can the university survive as a real university if its governance and teaching mission become the objects of scrutiny and direct interference not of its teachers but of powers outside the university?

I think not. I will go further and say that it is precisely the role of the contemporary academy to keep open the gap between itself and society, since society itself is too directly ruled by politics to serve so general and so finally intellectual and moral a role as the university plainly must. We must first, I think, accept that nationalism, whether it is the nationalism of the victim or of the victor, has its limits. For those of us just emerging from marginality and persecution, our traditions constitute a necessary thing: a long deferred and denied identity needs to come out into the open and take its place among other human identities. But that is only the first step. To make all or even most of education subservient to this goal is to limit human horizons without either intellectual or, I would argue, political warrant.

A single over-mastering identity guided by a religious or secular authority outside the academy at the core of the academic enterprise, whether that identity be Western, African, Islamic, Arab or Asian, is a confinement, a deprivation. The world we live in is made up of numerous identities, numerous ideas, lives, philosophies interacting, sometimes harmoniously, sometimes antithetically. Not to deal with that whole – which is in fact a contemporary version of the whole referred to by Newman as a true enlargement of mind – is not to have academic freedom. We cannot make our claim as seekers after justice if we advocate knowledge only of and about ourselves, knowledge only that is approved by a team of referees who decide what can and cannot be read. Who then will referee the referees?

Our model for academic freedom should be the migrant or traveller: for if, in the real world outside the academy, we must be ourselves and only ourselves, inside the academy we should be able to discover and travel among other selves, other identities, other varieties of the human adventure. But, most essentially, in this joint discovery of self and other, it is the role of the academy to transform what might be conflict, or contest, or assertion into reconciliation, mutuality, recognition, creative interaction. Rather than viewing the search for knowledge in the academy as the search for coercion and control over others, we should regard knowledge as something for which risks must be taken, and we should think of academic freedom as an invitation to explore knowledge in the hope of understanding and perhaps even assuming more than one kind. We must always view the academy as a place to voyage in, owning none of it but at home everywhere in it. There can be no forbidden knowledge if the modern university is to maintain its place, its mission, its power to educate.

An altogether different challenge to the concept of academic freedom is found in national universities in much of the contemporary Arab world. I speak here generally of most of the large public universities in countries all through the area. Most of these countries are in fact run by secular governments. What is important to understand, however, is that with few exceptions Arab universities are not only nationalist universities, but are also political institutions, for perfectly understandable reasons. In Palestine, Birzeit and Al-Najah, for instance, have resisted Israeli occupation and preserved Palestinian identity admirably. Elsewhere, the Arab world which had been dominated either by Ottoman or by European colonialism, became independent after World War II. National independence for countries like Egypt and Syria, meant that young people at last could be educated fully in the traditions, histories, languages and cultures of their own particular Arab countries.

When independence was achieved as a result of anti-colonial struggles one of the first things to be changed was education. I recall, for instance, that after the Revolution of 1952 in Egypt a great deal of emphasis was placed on the Arabisation of the curriculum, of intellectual norms, of values to be inculcated in schools and universities. The same was true of Algeria after 1962, where an entire generation of Muslims were for the first time entitled and enjoined to study Arabic, which had been forbidden except as a language in mosques while Algeria was considered and ruled as a department of France. It is important to understand, therefore, the justified passion that went into reclaiming the educational territory for so long dominated by foreign rulers in the Arab world, and it is equally important to understand the tremendous spiritual wound felt by many of us because of the sustained presence in our midst of domineering foreigners who taught us to respect distant norms and values more than our own.

Yet it is also true to say that in the newly independent countries of the Arab world, the national universities were often re-conceived, I believe, as (rightly or wrongly) extensions of the newly established national security state. Once again it is clear that all societies accord a remarkable privilege to the university and school as crucibles for the shaping of national identity. This is true everywhere at sometimes too high a price. In the US there was a great deal of pressure on universities to benefit the defence department especially during the Cold War.

In the Arab world true education has often been short-circuited so to speak. Whereas in the past young Arabs fell prey to the intervention of foreign ideas and norms, now they were to be remade in the image of the ruling party which, given the Cold War, and the Arab–Israeli struggle, became also the party of national security and, in some countries, the only party. Thus adding to the vastly increased pressure on universities to open their doors to everyone in the new society – an extremely admirable policy pioneered in Egypt – universities also became the proving ground for earnest patriots. Political conformity rather than intellectual excellence was often made to serve as a criterion for promotion and appointment, with the general result that timidity and conservatism came to rule intellectual practice. Consequently not only did many brilliant and gifted people leave the Arab world in a massive brain drain, but I would say that the whole notion of academic freedom underwent a significant downgrading. It became possible for one to be free in the university only if one completely avoided anything that might attract unwelcome attention or suspicion.

I do not want to make of this occasion a long, anguished recital of how demoralised a place the Arab world, in most of its contemporary aspects, has become, but I do think it is important to link its depressed situation with the lack of democratic rights, and of an atmosphere bereft of well-being and confidence in the society. Political repression has never been good for academic freedom and, perhaps more importantly, it has been disastrous for academic and intellectual excellence when such things as book banning and censorship are practised. My assessment as I said, is that too high a price has been paid where political or religious passions and an ideology of conformity dominate.

The Image that must guide us in inhabiting the academic and cultural space provided by the university is that of the traveller and not the Sultan. Travelers must suspend the claim of customary routine in order to live in new rhythms and rituals. Most of all, and most unlike the Sultan who must guard only one place and defend its frontiers, the traveller crosses over, traverses territory, abandons fixed positions, all the time. To do this with dedication and love as well as a realistic sense of the terrain is, I believe, academic freedom at its highest, since one of its main features is that you can leave authority and dogma to the Sultan. Academic freedom is risk and danger. It means allowing oneself a few years where the conventions of society are suspended so that the search for knowledge can go on for the love of knowledge alone.

Notes

Introduction

1 *Al-Ahram Weekly*, 11 August 2005.
2 There are a number of books, some specifically on Egypt and others more generally on the Middle East and Muslim societies, that focus on one subfield from among the many that this volume will bring together. Some of these titles deal exclusively with the literary field, or the field of gender, or mass media etc., focusing only on Egypt; others are equally focused with regard the field of study but provide a regional reading of that field. None, to my knowledge, bring together the variety of cultural subfields (especially the literary field for long studied on its own) that this volume proposes. For example, Richard Jacquemond's *Entre scribes et écrivains: le champ littéraire dans l'Egypte contemporaine*, Paris: Actes Sud, 2003 (English translation: *Conscience of the Nation: Writers, Power and Society in Modern Egypt*, trans. David Tresilian, Cairo: AUC Press, 2007) deals exclusively with the literary field; Viola Shafik's *Arab Cinema: History and Cultural Identity*, Cairo: AUC Press, 1998, provides extensive coverage of the history of cinema and its relationship to identity politics in the Arab world, while her more recent book *Popular Egyptian Cinema: Gender, Class and Nation*, Cairo: AUC Press, 2007, focuses on the development of national imaginings of identity and gender through Egyptian popular cinema in particular; Lila Abu-Lughod's *Dramas of Nationhood*, Cairo: American University in Cairo Press, 2005), dwells solely on the politics of television in contemporary Egypt; Walter Armbrust's *Mass Culture and Modernism in Egypt*, Cambridge: Cambridge University Press, 1996, focuses on television, popular music, the press and cinema but does not provide anything on the literary field; Sherifa Zuhur's *Images of Enchantment*, Cairo: AUC Press, 1998, focuses exclusively on the performing arts in the Middle East, while Dale Eickelman's and Jon W. Anderson's edited volume *New Media in the Muslim World: The Emerging Public Sphere*, Indiana: Indiana University Press, 2003, explores how new media have reshaped the understanding of gender, authority and identity in Muslim societies; and finally Jessica Winegar, *Creative Reckonings: The Politics of Art and Culture in Contemporary Egypt*, Stanford: Stanford University Press, 2006, delves into the structure and politics of the art world in Egypt.
3 For a comprehensive study of the modernizing trend of political and social thought in the Arab World see Albert Hourani, *Arab Thought in the Liberal Age: 1798–1939*, Cambridge: Cambridge University Press, 1983; see also the contributions listed above.
4 See Jacquemond, *Entre scribes et écrivains*.
5 See Gregory Starrett, *Putting Islam to Work: Education, Politics, and Religious Transformation in Egypt*, Berkeley: University of California Press, 1998. Starrett provides an excellent reading of the development of mass education and the mass media in Egypt and how they have transformed the contemporary Islamic tradition, and

demonstrates that today's Islamic resurgence is rooted in new ways of thinking about Islam that are based in the market, the media and the school.
6 See for example the euphoric description of the tumultuous spring and summer 2005 on the Egyptian streets in *Cairo Cosmopolitan*, Diane Singerman and Paul Amar (eds), Cairo: AUC Press, 2006, pp. 3–8.
7 Examples of major scandals include the tragedy of the *Al-Salam 98* ferry boat that caught fire and capsized, causing the death of at least a thousand people in February 2006; the repeated train accidents throughout the 1990s, the worst of which took the life of three hundred people in February 2002; the contaminated blood scandal that erupted in December 2006 in which an Egyptian MP was implicated, to mention only a few instances of the state's negligence and corruption.
8 Samer Shehata and Joshua Stacher, "The Brotherhood Goes to Parliament", *Middle East Report*, 240, autumn 2006. Online. Available at: merip.org/mer/mer240/shehata_stacher.html (accessed 20 January 2007).
9 For a brief history of this transformation and the changes that the Brotherhood has undergone since it was founded in 1928 by Hasan al-Banna see Mona El-Ghobashy, "The Metamorphosis of the Egyptian Muslim Brotherhood", *International Journal of Middle East Studies*, no. 37, 2005, pp. 373–395. See also Joel Campagna, "From Accommodation to Confrontation: The Muslim Brotherhood in the Mubarak Years", *Journal of International Affairs*, Vol. 50, 1996. Online. Available at: www.questia.com/PM.qst?a=o&se=gglsc&d=5000396998 (accessed 22 January 2007); Ahmed Abdalla, "Egypt's Islamists and the State: From Complicity to Confrontation", *Middle East Report*, no. 183, July–August 1993, p. 29. For a more comprehensive history of the Muslim Brotherhood see Richard P. Mitchell, *The Society of the Muslim Brothers*, Oxford: Oxford University Press, 1969.
10 Shehata and Stacher, "The Brotherhood goes to Parliament"; on the Egyptian judges' mobilization see "Egypt: Investigate Election Fraud, Not Judges", *Human Rights News*, hrw.org. Online. Available at: hrw.org/english/docs/2006/04/25/egypt13269.htm (accessed 20 January 2007).
11 For details on the crackdown on the Muslim Brotherhood see "Egypt: Crackdown on Muslim Brotherhood Deepens", *Human Rights News*, hrw.org. Available at: hrw.org/english/docs/2006/10/24/egypt14433.htm (accessed 20 January 2007); for a profile of Isam al-Iryan, one of the most prominent figures in the Brotherhood's new generation, see *Al-Ahram Weekly*, 5 October 2000 and 20 October 2005.
12 For more on the Brotherhood's renewed plans to constitute a political party see *The Daily Star*, 17 January 2007. The Brotherhood applied for official recognition with the government as a political party on several occasions without success after its electoral victories in 1984 and 1987.
13 Maye Kassem, "Egypt: Politics in the New Millennium", *UNISCI Discussion Papers*, no. 12, October 2006. Online. Available at: www.ucm.es/info/uisci/UNISCIKassem12.pdf (accessed 22 January 2007).
14 See the *Daily Star*, 24 January 2007.
15 Ayman Nur's case is discussed in detail in Kassem, "Egypt: Politics in the New Millennium".
16 There are hundreds of articles and sites on the internet about the crackdown on Egypt's bloggers. See for example Issandr El Amrani's excellent website, *The Arabist* at arabist.net/ throughout 2006.
17 For more on the changing political economy in Egypt under Mubarak see Robert Springborg, *Mubarak's Egypt: Fragmentation of the Political Order*, Boulder: Westview Press, 1989.
18 See Pierre Bourdieu, *Homo Academicus*, Paris: Les Editions de Minuit, 1984.
19 Pierre Bourdieu, *Les règles de l'art*, Paris: Editions du Seuil, 1992.
20 Ibid., p. 302.

278 Notes

21 For a detailed discussion on the receding power of the Egyptian state during the Mubarak era see Springborg, *Mubarak's Egypt*.
22 The most notorious example of such policing within the academic world is Campus Watch (www.campus-watch.org), founded in 2002 by the pro-Israel, neo-con Daniel Pipes, Director of the Middle East Forum Think Tank in Philadelphia. Campus Watch was launched to "monitor" Middle East Studies programmes and specialists in the US and has posted "dossiers" and lists of "unpatriotic" scholars who are critical of US foreign policy and the Israeli occupation, inciting students in its "Keep Us Informed" McCarthyite section to participate in the witch hunt and to inform on their professors. The first "blacklist" included Edward Said, Joseph Massad, Hamid Dabashi, among others. As a gesture of solidarity, more than 100 academics subsequently contacted the Middle East Forum asking to be added to its "blacklist" of academics.
23 One of the classics on the changing role of the university is Bill Readings, *The University in Ruins*, Cambridge, MA: Harvard University Press, 1997; see also Sheila Slaughter and Gary Rhoades, *Academic Capitalism and the New Economy: Markets, State and Higher Education*, Baltimore: Johns Hopkins University Press, 1999, and Derek Bok, *Universities in the Marketplace: The Commercialization of Higher Education*, Princeton: Princeton University Press, 2004.

Prologue: Take them out of the ball game – Egypt's cultural players in crisis

1 The three novels are *Qabla wa ba'd* (*Before and After*), by Tawfiq Abd al-Rahman, a 61-year-old retired civil servant; *Ahlam muharrama* (*Forbidden Dreams*), by Mahmud Hamid, a 34-year-old civil servant in the Ministry of Culture; and *Abna' al-khata' al-rumansi* (*Children of Romantic Error*) by Yasir Sha'ban, a 32-year-old psychiatrist and journalist. For a reading of the three novels see Ferial Ghazoul, "The Artist vs. the Commissar", *Al-Ahram Weekly*, 25 January 2001. For brief interviews with the writers see *Al-Ahram Weekly*, 18 January 2001.
2 *Al-Hayat*, 11 January 2001.
3 *Al-Usbu'*, 25 January 2001. The figure quoted above is Abd al-Sabur Shahin, perpetrator of the legal case against Nasr Abu Zayd. Shahine filed to divorce Abu Zayd from his wife, on the grounds that Abu Zayd's textual criticism of the Qur'an made him an apostate, and hence unfit to marry a Muslim. Abu Zayd and his wife eventually relocated to the Netherlands to escape the second, unfavourable verdict.
4 Yasir Sha'ban, *Abna' al-khata' al-rumansi*, Cairo: GOCP, 2000, p. 233. My translation.
5 Ghazoul, *Al-Ahram Weekly*, 25 January 2001.
6 *Al-Hayat*, 13 January 2001.
7 Gamal al-Ghitani, "Faltarhal anta!" (Why Don't You Leave!), *Akhbar al-Adab*, 21 January 2001.
8 *Al-Ahram Weekly*, 25 January 2001.
9 For a detailed analysis of the era of Muhammad Ali see Afaf Lutfy Al-Sayyid Marsot, *Egypt in the Reign of Muhammad Ali*, Cambridge: Cambridge University Press, 1984, and Khaled Fahmy, *All the Pasha's Men: Mehmed Ali, His Army and the Making of Modern Egypt*, London: Cambridge University Press, 1998.
10 For an excellent study of the Egyptian literary field see Richard Jacquemond, *Entre scribes et écrivains: Le Champ littéraire dans l'Egypte contemporaine* (*Between Scribes and Writers: The Literary Field in Contemporary Egypt*), Paris: Actes Sud, 2003.
11 Ghazoul, "The Artist vs. the Commissar".
12 For a detailed account of the Haydar Haydar affair see Sabry Hafez, "The Novel, Politics and Islam", *New Left Review*, no. 5, September–October 2000, pp. 117–141, and Max Rodenbeck, "Witch Hunt in Egypt", *New York Review of Books*, 16 Novem-

Notes 279

ber 2000. Haydar Haydar (1936–) is a prominent Syrian writer whose novel *Walima li a'shab al-bahr* (*Banquet for Seaweed*) appeared in 1983, in a limited edition published in Nicosia. It received immediate critical acclaim and was reprinted several times in Beirut and Damascus during the following years. As Sabry Hafez put it, *Banquet for Seaweed* unfolds what is essentially a political obituary – at once mordant and poignant – of both communist and nationalist movements in the Arab world of the 1960s and 1970s.

13 *Al-Usbu'*, 30 March 2000.
14 Muhammad Abbas, *Al-Sha'b*, 28 April 2000. Abbas condemned *Walima li a'shab al-bahr* as the blasphemy of an apostate, meriting death, for a sentence in the novel that read: "In the age of the atom, space exploration, and the triumph of reason, they rule us with the laws of the Bedouin gods and the teaching of the Qur'an. Shit!'" In "The Novel, Politics, and Islam", Hafez explains that "[w]hat provoked [Abbas's] fury was the juxtaposition on the same page, and in the same line, of the last two words, despite the full stop between them, and the fact that, in Arabic, the second could not grammatically be a qualifier of the first. To present the passage as a calculated insult to the faithful, Abbas also had to ignore a reference to the whole utterance as "big buzzing words emanating from the demented mind of Mr Bahili, in the following paragraph", p. 133.
15 *Akhbar al-Adab*, 21 January 2001.
16 This policy posits that 70 per cent of the manuscripts published by GOCP in a given year must be written by writers from the provinces. Manuscripts from Cairene writers in excess of the allotted 30 per cent – regardless of quality – go on the "waiting list" until the quota of writers from the provinces is filled.
17 Salah al-Din Muhsin is a writer and publisher who was arrested on 23 December 2000 and sentenced to three years' imprisonment with hard labour on charges of "denigration of revealed religions" and "threatening social peace". The indictment referred to Muhsin's publications *Musamarat al-sama'* (*Lecture of the heaven*), *Mudhakkirat muslim* (*Memoirs of a Muslim*) and *Irti'ashat tanwiriya* (*Shivers of Enlightenment*).
18 *Al-Hayat*, 11 January 2001.

1 Dr Ramzi and Mr Sharaf: Sonallah Ibrahim and the duplicity of the literary field

1 Sonallah Ibrahim was born in 1937. He studied law at Cairo University and became interested in drama criticism, which he studied for one year. He wrote for various Egyptian newspapers until his arrest, with hundreds of other Egyptian leftists and communists, in 1959. Upon his release in 1964, he worked in a small bookshop in Cairo and eventually returned to journalism, first as a reporter in the Egyptian press agency MENA and later as director of the Arabic bureau, in Berlin, of the ADN (the press agency of the German Democratic Republic) where he remained for three years. After Berlin, he lived for three years in Moscow where he studied film directing. From 1975 to 1976 he was editor-in-chief of an Egyptian publishing house and since then he has dedicated all his time to writing. He has published novels, short stories, translations and youth literature based on natural science. He is author of *Tilka l-ra'iha*, Cairo: Maktab Yulyu, 1966; *Najmat Aghustus*, Damascus: Ittihad al-Kuttab al-Arab, 1974; *Al-Lajna*, Beirut; Dar al-Kalima, 1981; *Bayrut, Bayrut*, Cairo: Dar al-Mustaqbal al-Arabi, 1984; *Dhat*, Cairo: Dar al-Mustaqbal al-Arabi, 1992; *Sharaf*, Cairo: Dar al-Hilal, 1997; *Warda*, Cairo: Dar al-Mustaqbal al-Arabi, 2000; *Amrikanli*, Cairo: Dar al-Mustaqbal al-Arabi, 2003; *Yawmiyyat al-wahat*, Cairo: Dar al-Mustqabal al-Arabi, 2005; *Al-Talassus*, Cairo: Dar al-Mustaqbal al-Arabi, 2007. For a longer profile of Sonallah Ibrahim see Richard Jacquemond's Ph.D. thesis, *Le champ littéraire égyptien depuis 1967*, Université de Provence, 1999, pp. 449–460. For more on Sonallah Ibrahim's position in the literary field see Chapters 2 and 4 below.

2 Sonallah Ibrhim, *"Sharaf"*, *Akhbar al-Adab*, 5 January 1997.
3 See my discussion of the publication history of Sonallah Ibrahim's novels in "Sonallah Ibrahim and the (Hi)story of the Book", *Egyptian Writers between History and Fiction: Essays on Naguib Mahfouz, Sonallah Ibrahim and Gamal al-Ghitani*, Cairo: AUC Press, 1994; 2005, pp. 39–57.
4 Sonallah Ibrahim, *Dhat*, p. 5.
5 See *Egyptian Writers between History and Fiction*, pp. 119–146.
6 Gamal al-Ghitani was born in 1945 to a poor family in a small village in the governorate of Suhaj in Upper Egypt. The family later moved to Cairo, where Al-Ghitani grew up in Gammaliyya, one of the historic districts in Old Cairo. From 1962 to 1968 al-Ghitani studied carpet design and worked as a designer, a short-lived career that has had great influence on his writing techniques. For him, the technical elements involved in carpet design have inspired the way he develops the construction of his literary works. Al-Ghitani started his writing career in 1963 with the publication of his first short story, in the Lebanese literary journal *Al-Adib*. His career as a journalist started in 1968. Today he is editor of the literary section in Cairo's weekly *Akhbar al-Yawm* and editor-in-chief of the weekly literary paper *Akhbar al-Adab*. His literary production includes works of both fiction and non-fiction, many of which have been translated into several European languages. For a long profile of Gamal al-Ghitani's career see Jacquemond's *Le champ littéraire égyptien*, pp. 461–468; see also Chapter 3 below.
7 Pierre Bourdieu, "Le champ littéraire", in *Actes de la Recherche en Sciences Sociales*, no. 89, September 1991, p. 4.
8 Bourdieu, "Le champ littéraire", p. 6.
9 Bourdieu, *Les règles de l'art*, Paris: Editions du Seuil, 1992; English translation, *Rules of Art: Genisis and Structure of the Literary Field*, trans. Susan Emanuel, Stanford: Stanford University Press, 1996.
10 Bourdieu, "Le champ littéraire", p. 6.
11 Gamal al-Ghitani, "Sharaf Sonʿallah"; for the complete English translation of the text of al-Ghitani's editorial see Appendix I below.
12 Ibid.
13 Nada Tomiche, *Histoire de la littérature romanesque de l'Egypte moderne*, Paris: Maisonneuve et Larose, 1981, p. 130.
14 Indeed, Ibrahim who had been a political prisoner from 1954 to 1965, was made to appear before high-ranking officials at the Information Agency who interrogated him about the content of his pseudo-autobiographical novel, *Tilka l-ra'iha*, which exposed his own inhuman experience of detention among a number of other taboo issues. The manuscript was then taken to President Nasser to make him witness the level of "decadence" to which the communists had descended. For a more detailed reading of the circumstances surrounding the publication and banning of *Tilka l-ra'iha* see Mehrez, "Sonallah Ibrahim and the (Hi) Story of the Book", pp. 39–57.
15 Ibid.
16 Yahya Haqqi (1905–1992) was one of Egypt's most established writers, who at the time of the publication of Ibrahim's *Tilka l-ra'iha* was the editor of the literary journal *Al-Majalla* and had acquired a reputation of openness and sympathy towards the younger literary talents. In his introduction to the first complete edition of *Tilka al-ra'iha*, Casablanca, 1986, Ibrahim quotes a passage from Haqqi's weekly editorial in the Egyptian newspaper *Al-Masa'*, where the latter had attacked *Tilka al-ra'iha*: "I am still upset by this short novel whose reputation has been spreading through literary circles recently. It would have been worthy of being considered among the best of our literature had its author not slipped into error, out of foolishness and decadent taste. He did not find it sufficient to present us with the hero as he is masturbating (had it been limited to this then it would have been relatively easy to bear). No, he went beyond that to describe the hero's return home one day later to see the traces of

semen spilled on the ground. I found this physiological description truly disgusting, and it left such an ill effect on me that I could not appreciate the story in the slightest, despite the outstanding skill evident in it. I am not attacking it in terms of its moral aspects, but rather on the basis of its flawed sensibility and vulgarity. This is a shameful repulsiveness which must be checked, and which the reader must be spared from having to swallow."
17 Al-Ghitani, "Sharaf Son'allah".
18 Ibid.
19 Bourdieu, "Le champ littéraire", p. 6.
20 Al-Ghitani, "Sharaf Son'allah".
21 Ibid. Here al-Ghitani is referring to Sonallah Ibrahim's withdrawal from the UNESCO conference in protest over the unannounced presence of Israeli writers.
22 The "Triangle of Horror" is located in downtown Cairo and represents the centre for literary scandal and rumour besides political small talk and the literati's sexual chitchat and gossip. For a full description of the "Triangle of Horror" see Sonallah Ibrahim and Jean Pierre Ribière, *Cairo from Edge to Edge*, trans. Samia Mehrez, Cairo: AUC Press, 1998, pp. 14–16.
23 Ibrahim Abdel Meguid, "Amrika umm al-dunya", *Al-Arabi*, 23 December 1997.
24 For a more detailed account of Sonallah Ibrahim's refusal of the AUC Naguib Mahfouz Medal for Literature see Chapter 2 below.
25 *Akhbar al-Adab*, 12 January 1997.
26 Al-Ghitani, "Sharaf Son'allah".
27 Bourdieu, "Le champ littéraire", p. 6.
28 See "Sonallah Ibrahim's *Dhat*: The Ultimate Objectification of the Self", in *Egyptian Writers*, p. 130.
29 Tala'at Harb (1876–1941) is the symbol of Egypt's modernity and economic prosperity. He was a leading Egyptian nationalist and lawyer who was a major force behind Egypt's twentieth-century industrial development. With a group of like-minded industrialists in 1920 he founded Bank Misr, Egypt's leading financial and industrial establishment at the time of the 1952 revolution.
30 *Al-Arabi*, 20 January 1997.
31 *Ruz al-Yusuf*, 27 January 1997.
32 For a more detailed reading of this issue see Richard Jacquemond, "Quelques débats récents autour de la censure", *Egypte/Monde Arabe*, no. 20, 4e trimestre 1994, pp. 25–41.
33 In fact, the publication of *Sharaf* in the Dar al-Hilal edition with an appended long list of acknowledgements of sources and works relied on by the author in his novel, including Fathi Fadl's *Al-Zinzana* (*The Cell*), ended the debate about plagiarism that had accompanied the publication of the first five chapters in *Akhbar al-Adab*. See the complete list of acknowledgements in *Sharaf*, pp. 471–472.

2 Children of our alley: the AUC Naguib Mahfouz Award and the Egyptian literary field

1 *Awlad haratina* transports us into a timeless, symbolic *hara* (alley), where the successive heroes (whose life histories parody those of the successive prophets), all descendants of the imposing Gebelawi, re-enact the human struggle for meaning, knowledge, and social justice. *Awlad haratina* can also be read as a symbolic history of Egypt after the revolution. It first appeared in 1959 in serialized form on the pages of *Al-Ahram*, whose editor-in-chief at the time was Muhammad Hasanayn Haykal, the man responsible for transforming Egypt's leading daily newspaper into an intellectual fortress by inviting the country's leading writers and intellectuals to join its editorial staff. Even though Mahfouz himself offers us a political reading of *Awlad haratina*, the prevailing reading at the time was overwhelmingly religious. Before the

282   *Notes*

whole serialized version of the novel was completed in *Al-Ahram*, all hell broke loose! Several petitions were sent to *Al-Azhar* protesting against references in the novel to the Prophet Muhammad, and accordingly the sheikhs condemned the work as blasphemous and demanded that it be banned. The novel itself was never published in Egypt until Mahfouz's death in 2006, but it was published in Beirut and was sold underground in Cairo with Mahfouz's knowledge. The serialized version of the novel was never discontinued. Haykal, who was a close friend of Nasser's, made sure that it went on, despite the protests by Al-Azhar. After Mahfouz's death, *Awlad haratina* was finally published in Egypt by Dar al-Shuruq in 2006, framed by an introduction by Kamal Abu al-Magd and an after word by Muhammad Salim al-Awwa, both prominent Islamic intellectuals.

2 For an interesting reading of *Awlad haratina* and Naguib Mahfouz's position within the literary field in Egypt before its publication see Richard Jacquemond, "Thawrat al-takhyiil wa takhyiil al-thawra: Qira'a jadida fi *Awlad haratina*" (Revolutionary Fiction and Fictional Revolution: A New Reading of *Children of Our Alley*), *Alif*, no. 23, 2003, pp. 118–132.

3 Naguib Mahfouz, *Children of the Alley*, trans. Peter Theroux, New York: Anchor Books, 1996, p. 5.

4 From the Director of AUC Press, Mark Linz, in his inaugural speech that has later served as a basis for the yearly announcement for the deadline for submissions.

5 Over the years, several noted scholars have served on the Naguib Mahfouz Award Committee, namely the late Dr Ali al-Ra'i, Professor Emeritus and former Professor of Drama Criticism at Ain Shams and Kuwait universities; the late Dr Abd al-Qadir al-Qitt, Professor Emeritus, Arabic Department, Ain Shams University; Dr Ferial Ghazoul, Professor of English and Comparative Literature at the American University in Cairo, editor of *Alif: Journal of Comparative Poetics* and Chair of the Naguib Mahfouz Award Committee from 1996 to 2002, and Raga' al-Naqqash, a distinguished critic and writer in the Al-Ahram Institute. Currently serving on the committee are: Dr Abd al-Mun'im Tallima, Professor of Literary Criticism at Cairo University; Dr Huda Wasfi, Professor of French literature, Adviser to the Minister of Culture and editor of the literary journal *Fusul*; Mr Ibrahim Fathi, a distinguished literary critic; Mr Fakhri Salih, head of the Jordanian association of critics and deputy director of the Arab Writers' Union; Dr Samia Mehrez, Associate Professor of Arabic Literature at the American University in Cairo and Chair of the Mahfouz Award Committee, and Mark Linz, Director of AUC Press (ex officio).

6 Ferial Ghazoul, "The Phenomenal Al-Kharrat", *Al-Ahram Weekly Literary Supplement*, 13–19 July 2000.

7 Ibid.

8 Edwar al-Kharrat, *Rama and the Dragon*, trans. Ferial Ghazoul and John Verlenden, Cairo: AUC Press, 2002.

9 Naguib Mahfouz Award Committee citations, 1999.

10 *Al-Ahram al-Arabi*, 18 December 1998, p. 10.

11 *Al-Musawwar*, 4 January 2002, p. 34. Somaya Ramadan is referring to the many crises that have surrounded literary texts during the 1990s, including the stabbing of Naguib Mahfouz in 1994 because of his "blasphemous" novel *Awlad haratina* as well as later crises like that surrounding Haydar Haydar's *Walima li-a'shab al-bahr* in April–May 2000. See the Prologue above.

12 The Saudi King Faysal Prize was established in 1977 and first awarded in 1979; the Sultan al-Uways Prize is named after the Gulf businessman Sultan ibn Ali al-Uways and is awarded every two years since its establishment in 1988.

13 For a complete list of the translated works see the AUC Press catalogue.

14 The words are those of the poet Abd al-Mun'im Ramadan in *Akhbar al-Adab*, 23 December 2001, p. 7. The accusation that the AUC Naguib Mahfouz Literary Award and its panel of judges represent a literary reality of their own making that does not

reflect literary developments in the field was again levelled by the writer and journalist Ibrahim Farghali at the press conference held on 10 December 2006 on the eve of the ceremony celebrating Sahar Khalifeh's 2006 award-winning novel *Sura wa ayquna wa ahdun qadim*. Indeed, Farghali, whose novel *Ibtisamat al-qiddisin* (*The Smile of Saints*) is being translated into English by AUC Press, insisted that the panel of judges catered to "western literary taste" that continued to seek the "storytelling" aspect of Arab literary works when more recent texts (referring to his own novel, among others) have shown a tendency to be more "philosophical", an accusation that can be easily dismantled by the diverse literary orientations of the award-winning texts to date.
15 Sayyid al-Bahrawi, "Latifa al-Zayyat tarfud al-ja'iza" (Latifa al-Zayyat Refuses the Prize), *Akhbar al-Adab*, 5 January 1997.
16 Sonallah Ibrahim, *Dhat*, Cairo: Dar al-Mustaqbal al-Arabi, 1992; English translation: *Zaat*, trans. Tony Colderbank, Cairo: AUC Press, 2001.
17 For a long discussion of Sonallah Ibrahim's unique position within the Egyptian if not the Arab literary field at large, see Chapters 1 and 3.
18 I was informed of Sonallah Ibrahim's refusal of the Naguib Mahfouz Award in private, first, by the former chair of the awarding committee, then by Sonallah Ibrahim himself. Ibrahim's refusal of the award was eventually made public and repeatedly used in the press to attack the award and delegitimate it.
19 It is noteworthy, however, that al-Zayyat did agree to be interviewed in AUC's literary journal *Alif* and later signed for a reprint of that interview in *The View from Within: Writers and Critics on Contemporary Arabic Literature*, Ferial Ghazoul and Barbara Harlow (eds), Cairo: AUC Press, 1994.
20 Sayyid al-Bahrawi, "Ghiwayat al-jawa'iz" (The Seduction of Prizes), *Akhbar al-Adab*, 22 December 1996.
21 Ibid.
22 Ibid.
23 Naguib Mahfouz Award Committee citations, 1996.
24 Al-Bahrawi, "Latifa al-Zayyat Tarfud al-ja'iza".
25 See Abbas al-Tunsi, "Ghiwayat al-tufula al-yasariyya" (The Seduction of the Infantile Left), *Akhbar al-Adab*, 29 December 1996, where Tunsi responds to Bahrawi by critiquing his simplistic and dangerous attempt to link the cultural and the political and calling on him to abandon these "petty coffee-shop" battles.
26 Al-Bahrawi, "Latifa al-Zayyat tarfud al-ja'iza".
27 For a more detailed discussion of Sayyid al-Bahrawi and Ibrahim Abdel Meguid's debate see Chapter 1 above.
28 Ibrahim Abdel Meguid, "Raddan ala Sayyid al-Bahrawi" (A Response to Sayyid al-Bahrawi), *Akhbar al-Adab*, 12 January 1997.
29 Naguib Mahfouz Award Committee citations, 2000.
30 For the full text of this statement see *Al-Qahira*, 19 December 2000. The writers who signed the statement were: Salwa Bakr, Yusuf al-Qaʿid, Muhammad Gibril and Abd al-Fattah Risq. Another group removed their signatures from the statement; those were Ibrahim Aslan, Khairy Shalaby and Abd al-Al al-Hamamsy.
31 Mansura Izz al-Din, "Jannat Amrika wa jahimuha" (America's Heaven and Hell), *Akhbar al-Adab*, 17 December 2000.
32 Ibid.
33 Alia Mamdouh, "The Master of Writing: Naguib Mahfouz Award Address", 11 December 2004.
34 These comments are made by Muhammad Badawi, Professor of Arabic literature, literary critic and poet, and the poet Abd al-Munʿim Ramadan, in *Akhbar al-Adab*, 23 December 2001, pp. 6–7.
35 Naguib Mahfouz Award Committee citations, 1997.
36 *Al-Ahram Weekly*, 19 December 2002.

37 Abdu Wazin, "Al-Dhakira al-mathquba" (A Memory Full of Holes), *Al-Hayat*, 23 December 1998.
38 *Akhbar al-Adab*, 23 December 2001.
39 Shehrazade al-Arabi, "Laysat al-riwaya al-nisa'iyya al-ula fi l-Jaza'ir" (This Is Not the First Novel by a Woman in Algeria), *Al-Hayat*, 23 December 1998.
40 Mahmud Khayrallah, "Riwaya tahtaqir al-misriyyin wa tuhajim Abd al-Nasir" (A Novel that Treats Egyptians with Contempt and Attacks Abdel Nasser), *Al-Arabi*, 23 December 2001.
41 Abdu Wazin, *Al-Hayat*, 23 December 1998, p. 18.
42 Mahmud Khayrallah, "Ma'raka sakhina hawla l-riwaya l-fa'iza bi ja'izat al-jami'a l-amrikiyya" (Heated Battle over the AUC Award-winning Novel), *Al-Arabi*, 6 January 2002, p. 15.
43 *Al-Hayat*, 23 December 1998, p. 18.
44 Mahmud Khayrallah, *Al-Arabi*, 23 December 2001, p. 15.
45 Yusuf al-Qa'id, "Raga' al-Naqqash yafdah al-ilaqa bayna *Dkakirat al-jasad* wa *l-Walima*" (Raga' al-Naqqash Reveals the Relationship between *Memory in the Flesh* and *A Banquet for Seaweed*), *Al-Hayat*, 4 March 2001, p. 16; Wahid Abd al-Maguid "Ahl al-thaqafa" (The People of Culture), *Al-Hayat*, 11 April 2001, p. 18.
46 Khalid Isma'il, "Hikayat *Awraq al-narjis*" (The story of *Leaves of Narcissus*), *Al-Ahrar*, 8 January 2002, p. 4.
47 Shawqi Bazi', "Al-Ahlam ... al-munbahira bi nafsiha" (Ahlam ... Enamoured by Herself), *Al-Hayat*, 30 January 1999, p. 17.
48 Mahmud Khayrallah, *Al-Arabi*, 23 December 2001, p. 15.
49 On the reception and battles surrounding women's writing within the literary field see Chapter 7 below.
50 Naguib Mahfouz Award Committee citations, 1998.
51 Naguib Mahfouz Award Committee citations, 2001.
52 See Samia Mehrez, "The Map of Writing: An Interview with Ahdaf Souief", *Alif*, no. 20, 2000, pp. 168–181.
53 Edwar al-Kharrat, Naguib Mahfouz Ceremonial Address, American University in Cairo, 11 December 1999.
54 *Cairo Times*, 23 December 1999, p. 33.
55 Ibid.
56 Naguib Mahfouz Award Committee citations, 2003.
57 Khairy Shalaby's acceptance speech, American University in Cairo, 11 December 2003.
58 *Akhbar al-Adab*, 23 December 2001, p. 7.
59 The novelist Khairy Shalaby's comments in *Akhbar al-Adab*, 23 December 2001, p. 7.
60 The poet Abd al-Mun'im Ramadan's comments in *Akhbar al-Adab*, 23 December 2001, p. 7. Ramadan's list includes some of the most prominent names of Egyptian writers who had not been translated.
61 Ferial Ghazoul's comments in *Akhbar al-Adab*, 23 December 2001, p. 6.
62 On the politics of translating Arabic literature see Richard Jacquemond, "Egyptian Translation in the Postcolonial Era: From Acculturation to Cultural Decolonization", in *Rethinking Translation: Discourse, Subjectivity, Ideology*, ed. Lawrence Venuti, London: Routledge, 1992, pp. 139–158; Amal Amireh, Publishing in the West: Problems and Prospects for Arab Women Writers", *Al-Jadid*, Vo. 2, no. 10, August 1996. Online. Available at: leb.net/~aljadid/features/0210amireh.thml (accessed 3 April 2006).
63 Lawrence Venuti, "Translation, Community, Utopia", in *The Translation Studies Reader*, ed. Lawrence Venuti, London: Routledge, 2000, p. 477.
64 Mark Linz, Cairo International Book Fair, 2002.
65 See Richard Jacquemond, "Min asr al-nahda ila zaman al-awlama" (Egyptian Trans-

lation in the Postcolonial Era: From Acculturation to Cultural Decolonization), *Al-Adab*, Beirut, July–August 1999, pp. 47–50; Amireh, "Publishing in the West: Problems and Prospects for Arab Women Writers", and Magda al-Nowaihi, "Unheard in English", *MIT EJMES*, Vol. 4, Fall 2004, pp. 23–29.
66 For more on Alaa al-Aswany and *Imarat Ya'qubyan* see Chapter 8 below.
67 Gilles Kepel, "L'immeuble Yacoubian, un concentré des tensions du Moyen-Orient" (The Yacoubian Building Brings Together Tensions in the Middle East), *Le Monde*, 28 April 2006.

3 The big one: the intellectual and the political in modern Egyptian literature

1 Gamal al-Ghitani, *Al-Zayni Barakat*, Damascus: Ministry of Culture, 1974. First published in serialized form in *Ruz al-Yusuf* (1970–71); English trans., Farouk Abdel Wahab, London: Penguin Books, 1988 and Cairo: AUC Press, 2004. All quotations from the text are from the AUC edition.
2 Ibrahim Issa, *Maqtal al-rajul al-kabir* (*The Assassination of the Big Man*), Cairo, privately published, 1999.
3 Richard Jacquemond, *Le champ littéraire égyptien depuis 1967*, Université de Provence, 1999. A shorter version of the dissertation has recently been published under the title *Entre scribes et écrivains: le champ littéraire dans l'Egypte contemporaine*, Paris: Actes Sud, 2003; Arabic trans. Bashir al-Siba'i, *Bayna kataba wa kuttab*, Cairo: Dar al-Mustaqbal al-Arabi, 2004. An English translation is forthcoming from AUC Press.
4 Jacquemond, *Le champ littéraire égyptien depuis 1967*, p. 464.
5 Al-Ghitani, *Al-Zayni*, p. 182.
6 Ibid., pp. 232–233.
7 Ibid., p. 234.
8 Ibid., p. 235.
9 *Le champ littéraire égyptien*, p. 468.
10 For a more detailed reading of *Al-Zayni Barakat* see Samia Mehrez, "*Al-Zayni Barakat*: Narrative as Strategy", *Egyptian Writers between History and Fiction: Essays on Naguib Mahfouz, Sonallah Ibrahim and Gamal al-Ghitani*, Cairo: AUC Press, 1994 and 2005, pp. 96–118.
11 See Ghali Shoukri, *Egypte, contre révolution* (*Egypt: Counter Revolution*), Paris: Le Sycamore, 1979, p. 551.
12 On 26 February the censorship office in the information ministry informed *Al-Dustur*, which was also licensed abroad, that its licence to print and distribute in Egypt had been revoked. This move effectively banned the newspaper from publishing. The editor-in-chief Ibrahim Issa said that the reason provided for this extreme measure was the paper's publication on 25 February of a statement issued by the Islamic Group that levelled various unsubstantiated accusations against Coptic Christian businessmen in Egypt and threatened to kill three of them. In addition to publishing the statement, the paper cited former security officials who cast doubt on the document's authenticity. Censors did not object to the publication of the material; authorities acted only after the issue of the newspaper had been published. The Information Minister Safwat al-Sharif reportedly defended the action by citing the law governing foreign publications, which he said prohibits "distribution in Egypt of publications which slur religions, spread subversive ideas, or propagate the tracts of terrorist groups". The Islamic Group since 1992 has claimed responsibility for acts of violence by its armed wing that have killed and injured hundreds of Egyptian civilians, foreigners and police and security forces.
13 Issa, *Maqtal al-rajul al-kabir*, p. 321.
14 Ibid., p. 59.

286 Notes

15 For more on the Haydar Haydar crisis see the Prologue above, Sabry Hafez, "The Novel, Politics and Islam", *New Left Review*, No. 5 September–October, 2000 and Max Rodenbeck, "Witch Hunt in Egypt", *New York Review of Books*, 16 November 2000.
16 *Akhbar al-Adab*, 14 May 2000, p. 15.
17 Dr Saad Eddin Ibrahim is Professor of Political Sociology at the American University in Cairo and the director of the Ibn Khaldun Center for Developmental Studies. He was arrested at midnight on Friday 30 June 2000 and some of his documents were confiscated. At the same time another force from the state security investigation bureau raided the Ibn Khaldun Center and arrested two of the centre's staff. Dr Saad Eddin was charged with collecting funds without a permit from the official authorities, misappropriation of funds in a fraudulent manner to prepare forged voting lists and cards, co-operation with others to prepare forged voting lists and cards, preparing public media containing false phrases and rumours and disseminating provocative propaganda that could cause damage to the public interest, accepting funds from a foreign country with the purpose of carrying out work harmful to the national interest by producing a film (entitled: *Be a Partner and Participate*) that damaged Egypt's reputation abroad. He was released on bail on 10 August 2000 and was subsequently rearrested and imprisoned for one year before he was finally tried and cleared of all alleged charges against him.
18 *Akhbar al-Adab*, 20 August 2000.
19 *Akhbar al-Adab*, 14 May 2000.
20 *Al-Zayni*, p. 235.
21 *Maqtal al-rajul al-kabir*, p. 328.
22 Ahmad Abul-Wafa *et al.*, "Comeback Kid", *Cairo Magazine*, 20 October 2005, pp. 16–18.
23 Dream TV is primarily owned by the Egyptian businessman Ahmed Bahgat. Since its establishment in 2001 it has ventured openly into controversial topics both social and political and has become the target of state criticism and punitive measures. For more details on the controversies surrounding Dream TV see *Al-Ahram Weekly*, 7 November 2002.
24 See the interview with Ibrahim Issa in *Akhbar al-Adab*, 28 August 2005.
25 Ibid.
26 Ibid.
27 Ibrahim Issa, *Ashbah wataniyya*, Cairo: Merit, 2005, p. 325.
28 On 26 June 2005 a court in the village of Al-Warrak, near Cairo, sentenced Ibrahim Issa and Sahar Zaki, a journalist in *Al-Dustur*, to one year in prison for "insulting the president" and "spreading false or tendentious rumours", after they reported on an anti-government lawsuit. The court ruled on a complaint brought by the "ordinary people of al-Warrak" who were purportedly offended by an April 2005 *Al-Dustur* article reporting on a lawsuit brought in the same village. The suit accused President Hosni Mubarak and his son Gamal Mubarak, as well as the first lady, Suzanne Mubarak, and high officials, of unconstitutional conduct and "wasting foreign aid" in connection with economic privatization efforts. The court also sentenced Sa'id Muhammad Abdullah Sulayman, the man who brought the suit, to one year in prison. All three released on bail of £E10,000.

4 The value of freedom: the writer against the establishment

1 Sonallah Ibrahim, Introduction to *Tilka l-ra'iha*, Casablanca, 1986, pp. 15–16.
2 The complete text of Sonallah Ibrahim's speech was published in *Akhbar al-Adab*, 26 October 2003, pp. 2–3.
3 Sonallah Ibrahim, George Antonius Memorial Lecture, 9 June 2005, unpublished document, p. 3.

4 Ibid., p. 1.
5 Sonallah Ibrahim, *Yawmiyyat al-wahat*, Cairo: Dar al-Mustaqbal al-Arabi, 2005.
6 Ibrahim, *George Antonius Memorial Lecture*, p. 6.
7 For more details on the banning of *Tilka l-ra'iha* see Samia Mehrez, "Sonallah Ibrahim and the (Hi)story of the Book", *Egyptian Writers between History and Fiction*, Cairo: AUC Press, 1994 and 2005, pp. 39–58.
8 Ibrahim, George Antonius Memorial Lecture, p. 8.
9 Ibid., p. 11.
10 *Al-Ahali*, Wednesday 29 October 2003.
11 The al-Uways Award was established by a wealthy, independent arts patron from the Emirates. Some of the Arab world's most distinguished intellectuals have received al-Uways: Saʿdi Yusuf, Faruq Abd al-Qadir, Yumna l-Id, Gamal al-Ghitani, Alfrid Farag, Edwar al-Kharrat. Sonallah Ibrahim has argued throughout that he accepted always because it was an independent award.
12 Charles Levinson, "Outside the Barn", *Cairo Times*, 30 October 2003, p. 9.
13 *Akhbar al-Adab*, 13 February 2005.
14 For more on the Saad Eddin Ibrahim accusations and trial see Chapter 3 above. Ayman Nur is a former lawyer and parliamentarian who formed his political party in October 2004 with a view to contesting presidential elections the following year. Three months later, prosecutors in Cairo charged him with forging signatures to register the Al-Ghadd Party. He was stripped of parliamentary immunity and brought to trial. The government has rejected all allegations that the trial was politically motivated. His trial was delayed, enabling him to take part in the 2005 presidential elections. He polled 8 per cent – a result Nur alleged was rigged. His trial went ahead in December, delivering a guilty verdict and handing him a five-year prison sentence.
15 *Al-Multaqa*, 6 November 2003, p. 7.
16 Steven Negus, "A Rejection of Patronage", *Cairo Times*, 12 November 2003, p. 4.
17 Ibid., p. 7.
18 *Al-Safir*, 25 October 2003.
19 *Akhbar al-Yawm*, 25 October 2003, p. 17.
20 Ibid., p. 17.
21 Ibid., p. 17.
22 *Al-Akhbar*, 27 October 2003, p. 19.
23 Idris Ali, "Waqaʾiʿ laylat Sonʿalla Ibrahim min al-sufuf al-khalfiya" (Details of Sonallah Ibrahim's Evening from the Backseats), *Al-Qahira*, 4 November 2003.
24 The members of the jury who applauded Sonallah Ibrahim's speech were Mahmud Amin al-Alim, Ferial Ghazoul and Ceza Draz.
25 *Akhbar al-Yawm*, 25 October 2003.
26 Initially the Arab Novel Award was to be given every two years. However, when Sonallah Ibrahim rejected the award in its second round, the Minister of Culture decided to make it a yearly event in order to counter Ibrahim's snub quickly.
27 The internet version of the statement was sent by the Free Egyptian Writers Union, 31 October 2003.
28 *Al-Arabi*, 26 October 2003, and *Al Jil*, 4 November 2003.
29 Sonallah Ibrahim, *Amrikanli*, Cairo: Dar al-Mustaqbal al-Arabi, 2003, p. 46.
30 Hanan Samaha, "Word Play", *Cairo Times*, 6 November 2003, p. 29.
31 Ibrahim, *Amrikanli*, p. 476.
32 Sonallah Ibrahim and Jean-Pierre Ribière, *Cairo from Edge to Edge*, Cairo: AUC Press, 1998.
33 Compare, for example, the passage I quote in this chapter from Ibrahim's George Antonius Memorial Lecture about the beginnings of his obsession with newspaper clippings and Shukri's same obsession in *Amrikanli*, p. 79.
34 Ibrahim, *Amrikanli*, pp. 456–458.
35 Youssef Rakha, "The Smell of Dissent", *Al-Ahram Weekly*, 27 November 2003.

36 Wa'il Abd al-Fattah, "Indama yakhruj al-muthaqqaf an al-nass fi isti'rad al-amir" (When the Intellectual Improvises at the Spectacle of the Prince), *Sawt al-Umma*, 3 November 2003.
37 Ibid., p. 19.
38 *Al-Jil*, 4 November 2003.
39 *Al-Arabi*, 26 October 2003.
40 Ferial Ghazoul, "Son'alla Ibrahim wa jamaliyyat al-irbak" (Sonallah Ibrahim and the Poetics of Confusion), *Akhbar al-Adab*, 9 November 2003.
41 *Al-Arabi*, 2 November 2003.
42 See Samia Mehrez, "Sonallah Ibrahim's *Dhat*: The Ultimate Objectification of the Self", *Egyptian Writers between History and Fiction*, pp. 119–120.
43 Youssef Rakha, "The Smell of Dissent", *Al-Ahram Weekly*, 27 November 2003.
44 *Al-Arabi*, 2 November 2003.
45 For more details on Ibrahim's *Sharaf* see Chapter 1 above.
46 *Akhbar al-Yawm*, 25 October 2003, p. 17. Later, in *Al-Hayat*, 6 November 2003, the Minister of Culture denied that he had used the words "discipline and reform".
47 *Akhbar al-Adab*, 2 November 2003.
48 Ibid.
49 *Al-Hayat*, 6 November 2003. More recently during a lecture in Bahrain, the Minister of Culture reiterated the same position, declaring that since his tenure he has tried to "politicize the cultural", *Al-Hayat*, 26 January 2006.
50 *Al-Arabi*, 2 November 2003.
51 Edward Said, *Representations of the Intellectual: The 1993 Reith Lectures*, New York, Pantheon Books, 1994, p. 89.

5 Lost in globalization: education and the stranded Egyptian elite

1 Edward W. Said, "Commencement Address", American University in Cairo, 17 June 1999.
2 Ibid., p. 5.
3 Ibid., p. 5.
4 Ibid., p. 10.
5 Ibid., p. 12.
6 Ibid., p. 13.
7 See Edward Said, *Out of Place*, New York: Alfred A. Knopf, 1999, pp. 38–46 and 179–193.
8 I am referring specifically to the Maxime Rodinson crisis of May 1998 and the *Al-Kubz al-hafi* crisis of December 1998 at the American University in Cairo, both of which are discussed in detail in Chapter 12.
9 Lawrence R. Murphy, *The American University in Cairo*, Cairo: AUC Press, 1987, p. 6.
10 Donald Malcolm Reid, *Cairo University and the Making of Modern Egypt*, Cairo: AUC Press, 1990, pp. 23–24.
11 Ibid., p. 164.
12 Ibid., pp. 164–165.
13 Bassam Tibi, *Arab Nationalism: A Critical Enquiry*, edited and translated by Marion Farouk-Sluglett and Peter Sluglett, London: Macmillan, 1981, p. 74.
14 See *The American University in Cairo Catalog: 1989–1990*, p. 13.
15 Murphy, *The American University in Cairo*, p. 172.
16 Al-Azhar University, which is considered the bastion of Islamic knowledge in Egypt, was founded in AD 970. The Al-Azhar system, which maintains separate facilities for male and female students from primary to university level, enrols 4 per cent of the country's total students, In order to be admitted to the Al-Azhar University system, students must hold a Secondary School Certificate from the Al-Azhar education

system and a Certificate of Qur'an Recitation from a Qur'an Recitation Institute or hold an Al-Azhar diploma.
17 For more on the notions of "order" and "disorder" that permeated practically all the aspects of "modernizing" and colonizing Egypt throughout the nineteenth century, from the surveillance and control of agricultural wealth in Egyptian villages to the nineteenth-century concept of *"tarbiya"* (education) and the actual physical transformations of the city of Cairo, see Timothy Mitchell, *Colonizing Egypt*, Cairo: AUC Press, 1988, pp. 63–127. Mitchell complicates the notion of "disorder" associated with Al-Azhar, for unlike modern pedagogical strategies organized around the group, traditional religious teaching was based on the individual relationship between master and student and therefore offered an alternative form of order that has sustained this pre-modern institutional learning (pp. 80–81). For more on Muhammad Ali's educational policies see Afaf Lutfy Al-Sayyid Marsot, *Egypt in the Reign of Muhammad Ali*, Cambridge: Cambridge University Press, 1984, and Khaled Fahmy, *All the Pasha's Men: Mehmed Ali, His Army and the Making of Modern Egypt*, London: Cambridge University Press, 1998 see also Omnia Shakry, "Schooled Mothers and Structured Play: Child Rearing in Turn-of-the-Century Egypt", and Khaled Fahmy, "Women, Medicine, and Power in Nineteenth-Century Egypt", in *Remaking Women: Feminism and Modernity in the Middle East*, Lila Abu-Lughod (ed.), Cairo: AUC Press, 1998, pp. 126–170 and 35–72 respectively.
18 See Reid, *Cairo University*, p. 164.
19 Mohsen Elmahdy Said, Country Higher Education Profiles: Egypt. Online. Available at: tp:// (accessed 4 April 2006).
20 Reid, *Cairo University*, p. 12.
21 For a detailed account of the various restrictions on the autonomy of Cairo University and the different laws that control the academy and academic freedom see Reid, Cairo University, pp. 169–173; Muhammad Abul-Ghar, *Ihdar istiqlal al-jami'at*, Cairo, 2001, Ra'uf Abbas, *Mashaynaha khutan*, Cairo: Dar al-Hilal, 2004, and Ahmed Abdallah, *The Student Movement and National Politics in Egypt*, London: Al-Saqi, 1985. The first two are personal accounts of the history of Cairo University by two of its faculty: Abul-Ghar teaches in Cairo University's Medical School and Ra'uf Abbas is in the Department of History, Faculty of Letters, Cairo University; Ahmed Abdallah was a leader of the student movement in Egypt during the 1970s. See also *Reading between the "Red Lines": The Repression of Academic Freedom in Egyptian Universities*, Human Rights Watch, Vol. 17, no. 6 (E). Online. Available at: hrw.org/reports/2005/egypt0605/ (accessed 10 April 2006).
22 Reid, *Cairo University*, p. 171.
23 Ibid.
24 Ibid., pp. 169–170.
25 Reid, p. 189.
26 Ibid., p. 175.
27 The figures are according to *A Brief Description of the Higher Education System in Egypt*, a country profile in progress report on Egypt, p. 2. Online. Available at: www.gse.buffalo.edu/org/IntHigherEdFinance/Egypt.pdf (accessed 25 April 2006).
28 See the UNDP Arab Fund for Economic and Social Development, *Arab Human Development Report 2003: Building a Knowledge Society*, New York: United Nations Publications, 2003. The UNDP *Arab Human Development Report* of 2003 focuses on the decline in the quality of national education, citing insufficient sources, lack of policies and vision, poor curricula, absence of modern methodologies, and poor educators' working conditions, among other things, p. 52.
29 See the World Bank's *Arab Republic of Egypt Higher Education Enhancement Project* (HEEP) 2002. Online. Available at: wds.worldbank.org/servlet/WDSContentServer/WDSP/IB/2002/04/12/000094946_02033004305220/Rendered/PDF/multi0page.pdf (accessed 12 January 2007).

290 Notes

30 Except for elite faculties such as the Faculty of Medicine, the Faculty of Political Science and the foreign language sections in the Faculty of Letters.
31 *Al-Ahram Weekly*, 1 July 2004.
32 Ibid.
33 Ibid.
34 See Leadership for Education and Development Program (LEAD) description on the AUC website www.aucegypt.edu. Online. Available at: www.aucegypt.edu/students/lead/about.htm (accessed 4 June 2006).
35 Ibid.
36 Yasir Suleiman, "Introduction", *Arabic Sociolinguistics: Issues and Perspectives*, Yasir Soleiman (ed.), Richmond: Curzon Press, 1994, p. 1.
37 Ibid., p. 8.
38 *Arab Human Development Report* (AHDR), p. 125.
39 See Arabic text of the ALESCO report at . Available at: www.aticm.org.eg/admin/Farek_kema/REPAWSIS17%D8%B1%D8%B6%D8%A7.doc (accessed 10 June 2006).
40 Niloofar Haeri, "Introduction", *Sacred Language Ordinary People*, London: Palgrave Macmillan, 2003, p. 5.
41 Niloofar Haeri, "Arabs Need to Find Their Tongue", *Guardian*, 14 June 2003.
42 Ibid.
43 Quoted in Haeri, "Introduction", *Sacred Language Ordinary People*, p. 10.
44 Ibid., p. 3.
45 Benedict Anderson, *Imagined Communities*, London and New York: Verso, 1983.
46 Fatma H. Sayed, *Transforming Education: Western Influence and Domestic Policy Reform*, Cairo: AUC Press, 2006, p. 27.
47 Ibid., p. 29.
48 *Arab Human Development Report*, p. 53.
49 See Sayed, *Transforming Education*, p. 3.
50 Ibid., pp. 9–22.
51 In *Transforming Education* Sayed states that, given the political sensitivity of the rise of Islamic fundamentalism in Egypt, foreign development assistance has never acknowledged or publicized it as a formal objective of its educational development programmes (p. 34).
52 G. Starrett, *Putting Islam to Work: Education, Politics, and Religious Transformation in Egypt*, Berkeley: University of California Press, 1998, p. 199.
53 Ibid., p. 199.
54 Ibid., p. 3.
55 Ibid., p. 221.
56 Sayed, *Transforming Education*, p. 2.
57 Nancy Beth Jackson, "Despite Barriers, Private Schools Gain in Egypt", *Herald Tribune*, 16 February 1994. See also Karim Alrawi, "The War on Education: The Devil or the Dustbowl", *New Internationalist*, 248, October 1993. Online. Available at: www.newint.org/issue248/devil.htm (accessed 10 January 2006).
58 Sayed, *Transforming Education*, pp. 33–34.
59 For more on Islamic schools and dress within the educational system in Egypt see Linda Herrera, "Downveiling: Gender and the Contest over Culture in Cairo", *Middle East Report*, 219, Summer 2001, pp. 16–19.
60 LEAD programme description.
61 Egypt legalized Egyptian private universities only in 1992 when the People's Assembly passed a Law no. 101 allowing the establishment of private universities. The Law sets forth various regulations to exert a minimal level of government control. For example, the Minister for Education must approve the appointment of private university presidents, and non-Egyptians cannot occupy leading posts in private universities without the ministry's approval. In addition, the Supreme Council of Universities

indirectly supervises private universities and is responsible for monitoring standards to ensure that graduation certificates from state and private universities represent an equal education level. In May 2002 the private universities' committee was replaced with the Private Universities' Council. The council has the same powers as the Supreme Council of Universities, which regulates public universities.
62 See Iman Farag, "Higher Education in Egypt: The Realpolitik of Privatization", *International Higher Education*, Winter 2000. Online. Available at: www.bc.edu/bc_org/avp/soe/cihe/newsletter/News18/text11.html (accessed 20 June 2006).
63 These new changes were approved by the University Senate in 2006.
64 Open letter to the AUC President from faculty and students, March 2006.
65 Larry Gordon, "Arabic Soars at U.S. Colleges", *Los Angeles Times*, 21 March 2006. See also Faiza Elmasry, "US College Students Crowd Into Arabic Language Classes", VOANews.com, 17 February 2005. Online. Available at: www.voanews.com/english/archive/2005-02/2005-02-17-voa28.cfm?CFID=86250320&CFTOKEN=37524210 (accessed 16 January 2007).
66 Ibid.

6 Translating gender between the local and the global

1 A shorter version of this chapter was delivered as a keynote address at the international workshop on Gendered Bodies, Transnational Politics: Modernities Reconsidered, organized by the Institute for Gender Studies at the American University in Cairo and the Center for Gender and Sexuality Studies at New York University", 12–14 December 2003, Cairo. I am grateful to many of the colleagues whose comments were invaluable in the revision of this manuscript. I particularly wish to thank Professor Rabab Abdel Hadi, whose questions during that session inspired the entire section on the Arab Human Development Report 2003 included in this revised version.
2 Samia Mehrez, "Translation and the Postcolonial Experience: The Francophone North African Text", *in Rethinking Translation: Discourse, Subjectivity, Ideology*, Lawrence Venuti (ed.), London: Routledge, 1992, p. 120.
3 I am thinking of examples of works that have redefined and repositioned "the women's question" in Islamic societies and have historicized for women's movements and feminism(s) as well as the contested terms of women's empowerment and emancipation in the modern Arab Middle East such as Judith Tucker, *Women in Nineteenth Century Egypt*, Cambridge: Cambridge University Press, 1985, Deniz Kandiyoti (ed.), *Women Islam and the State*, Philadelphia: Temple University Press, 1991, Margo Badran, *Feminists Islam and Nation: Gender and the Making of Modern Egypt*, Cairo: AUC Press, 1996, Leila Ahmed, *Women and Gender in Islam: Historical Roots of a Modern Debate*, Cairo: AUC Press, 1992, Beth Baron, *The Women's Awakening in Egypt: Culture Society and the Press*, New Haven and London: Yale University Press, 1994, Lila Abu-Lughod (ed.), *Remaking Women: Feminism and Modernity in the Middle East*, Cairo: AUC Press, 1998, to mention only a handful of examples from an increasing body of scholarship that over the past two decades has constituted new ways of thinking about women and gender relations in the Arab World and have indeed redefined the parameters of the debate on the "women's question" in the western academy.
4 Lawrence Venuti, *The Translator's Invisibility: A History of Translation*, London: Routledge, 1995, p. 19.
5 Lawrence Venuti, "Introduction", *Rethinking Translation Discourse, Subjectivity, Ideology*, L. Venuti (ed.), London: Routledge, 1992, p. 10.
6 For a historical and theoretical overview of the development of the concept of gender in western scholarship see David Glover and Cora Kaplan, *Genders*, London: Routledge, 2000, p. ix.

292 *Notes*

7 Sherry Simon, *Gender in Translation: Cultural Identity and the Politics of Transmission*, London: Routledge, 1996, p. 143.
8 See for example Gayatri Spivak's conversation with Farida Akhter about translating the word "gendering" into Bengali where Akhter, who is profoundly involved in international feminism, argued that, in Bangladesh, the real work of the women's movement and of feminism was being undermined by talk of "gendering", mostly deployed by the women's development wings of transnational non-government organizations, in conjunction with some local academic feminist theorists. Spivak recounts that one of Akhter's intuitions was that "gendering" could not be translated into Bengali. Spivak's response was that "gendering" is an awkward new word in English as well, acknowledging the difficulty of translating "gender" into the US feminist context for her. See Gayatri Spivak, "The Politics of Translation", in *The Translation Studies Reader*, Lawrence Venuti (ed.), London: Routledge, 2000, pp. 404.
9 Spivak, "The Politics of Translation", pp. 397–416. Spivak emphasizes that the task of the feminist translator is to consider language as a clue to the workings of gendered agency for the writer herself "writes agency" in accordance with her ideological position.
10 Ferial Ghazoul, "Editorial", *Alif*, vol. 19, 1999, p. 6.
11 Spivak, "The Politics of Translation", p. 397.
12 *Arab Human Development Report*, New York: United Nations Publications, 2003, p. 122.
13 Ibid., p. 67.
14 Ibid., p. 66.
15 Ibid., p. 52.
16 Ibid., p. 114.
17 Ibid., p. 53.
18 Ibid., p. 56.
19 Ibid., p. 76.
20 Ibid., p. 82.
21 Ibid., p. 75.
22 Ibid., p. 67.
23 Ibid., p. 75.
24 Ibid., p. 54.
25 Ibid., p. 124.
26 Ibid., p. 125.
27 Simon, *Gender in Translation*, p. 143.
28 Pierre Bourdieu, *Masculine Domination*, Stanford: Stanford University Press, 2000, p. viii.
29 *Al-Ahram*, 19 December 2003.
30 *Al-Hayat*, 21 December 2003.
31 Hoda Elsadda's own account in the Arabic interview with her in *Alif*, Vol. 19, 1999, p. 212. This and the following quotations are my translation.
32 Hoda Elsadda, "Women and Memory", *Alif*, Vol. 19, pp. 210–230 (an interview in Arabic).
33 Ibid., pp. 219–220.
34 Ibid., pp. 222–223.
35 Ibid., pp. 255–256 (English abstract of the Arabic interview).
36 Heba Raouf Ezzat, "Women and Ijtihad: Towards a New Islamic Discourse", *Alif*, vol. 19, pp. 96–120 (citations are from the English abstract to the Arabic article, p. 257).
37 Elsadda, "Women and Memory", p. 217.
38 Ibid., p. 223.
39 Ibid., p. 216.
40 Ibid., pp. 218–219.

41 Ibid., p. 217.
42 Ibid., p. 216.
43 Ibid., p. 224.
44 Elsadda, pp. 224–225.
45 Lawrence Venuti, "Translation, Community, Utopia", in *The Translation Studies Reader*, Lawrence Venuti (ed.), London: Routledge, 2000, pp. 468–487.

7 Where have all the families gone? Egyptian literary texts of the 1990s

1 By dominant cultural representations of the family I am referring particularly to those prevalent through television soap operas and serials as well as the majority of Egyptian films. For representations of the family in television serials see Chapter 9 below and Lila Abu-Lughod, *Dramas of Nationhood*, Cairo: American University in Cairo Press, 2005; for representations of the family in film see Chapter 10 below.
2 Naguib Mahfouz, *Bayn al-Qasrayn, Qasr al-Shawq, Al-Sukkariyya*, Cairo: Maktabat Misr, 1956 and 1957.
3 See also Soraya Altorki, "Patriarchy and Imperialism: Father–Son and British–Egyptian Relations in Najib Mahfuz's *Trilogy*", in *Intimate Selving in Arab Families*, Suad Joseph (ed.), Syracuse: Syracuse University Press, 1999, pp. 215–234.
4 Naguib Mahfouz, *Awlad haratina*, Beirut: Dar al-Adab, 1967. It appeared in serialized form in the Egyptian daily *Al-Ahram* in 1959.
5 See Altorki, "Patriarchy and Imperialism", for further discussion of the significance of the death of the patriarch in *The Trilogy* in particular.
6 See Samia Mehrez, "Kitabat al-watan: Latifa al-Zayyat bayn *Al-Bab al-maftuh* wa *Hamlat taftish awraq shakhsiyya*" (Writing the Nation: Latifa al-Zayyat between *The Open Door* and *The Search*) in *Latifa al-Zayyat: Al-Adab wa l-watan*, Sayyid al-Bahrawi (ed.), Cairo: Dar al-Mar'a al-Arabiyya, Marqaz al-Buhuth al-Arabiyya, 1996, pp. 137–141. See also Marilyn Booth's introduction to the English translation of *Al-Bab al-maftuh* (*The Open Door*), Cairo: AUC Press, 2000, pp. ix–xxxi.
7 *Al-Bab al-maftuh* ends with the prospect of a unity or marriage between Layla and Husayn with the blessing of her brother, Mahmud (also Husayn's friend and fellow revolutionary) who has himself married Layla's school friend, Sana'. Both young couples are constituted against the will of the patriarch, Layla's father, who is twice defeated: once by their violation of traditional family rules, and again by their direct involvement in the national resistance to the British.
8 Sonallah Ibrahim, *Dhat*, Cairo: Dar al-Mustaqbal al-Arabi, 1992.
9 See Samia Mehrez, "Sonallah Ibrahim's Dhat: The Ultimate Objectification of the Self", in *Egyptian Writers between History and Fiction*, Cairo: AUC Press, 1994 and 2005, pp. 119–146; see also Chapter 8 below.
10 Sabry Hafez, "Jamaliyyat al-riwaya al-jadida: al-qatiʿa al-maʿrifiyya wa l-nazʿa al-mudadda" (Poetics of the New Novel) in *Alif*, Vol. 21, 2000, pp. 184–246.
11 May Telmissany, "Al-Kitaba ala hamish al-tarikh" (Writing on the Margin of History) in *Latifa al-Zayyat: al-Adab wa l-watan*, pp. 97–106.
12 Hafez, "Jamaliyyat al-riwaya al-jadida".
13 Mahmud al-Wardani, *Al-Rawd al-atir*, Cairo: Dar al-Hilal, 1998; Ibrahim Abdel Meguid, *La ahad yanam fi l-Iskandariyya*, Cairo: Dar al-Hilal, 1996, and *Tuyur al-Anbar*, Cairo: Dar al-Hilal, 2001.
14 Bahaa Taher, *Nuqtat nur*, Cairo: Dar al-Hilal, 2001.
15 Edwar al-Kharrat, *Sukhur l-sama'*, Cairo: Markaz al-Hadara l-Arabiyya, 2001.
16 See Richard Jacquemond's reading of this novel, "Samir Gharib Ali, une neutralité qui dérange", *Le Monde des Livres*, 30May 1997.
17 Mahmud Hamid, *Ahlam muharrama* (*Forbidden Dreams*), Cairo: GOCP, 2000.

18 Yasir Shaʿban, *Abnaʾ al-khataʾ al-rumansi* (*Children of Romantic Error*), Cairo: GOCP, 2000.
19 See Ferial Ghazoul, "The Artist vs. the Commissar", *Al-Ahram Weekly*, 25 January 2001; see also the Prologue above.
20 The first novels of some of the "girls" have already been translated into English: Miral al-Tahawy, *The Tent*, Tony Colderbank, trans., Cairo: AUC Press, 1996; May Telmissany, *Dunyazad*, Roger Allen, trans., London, Saqi Books, 2000; Somaya Ramadan, *Leaves of Narcissus*, Marilyn Booth, trans. Cairo: AUC Press, 2002.
21 Mona Prince, *Thalath haqaʾib li l-safar*, Cairo: Marqaz al-Hadara l-Arabiyya, 1998. Mona Prince was born in 1970 and has already published one collection of short stories and one short novel, besides uncollected short stories and essays in different local and regional magazines and newspapers. Both her novel and her short story collection have been awarded distinguished local and regional literary prizes. Her novel, *Thalath haqaʾib li l-safar*, has been awarded the second prize of the nation-wide literary award of the General Organization of Cultural Palaces (1998). Her collection of short stories, *Qitʿat al-tin al-akhira* (2000), earned her second place in the regional literary contest for young Arab women writers organized by The Sharja Women's Club in 1999. She has participated in successful experimental theatre and dance productions both in Cairo and abroad. She is currently assistant professor in the English Department, Faculty of Education, Suez Canal University. She obtained a B.A. in English Language and Literature from Ain Shams University in 1991 and was awarded an M.A. in 1991 with distinction from the same university, for her thesis on Chinua Achebe's novels. All references to the text of *Thalath haqaʾib* that appear in this chapter are my translations.
22 Somaya Ramadan, *Awraq al-narjis*, Cairo: Dar Sharqiyyat, 2001. Somaya Ramadan was born in Cairo in 1951. She studied in Cairo and Dublin and earned a Ph.D. in Irish Literature. She has taught English and Arabic Literature at the American University in Cairo and is currently Professor of English at the Academy of Arts, Cairo. She has published two collections of short stories: *Khashab wa nahas*, Cairo: Dar Sharqiyyat, 1995, *Manazil al-ruh*, Cairo: GEBO, 1999, and her novel *Awraq al-narjis*. She has also published numerous articles in English and in Arabic and recently translated Virginia Woolf's *A Room of One's Own* into Arabic, Cairo: Supreme Council for Culture, 1999. She was awarded the AUC Naguib Mahfouz Prize for *Awraq al-narjis* in 2001: this has been translated into English by Marilyn Booth and published by AUC Press in 2002. All references to *Awraq al-narjis* that appear in this chapter are my translations; page references are to the original Arabic text.
23 Adil Ismat, *Hajis mawt*, Cairo: Dar Sharqiyyat, 1995. Adil Ismat was born in 1959 in a small village near Tanta. He spent ten years in the village *kuttab* (Qurʾanic school) before he went to a primary school in Tanta. He earned a B.A. in Philosophy from Ain Shams University in 1984 and an M.A. in library science from the University of Tanta. He spent some years working for an oil company in the Eastern desert before returning to Tanta as a librarian in one of its secondary schools. He has published *Hajis mawt* and *Al-Rajul al-ari*, Cairo: Dar Sharqiyyat, 1998. He resides in Tanta with his family. All references to *Hajis mawt* that appear in this chapter are my translations.
24 Mustafa Zikri, *Ma yaʿrifuhu Amin*, in *Huraʾ mataha qutiyya*, Cairo: Dar Sharqiyyat, 1997. Mustafa Zikri was born in 1966. He studied philosophy for two years in Beirut during the 1980s. He then returned to Cairo where he obtained a B.A. at the Institute of Cinema. He has written the screenplay for two of Egypt's widely acclaimed recent feature films: *Afarit al-asfalt* (1995) and *Jannat al-shayatin* (1999). He has published *Huraʾ mataha qutiyya*, *Al-Khawf yaqtul al-ruh*, Cairo: Sharqiyyat, 1998 and *Lamsa min alam gharib*, Cairo: Sharqiyyat, 2000, and *Miraʾat 202*, Cairo: Merit, 2003 for which he was awarded the Sawiris Literary Prize, 2006. References

Notes   295

to *Ma ya'rifuhu Amin* that appear in this chapter are my translations. He lives in the Cairo suburb of Helwan. All references to *Ma ya'rifuhu Amin* that appear in this chapter are my translations.

25 See for example the short biographies provided in this chapter about the four authors under study. If read within a comparative framework these show that the "imminent death of the individual" that looms large in their literary works cuts across their differences in age, gender, educational background, professional orientation and class.
26 *Thalath haqa'ib*, p. 7.
27 Ibid., p. 8.
28 Ibid., p. 13.
29 Ibid., p. 88.
30 Ibid., pp. 40–41.
31 Ibid., p. 40.
32 Ibid., p. 31.
33 Ibid., p. 46.
34 Ibid., p. 42.
35 Ibid., p. 42.
36 Ibid., p. 46.
37 Ibid., p. 46.
38 Ibid., p. 47.
39 Ibid., p. 76.
40 Ibid., p. 86.
41 Ibid., p. 31.
42 Ibid., p. 61.
43 Ibid., p. 89.
44 *Awraq al-narjis*, p. 25.
45 Ibid., p. 9.
46 Ibid., pp. 9–10.
47 Ibid., pp. 10–11.
48 Ibid., p. 61.
49 Ibid., p. 61.
50 Ibid., p. 30.
51 Ibid., pp. 14–15.
52 Ibid., p. 16.
53 Ibid., p. 16.
54 Ibid., p. 21.
55 Ibid., p. 17.
56 Ibid., p. 62.
57 Ibid., p. 25.
58 Ibid., p. 34.
59 Ibid., p. 38.
60 Ibid., p. 68.
61 Ibid., p. 72.
62 Ibid., pp. 15–16.
63 Ibid., p. 100.
64 Ibid., p. 12.
65 Ibid., p. 117.
66 Ibid., p. 65.
67 Ibid., p. 65.
68 Ibid., p. 48.
69 Ibid., p. 30.
70 Ibid., p. 48.
71 Ibid., p. 69.
72 Ibid., p. 74.

73 *Hajis mawt*, p. 114.
74 Ibid., p. 12.
75 Ibid., p. 9.
76 Ibid., p. 11.
77 Ibid., p. 32.
78 Ibid., p. 26.
79 Ibid., p. 20.
80 Ibid., p. 14.
81 Ibid., p. 13.
82 Ibid., p. 15.
83 Ibid., pp. 15–16.
84 Ibid., p. 18.
85 Ibid., p. 59.
86 Ibid., p. 26.
87 Ibid., p. 27.
88 Ibid., p. 39.
89 Ibid., p. 40.
90 Ibid., p. 52.
91 *Ma yaʿrifuhu Amin*, p. 60.
92 See Richard Jacquemond, *Le champ littéraire égyptien depuis 1967*, Ph.D. dissertation, Université de Provencé, 1999.
93 See *Banipal: Magazine of Modern Arab Literature*, no. 25, Spring 2006, pp. 22–116.
94 Marie-Thérèse Abdel-Messih, "Debunking the Heroic Self", *Banipal*, no. 25, Spring 2006, pp. 22–23.
95 Ahmed Alaidy, *An takun Abbas al-Abd*, Cairo: Merit, 2003; English translation *Being Abbas El Abd*, trans. Humphrey Davies, Cairo: AUC Press, 2006; described as such by Youssef Rakha in *Al-Ahram Weekly*, 5 February 2004.
96 See Chapter 1 above; see also Samia Mehrez, "Sonallah Ibrahim and the (Hi)Story of the Book", *Egyptian Writers between History and Fiction: Essays on Naguib Mahfouz, Sonallah Ibrahim, and Gamal al-Ghitani*, Cairo: AUC Press, 1994, 2005, pp. 39–57.
97 See Youssef Rakha, "Pop Power: On Ahmed al-Aidi and *Abbas al-Abd*", *The Daily Star*, 15 May 2004.
98 The Egyptian writer Ahmed Alaidy was born in Saudi Arabia in 1974. He returned to Cairo at the age of fifteen and failed to score in the notorious Thanawiyya Amma (national high school certificate). He eventually enrolled in a marketing degree at the Open University, a drawn-out programme that gives him plenty of time to "stare at the computer screen, talk to the computer and listen to it talking back". Alaidy has worked as a graphic designer, a satellite television show script-writer and editor. *An takun Abbas al-Abd* is his first novel.
99 Leslie Boktor, "Being Ahmed Al Aidi: A Young Author Shares a Lot with His Audience", *Cairo Magazine*, September 2005, www.cairomagazine.com/?module=display&story_id=1358&format=html (accessed 5 January 2007).
100 Rakha, "Pop Power".
101 See Rakha, "Pop Power"; see also Mona Abaza, *The Changing Consumer Cultures of Modern Egypt: Cairo's Urban Reshaping*, Cairo: AUC Press, 2006, pp. 229–285, and Humphrey Davies's comments on the challenges of translating Alaidy's text in the "Translator's Note", *Being Abbas El Abd*, pp. 127–131.
102 Ahmed Alaidy, *Being Abbas El Abd*, trans. Humphrey Davies, Cairo: AUC Press, 2006, pp. 34–35.
103 Ibid., p. 51.
104 Ibid., p. 1.
105 Ibid., pp. 123–124.

106 See Rakha, "Pop Power".
107 Alaidy, *Being Abbas El Abd*, p. 36.

8 From the *hara* to the *imara*: emerging urban metaphors in the literary production on contemporary Cairo

1 A shorter version of this chapter was delivered at the American University in Cairo, during the Cairo Papers Symposium entitled Transformations in Middle Eastern Urban Landscapes: From Modernism to Neoliberalism, 14 May 2005. I wish to thank my colleagues at AUC, Martina Rieker, Director of the Cynthia Nelson Institute for Gender Studies and co-ordinator of *Shehr Comparative Urban Landscapes Network*, and Iman Hamdi, Professor of Political Science at AUC and editor of *Cairo Papers in Social Science*, for inviting me to think about urban space in literary texts. I also wish to thank Nicholas Hopkins, Professor of Anthropology at AUC, whose challenging comments on my discussion of the *hara* in Naguib Mafouz's works have led me to rethink and reformulate part of my discussion in this chapter.
2 I borrow the expression "architect of history" from Blanche Housman Gelfant, *The American City Novel*, Norman: Oklahoma University Press, 1965, where she uses it to describe John Dos Passos's achievement in *Manhattan Transfer*. For her Dos Passos's accomplishment in this novel is that he provides the reader with not only a brilliant creation of New York as a physical place but also a social and ideological reading of the modern metropolis. It is this last achievement which makes of Dos Passos, whose works are parallel to some of those by Naguib Mahfouz, an "architect of history"; "a shaper of moral opinion who influences the group mind".
3 Franco Moretti, *Atlas of the European Novel: 1800–1900*, London and New York: Verso, 1998, p. 3.
4 André Raymond, *Cairo: City of History*, trans. Willard Wood, Cairo: AUC Press, 2001, p. 361.
5 Tarek Aboul Atta and Mahmoud Yousry, "The Challenge of Urban Growth in Cairo", in *The Urban Challenge in Africa: Growth and Management of its Large Cities*, Carole Rakodi (ed.), New York: United Nations University Press, 1997, pp. 111–149. See also Raymond, *Cairo: City of History*, pp. 337–377 and Eric Denis, "Urban Planning and Growth in Cairo", in *Middle East Report*, 202, Winter 1997. Online. Available at: www.jstor.org/view/082851/di011543/01p00442/0 (accessed 20 May 2006).
6 Sonallah Ibrahim, *Dhat*, Cairo: Dar al-Mustaqbal al-Arabi, 1992; English translation *Zaat*, trans. Tony Colderbank, Cairo: AUC Press, 2001 (references are to the English translation).
7 Hamdi Abu Golayyel, *Lusus mutaqaʿidun*, Cairo: Merit, 2002; English translation, *Thieves in Retirement*, trans. Marilyn Booth, Syracuse: Syracuse University Press, 2006 (references are to the English translation).
8 Alaa al-Aswany, *Imarat Yaʿqubyan*, Cairo: Merit, 2002. English translation, *Yacoubian Building*, trans. Humphrey Davies, Cairo: AUC Press, 2004 (references are to the English translation).
9 Mohamed Tawfik, *Tifl shaqi ismuhu Antar*, Cairo: Merit, 2003 (references are to the Arabic original; my translation).
10 Sonallah Ibrahim and Jean Pierre Ribière, *Cairo from Edge to Edge*, Cairo: AUC Press, 1998.
11 Ayşe Öncü and Petra Weyland, *Space, Culture and Power: New Identities in Globalizing Cities*, London: Zed Books, 1997, p. 2.
12 Samia Mehrez, *Egyptian Writers between History and Fiction: Essays on Naguib Mahfouz, Sonallah Ibrahim and Gamal al-Ghitani*, Cairo: AUC Press, 1994; see also Chapters 1 and 4 above.
13 For more on Abu Golayyel's background see Dina Hishmat, "*Lusus mutaqaʿidun*

de Hamdi Abu Gulayl: autonomisation des éspaces ruralisés dans la ville", in *L'évolution des représentations de la ville du Caire dans la littérature égyptienne moderne et contemporaine*, Ph.D. thesis, Paris: Université de Paris 3 (Sorbonne Nouvelle), 2004.
14 Humphrey Davies, "Translator's Note", *Yacoubian Building*.
15 For more on Mohamed Tawfik, who also writes and publishes in English, see his biographical sketch on the Arab World Books website. Online. Available at: www.arabworldbooks.com/authors/mohamed_tawfik.html (accessed 3 May 2005).
16 Mona El-Ghobashy, "Dreams Deferred", *Cairo Times*, 20–26 June 2002.
17 Eliott Colla, "Anxious Advocacy: The Novel, the Law, and Extrajudicial Appeals in Egypt", *Public Culture*, Vol. 17 no. 3, 2005, pp. 417–443. See also Chapter 3 above.
18 See Mehrez, *Egyptian Writers between History and Fiction*, and Richard Jacquemond, *Entre scribes et écrivains: le champ littéraire dans l'Egypte contomporaine*, Paris: Actes Sud, 2003. See also Chapters 1 and 2 above
19 On the relationship between the rise of the novel and imagined community see Benedict Anderson, *Imagined Communities*, London and New York: Verso, 1983.
20 Moretti, *Atlas of the European Novel*, p. 5.
21 Luc Barbulesco and Philippe Cardinal, *L'Islam en questions*, Paris: Grasset, 1986, p. 143. For more on Gamal al-Ghitani and the place he occupies in the Egyptian literary field see Chapters 1 and 3 above.
22 Naguib Mahfouz, *Midaq Alley*, trans. Trevor Le Gassick. London: Heinemann, 1966, p. 1.
23 Mahfouz, *Midaq Alley*, p. 244.
24 Gamal Al-Ghitani, *Najib Mahfudh yatadhakkar* (*Naguib Mahfouz Remembers*), *Akhbar al-Yawm*, 1987, p. 19.
25 For more on transformations that have taken place in Islamic Cairo see Raymond, *Cairo: City of History*, pp. 364–367; Caroline Williams, "Reconstructing Islamic Cairo: Forces at Work", and Yasser Elsheshtawy, "Urban Transformations: Social Control at al-Rifaʿi Mosque and Sultan Hasan Square", in *Cairo Cosmopolitan: Politics, Culture, and Urban Space in the New Globalized Middle East*, Diane Singerman and Paul Amar (eds), Cairo: AUC Press, 2006, pp. 269–294 and 295–312 respectively.
26 There are earlier manifestations of the *imara* in modern Egyptian literature, notably Yusuf Idris's 1969 *Al-Naddaha* (English translation, *The Siren* 1984) for example. However, Idris's text focuses more on rural–urban migration without using the space of the apartment building itself as a metaphor for and of the city.
27 For consumer patterns during the 1960s and 1970s *infitah* periods in Egypt see *Mona Abaza, The Changing Consumer Cultures of Modern Egypt: Cairo's Urban Reshaping*, Cairo: AUC Press, 2006, pp. 89–164; for the representation of theses changes in literary texts see Samia Mehrez, "Sonallah Ibrahim's *Dhat*: The Ultimate Objectification of the Self", *Egyptian Writers between History and Fiction*, pp. 119–146.
28 Ibrahim, *Zaat*, p. 47.
29 Ibid., p. 6.
30 Ibid., pp. 43–44.
31 For more on special transformations in post-*infitah* Cairo see Farha Ghannam, "Relocation and the Use of Urban Space", *Middle East Report*, 202, Winter 1997. Online. Available at: www.jstor.org/view/08992851/di011543/01p00475/0 (accessed 20 May 2006); Petra Kuppinger, "Giza Spaces", *Middle East Report*, 202, Winter, 1997. Online. Available at: www.jstor.org/view/08992851/di011543/01p00475/0 (accessed 20 May 2006); and Assef Bayat, "Cairo's Poor: Dilemmas of Survival and Solidarity", *Middle East Report*, 202, Winter, 1997. Online. Available at: www.jstor.org/view/08992851/di011543/01p00432/0 (accessed 20 May 2006).
32 Ibrahim, *Zaat*, p. 47.
33 Ibid., p. 49.
34 Ibid., p. 50.

Notes 299

35 Ibid., p. 61.
36 Ibid., p. 60.
37 Ibid., p. 83.
38 These figures are based on Assef Bayat's 1996 findings in "Cairo's Poor: Dilemmas of Survival and Solidarity"; see also Manal El-Batran and Christian Arandel, "A Shelter of Their Own: Informal Settlement Expansion in Greater Cairo and Government Responses", *Environment and Urbanization*, Vol. 10, no. 1, 1998, pp. 217–232. Online. Available at: eau.sagepub.com/cgi/content/abstract/10/1/217 (accessed May 2006).
39 Eric Denis, "Cairo as a Neoliberal Capital? From Walled City to Gated Community", in *Cairo Cosmopolitan*, p. 51.
40 Abu Golayyel, *Thieves in Retirement*, pp. 77–78.
41 Ibid., p. 78.
42 Ibid., p. 78.
43 Ibid., p. 57.
44 Ibid., p. 11.
45 Ibid., p. 30.
46 Catherine Miller, "Upper Egyptian Regionally Based Communities in Cairo: Traditional or Modern Forms of Urbanization?" in *Cairo Cosmopolitan*, pp. 375–397.
47 See Yasmine Fathi, "The Lodgers' Discontent", *Al-Ahram Weekly*, 3 March 2005.
48 ? Abdallah, "Faces: Alaa al-Aswany", *Egypt Today*, August 2004. Online. Available at: www.egypttoday.com/article.aspx?ArticleID=1797 (accessed 10 June 2006).
49 Al-Aswany, *Yacoubian Building*, p. 11.
50 Ibid., pp. 11–12.
51 Ibid., p. 11.
52 Ibid., pp. 12–13.
53 Joseph Massad, *Desiring Arabs*, Chicago: Chicago University Press, 2007.
54 Abdallah, *Egypt Today*, 2004.
55 Tawfik, *Tifl shaqi ismuhu Antar*, p. 7.
56 Written interview (by email) with Mohamed Tawfik, 22 July 2005, where he states: "My perspectives of Egypt have been enriched because of greater distance and less clutter"; "Distance is often compensated by a higher degree of alertness."
57 Tawfik, *Tifl shaqi ismuhu Antar*, p. 48.
58 Ibid., p. 9.
59 I am grateful to Paul Amar for this coinage.
60 Tawfik, *Tifl shaqi ismuhu Antar*, pp. 103–104.
61 Tawfik, written interview (by email), 22 July 2005.
62 Ibrahim, *Zaat*, p. 197.
63 Abu Golayyel, *Thieves in Retirement*, p. 74.
64 Diane Singerman and Paul Amar, "Introduction", *Cairo Cosmopolitan*, p. 21.
65 Singerman and Amar, "Introduction", p. 10.
66 Mahfouz, *Midaq Alley*, p. 244.
67 Ibid, p. 246.

9 Taking the soap out of the opera: the case of *Hagg Mitwalli's Family*

1 James Lull, ed., *World Families Watch Television*, Newbury Park: Sage Publications Inc., 1988, p. 17.
2 Lull, *World Families*, p. 17; see also Barrie Gunter and Michael Svennevig, *Behind and In Front of the Screen: Television's Involvement with Family Life*, London: John Libbey, 1987.
3 Ibid., p. 17.
4 For an excellent and detailed discussion of such controversies, whether social,

economic or religious, see Lila Abu-Lughod, *Dramas of Nationhood*, Cairo: AUC Press, 2005.
5 Lila Abu-Lughod, "Finding a Place for Islam: Egyptian Television Serials and the National Interest", *Public Culture*, Vol. 5, 1993, p. 500.
6 Walter Armbrust, *Mass Culture and Modernism in Egypt*, Cambridge: Cambridge University Press, 1996, p. 7.
7 Abu-Lughod, *Dramas of Nationhood*, p. 43.
8 Abu-Lughod, "Finding a Place for Islam", p. 494.
9 Abu-Lughod, *Dramas of Nationhood*, p. 43.
10 Ibid., p. 43.
11 Larry Strelitz, "Where the Global Meets the Local: Media Studies and the Myth of Cultural Homogenization", *TBS*, No. 6, Spring/Summer, 2001. Online. Available at: www.tbsjournal.com/Archives/Spring01/strelitz4.html (accessed 15 July 2006).
12 Farah Ghannam, "Keeping Him Connected: Globalization and the Production of Locality in Cairo", in *Cairo Cosmopolitan: Politics, Culture and the Urban Space in the New Globalized Middle East*, Diane Singerman and Paul Amar (eds), Cairo: AUC Press, 2006, p. 252.
13 On Egypt's role as a primary producer and exporter of television serials in the Arab world see Abu-Lughod *Dramas of Nationhood*, Armbrust, *Mass Culture and Modernism in Egypt*, Said Sadek, "Cairo as Global/Regional Cultural Capital?" in *Cairo Cosmopolitan*, Marlin Dick, "The State of the Musalsal: Arab Television Drama and Comedy and the Politics of the State", *TBS*, No. 15, Fall 2005. Online. Available at: www.tbsjournal.com/Archives/Fall05/Dick.html (accessed 3 June 2006).
14 For a wealth of information on Arab transnational media see *TBS* (Transnational Broadcasting Studies), www.tbsjournal.com. For an early reading of Pan Arab media see Abdallah Schleifer, "Media Explosion in the Arab World: The Pan-Arab Satellite Broadcasters", *TBS*, No. 1, Fall 1998. Online. Available at: www.tbsjournal.com/Archives/Fall98/Articles1/Pan-Arab_bcasters/pan-arab_bcasters.html (accessed 10 June 2006), and Joe S. Foote, "CNE in Egypt: Some Light at the End of an Arduous Tunnel", *TBS*, No. 1, Fall 1998. Online. Available at: www.tbsjournal.com/Archives/Fall98/Articles1/CNE/cne2.html (accessed 10 June 2006).
15 "Arab Satellite Television: The World Through Their Eyes", *The Economist*, 24 February 2005. Online. Available at: www.economist.com/displayStory.cfm?story_id=3690442 (accessed 5 June 2006).
16 Sadek, "Cairo as Global/Regional Cultural Capital?" p. 163.
17 Jon B. Alterman, "Transnational Media and Social Change in the Arab World", *TBS*, No. 2, Spring 1999. Online. Available at: www.tbsjournal.com/Archives/Spring99/spr99.html (accessed 12 June 2006).
18 Ibid.
19 Ibid.
20 Ibid.
21 Dick, "The State of Musalsal" (accessed 6 June 2006).
22 Ibid.
23 Schleifer, "Media Explosion in the Arab World" (accessed 4 June 2006).
24 Quoted in Larry Strelitz, "Where the Global Meets the Local".
25 Ursula Lindsey, "TV Versus Terrorism: Why This Year's Ramadan Shows Tackled One 'Controversial' Subject, But Were Barred from Broaching Others", *TBS*, No. 15, Fall 2005. Online. Available at: www.tbsjournal.com/Archives/Fall05/Lindsey.html (accessed 6 June 2006).
26 See Lila Abu-Lughod's discussion of these TV dramas and the debates surrounding them in *Dramas of Nationhood*.
27 *Al-Hayat*, 30 June 2005. See also for example Sakina al-Sadat, "Thawrat nisa' misr ala musalsalat Ramadan hadha l-am" (Egyptian Women's Rebellion against Ramadan Serials), *Al-Musawwar*, 14 December 2001.

Notes 301

28 *Al-Hayat*, 2 April 2002, as reported by the Iraqi newspaper *Al-Ittihad*.
29 Ahmad Ghanim, "Taʿaddud al-zawjat bayn al-shariʿa wa l-waqiʿ" (Polygamy between Islamic Law and Reality), Islamweb.net. Online. Available at: www.islamweb.net/ver2/archive/readArt.php?lang=A&id=16238 (accessed 16 June 2006).
30 *Ruz al-Yusuf*, 28 December 2001.
31 Rachel Noeman, "Egypt Soap Opera Slammed for Glorifying Polygamy", Reuters, MaghrebOnLine.Net, 21 August 2002. Online. Available at: forum2002.maghrebonline. nl/viewtopic.php?p=19558&sid=0ff12922126b922f8d6111c599873373 (accessed 17 June 2006).
32 Ibid.
33 Ibid.
34 Adil Hammuda, "Hukuma jadida bi ri'asat al-hagg 'Mito'" (A new government Headed by Hagg Meeto), *Sawt al-Umma*, 26 December 2001.
35 Safinaz Kazim, "Al-Shabah bayn al-Hagg Mitwalli wa Jurj Bush" (The Similarity between Hagg Mitwalli and George Bush), *Sawt al-Umma*, 26 December 2001.
36 *Ruz al-Yusuf*, 28 December 2001.
37 Ibid.
38 Ibid.
39 Ibid.
40 Ibid.
41 Ibid.
42 Ibid.
43 Ibid.

10 The new kid on the block: *Bahibb issima* and the emergence of the Coptic community in the Egyptian public sphere

1 For an overview of the Coptic community's history in Egypt see Saad Eddin Ibrahim *et al.*, *The Copts of Egypt*, London: Minority Rights Group International in co-operation with the Ibn Khaldun Center for Development Studies in Cairo, 1996, Online. Available at: www.minorityrights.org/admin/Download/Pdf/Coptreport.pdf (accessed 10 January 2007). The Copts are Egypt's largest and oldest Christian community dating back to AD 42 with the formation of the first church in Alexandria by St Mark the Evangelist. As Ibrahim states in *The Copts of Egypt*, from the outset the Copts have been socially, economically and culturally integrated and are represented in all classes of Egyptian society. However, it is the political integration of the community that leaves much to be desired. According to official, conservative estimates the Copts represent about 6–7 per cent of the Egyptian population, though some enthusiastic Copts will put the proportion as high as 25 per cent. It has been recommended by members of the Coptic community that the Egyptian state undertake proper and reliable statistics to prevent exaggeration and misuse of existing statistics (see Karim al-Gawhary, "Copts in the 'Egyptian Fabric'", *Middle East Report*, 200 (*Minorities in the Middle East and the Politics of Difference*), July–September 1996, pp. 21–22. For a more general overview of the Christian communities in the Arab Middle East and their historic role in Arab Islamic civilization and culture as well as the political changes that have impacted their position within the context of Muslim societies see for example Andrea Pacini, ed., *Christian Communities in the Arab Middle East: The Challenge of the Future*, Oxford: Clarendon Press, 1988.
2 Eleven priests, a Coptic lawyer and reportedly one Muslim lawyer filed a lawsuit against the film after its release in July 2004 at the court for expedited procedures calling for its banning, and demanding that in the future the church be granted the right to pre-screen such movies. See *Al-Ahram Weekly*, 15 July 2004.

302   *Notes*

3 See Vickie Langohr, "Frosty Reception for US Religious Freedom Commission", in *Middle East Report*, 29 March 2001. Online. Available at: www.merip.org/mero/mero032901.html (accessed 11 January 2007), where among the internal and external factors cited that have impacted the Egyptian state's efforts to contain further exposure of the Coptic question are: the unprecedented number of instances of sectarian violence, pressures from the Christian right in the US (to whom the Bush administration is indebted) that together with the immigrant Coptic community in the US have expressed concerns over equal religious rights and freedom of religious expression in Egypt and Egypt's dependence on US aid, as well as US pressures on the Mubarak regime to influence Egypt's positions on the Palestinian and US-led sanctions on Iraq.

4 See David Zeidan, "The Copts – Equal, Protected or Persecuted? The Impact of Islamization on Muslim-Christian Relations in Modern Egypt", in *Islam and Christian–Muslim Relations*, Vol. 10, no. 1, 1999, pp. 53–65, where he argues like many other scholars who have dealt with the Coptic question in Egypt, that President Sadat's policy of appealing to Islamists, publicly attacking the Coptic Church and detaining the Coptic Patriarch, Shenouda III, in 1980–81 alienated the Coptic community that during the first half of the twentieth century was part of the secular, liberal and pan-Arab nationalist ideology and movement (pp. 56–57). He also enumerates several discriminatory practices against the Copts that include the lack of permits for building new churches, the confiscation of Coptic *waqf* lands for Islamic purposes, disadvantages in personal law and conversions, and the imposition of *Shariʿa* (Islamic law) on non-Muslims, as well as discrimination in government and public service (p. 57). For a reading of the Coptic community's efforts to preserve its unity and identity in face of the rising re-Islamization or Islamic trend in Egyptian society and the state's implementation of Islamic leaning policies see Dina el Khawaga, "The political Dynamics of the Copts: Giving the Community an Active Role", in *Christian Communities in the Arab Middle East: The Challenge of the Future*, pp. 172–190, where she argues that, rather than seeking explicit forms of political expression, the renewal movement within the Coptic Church was able to organize the faithful and mobilize them not only through the institution of the clergy but also by its ability to provide them with a space which compensated for their status as a minority and served to exclude the (Muslim) other.

5 For an overview of the Coptic community's political and cultural role in national politics and cultural renewal since the nineteenth century *nahda* see Andrea Pacini, "Introduction", and Samir Khalil Samir, "The Christian Communities, Active Members of Arab Society throughout History", in *Christian Communities in the Arab Middle East: The Challenge of the Future*, pp. 1–24 and 67–91 respectively. For the perception of Copts as colonial collaborators, a potential "fifth column" under British rule in Egypt, and as traitors, exploiters and betrayers see Zeidan, "The Copts", pp. 55–56 and 61–62.

6 All of the literature I have consulted confirms that the Copts do not think of themselves as a minority but rather as Egyptians and Arabs sharing a common history and culture with Muslim Egyptians as part of an Islamic world and a pan-Arab nation and that their participation in moments of national crises has always been motivated by their sense of national belonging. This nationalistic integration of the Coptic community is contradicted by their actual legal status. In the modern Egyptian nation-state, whose legal system is informed by *Shariʿa*, the Coptic community continues to be granted privileges rather than given rights. There are obvious contradictions between the modern concept of citizenship that stipulates legal equality between all citizens and the premodern concept of *dhimmi* which defined the special minority status of the Copts under the Islamic Empire. For a reading of the Coptic community's legal status see Bernard Botiveau, "The Law of the Nation-State and the Status of non-Muslims in Egypt and Syria", in *Christian Communities in the Arab Middle East: The Challenge of the Future*, pp. 111–126.

7 On the underrepresentation of Copts in the public sphere see Karim al-Gawhary, "Copts in the Egyptian Fabric". On the basis of 1996 figures provided by Maurice Sadiq, director of the Center of Egyptian Human Rights for the Consolidation of National Unity, a Cairo-based human rights centre focusing on Coptic issues, there is not a single Coptic governor in the 26 Egyptian provinces, only ten Copts head the boards of the 3600 public sector companies, only one Copt served as ambassador, and not a single Copt is president of a university. The same figures are provided in the 1996 Ibn Khaldoun Center report, *The Copts of Egypt*, p. 23. Underrepresentation of the Copts in educational institutions and curricula include restricted admission to universities and colleges and military and police academies as well as medical school (gynaecology and obstetrics) among others (Zeidan, "The Copts", p. 58). In *The Copts of Egypt*, it is stated that there is hardly any representation of Coptic history or culture and no representation of Christian doctrines and creeds; with the rise of Islamic religious extremism educational curricula have tended to increase the schism between Muslims and Christians (pp. 23 and 27).
8 For more details on these instances of violence against the Coptic community see Ibrahim, *The Copts of Egypt*, p. 21, and Langohr, "Frosty Reception for US Freedom Commission".
9 See Karim al-Gawhary, "Copts in the Egyptian Fabric". The initial attack against the conference on minorities in the Middle East came from the prominent journalist Muhammad Hassanayn Haykal, former editor-in-chief of the largest and oldest Arabic daily, *Al-Ahram*, and a close confident of the late Egyptian President Gamal Abdel Nasser. In an article entitled "Citizens or Protected Minority?" Haykal refuted the "minority" status of the Copts and described them as "part of Egypt's unbreakable fabric", warning against politically motivated foreign funding and foreign intervention in national affairs. Similarly, Pope Shenouda III issued a statement rejecting the designation of Copts as a "minority", and stressing that they are "part and parcel of the Egyptian nation". The public debate surrounding the conference involved at least two hundred intellectuals both Coptic and Muslim who all supported Haykal's position through articles in the Egyptian press. These nationalistic arguments by consecrated public figures rang hollow when compared to actual discriminatory policies and realities with regard to the Coptic community on the ground.
10 In 1998 the murder of two Copts in Kosheh village in Upper Egypt led to the arrest by police of hundreds of Copts, many of whom claimed to have been tortured, though the local Copts had insisted that the killers had been Muslims. Again in January 2000 Kosheh witnessed more violence: an argument between a Coptic merchant and a Muslim customer escalated into bloodshed, and the Muslims burned and looted Coptic shops. At least 23 people died: twenty Copts, one Muslim and two unidentified burned bodies. Kosheh Copts have blamed the local security forces for simply standing aside while Muslims mob burned Coptic shops and killed members of the Coptic community.
11 Indeed, as Langohr points out in "Frosty Reception for the US Religious Freedom Commission in Egypt", the Sheikh of Al-Azhar, Sayyid Tantawi, gave an interview to the commission in which he stressed that Copts reject interference in their internal affairs, while Pope Shenouda III met with the commission but did not make a public statement.
12 As Langohr explains in "Frosty Reception for US Religious Freedom Commission in Egypt", The United States Commission on International Religious Freedom (USCIRF) was created in 1998 by the International Religious Freedom Act (IRFA) to advice the president of the US, the State Department and the Congress on religious freedom worldwide. The impetus to make the US government a crusader for religious liberty came from the Christian right, and the USCIRF – despite its current multi-faith composition – still bears the imprint of its evangelical and partisan origins. The delegation came to Egypt to investigate claims made by the Coptic community in the US that Egyptian Copts are victims of discrimination and religiously motivated attacks on their property and lives.

304 *Notes*

13 For a detailed reading of the representation of the Copts and other minorities (Nubians and Jews) in Egyptian cinema see Viola Shafik, "Variety or Unity: Minorities in Egyptian Cinema", *Orient*, Vol. 39, no. 4, December 1998, pp. 627–648. Shafik argues that the strategies of Othering have been applied in the Egyptian cinematic context at different levels regarding local minorities such as Copts, Jews and Nubians. Shafik states that the objects of laughter in Egyptian films were likely to be non-Muslim, non-Whites and non-Arabs even when their comic function in film did not necessarily reflect their real status as members of the various minorities in Egyptian society. She further argues that the depiction and roles of these minorities in cinematic representation have changed over the course of the twentieth century depending on their position within the evolving national narrative, citing specifically the example of the Nubians and the Jews. The former were predominantly represented as honest, loyal, heavily accented house servants (which basically reflected their general dominated and underprivileged position within Egyptian society) while the latter were cast in more varied roles owing to the heterogeneity of the Jewish community itself. Hence they were cast at once as rich store owners but also poor, *ibn balad* (urban, lower-class Egyptian) types. With the establishment of the state of Israel and the Jewish exodus from Egypt, the Copts, whose community is as heterogeneous as the former Jewish one, were cast in the same roles as the now absent Jews. In these roles they remained one-dimensional, stereotypical characters lacking realistic representation.
14 For a reading of Alaa al-Aswany's novel *Imarat Ya'qubyan* see Chapter 8 above.
15 For a detailed reading of the TV serial *Khalti Safiya wa l-dir* see Lila Abu-Lughod, *Dramas on Nationhood*, Cairo: AUC Press, 2005, pp. 178 and 180–181.
16 For example, Viola Shafik notes that *Hasan wa Murqus wa Kuhin* was produced in 1954 in the wake of the Cairo Trial of the Operation Susannah when tensions between Egypt and Israel because of increased Zionist activities in Egypt arose, while Lila Abu-Lughod notes that *Khalti Safiya wa l-dir* coincided with eruption of several instances of "communal strife" between Muslims and Copts in the late 1980s and early 1990s. See Shafik, "Unity or Diversity", p. 639, and Abu-Lughod, *Dramas of Nationhood*, p. 178.
17 Shafik, "Unity or Diversity", p. 644.
18 For a detailed reading of *Awan al-ward* see Lila Abu-Lughod, *Dramas on Nationhood*, pp. 176–179.
19 Abu-Lughod, *Dramas of Nationhood*, p. 164.
20 Stories about conversions of Copts to the Islamic faith strike a highly sensitive chord for the Coptic community since they threaten its historic efforts of self-preservation. Public representations of such conversions in the media are therefore bound to be contested and resisted by members of the Coptic community.
21 See Abu-Lughod's discussion of various problems caused by other TV serials representing Copts in *Dramas of Nationhood*, p. 177.
22 See Amina Elbendary, "Love Lost in Shubra", *Al-Ahram Weekly*, 31 July 2003.
23 For more details on the censored segments of *Film hindi* see Viola Shafik, "Unity or Diversity", p. 646.
24 See *Nahdat Misr*, 8 June 2004.
25 *Bahibb issima* has been compared to both Giuseppe Tornatore's *Nuovo Cinema Paradiso* (1989), which also used a child's perspective, and Volker Schlöndorff's *Die Blechtrommel* (The Tin Drum, 1979) whose child narrator deliberately stops growing. See Mohamed El-Asyouti, "A Permissive Tyranny", *Al-Ahram* Weekly, 17 June 2004.
26 These are the words that Na'im as an adult says in the film as he comments on himself as a child.
27 For more on other cultural crises and committees that are set up to resolve or dissolve them see the Prologue above.
28 This committee included a majority of Copts – Dr Yunan Labib Rizq (historian),

General Nabil Luqa Bibawy (member of the National Democratic ruling party), Dr Nagi Fawzi (professor in the Academy of Arts), Ms Isis Nazmi (journalist), Mr Nadir Adli (journalist) – and one Muslim: Ahmad Salih (cultural critic in the *Al-Akhbar* newspaper).
29 My interview with Hani Fawzi and Usama Fawzi, Cairo, 24 September 2004.
30 In addition to Al-Azhar's purview over publications dealing with "religious affairs" it was granted in 1994 through a fatwa (religious decree) issued by the State Council the right to ban audio and video materials that "violate the principles of Islam". These fluid and vaguely defined powers have allowed for Al-Azhar's increased interventions in the cultural field. Its recommendations to ban cultural products have routinely caused crackdowns within the cultural field, for example the confiscation of dozens of literary and intellectual works at the 2002 Cairo International Book Fair. When Al-Azhar receives reports that a book in circulation is blasphemous, a committee of the members of the Islamic Research Academy (IRA), the think tank of Al-Azhar, is appointed to study the publication in question. Its decisions to ban are advisory to the Ministry of Culture and of the Interior that actually impose the ban.
31 In May 2004 the Islamic Research Academy (IRA), of Al-Azhar decided to ban Nawal El Saadawi's well known novel *The Fall of the Imam*, which had been published in Arabic in 1987 and was later translated into fourteen languages before its second Arabic edition appeared in 2002. The reason given for this decision was that the novel violated the principles of Islam. Intellectuals and writers in Egypt immediately launched a campaign of protest in the press against Al-Azhar's repeated interventions in cultural affairs. However, the novel was still banned. On another level, the sudden, ill-defined and therefore highly controversial decision by the Minister of Justice to grant "search and seizure powers" to certain members of the IRA in June 2004, thereby coinciding with the Saadawi case, was massively contested by Egyptian secular intellectuals and human rights activists who feared that the minister's action further extended the purview and power of Al-Azhar in the cultural field. After dozens of articles in the press expressing concern over the implications of the ministerial decision for the cultural field, the Minister of Justice assured intellectuals that "search and seizure powers" involved unlicensed religious publications, like copies of the Qur'an or the Prophet Muhammad's sayings (*hadith*) only. Al-Azhar has traditionally played a consultative role, with no executive legal powers, when reviewing cultural material deemed sexually explicit or religiously unacceptable. For more on this debate see *Al-Ahram Weekly*, 17 June 2004.
32 See for example Sheikh Al-Azhar's reaction when consulted on Haydar Haydar's allegedly "blasphemous" novel *Walima li a'shab al-bahr* in the Prologue above.
33 For more comments on this private screening that was held at the Cairo Sheraton on 4 June, i.e. five days before the commercial release of the film, see *Sawt al-Umma*, 7 June 2004.
34 See *Al-Hayat*, 8 June 2004.
35 *Al-Ahram*, 23 June 2004.
36 *Al-Musawwar*, 18 June 2004.
37 The term *sinima nadhifa* (clean cinema) is a recently coined expression that designates films that steer clear from major taboos such as religion and sex.
38 See the strategy used by *Al-Sha'b* newspaper to incriminate Hydrar Haydar's *Walima li a shab al-bahr* in the Prologue above.
39 See the article by Bishop Murqus Aziz Khalil in *Al-Mussawar*, 18 June 2004.
40 Ibid.
41 See the survey of movie theatres conducted by *Al-Mussawar*, 2 July 2004.
42 See *Watani*, 27 June 2004.
43 See *Al-Hayat*, 6 July 2004.
44 See also Shafik, "Unity or Diversity", pp. 645–646.

306 *Notes*

45 See for example the article in *Ruz al-Yusuf*, 3 July 2004 by a Protestant priest against the intervention of any religious authorities in the cultural field.
46 See *Al-Ahram al-Arabi*, 19 June 2004.
47 See *Al-Wafd*, 20 June 2004.
48 In fact, besides the enormous support that the film received in the press, a group of Muslim and Coptic intellectuals filed a counter-lawsuit on 11 September 2004 against the attackers of *Bahibb issima* on the basis that censorship of the film would curtail their civic rights as citizens and public figures involved in the cultural scene. I am grateful to the Hisham Mubarak Legal Center for providing me with a copy of the documentation for this case.

11 *Found in Cairo*: the limits of representation in the visual field

1 For a historical overview of modern Egyptian art and questions of modernity, identity, and authenticity see Liliane Karnouk, *Modern Egyptian Art: 1910–2003*, Cairo: AUC Press, 2005; Jessica Winegar, *Creative Reckonings: The Politics of Art and Culture in Contemporary Egypt*, Stanford: Stanford University Press, 2006.
2 Peter van der Veer, "Visual Practices in South Asian Nationalisms", paper presented at the conference on Visual Practices and Public Subjects: Secularism, Religious Nationalism and the State, AUB, April 2005, p. 15.
3 For a more extensive discussion of the forms of "street censorship" see Richard Jacquemond, "The Shifting Limits of the Sayable in Contemporary Egyptian Fiction", *MIT EJMES*, Vol. 4, Fall 2004, pp. 41–52.
4 Ibid., p. 41.
5 For actual examples of interventions by these self-proclaimed censors that represent what the cultural milieu has labelled "street censorship" see the Prologue, Chapters 10 above and Chapter 12 below.
6 For a panorama of some of the recent censorship cases in Egypt see the Prologue, Chapter 3, Chapter 9, Chapter 10 above and Chapter 12 below; see also the special issue of *Al-Adab* on censorship in Egypt, Vol. 50, no. 11–12, 2002.
7 Jessica Winegar, "Cultural Sovereignty in a Global Art Economy: Egyptian Cultural Policy and the New Western Interest in Art from the Middle East", *Cultural Anthropology*, Vol. 21, no. 2, May 2006, p. 182.
8 See the Prologue above.
9 Ibid.
10 See Chapter 4 above.
11 See Adil al-Siwi, "Representing the Body", *Ain: Journal of Plastic Arts*, Vol. 1, 1997, p. 6. This is the only published volume of this independent journal.
12 See the "Testimonies by Young Artists", ibid., pp. 76–85.
13 Ibid., p. 285.
14 For more details on these forgery and fraud scandals that involved paintings by some of Egypt's most renowned modern painters including Abd al-Hadi al-Ghazzar, Mahmud Sa'id and Hamid Nada among others, and the ensuing debates, see *Al-Misri al-Yawm*, 26 June 2005; *Al-Fajr* 16 July 2005 and 22 July 2005; *Ruz al-Yusuf*, 22 July 2005; *Egypt Today*, July 2005; *Al-Qahira*, 19 July 2005; see also Mona Abaza's discussion of art scandals and frauds in the visual field in her book *The Changing Consumer Cultures of Modern Egypt: Cairo's Urban Reshaping*, Cairo: AUC Press, 2006, pp. 219–222.
15 See Muhammad Abla's comments in *Al-Qahira*, 19 July 2005.
16 This was the case of the poet Iman Mirsal, for example, who published a statement in *Akhbar al-Adab* declining the ministry's invitation to Frankfurt.
17 See the article on Huda Lutfi by Judith Staines, "Cultural Play and Metamorphosis", culturebase.net, The International Artist Database. Online. Available at: www.culturebase.net/artist.php?158 (accessed 20 October 2005).

18 Huda Lutfi, "Women, History, Memory", interview by Samia Mehrez and James Stone, *Alif*, Vol. 19, 1999, p. 227.
19 Ibid., pp. 226–227.
20 Ibid., p. 236.
21 Huda Lutfi, "Found in Cairo: Representation and Reception in the Contemporary Egyptian Visual Field", unpublished testimony, delivered by the artist at a workshop entitled From Local to Global: Visual Arts in the Eastern Mediterranean between International Markets and Local Expectations, Florence, March 2006, p. 3.
22 Ibid., p. 229.
23 Lutfi, "Women, History, Memory", p. 228.
24 For a truly lyrical description of *Suq al-Iman* in the City of the Dead see, Nur Elmessiri and Nigel Ryan, "Arms Full of Things: Souq Al-Imam Al-Shafei at the Southern Cemetery" (photographs by Mary Cross), *Alif*, Vol. 21, 2001, pp. 9–24.
25 Lutfi, "Found in Cairo", p. 14.
26 For a more detailed description of the *Found in Cairo* exhibit see Lutfi's "Found in Cairo", pp. 14–20.
27 See Winegar, "Cultural Sovereignty in a Global Art Economy", p. 192.
28 Ibid., p. 196.
29 Ibid., p. 196.
30 Quoted in ibid., p. 197.
31 Lutfi, "Found in Cairo", p. 21.
32 One of the administrators at the Ministry of Culture describes young artists' engagement with private galleries in these terms. See Winegar, "Cultural Sovereignty in a Global Art Economy" for more examples of this attitude toward the private art world in Egypt.
33 See the coverage of this story of conversion and the tensions that arose between the Coptic and Muslim communities in *Al-Ahram Weekly*, 23–9 December 2004.
34 Lutfi, pp. 23–24.
35 See the Prologue and Chapter 3 above.
36 The prominent feminist Nawal Saadawi faced a *hisba* case in Egyptian civil courts in summer 2001 because of her views on Islamic pilgrimage and inheritance laws. The lawyer who launched the case against her sought to force a divorce between her and her husband. The *hisba* law is a legal procedure which allows an individual to file a complaint on behalf of society against another individual. The Public Prosecutor is the sole authority competent to decide whether or not a complaint under the *hisba* law, introduced in 1996, can lead to prosecution. On 23 May 2001 the Public Prosecutor publicly stated that there was no justification for any such charge to be brought against Nawal al-Saadawi. On 18 June the Personal Status Court of North Cairo briefly examined the complaint against Nawal al-Saadawi and postponed its decision. On July 30 July 2001 the court dismissed the case.
37 Jacquemond, "The Shifting Limits of the Sayable in Egyptian Fiction", p. 1.
38 Lutfi, "Found in Cairo", p. 19.
39 Ibid., p. 25.
40 Ibid., p. 30.

12 Literature and literalism: *Al-Khubz al-hafi* reconsidered

1 The *Al-Khubz al-hafi* crisis is but one example of many cases of censorship on university campuses in Egypt that have taken many guises and have involved, depending on the case, both state and non-state actors. For other cases and levels of censorship in the Egyptian academy see the Human Rights Watch Report, "Reading between the 'Red Lines': The Repression of Academic Freedom in Egyptian Universities", Human Rights Watch Report, June 2005. Online. Available at: hrw.org/reports/2005/egypt0605/7.htm#_Toc104800438 (accessed 21 October 2006),

and CAFMENA letter to President Hosni Mubarak on 16 June 1998, concerning the banning of Maxime Rodinson's *Muhammad*. Online. Available at: fpnew.ccit.arizona.edu/mesassoc/CAFMENAletters.htm#061698Egypt (accessed 23 October 2006).
2 Pierre Bourdieu, *Homo Academicus*, Paris: Les Editions de Minuit, 1984; English translation by Peter Collier, Stanford: Stanford University Press, 1988. References are to the French edition, p. 112.
3 Bourdieu, *Homo Academicus*, pp. 147–154.
4 Salah Muntasir, "Kitab yajib waqfuhu" (A Book that Must Be Stopped), *Al-Ahram*, 13 May 1998.
5 Maxime Rodinson (1915–2004) was a French Marxist historian, sociologist and orientalist. Rodinson became well known in France when he expressed a certain reticence about Israel, despite himself being Jewish. He had always been suspicious of Zionism and considered those who expressed enthusiasm for Israel as indulging in a belated form of colonialism. After the 1967 Arab–Israeli war, Rodinson distinguished himself as a leading champion of the Palestinian struggle for self-determination. While he regarded Israel as a colonial-settler state, the creation of the state was now a fact, and the time for questioning its wisdom is past, as he put it in his *Israel and the Arabs* (1968).
6 As explained in a memorandum by the Dean of Humanities and Social Science at AUC, 13 May 1998. See also "Rodinson Banned at AUC", *Middle East Report*, Winter 1998, p. 11; "Reading between the 'Red Lines'.
7 As explained in a memorandum by the Dean of Humanities and Social Science at AUC, 13 May 1998.
8 For a history of the American University's crises with the Egyptian state and society at large see Lawrence R. Murphy, *The American University in Cairo*, Cairo: AUC Press, 1987.
9 See "Reading between the 'Red Lines' (accessed 21 October 2006). See also *Ruz al-Yusuf*, 27 March 1999, where in a long article about censorship of books the AUC Press Director is quoted as saying that the Censor had asked "to review" 450 titles since the Rodinson affair. See also a similar article about censorship at AUC in *Al-Safir*, 20 March 1999.
10 Mohamed Choukri (1935–2003) was born on 15 July in Beni Chiker in the Rif Mountains of northern Morocco near the city of Nador, during a time of famine. Eight of his siblings died of malnutrition. He fled home to escape his tyrannical father at the age of eleven. At the age of twenty he began to teach himself how to read and write and eventually started writing short stories. In the mid-1970s Choukri met the expatriate writer Paul Bowles, who encouraged his creative talent and translated his autobiography under the title *For Bread Alone* in 1972. In 1981 Choukri's autobiography was translated into French by the prominent Moroccan francophone writer Taher Ben Jelloun, under the title *Le pain nu*. The autobiography was finally published in Arabic in 1982 as *Al-Khubz al-hafi* and was banned in Morocco until 2000 because of its daring and vivid descriptions of Choukri's life of petty crime, prostitution and drug use. For more detailed information on Mohamed Choukri and his works see *The Authorized Paul Bowles Web Site*, www.paulbowles.org/booksbest2.html (accessed 21 October 2006). For a critical reading of the original Arabic text *Al-Khubz al-hafi* and Bowles' translation into English see Nada Tanoukhi "Rewriting Political Commitment for International Canon: Paul Bowles's *For Bread Alone* as Translation of Mohamed Choukri's *Al-Khubz Al-hafi*", *Research in African Literatures*, Vol. 34, no. 2, Summer 2003, pp. 127–144.
11 *For Bread Alone*, the English translation of *Al-Khubz al-hafi*, had been taught by my colleague Dr Ferial Ghazoul of the Department of English and Comparative Literature in her class on Third World Literature. It was again on her reading list for that same class during spring 1999 when, in solidarity with me during *Al-khubz al-hafi*

crisis she refused to remove it from her list and made sure that her students could read it in the library after the AUC administration had "complied" with the Censor's decision to "prohibit [its] circulation" (*man' min al-tadawul*). In fact, since *Al-Khubz al-hafi* was not a banned book and had been in bookstores and in circulation in Egypt during the crisis, the AUC administration had written to the Censor's office to "inquire" about the status of the book, an "inquiry" that effectively extracted from the Censor the prohibition from circulation of the book. The Censor's office responded to the AUC administration's "inquiry" in a brief and rather vague letter dated 22 April 1999 (i.e. four months after the crisis had started), saying: "In response to your letter concerning *Al-Khubz al-hafi* we wish to inform you that the book has been prohibited from circulation due to the blatant sexual scenes that violate our religious and social traditions." I have been given a copy of the original letter in Arabic by the administration when repeated efforts to extract a promise or declaration from me not to teach the book again had failed and I continued to insist that as long as the book was not officially banned I would retain the right to use it again in my courses.

12 *Al-Khubz al-hafi* was eventually made into a highly successful film in 2005 by Rachid Bin Haj, the Italian filmmaker of Algerian origin, in a joint Italian, French, Moroccan production. It was shown at several international film festivals including the Cairo International Film Festival, 2005. It also subsequently received recognition by the Moroccan Ministry of Culture, including a complimentary letter from His Majesty Muhammad VI.

13 For example, in 2006 the Egyptian documentary filmmaker, Tahani Rached made a film about street girls in Cairo (*Al-Banat dul*; English translation *These Girls*) that exposed the cruelty of these women's lives on the streets. It was produced by Studio Misr and was shown at Cannes Film Festival in 2006. The film created a controversy among Egyptian parliamentarians, some of whom called for banning it because of its shockingly candid and audacious representation of the reality of street children's lives in Cairo.

14 For more on Sonallah Ibrahim's *Tilka l-ra'iha* and its status in the literary field see Samia Mehrez, *Egyptian Writers between History and Fiction*, Cairo: AUC Press, 1994, 2005, pp. 39–57.

15 Normally complaints are first discussed with the instructor. If not resolved directly they may be taken to the chair of the department and further up the administrative level (Dean, Provost and President) if necessary.

16 I actually made a point of purchasing copies of *Al-Khubz al-hafi* from the state-run Ruz al-Yusuf bookstore downtown Cairo and at the Cairo International Book Fair that is held annually during the month of January, hence after the crisis at AUC. The receipts for these purchases are dated 23 January and 30 January 1999 respectively. Indeed, because of the crisis at AUC and its eventual press coverage all copies of *Al-Khubz al-hafi* were sold out at the Cairo Book Fair in 1999. See Appendix II for copies of the two receipts.

17 For example: Muhammad Barrada, Professor of Arabic Literature at Mohammed V University, Morocco, who was instrumental in publishing Choukri's first collection of short stories *Majnun al-ward* (*Madman of Roses*), Beirut: Dar Al-Adab, 1979 and has since been Choukri's literary godfather. Together they published a volume of their correspondence entitled *Ward wa ramad* (*Roses and Ashes*), Rabat Al-Manahil, 2000. Also Sabri Hafez, Professor of Arabic Literature at SOAS, England, wrote an introduction to Choukri's second part of the autobiography, *Al-Shuttar*, London: Dar Al-Saqi, 1992, pp. 219–242.

18 Ferial Ghazoul and Barbara Harlow, *The View from Within: Writers and Critics on Contemporary Arabic Literature*, Cairo: AUC Press, 1994, pp. 220–227.

19 For the complete text of the memorandum I circulated by email to all AUC faculty recounting the details of this meeting see Appendix III. The names of individuals implicated in the *Al-Khubz al-hafi* crisis have been blocked out.

310 *Notes*

20. In a memo circulated to all AUC faculty the AUC administration challenged my account of the meeting, arguing that they did not ask me to apologize to my students for teaching the book but rather to apologize for "the hurt" it might have caused them. See Appendix IV.
21. See Appendix III.
22. My open letter to all AUC faculty is dated 27 December 1998. See Appendix III.
23. See Appendix IV.
24. See Appendix V.
25. Two top administrators presented their apologies to me in a meeting of our department on 11 February 1999.
26. See anonymous parents' letter to the AUC Affirmative Action Office, Appendix VI.
27. The January 4 meeting with members of AUC administration was attended by two top officials and Huda Lutfi, my colleague in the department.
28. More than one article in the Egyptian press covered the urgent meeting of the Parliamentary Committee for Education and Academic Research called into session by the National Democratic MP, Ahmad Shiha to question the Minister of Higher Education on the *Al-Khubz al-hafi* crisis and to call for disciplinary action against me. See for example *Al-Gumhuriyya*, 2 March 1999; *Al-Arabi*, 8 March 1999; *Al-Ahali*, 24 March 1999.
29. A short article in *Al-Gumhuriyya*, 2 March 1999 reported that I had threatened to sue the AUC *administration*; *Al-Arabi* 8 March 1999, reported that the Minister of Higher Education had denied allegations that he would seek disciplinary action against me.
30. Muhammad Mustafa Shurdi, "*Al-Khubz al-hafi* ... fi l-Jamiʿa al-amrikiya" (*Al-Khubz al-hafi* in the American University), *Al-Wafd*, 7 January 1999.
31. A high university official told me during a department meeting on 11 February 1999 that the administration was against replying to the press and the first attack it launched against me.
32. *Al-Wafd*, 11 January 1999. The complete text of the translated letter may be consulted in Appendix VII.
33. The AUC administration eventually released a statement on *Al-Khubz al-hafi* on 3 March 1999, i.e. more than two months after the beginning of the crisis. For the text of the statement see Appendix VIII. The text of the statement is also available at www.library.cornell.edu/colldev/mideast/mehr.htm.
34. For interesting coverage of and positions on the *Al-Khubz al-hafi* crisis case see Judith Gabriel, "Mohammed Shukri's 'The Plain Bread' Is Target of Hostile Press, Academic Furor in Egypt", *Al-Jadid*, Vol. 5, no. 26, Winter 1999, pp. 4, 5, 30; Salama Ahmad Salama, "Al-Fikr al-hafi" (Barefoot Thought), *Al-Kutub Wijhat Nadhar*, April 1999; Joseph Logan, "Morality Cops in the Classroom", *Cairo Times*, 18–30 March 1999; Joseph Logan, "Banned in Cairo", *Lingua Franca*, July/August 1999; Shahnaz Rouse, "Policing Voices, (En) Gendering Censorship, *The Review*, Association for Middle East Women's Studies (AMEWS)", Vol. VIX, no. 4, Winter 2000, pp. 9–11, 19.
35. I am particularly grateful to Ferial Ghazoul (Department of English and Comparative Literature) and Nicholas Hopkins (Department of Sociology, Anthropology, Psychology and Egyptology) with whom I consistently consulted. I remain indebted to their wisdom, vision, friendship and professional integrity.
36. I owe special thanks to my colleagues in the Department of Arabic Studies – Huda Lutfi, Shahab Ahmed, Clarissa Burt and Teirab AshShareef – whose friendship, warmth and solidarity day in and day out throughout the crisis have provided me with indispensable confidence and conviction. Without their support and selflessness it would have been impossible for me to sustain the battle that lasted for six months. I particularly appreciate the courageous outspokenness of Shahab Ahmed, Clarrisa Burt and Teirab AshShareef, who as junior colleagues in the department subjected themselves to potential reprisals because of their support for me. All three have subsequently left AUC. I am equally grateful to Richard Jacquemond, my husband and

Notes 311

colleague, whose presence, energy, insight and advice have helped me survive the six-month-long crisis.
37 Gamal al-Ghitani, "Tilka l-dajja" (That Fuss), *Al-Akhbar*, 18 January 1999.
38 *Al-Ahram al-Arabi*, 3 March 1999.
39 See *Al-Itihad al-Ishtiraki*, February 1999, *Al-Sharq al-Awsat*, 18 February 1999, and *Al-Hayat*, 22 February 1999.
40 Mohamed Choukri, Letter to the President of the American University in Cairo, 8 February 1999.
41 Hasan Daoud, "Qadiyyat *al-Khubz al-hafi*" (The Case of *Al-Khubz-al-hafi*), *Al-Hayat*, 4 February 1999.
42 Magda al-Nowaihi (1958–2002) taught Arabic literature at Columbia University. We had known each other since our undergraduate years in the Department of English Literature at AUC. Over these long years we were able to establish a remarkably strong bond both personally and professionally despite the long distance that separated us.
43 This letter was posted on the internet on 20 January 1999. For the text of Magda al-Nowaihi's and Muhammad Siddiq's letter see Appendix IX.
44 For the text of Magda al-Nowaihi's letter see Appendix X.
45 I first met Edward Said at UCLA in 1979 where I had just enrolled in the Program of Comparative Literature. He was the mentor of my own MA mentor at AUC, Ferial Ghazoul, who had written to him about my MA thesis, recommending its publication in *Arab Studies Quarterly* on whose board he served. After then our paths crossed more than once: at Cornell during the 1980s where I taught Arabic Literature and then many times in Cairo specifically while he was writing his autobiography *Out of Place* and happened to be my next-door neighbour at the AUC Hostel in Zamalek.
46 Edward Said, "Literature and Literalism", *Al-Ahram Weekly*, 28 January 1999.
47 Ibid. For an interesting reading of Said's article in *Al-Ahram Weekly* and the different positions taken during the *Al-Khubz al-hafi* crisis see Richard Jacquemond, "The Shifting Limits of the Sayable in Contemporary Egyptian Fiction", *The MIT Electronic Journal of Middle East Studies*, Vol. 4, Fall 2004, pp. 41–52. web.mit. edu/CIS/www/mitejmes/issues/200412/MITEJMES_Vol_4_Fall.pdf (accessed 23 October 2006).
48 For the text of the entire interview with the President of AUC see *Al-Ahram Weekly*, 28 January 1999.
49 Part of the text of Edward Said's commencement address was published in *AL-Ahram Weekly*, 24 June 1999. The entire text was published in *Alif* Vol. 25, 2005, pp. 26–36. It is also reproduced as Appendix XI.
50 The CAFMENA letter was sent to the AUC President with a copy to me on 25 May 1999. It was later published in the autumn 1999 *MESA Newsletter*. See also CAFMENA letters website at: fpnew.ccit.arizona.edu/mesassoc/CAFMENAletters. htm#0521AUC (accessed 23 October 2006).
51 CAFMENA letter to President Husni Mubarak, 21 May 1999. The text of the letter was later published in the autumn 1999 *MESA Newsletter*. It is also available on the CAFMENA letters website at: fpnew.ccit.arizona.edu/mesassoc/CAFMENAletters. htm#052199Egypt (accessed 23 October 2006).
52 This was the position of the AUC Professor Saad Eddin Ibrahim, whose public intervention in the *Caravan*, the AUC weekly student paper, in its issue of 14 February 1999 was the first. His defence of liberal education and my academic freedom as an instructor opened a long debate on the pages of *Caravan* for another three months.
53 This was the argument put forth by the AUC Professor Yahya El Ezabi on the pages of the weekly student paper the *Caravan*, 21 February 1999. It is instructive to note that El Ezabi's position echoed that of the AUC President which he had articulated only a couple of weeks earlier in *Al-Ahram Weekly*'s 28 January issue when he stated that: "[*Al-Khubz al-hafi*] has sexually explicit passages that are very offensive. I was offended when I read them. I couldn't read them aloud."

54 See the *Caravan* issues of 14 February, 21 February, 28 February, 14 March, 21 March, 26 April 1999.
55 Salwa Bakr, "The Monkey Trainer", in *The Wiles of Men and Other Stories*, Austin: University of Texas Press, 1993, pp. 83–96.
56 Bakr, "The Monkey Trainer", p. 96.
57 Two articles appeared in the 14 March student paper, *Caravan*: "Mehrez's Monkey Provides Powerful Parable", and a letter to the editor entitled "Thank You Dear Teacher", in which a student who had attended my talk deemed it "inspiring" and concluded that "to teach is to touch lives forever".
58 See for example Abbas al-Tunsi (AUC Senior Lecturer in the Arabic Language Institute), who participated in the debate several times. The first was "Libraliyun min naw'in khass" (A Special Breed of Liberals), *Akhbar al-Adab*, 24 January 1999, where he basically defended the Chair of Arabic Studies and attacked the "liberal" paper *Al-Wafd* for rushing to demand banning and censorship of a well known literary text, but still openly declared that he was against teaching Choukri's text in an introductory class, deeming it appropriate for graduate students only. See also Ferial Ghazoul (AUC Professor of Comparative Literature), "When the Subaltern Speaks", *Ahram Weekly*, 18 February 1999, where she defends *Al-Khubz al-hafi* as a "classic of modern Arabic literature" that denudes the immorality of social reality and as such has an ultimate moral goal; Mahmud al-Rabi'i (AUC Professor of Arabic Literature), "Hurriyyat al-ibda' wa hurriyyat al-talaqqi" (Creative Freedom and Freedom of Reception), who basically argued that the teacher of a controversial work does not have the same freedom as the writer who created it since her or his students, whose sensibilities should be respected, do not participate in the choice of the work, and finally Galal Amin (AUC Professor of Economics), "Fasl al-maqal fi ma bayn *al-Khubz al-hafi* wa *Mawsim al-hijra* min infisal" (A Definitive Demonstration of the Difference between *Al-Khubz al-hafi* and *Season of Migration to the North*), *Al-Kutub Wijhat Nadhar*, no. 4, May 1999, pp. 60–63.
59 Jacquemond, "The Limits of the Sayable in Egyptian Fiction".
60 Ibid., p. 48.
61 Galal Amin, "Fasl al-maqal".
62 See Ferial Ghazoul, "Laysat al-riwaya mashhadan jinsiyan illa idha iktafa qari'uha bi l-talassus ala hadha al-janib" (The Novel Is Not Pornographic unless the Reader Chooses a Voyeuristic Perspective), *Al-Hayat*, 11 May 1999.
63 Ghazoul, "When the Subaltern Speaks".
64 See Muhammad Salmawi, "Ma bayn al-takhassus wa wijhat al-nadhar" (Between Specialization and Personal Opinion), *Al-Ahram*, 24 May 1999; "Al-takhassus marra ukhra" (Specialization Once More), *Al-Ahram*, 31 May 1999; "Fann al-sira al-dhatiyya" (The Art of Autobiography), *Al-Ahram*, 14 June 1999; and Galal Amin's reply, "Al-Irhab bi-sm al-hurriyya asra' wasila li qatl al-hurriyya dhatiha" (Terrorism in the Name of Freedom is the Quickest Way to Killing Freedom Itself), *Al-Arabi*, 6 June 1999.
65 Galal Amin, "Fasl al-maqal", p. 61.
66 Jacquemond, "The Shifting Limits of the Sayable", p. 49. Indeed Jacquemond cites the example of Galal Amin's intervention against another Egyptian literary text, *Al-Saqqar (The Hawker)* by Samir Gharib Ali. For more details on this episode see Jacquemond, "The Shifting Limits of the Sayable".
67 Edward Said, "Literature and Literalism".
68 See "*Al-Khubz al-hafi*: Wathiqat al-idana" (*Al-Khubz al-hafi*: The Document of Incrimination) in *Al-Adab*, November 2002, pp. 58–68.
69 These accusations are in the minutes of a departmental meeting on 27 December 1998 which took place just before I circulated by email my open letter to all AUC faculty (Appendix III). Referring to the *Al-Khubz al-hafi* incident, one of my senior colleagues said during the 27 December meeting: "What happened does come within the

purview of sexual harassment. I have looked it up a bit. People are sued for the discussion of rape and even giving sexual examples in class." Another senior colleague commented: "We should strike a balance between academic freedom and mental or sexual harassment. There is a difference between sex in a classic and a non-classic work of literature." These comments, along with sexual harassment materials circulated for "discussion" by the chair of the department prior to a meeting on 11 February 1999, became the subject of several hostile memos between me and the accusing colleagues until 25 February 1999 when the Provost, in a memo to me, copied to the President, the Chair of my department, the Affirmative Action Office and the accusing senior colleague, after legal council, intervened to dismiss the validity of the accusations, saying: "Thank you for your recent memo regarding the issue of sexual harassment. We consulted AUC's lawyer about the anonymous complaint charging you with sexual harassment. In his opinion, the circumstances of this case do not constitute sexual harassment. I trust that this will put an end to all discussion of what has proven to be a false issue."

70 See *Wikipedia: The Free Encyclopedia*, "The Nasr Abu Zayd Case", /en.wikipedia.org/wiki/Nasr_Abu_Zayd#The_Nasr_Abu_Zayd_case suffered major religious persecution for his views on the Qur'an as a religious, mythical literary work. In 1995, he was promoted to the rank of Professor, but Islamic controversies about his academic work led to a court decision of apostasy and the denial of the appointment. A hisba trial was started against him by fundamentalist Islamic scholars, he was declared a heretic (*murtadd*) by an Egyptian court, was consequently declared divorced from his wife (since she is not allowed to be married to a non-Muslim) and, in effect, forced out of his homeland." For more details on the Abu Zayd case see the text of the article in Wikipedia.

71 For example, in their letter, the anonymous parents stated that most of the books on my reading list for the course were "sexually oriented", echoing the exact words of one of my senior colleagues in the department. The parents also demanded (in bold print) of the AUC President to: "Make sure that the heads of the departments know the material taught and do not leave the teacher to destroy the minds of our children". The surveillance issue was at the core of the faculty battle during *Al-Khubz al-hafi* crisis since the Chair of Arabic Studies had volunteered, without consultation with the faculty, to state in his 11 January 1999 letter to *Al-Wafd* that: "The truth is that the university [administration] did intervene, and that the concerned department held several meetings where it was decided that books taught to new students in any course must be chosen by the instructors from a list of books prepared by the department for this course. This in order to guarantee that what happened will not be repeated."

72 See Appendix VI for full text of the letter. I have not attempted to correct the poor grammar, punctuation etc. of the original document.
73 See Appendix VI.
74 Edward Said, AUC Commencement Address, 17 June 1999. Appendix XI.
75 See Appendix VI.
76 See Appendix VI.
77 Edward, Appendix XI.
78 See Appendix VI.
79 *Kutub mamnu'a* (*Banned Books*), Nile Cultural Channel, 16 November 2006.

Bibliography

Literary works in Arabic and in translation

Abdel Meguid, I., *Tuyur al-anbar*, Cairo: Dar al-Hilal, 2001; English translation: *Birds of Amber*, Abdel Wahab, F. (trans.), AUC Press, 2005
——, *Al-Balda al-ukhra*, London: Dar Riad al-Raiyyis, 1991; English translation: *The Other Place*, Abdel Wahad, F. (trans.), AUC Press, 1997
——, *La ahad yanam fi l-Iskandariya*, Cairo: Dar al-Hilal, 1996; English translation: *No One Sleeps in Alexandria*, Abdel Wahab, F. (trans.), AUC Press, 1999
Abu Golayyel, H., *Lusus mutaqa'idun*, Cairo: Merit, 2002; English translation: *Thieves in Retirement*, Booth, M. (trans.), Syracuse: Syracuse University Press, 2006
Abu Rayya, Y., *Laylat urs*, Cairo: Dar al-Hilal 2002; English translation: *Wedding Night*, Hewison, N. (trans.), Cairo: AUC Press, 2006
Alaidy, A., *An Takun Abbas al-Abd*, Cairo: Merit, 2003; English translation: *Being Abbas El Abd*, Davies, H. (trans.), Cairo: AUC Press, 2006
Al-Aswany, A., *Imarat Ya'qubyan*, Cairo: Merit, 2002; English translation: *Yacoubian Building*, Davies, H. (trans.), Cairo: AUC Press, 2004
Al-Ghitani, G., *Al-Zayni Barakat*, Damascus: Ministry of Culture, 1974: English translation: *Zayni Barakat*, Abdel Wahab, F. (trans.), London: Penguin Books, 1988 and Cairo: AUC Press, 2004
Al-Kharrat, E., *Rama wa l-tinnin*, Beirut: Dar Al-Adab, 1992; English translation: *Rama and the Dragon*, Ghazoul, F., and Verlenden, J. (trans.), Cairo: AUC Press, 2002
——, *Sukhur al-Sama'* (*The Rocks of Heaven*), Cairo: Markaz al-Hadara l-Arabiyya, 2001
Al-Tahawy, M., *Al-Khiba'*, Cairo: Dar Sharqiyyat 1996: English translation: *The Tent*, Colderbank, T. (trans.), Cairo: AUC Press, 1996
Al-Wardani, M., *Al-Rawd al-atir* (*Perfumed gardens*), Cairo: Dar al-Hilal, 1998
Al-Zayyat, L., *Al-Bab al-maftuh*, Cairo: GEBO, 1960; English translation: *The Open Door*, Booth, M. (trans.), Cairo: AUC Press, 2002
Bakr, S., "The Monkey Trainer", in *The Wiles of Men and Other Stories*, Austin: University of Texas Press, 1993
Barakat, H., *Harith al-miyah*, Beirut: Dar Al-Nahar, 1998; English translation: *The Tiller of Waters*, Booth, M. (trans.), Cairo: AUC Press, 2004
Barghouti, M., *Ra'aytu Ramalla*, Cairo: Dar al-Hilal 1997; English translation: *I Saw Ramallah*, Souief, A. (trans.), Cairo: AUC Press, 2003
Choukri, M., *Al-Khubz al-hafi*, Tangiers, privately published, 1982; Dar al-Saqi, 1993; English translation: *For Bread Alone*, Bowles, P. (trans.), London: Peter Owen

Publishers, 1971; French translation: *Le pain nu*, Ben Jelloun, T. (trans.), Paris: Maspéro, 1980
——, *Majnun al-ward* (*Madman of the Roses*), Beirut: Dar Al-Adab, 1979
Choukri, M., and Barrada, M., *Ward wa ramad* (*Roses and Ashes*), Rabat: Al-Manahil, 2000
Hamid, M., *Ahlam muharrama* (*Forbidden Dreams*), Cairo: GOCP, 2000
Haydar, H., *Walima li-a'shab al-bahr* (*Banquet for Seaweed*), Nicosia, privately published, 1983
Himmich, B., *Al-Allama*, Rabat: Dar al-Ma'arif, 2001; English translation, *The Polymath*, Allen, R. (trans.), Cairo: AUC Press, 2004
Ibrahim, S., *Al-Talassus* (*Evesdropping*), Cairo: Dar al Mustqabal al-Arabi, 2007
——, *Yawmiyyat al-wahat* (*Memoirs of Al-Wahat*), Cairo: Dar al-Mustqabal al-Arabi, 2005
——, *Amrikanli*, Cairo: Dar al-Mustaqbal al-Arabi, 2003
——, *Dhat*, Cairo: Dar al-Mustaqbal al-Arabi, 1992; English translation: *Zaat*, Colderbank, T. (trans.), Cairo: AUC Press, 2001
——, *Warda*, Cairo: Dar al-Mustaqbal al-Arabi, 2000
——, *Sharaf*, Cairo: Dar al-Hilal, 1997
——, *Bayrut, Bayrut*, Cairo: Dar al-Mustaqbal al-Arabi, 1984
——, *Al-Lajna*, Beirut; Dar al-Kalima, 1981; English translation: *The Committee*, St Germain, M., and Constable, C. (trans.), Cairo: AUC Press, 2002
——, *Najmat Aghustus* (*Star of August*), Damascus: Ittihad al-Kuttab al-Arab, 1974
——, *Tilka l-ra'iha*, Cairo: Maktab Yulyu, 1966; English translation: *The Smell of It*, Johnson-Davies, D. (trans.), London: Heinemann, 1971
Ismat, A., *Al-Rajul al-ari* (*The Naked Man*), Cairo: Dar Sharqiyyat, 1998
——, *Hajis mawt* (*Fear of Death*), Cairo: Dar Sharqiyyat, 1995
Issa, I., *Ashbah wataniyya* (*Nationalistic Ghosts*), Cairo: Merit, 2005
——, *Maqtal al-rajul al-kabir* (*The Assassination of the Big Man*), Cairo, 1999
Khalifeh, S., *Sura wa ayquna wa ahdun qadim* (*An Image, an Icon and a Covenant*) Beirut: Dar al-Adab, 2002
Mahfouz, N., *Awlad haratina*, Beirut: Dar al-Adab, 1967; Cairo: Dar al-Shuruq, 2006; English translation: *Children of the Alley*, Theroux, P. (trans.), New York: Anchor Books, 1996
——, *Zuqaq al-midaqq*, Cairo: Lajnat al-nashr li l-jami'iyyin, 1947: English translation: *Midaq Alley*, Le Gassick, T. (trans.), London: Heinemann, 1966
——, *Bayn al-Qasrayn, Qasr al-Shawq, Al-Sukkariyya*, Cairo: Maktabat Misr, 1956 and 1957; English translation: *The Cairo Trilogy*, Hutchins, M. W., Kenny, E. O., Kenny, M. L., Samaan, B. A. (trans.), Cairo: AUC Press, 2001
Mamdouh, A., *Al-Mahbubat*, Dar al-Saqi, 2003; English translation: *The Loved Ones*, Booth, M. (trans.), Cairo: AUC Press, 2006
Mosteghanemi, A., *Dhakirat al-jasad*, Beirut: Dar al-Adab, 1996; English translation: *Memory in the Flesh*, Ahmar, B. (trans.), Cairo: AUC Press, 2003
Prince, M., *Thalath haqa'ib li l-safar* (*Three Suitcases for Departure*), Cairo: Marqaz al-Hadara l-Arabiyya, 1998
Ramadan, S., *Awraq al-narjis*, Cairo: Dar Sharqiyyat, 2001; English translation: *Leaves of Narcissus*, Booth, M. (trans.), Cairo: AUC Press, 2002
——, *Manazil al-ruh* (*Homes of the Soul*), Cairo: GEBO, 1999
——, *Khashab wa nahas* (*Wood and Brass*), Cairo: Dar Sharqiyyat, 1995
Sha'ban, Y., *Abna' al-khata' al-rumansi* (*Children of Romantic Error*), Cairo: GOCP, 2000

Shalaby, K., *Wikalat Atiyya*, Cairo: Dar Sharqiyyat, 1992; English translation: *The Lodging House*, Abdel Wahad, F. (trans.), Cairo: AUC Press, 2006
Taher, B., *Nuqtat nur (A Spot of Light)*, Cairo: Dar al-Hilal, 2001
Tawfik, M., *Tifl shaqi ismuhu Antar (A Naughty Boy Called Antar)*, Cairo: Merit, 2003
Telmissany, M., *Dunyazad*, Cairo: Dar Sharqiyyat, 1997: English translation: *Dunyazad*, Allen, R. (trans.), London: Saqi Books, 2000
Zikri, M., *Mir 'at 202 (202 Mirror)*, Cairo: Merit, 2003
——, *Lamsa min alam gharib (A Touch from a Strange World)*, Cairo: Sharqiyyat, 2000
——, *Al-Khawf ya'qul al-ruh (Fear Eats the Soul)*, Cairo: Sharqiyyat, 1998
——, "Ma ya'rifuhu Amin", in *Hura' mataha qutiyya* ("What Amin Knows", in *Hallucinations in a Gothic Labyrinth*), Cairo: Dar Sharqiyyat, 1997

Other sources: English and Arabic

Abaza, M., *The Changing Consumer Cultures of Modern Egypt: Cairo's Urban Reshaping*, Cairo: AUC Press, 2006
Abbas, R., *Mashaynaha khutan*, Cairo: Dar al-Hilal, 2004
Abdallah, A., *The Student Movement and National Politics in Egypt*, London: Al-Saqi, 1985
——, "Egypt's Islamists and the State: From Complicity to Confrontation", *Middle East Report*, no. 183, July–August 1993
Abdel Meguid, I., "Raddan ala Sayyid al-Bahrawi" (A Response to Sayyid al-Bahrawi), *Akhbar al-Adab*, 12 January 1997
Abdel-Messih, M. T., "Debunking the Heroic Self", *Banipal*, no. 25, Spring 2006
Aboul Atta, T., and Yousry, M., "The Challenge of Urban Growth in Cairo", in *The Urban Challenge in Africa: Growth and Management of its Large Cities*, Rakodi, C. (ed.), New York: United Nations University Press, 1997
Abul-Ghar, M., *Ihdar istiqlal al-jami'at*, Cairo, privately published, 2001
Abu-Lughod, L., *Dramas of Nationhood*, Cairo: American University in Cairo Press, 2005
Abu-Lughod, L., "Finding a Place for Islam: Egyptian Television Serials and the National Interest", *Public Culture*, Vol. 5, 1993
Ahmed, L., *Women and Gender in Islam: Historical Roots of a Modern Debate*, Cairo: AUC Press, 1992
ALESCO report. Online. Available at: www.aticm.org.eg/admin/Farek_kema/REPAW-SIS17%D8%B1%D8%B6%D8%A7.doc (accessed 10 June 2006)
Al-Bahrawi, S., "Ghiwayat al-jawa'iz" (The Seduction of Prizes), *Akhbar al-Adab*, 22 December 1996
——, "Latifa al-Zayyat tarfud al-ja'iza" (Latifa al-Zayyat Refuses the Prize), *Akhbar al-Adab*, 5 January 1997
Al-Gawhary, K., "Copts in the 'Egyptian Fabric'", *Middle East Report*, 200, July–September 1996
Al-Ghitani, G., "Faltarhal anta!" (Why Don't You Leave!), *Akhbar al-Adab*, 21 January 2001
——, "*Sharaf Son'alla*", *Akhbar al-Adab*, 5 January 1997
——, *Najib Mahfudh yatadhakkar*, Cairo: *Akhbar al-Yawm*, 1987
Al-Nowaihi, M., "Unheard in English", *MIT EJMES*, Vol. 4, Fall 2004. Online. Available at: www.web.mit.edu/CIS/www/mitejmes/issues/200412/MITEJMES_Vol_4_Fall.pdf (accessed 3 January 2006)

Al-Rabi'i, M., "Hurriyyat al-ibda' wa hurriyyat al-talaqqi" (Freedom of Creation and Freedom of Reception), *Ibda'*, June 1999

Alrawi, K., "The War on Education: The Devil or the Dustbowl", *New Internationalist* 248, October 1993. Online. Available at: www.newint.org/issue248/devil.htm (accessed 10 January 2006)

Al-Siwi, A., "Representing the Body", *Ain: Journal of Plastic Arts*, Vol. 1, 1997

Altorki, S., "Patriarchy and Imperialism: Father–Son and British–Egyptian Relations in Najib Mahfuz's *Trilogy*", in *Intimate Selving in Arab Families*, Joseph, S. (ed.), Syracuse: Syracuse University Press, 1999

Al-Tunsi, A., "Ghiwayat al-tufula al-yasariyya" (The Seduction of the Infantile Left), *Akhbar al-Adab*, 29 December 1996

Alterman, J. B., "Transnational Media and Social Change in the Arab World", *TBS*, no. 2, Spring 1999. Online. Available at: www.tbsjournal.com/Archives/Spring99/spr99.html (accessed 12 June 2006)

Amin, G., "Al-Irhab bi-sm al-hurriyya asra' wasila li qatl al-hurriyya dhatiha" (Terrorism in the Name of Freedom is the Quickest Way to Killing Freedom Itself), *Al-Arabi*, 6 June 1999

——, "Fasl al-maqal fi ma bayn *al-Khubz al-hafi* wa *Mawsim al-hijra* min infisal" (A Definitive Demonstration of the Difference between *Al-Khubz al-hafi* and *Season of Migration to the North*), *Al-Kutub Wijhat Nadhar*, no. 4, May 1999

Amireh, A., "Publishing in the West: Problems and Prospects for Arab Women Writers", *Al-Jadid*, Vol. 2, no. 10, August 1996

Anderson, B., *Imagined Communities*, London and New York: Verso, 1983

Arab Human Development Report 2003: Building a Knowledge Society, New York: United Nations Publications, 2003. Online. Available at: www.miftah.org/Doc/Reports/Englishcomplete2003.pdf (accessed 5 January 2005)

Arab Republic of Egypt: Higher Education Enhancement Project (HEEP), 2002. Online. Available, at: wds.worldbank.org/servlet/WDSContentServer/WDSP/IB/2002/04/12/000094946_02033004305220/Rendered/PDF/multi0page.pdf (accessed 12 January 2007)

Armbrust, W., *Mass Culture and Modernism in Egypt*, Cambridge: Cambridge University Press, 1996

Badran, M., *Feminists Islam and Nation: Gender and the Making of Modern Egypt*, Cairo: AUC Press, 1996

Barbulesco, L., and Cardinal, P., *L'Islam en questions*, Paris: Grasset, 1986

Baron, B., *The Women's Awakening in Egypt: Culture Society and the Press*, New Haven and London: Yale University Press, 1994

Bayat, A., "Cairo's Poor: Dilemmas of Survival and Solidarity", *Middle East Report* 202, Winter 1997, Online. Available at: www.jstor.org/view/08992851/di011543/01p00432/0 (accessed 20 May 2006)

Bok, D., *Universities in the Marketplace: The Commercialization of Higher Education*, Princeton: Princeton University Press, 2004

Booth, M., "Introduction", *The Open Door*, Cairo: AUC Press, 2000

Botiveau, B., "The Law of the Nation-State and the Status of non-Muslims in Egypt and Syria", in *Christian Communities in the Arab Middle East: The Challenge of the Future*, Pacini, A. (ed.), Oxford: Clarendon Press, 1988

Bourdieu, P., *Masculine Domination*, Stanford: Stanford University Press, 2000

——, *Rules of Art: Genisis and Structure of the Literary Field*, Emanuel, S. (trans.), Stanford: Stanford University Press, 1996

318 Bibliography

——, *Les règles de l'art*, Paris: Editions du Seuil, 1992

——, "Le champ littéraire", *Actes de la Recherche en Sciences Sociales*, no. 89, 1991

——, *Homo Academicus*, Paris: Les Editions de Minuit, 1984; English translation, Collier, P., Stanford: Stanford University Press, 1988

Brief Description of the Higher Education System in Egypt. Online. Available at: www.gse.buffalo.edu/org/IntHigherEdFinance/Egypt.pdf (accessed 25 April 2006)

CAFMENA letter to President Hosni Mubarak, 16 June 1998. Online. Available at: fpnew.ccit.arizona.edu/mesassoc/CAFMENAletters.htm#061698Egypt (accessed 23 October 2006)

CAFMENA letter to AUC President, 25 May 1999. Online. Available at: fpnew.ccit.arizona.edu/mesassoc/CAFMENAletters.htm#0521AUC (accessed October 2006)

Campagna, J., "From Accommodation to Confrontation: The Muslim Brotherhood in the Mubarak Years", *Journal of International Affairs*, Vol. 50, 1996. Online. Available at: www.questia.com/PM.qst?a=o&se=gglsc&d=5000396998 (accessed 22 January 2007)

Choukri, M., *The Authorized Paul Bowles Web Site*. Online: Available at: www.paulbowles.org/booksbest2.html (accessed 21 October 2006)

Colla, E., "Anxious Advocacy: The Novel, the Law, and Extrajudicial Appeals in Egypt", *Public Culture*, Vol. 17, no. 3, 2005

Davies, H., "Translator's Note", *Yacoubian Building*, Davies, H. (trans.), Cairo: AUC Press, 2004

Denis, E., "Cairo as a Neoliberal Capital? From Walled City to Gated Community", in *Cairo Cosmopolitan: Politics, Culture, and Urban Space in the New Globalized Middle East*, Singerman, D., and Amar, P. (eds), Cairo: AUC Press, 2006

——, "Urban Planning and Growth in Cairo", *Middle East Report*, 202, Winter, 1997. Online. Available at: www.jstor.org/view/08992851/di011543/01p00442/0 (accessed 20 May 2006)

Dick, M., "The State of the Musalsal: Arab Television Drama and Comedy and the Politics of the State", *TBS*, no. 15, Fall 2005. Online. Available at: www.tbsjournal.com/Archives/Fall05/Dick.html (accessed 3 June 2006)

Eickelman, D., *New Media in the Muslim World: The Emerging Public Sphere*, Indiana: Indiana University Press, 2003

El-Batran, M., and Arandel, C., "A Shelter of Their Own: Informal Settlement Expansion in Greater Cairo and Government Responses", *Environment and Urbanization*, Vol. 10, no. 1, 1998, Online. Available at: eau.sagepub.com/cgi/content/abstract/10/1/217 (accessed 30 May 2006)

El-Ghobashy, M., "The Metamorphosis of the Egyptian Muslim Brotherhood", *International Journal of Middle East Studies*, 37, 2005

"Egypt: Investigate Election Fraud, Not Judges", *Human Rights News*, hrw.org. Online. Available at: hrw.org/english/docs/2006/04/25/egypt13269.htm (accessed 20 January 2007)

El Amrani, I., *The Arabist website* at http://arabist.net/

El Khawaga, D., "The Political Dynamics of the Copts: Giving the Community an Active Role", in *Christian Communities in the Arab Middle East: The Challenge of the Future*, Pacini, A. (ed.), Oxford: Clarendon Press, 1988

Elmasry, F., US College Students Crowd Into Arabic Language Classes, VOANews.com 17 February 2005. Online. Available at: www.voanews.com/english/archive/2005-02/2005-02-17-voa28.cfm?CFID=86250320&CFTOKEN=37524210 (accessed 16 January 2007)

Elmessiri, N., and Ryan, N., "Arms Full of Things: Souq Al-Imam Al-Shafei at the Southern Cemetery", *Alif*, Vol. 21, 2001

Elsadda, H., "Women and Memory", *Alif*, Vol. 19, 1999

Elsheshtawy, Y., "Urban Transformations: Social Control at al-Rifa'i Mosque and Sultan Hasan Square", in *Cairo Cosmopolitan: Politics, Culture, and Urban Space in the New Globalized Middle East*, Singerman, D., and Amar, P. (eds), Cairo: AUC Press, 2006

Ezzat, H. R., "Women and Ijtihad: Towards a New Islamic Discourse", *Alif*, Vol. 19, 1999

Fahmy, K., "Women, Medicine, and Power in Nineteenth-Century Egypt", in *Remaking Women: Feminism and Modernity in the Middle East*, Abu-Lughod, L. (ed.), Cairo: AUC Press, 1998

———, *All the Pasha's Men: Mehmed Ali, His Army and the Making of Modern Egypt*, London: Cambridge University Press, 1998

Farag, I., "Higher Education in Egypt: The Realpolitik of Privatization", *International Higher Education*, Winter 2000. Online. Available at: www.bc.edu/bc_org/avp/soe/cihe/newsletter/News18/text11.html (accessed 20 June 2006)

Foote, J. S., "CNE in Egypt: Some Light at the End of an Arduous Tunnel", *TBS*, No. 1, Fall 1998. Online. Available at: www.tbsjournal.com/Archives/Fall98/Articles1/CNE/cne2.html (accessed 10 June 2006)

Gabriel, J., "Mohammed Shukri's 'The Plain Bread' Is Target of Hostile Press, Academic Furor in Egypt", *Al-Jadid*, Vol. 5, no. 26, Winter 1999

Gelfant, B. H., *The American City Novel*, Norman: Oklahoma University Press, 1965

Ghanim, A., "Ta'addud al-zawjat bayn al-shari'a wa l-waqi'" (Polygamy between Islamic Law and Reality), Islamweb.net. Online. Available at: www.islamweb.net/ver2/archive/readArt.php?lang=A&id=16238 (accessed 16 June 2006)

Ghannam, F., "Relocation and the Use of Urban Space", *Middle East Report* no. 202, Winter 1997. Online. Available at: www.jstor.org/view/08992851/di011543/01p00475/0 (accessed 20 May 2006)

———, "Keeping Him Connected: Globalization and the Production of Locality in Cairo", in *Cairo Cosmopolitan: Politics, Culture and the Urban Space in the New Globalized Middle East*, Singerman, D., and Amar, P. (eds). Cairo: AUC Press, 2006

Ghazoul, F., "Son'alla Ibrahim wa jamaliyyat al-irbak" (Sonallah Ibrahim and the Poetics of Confusion), *Akhbar al-Adab*, 9 November 2003

———, "The Artist vs. the Commissar", *Al-Ahram Weekly*, 25 January 2001

———, "The Phenomenal Al-Kharrat", *Al-Ahram Weekly Literary Supplement*, 13–19 July 2000

———, "Editorial", *Alif*, Vol. 19, 1999

———, "When the Subaltern Speaks", *Al-Ahram Weekly*, 18 February 1999

Ghazoul, F., and Harlow, B. (eds), *The View from Within: Writers and Critics on Contemporary Arabic Literature*, Cairo: AUC Press, 1994

Glover, D., and Kaplan, C., *Genders*, London: Routledge, 2000

Gordon, L., "Arabic Soars at U.S. Colleges", *Los Angeles Times*, 21 March 2006

Gunter, B., and Svennevig, M., *Behind and In Front of the Screen: Television's Involvement with Family Life*, London: John Libbey, 1987

Haeri, N., "Arabs Need to Find Their Tongue", *The Guardian*, 14 June 2003

———, "Introduction", *Sacred Language Ordinary People*, London: Palgrave Macmillan, 2003

Hafez, S., "Jamaliyyat al-riwaya al-jadida: al-qati'a al-ma'rifiyya wa l-naz'a al-mudadda (Poetics of the New Novel), *Alif*, Vol. 21, 2000

320 Bibliography

——, "The Novel, Politics and Islam", *New Left Review*, no. 5, September–October 2000
Hafez, S., "Introduction", Choukri, M., *Al-Shuttar*, London: Dar Al-Saqi, 1992
Herrera, L., "Downveiling: Gender and the Contest over Culture in Cairo", *Middle East Report*, no. 219, Summer 2001
Hishmat, D., *L'évolution des représentations de la ville du Caire dans la littérature égyptienne moderne et contemporaine*, Ph.D. thesis, Paris: Université de Paris 3 (Sorbonne Nouvelle), 2004
Hourani, A., *Arab Thought in the Liberal Age: 1798–1939*, Cambridge: Cambridge University Press, 1983
Ibrahim, S., *George Antonius Memorial Lecture*, 9 June 2005, unpublished
Ibrahim, S., and Ribière, J.-P., *Cairo from Edge to Edge*, Mehrez, S. (trans.), Cairo: AUC Press, 1998
Ibrahim, S.E., et al., *The Copts of Egypt*, London: Minority Rights Group International and Ibn Khaldun Center for Development Studies in Cairo, 1996. Online. Available at: www.minorityrights.org/admin/Download/Pdf/Coptreport.pdf (accessed 10 January 2007)
Jacquemond, R., *Entre scribes et écrivains: le champ littéraire dans l'Egypte contemporaine*, Paris: Actes Sud, 2003; Arabic translation: *Bayna Kataba wa Kuttab*, Al-Siba'i, B. (trans.), Cairo: Dar al-Mustaqbal al-Arabi, 2004; English translation: *Conscience of the Nation: Writers, Power and Society in Modern Egypt*, David Tresilian (trans.), Cairo: AUC Press, 2007
——, "Thawrat al-takhyiil wa takhyiil al-thawra: Qira'a jadida fi *Awlad haratina*" (Revolutionary Fiction and Fictional Revolution: A New Reading of *Children of Our Alley*), *Alif*, Vol. 23, 2003
——, *Le champ littéraire égyptien depuis 1967*, Ph.D. thesis, Université de Provence, 1999
——, "Samir Gharib Ali, une neutralité qui dérange", *Le Monde des Livres*, 30 May 1997
——, "Quelques débats récents autour de la censure", *Egypte/Monde Arabe*, No. 20, 4e trimester, 1994
——, "Egyptian Translation in the Postcolonial Era: From Acculturation to Cultural Decolonization", *Rethinking Translation: Discourse, Subjectivity, Ideology*, Venuti, L. (ed.), London: Routledge, 1992
Kandiyoti, D. (ed.), *Women Islam and the State*, Philadelphia: Temple University Press, 1991
Karnouk, L., *Modern Egyptian Art: 1910–2003*, Cairo: AUC Press, 2005
Kassem, M., "Egypt: Politics in the New Millennium", *UNISCI Discussion Papers*, No. 12, October 2006. Online. Available at: www.ucm.es/info/uisci/UNISCIKassem12.pdf (accessed 22 January 2007)
Kepel, G., "*L'immeuble Yacoubian*, un concentré des tensions du Moyen-Orient," (*The Yacoubian Building* Brings together Tensions in the Middle East), *Le Monde*, 28 April 2006
Kuppinger, P., "Giza Spaces", *Middle East Report*, no. 202, Winter 1997. Online. Available at: www.jstor.org/view/08992851/di011543/01p00464/0 (accessed 20 May 2006)
Langohr,V., "Frosty Reception for US Religious Freedom Commission", in *Middle East Report*, 29 March 2001. Online. Available at: www.merip.org/mero/mero032901.html (accessed 11 January 2007)
Leadership for Education and Development Program (LEAD), Online. Available at: www.aucegypt.edu/students/lead/about.htm (accessed 4 June 2006)
Lindsey, U., "TV Versus Terrorism: Why This Year's Ramadan Shows Tackled One

'Controversial' Subject, But Were Barred from Broaching Others", *TBS*, no. 15, Fall 2005. Online. Available at: www.tbsjournal.com/Archives/Fall05/Lindsey.html (accessed 6 June 2006)

Logan, J., "Banned in Cairo", *Lingua Franca*, July–August 1999

Lull, J. (ed.), *World Families Watch Television*, Newbury Park: Sage Publications Inc., 1988

Lutfi, H., "Women, History, Memory", interview by Samia Mehrez and James Stone in *Alif*, Vol. 19, 1999. Online. Available at: www.jstor.org/view/11108673/ap020019/02a00120/0 (accessed 8 March 2006)

——, "Found in Cairo: Representation and Reception in the Contemporary Egyptian Visual Field", From Local to Global: Visual Arts in the Eastern Mediterranean between International Markets and Local Expectations, Florence, March 2006, unpublished testimony

Marsot, A. L. A., *Egypt in the Reign of Muhammad Ali*, Cambridge: Cambridge University Press, 1984

Massad, J., *Desiring Arabs*, Cambridge, MA: Harvard University Press, forthcoming

Mehrez, S., *Egyptian Writers between History and Fiction: Essays on Naguib Mahfouz, Sonallah Ibrahim and Gamal al-Ghitani*, Cairo: AUC Press, 1994 and 2005

——, "The Map of Writing: An Interview with Ahdaf Souief", *Alif*, Vol. 20, 2000

——, "*Al-Khubz al-hafi*: Wathiqat al-idana" (*Al-Khubz al-hafi*: The Document of Incrimination), *Al-Adab*, Vol. 50, 11–12, 2002

——, "Kitabat al-watan: Latifa al-Zayyat bayn *al-Bab al-maftuh* wa *Hamlat taftish awraq shakhsiyya*, *Latifa al-Zayyat: al-Adab wa l-watan* (Writing the Nation: Latifa al-Zayyat between *The Open Door* and *The Search*), in *Al-Adab wa twatan*, Bahrawi, S. (ed.), Cairo: Dar al-Mar'a al-Arabiyya, Marqaz al-Buhuth al-Arabiyya, 1996

——, "Translation and the Postcolonial Experience: The Francophone North African Text", in *Rethinking Translation: Discourse, Subjectivity, Ideology*, Venuti, L. (ed.), London: Routledge, 1992

Miller, C., "Upper Egyptian Regionally Based Communities in Cairo: Traditional or Modern Forms of Urbanization?", *Cairo Cosmopolitan: Politics, Culture and the Urban Space in the New Globalized Middle East*, Singerman, D., and Amar, P. (eds), Cairo: AUC Press, 2006

Miskin, A., "Rodinson Banned at AUC", *Middle East Report*, no. 209, Winter 1998

Mitchell, R. P., *The Society of the Muslim Brothers*, Oxford: Oxford University Press, 1969

Mitchell, T., *Colonizing Egypt*, Cairo: AUC Press, 1988

Moretti, F., *Atlas of the European Novel: 1800–1900*, London and New York: Verso, 1998

Murphy, L. R., *The American University in Cairo*, Cairo: AUC Press, 1987

Noeman, R., "Egypt Soap Opera Slammed for Glorifying Polygamy", Reuters, MaghrebOnLine.Net, 21 August 2002. Online. Available at: forum2002.maghrebonline.nl/viewtopic.php?p=19558&sid=0ff12922126b922f8d6111c599873373 (accessed 17 June 2006)

Öncü, A., and Weyland, P. (eds), *Space, Culture and Power: New Identities in Globalizing Cities*, London: Zed Books, 1997

Pacini, A., "Introduction", in *Christian Communities in the Arab Middle East: The Challenge of the Future*, Pacini, A. (ed.), Oxford: Clarendon Press, 1988

Pipes, D., *Campus Watch* at www.campus-watch.org

Rakha, Y., "Pop Power: On Ahmed al-Aidi and *Abbas al-Abd*", *The Daily Star*, 15 May

2004. Online. Available at: www.arabworldbooks.com/Readers2004/articles/Ahmed_alaidi2.htm (accessed 4 January 2007)

Raymond, A., *Cairo: City of History*, Wood, W. (trans.), Cairo: AUC Press, 2001

Reading between the "Red Lines": The Repression of Academic Freedom in Egyptian Universities, Human Rights Watch, Vol. 17, no. 6 (E). Online. Available at: hrw.org/reports/2005/egypt0605/ (accessed 10 April 2006)

Readings, B., *The University in Ruins*, Cambridge, MA: Harvard University Press, 1997

Reid, D. M., *Cairo University and the Making of Modern Egypt*, Cairo: AUC Press, 1990

Rodenbeck, M., "Witch Hunt in Egypt", *New York Review of Books*, 16 November 2000

Rouse, S., "Policing Voices, (En) Gendering Censorship", *The Review*, Association for Middle East Women's Studies (AMEWS), Vol. VIX, no. 4, Winter 2000

Sadek, S., "Cairo as Global/Regional Cultural Capital?", in *Cairo Cosmopolitan: Politics, Culture and the Urban Space in the New Globalized Middle East*, Singerman, D., and Amar, P. (eds), Cairo: AUC Press, 2006

Said, E. W., *Out of Place*, New York: Alfred A. Knopf, 1999

——, *Representations of the Intellectual: The 1993 Reith Lectures*, New York, Pantheon Books, 1994

——, "Literature and Literalism", *Al-Ahram Weekly*, 28 January 1999

——, "On the University", *Alif*, Vol. 25, 2005

Said, M. E., *Country Higher Education Profiles: Egypt*. Online. Available at: www.bc.edu/bc_org/avp/soe/cihe/inhea/profiles/Egypt.htm (accessed 4 April 2006)

Salama, S. A., "Al-Fikr al-hafi" (Barefoot Thought), *Al-Kutub Wijhat Nadhar*, April 1999

Salmawi, M., "Ma bayn al-takhassus wa wijhat al-nadhar" (Between Specialization and Personal Opinion), *Al-Ahram*, 24 May 1999;

——, "Al-takhassus marra ukhra" (Specialization Once More), *Al-Ahram*, 31 May 1999

——, "Fann al-sira al-dhatiyya" (The Art of Autobiography), *Al-Ahram*, 14 June 1999

Samir, S. K., "The Christian Communities, Active Members of Arab Society throughout History", in *Christian Communities in the Arab Middle East: The Challenge of the Future*, Pacini, A. (ed.), Oxford: Clarendon Press, 1988

Sayed, F. H., *Transforming Education: Western Influence and Domestic Policy Reform*, Cairo: AUC Press, 2006

Schleifer, A., "Media Explosion in the Arab World: The Pan-Arab Satellite Broadcasters", *TBS*, no. 1, Fall 1998. Online. Available at: www.tbsjournal.com/Archives/Fall98/Articles1/Pan-Arab_bcasters/pan-arab_bcasters.html (accessed 10 June 2006)

Shafik, V., *Popular Egyptian Cinema: Gender, Class and Nation*, Cairo: AUC Press, 2007

——, *Arab Cinema: History and Cultural Identity*, Cairo: AUC Press, 1998

——, "Variety or Unity: Minorities in Egyptian Cinema", *Orient*, Vol. 39, no. 4, December 1998

Shehata, S., and Stacher, J., "The Brotherhood Goes to Parliament", *Middle East Report* 240, Fall 2006. Online. Available at: merip.org/mer/mer240/shehata_stacher.html (accessed 20 January 2007)

Shoukri, G., *Egypte, contre révolution*, Paris: Le Sycamore, 1979

Simon, S., *Gender in Translation: Cultural Identity and the Politics of Transmission*, London: Routledge, 1996

Singerman, D., and Amar, P., "Introduction", in *Cairo Cosmopolitan: Politics, Culture and the Urban Space in the New Globalized Middle East*, Singerman, D., and Amar, P. (eds), Cairo: AUC Press, 2006

Slaughter, S., and Rhoades, G., *Academic Capitalism and the New Economy: Markets, State and Higher Education*, Baltimore: Johns Hopkins University Press, 1999

Spivak, G., "The Politics of Translation", in *The Translation Studies Reader*, Venuti L. (ed.), London: Routledge, 2000

Springborg, R., *Mubarak's Egypt: Fragmentation of the Political Order*, Boulder: Westview Press, 1989

Staines, J., "Cultural Play and Metamorphosis", *The International Artist Database*. Online. Available at: www.culturebase.net/artist.php?158 (accessed 20 October 2005)

Starrett, G., *Putting Islam to Work: Education, Politics, and Religious Transformation in Egypt*, Berkeley: University of California Press, 1998

Strelitz, L., "Where the Global Meets the Local: Media Studies and the Myth of Cultural Homogenization", *TBS*, no. 6, Spring/Summer, 2001. Online. Available at: www.tbsjournal.com/Archives/Spring01/strelitz4.html (accessed 15 July 2006)

Suleiman, Y., "Introduction"', in *Arabic Sociolinguistics: Issues and Perspectives*, Suleiman, Y. (ed.), Richmond: Curzon Press, 1994

Tawfik, M., "Written interview", email (22 July 2005)

Telmissany, M., "Al-Kitaba ala hamish al-tarikh" (Writing on the Margin of History), in *Latifa al-Zayyat: al-Adab wa l-watan*, Bahrawi, S. (ed.), Cairo: Dar al-Mar'a al-Arabiyya, Marqaz al-Buhuth al-Arabiyya, 1996

Tibi, B., *Arab Nationalism: A Critical Enquiry*, Farouk-Sluglett, M., and Sluglett, P. (eds and trans.), London: Macmillan, 1981

Tomiche, N., *Histoire de la littérature romanesque de l'Egypte moderne*, Paris: Maisonneuve et Larose, 1981

Tucker, J., *Women in Nineteenth Century Egypt*, Cambridge: Cambridge University Press, 1985

Van der Veer, P., "Visual Practices in South Asian Nationalisms", paper presented at the conference on Visual Practices and Public Subjects: Secularism, Religious Nationalism and the State, AUB, April 2005

Venuti, L., "Translation, Community, Utopia", *The Translation Studies Reader*, Venuti, L. (ed.), London: Routledge, 2000

——, *The Translator's Invisibility: A History of Translation*, London: Routledge, 1995

——, "Introduction", *Rethinking Translation Discourse, Subjectivity, Ideology*, Venuti, L. (ed.), London: Routledge, 1992

Wikipedia: The Free Encyclopedia, "The Nasr Abu Zayd Case". Online. Available at: en.wikipedia.org/wiki/Nasr_Abu_Zayd#The_Nasr_Abu_Zayd_case (accessed 16 November 2006)

Williams, C., "Reconstructing Islamic Cairo: Forces at Work", in *Cairo Cosmopolitan: Politics, Culture, and Urban Space in the New Globalized Middle East*, Singerman, D., and Amar, P. (eds), Cairo: AUC Press, 2006

Winegar, J., *Creative Reckonings: The Politics of Art and Culture in Contemporary Egypt*, Stanford: Stanford University Press, 2006

——, "Cultural Sovereignty in a Global Art Economy: Egyptian Cultural Policy and the New Western Interest in Art from the Middle East", *Cultural Anthropology*, Vol. 21, no. 2

Woolf, V., *A Room of One's Own*, Ramadan, S. (trans.), Cairo: Higher Council for Culture, 1999

Zeidan, D., "The Copts – Equal, Protected or Persecuted? The Impact of Islamization on Muslim–Christian Relations in Modern Egypt", *Islam and Christian–Muslim Relations*, Vol. 10, No. 1, 1999

Zuhur, S. (ed.) *Colors of Enchantment: Theatre, Dance, Music and the Visual Arts of the Middle East*, Cairo: AUC Press, 2001

——, *Images of Enchantment: Visual and Performing Arts of the Middle East*, Cairo: AUC Press 1998

Arabic and English periodicals

Al-Adab
Al-Ahali
Al-Ahram
Al-Ahram al-Arabi
Al-Ahram Weekly
Akhbar al-Adab
Akhbar al-Yawm
Al Jil
Al-Akhbar
Al-Arabi
Al-Dustur
Al-Fajr
Al-Gumhuriyya
Al-Hayat
Al-Ittihad al-Ishtiraqi
Al-Majalla
Al-Masa'
Al-Misri al-Yawm
Al-Multaqa
Al-Qahira
Al-Safir
Al-Sha'b
Al-Sharq al-Awsat
Al-Usbu'
Ruz al-Yusuf
Sawt al-Umma
Watani

Cairo Magazine
Cairo Times
Caravan, AUC Student Paper
Daily Star
Guardian
Herald Tribune
The Economist

Index

6 October victory 39
"9/11" September 11 2001 13, 171, 181, 206
1952 Revolution 41, 161, 281

A λ-Γαςηαρυ, Καριμ 301 n1, 303n7, 303n9
A Portrait of the Artist as a Young Man 73, 244
A[[xxx]]ilat al-Hagg Mitwalli (*Hagg Mitwalli's Family*) 171, 178, 301n35
Abaza, Mona 296n101, 298n27, 316n14
Abbas, Muhammad 19, 279n14
Abbas, Ra[[xxx]]uf 289n21
Abd al-Fattah, Wa[[xxx]]il 35, 288n36
Abd al-Hafiz, Wa[[xxx]]il 140
Abd al-Qadir, Faruq 287n11
Abd al-Quddus, Ihsan 63
Abd al-Rahman, Tawfiq 278n1
Abdallah, Ahmed 289n21
Abdallah, Yahya al-Taher 269
Abdel Hadi, Rabab 291n1
Abdel Meguid, Ibrahim 31–2, 45–7, 125, 281n23, 283n27, 283n28, 293n13
Abdel-Messih, Marie-Thérèse 140, 296n94
Abla, Muhammad 213, 306n15
Abna' al-khata' al-rumansi (*Children of Romantic Error*) 15, 278, 294n18
Aboul Atta, Tarek 297n5
Abu Golayyel, Hamdi 19, 146–7, 152–3, 158–9, 297n7, 297n13, 299n40, 299n63
Abu Nuwwas 15
Abu Rayya, Yusuf 45
Abu Shadi, Ali 14
Abu Zayd, Nasr Hamid 17–18, 230, 247
Abu-Lughod, Lila 173–4, 192, 276n2, 289n17, 291n3, 293n1, 300n4, 300n5, 300n7, 300n8, 300n9, 300n13, 300n26, 304n13, 304n15, 304n16, 304n18, 304n19, 304n21

Abul-Ghar, Muhammad 289n21
academic freedom 12, 91, 96, 229, 231–2, 236–43, 260, 262, 268, 270–2, 274–5, 289n21, 307n1, 311n52, 313n69
Afarit al-asfalt 195, 294n24
Ahlam muharrama (*Forbidden Dreams*) 278, 293n17
Ahmed, Leila 291n3
Akhbar al-Adab 15, 25–6, 30–4, 36–7, 40, 46, 48, 52, 59, 66, 68, 126, 141, 239, 253, 255, 278n7, 279n15, 280n2, 280n6, 281n25, 281n33, 282n14, 283n15, 283n20, 283n25, 283n28, 283n31, 283n34, 284n38, 284n58, 284n59, 284n60, 284n61, 286n16, 286n18, 286n19, 286n24, 287n13, 288n40, 288n47, 306n16, 312n58
Akhbar al-Yawm 280n6, 287n19, 287n25, 288n46, 298n24
Akhter, Farida 292n8
Al Haya al-Jadida 35
Al Jil 287n28, 288n38
al Raʿi, Ali 282n5
Al-Ahali 287n10, 310n28
Al-Ahram, daily newspaper 41, 63, 86, 114–15, 230–1, 250, 281n1, 282n1, 282n5, 292n29, 293n4, 303n9, 305n35, 308n4, 312n64
Al-Ahram Al-Arabi 44, 282n10, 306n46, 311n38
Al-Ahram Weekly 2, 50, 194, 241–2, 276n1, 277n11, 278n1, 278n5, 278n8, 282n6, 283n36, 286n23, 287n35, 288n43, 290n31, 294n19, 296n95, 299n47, 301n2, 304n2, 304n25, 305n31, 307n33, 311n46, 311n47, 311n48, 311n49, 311n53, 312n58
Al-Akhbar 59–60, 62, 287n22, 305n28, 311n37

326 Index

al-Alim, Mahmud Amin 73, 287n24
Al-Allama (The Polymath) 45
Al-Arabi 31–2, 35, 279n1, 281n23, 281n30, 284n40, 284n42, 284n44, 284n48, 287n28, 288n39, 288n41, 288n44, 288n50, 310n28, 310n29, 312n64
al-Arabi, Shehrazade 284n39
al-Ashri, Waʾil 140
Al-Asifa (The Storm) 98
al-Aswany, Abbas 147
al-Aswany, Alaa 56, 146–7, 160, 162, 166, 191, 285n66, 297n8, 299n48, 299n49, 304n14
Al-Azhar 5, 19, 35, 60, 62, 92, 94, 101, 103, 190, 201, 205, 212, 282n1, 282n16, 289n16, 289n17, 303n11, 305n30, 305n31, 305n32
Al-Bab al-maftuh (The Open Door) 31, 45, 47, 124, 130, 152, 293n6, 293n7
al-Bahrawi, Sayyid 32, 46–7, 283n15, 283n20, 283n24, 283n25, 283n26, 283n27, 283n28, 293n6
Al-Balda l-ukhra (The Other Place) 31, 45, 47
al-Bisati, Muhammad 54
al-Daramali, Nariman 184
Al-Dustur 62–3, 66, 68–9, 86, 285n12, 286n28
al-Gazzar, Abd al-Hadi 215
Al-Ghadd 5, 287n14
al-Ghitani, Gamal 9, 15, 21, 26–7, 31, 36, 58–9, 70, 87, 148–9, 209, 253, 278n7, 280n3, 280n6, 280n11, 281n17, 281n20, 281n21, 281n26, 285n1, 285n5, 285n10, 287n11, 296n6, 297n12, 298n21, 298n24, 311n37
al-Hakim, Tawfik 52, 62
al-Hamamsy, Abd al- Al 283
Al-Hayat 21, 80, 115, 240, 278n2, 278n6, 279n18, 284n37, 284n39, 284n41, 284n43, 284n45, 284n47, 288n46, 288n49, 292n30, 300n27, 301n28, 305n34, 305n43, 311n39, 311n41, 312n62
Al-Jadid 284n62, 310n34
al-Kharrat, Edwar 43–5, 50, 52–3, 125, 282n6, 282n8, 284n53, 287n11, 293n15
Al-Khawf yaqtul al-ruh 294n24
Al-Khubz al-hafi (For Bread Alone) 12, 229–30, 232–5, 237–51, 255, 257–8, 263, 266–9, 307n1, 308n10, 308n11, 309n12, 309n16, 309n19, 310n28, 310n29, 310n30, 310n33, 310n34, 311n41, 311n47, 311n53, 312n58, 312n68, 312n69, 313n71
Al-Khutuba 140
Al-Lajna (The Committee) 37, 39, 72, 74, 279n1, 315
Al-Mahbubat (The Loved Ones) 45, 48, 315
al-Mahgub, Rifʿat 17
Al-Majalla 280n16
Al-Masaʾ 280n16
Al-Masamir 266
Al-Muhajir (The Immigrant) 205
Al-Multaqa 287n15
Al-Mussawar 282n11, 300n27, 305n36
al-Nadim, Abdallah 266
al-Naggar, Safaʾ 140
al-Naqqash, Ragaʾ 282n5, 284n45
al-Nowaihi, Magda 56, 240–2, 251, 267–9, 271, 285n65, 311n42, 311n43, 311n44
al-Nuqali, Muhammad 178
al-Qaʿid, Yusuf 283n30, 284n45
Al-Qahira 81, 221, 283n30, 287n23, 306n14, 306n15
Al-Rajul al-ari 294n23
Al-Rawd al-atir 125, 293n13
Al-Safir 287n18, 308n9
Al-Saqqar (The Hawker) 126, 312n66
al-Shaʿb 18–19, 211
al-Sharif, Nur 172, 178, 180, 183, 186
al-Sharif, Safwat 177, 184, 285n12
al-Sheikh, Hanan 233, 247, 258
al-Shuryan, Dawud 21
al-Siwi, Adil 2, 6, 306n11
al-Siwirki, Midhat 182
Al-Sukkariyya 293n1
al-Tahawy, Miral 125, 258–9, 294n20
Al-Tawq wa-al-Iswira 269
Al-Thulathiyya (The Trilogy) 123–4, 293n3, 293n5
al-Tunsi, Abbas 283n25, 312n58
Al-Usbuʿ 278n3, 279n13
al-Uways Award 45, 52, 78, 80, 282n12, 287n11
Al-Wafd 189, 238–9, 247, 266, 306n47, 310n30, 310n32, 312n58, 313n71
al-Wardani, Haytham 140
al-Wardani, Mahmud 125, 293n13
Al-Warsha Theatre Company 214
Al-Zayni Barakat 58–61, 64–5, 67–8, 70, 285n1, 285n5, 285n10, 286n20
al-Zayyat, Latifa 31, 45–7, 124, 129, 283n15, 283n19, 283n24, 283n26, 293n6, 293n11

Alaidy, Ahmed 140–1, 143, 296n95, 296n98, 296n101, 296n102, 297n107
ALECSO (Arab League Educational, Cultural and Scientific Organization) 99
Ali, Idris 81, 287n23
Ali, Muhammad 16, 94, 112, 150, 209, 278n9, 289n17
Ali, Samir Gharib 126, 293n16, 312n66
Alif: Journal of Comparative Poetics 110–11, 118, 235, 258, 282n2, 282n5, 283n19, 284n52, 292n10, 292n31, 292n32, 292n36, 293n10, 307n18, 307n24, 311n49
All the Pasha's Men: Mehmed Ali, his Army and the Making of Modern Egypt 278n9, 289n17
Allouise 215
Alrawi, Karim 290n57
Alterman, Jon 174
Amar, Paul 166, 277n6, 298n25, 299n59, 299n64, 300n12
American hegemony 181, 184
American International School 103
American policy 32
American University in Beirut 92
American University in Cairo 12, 31–2, 41, 43, 46, 48, 91–2, 97, 110, 114–15, 214, 222, 224, 228–30, 233, 248, 260, 263–9, 276n2, 282n5, 284n53, 284n57, 286n17, 288n1, 288n8, 288n9, 288n14, 288n15, 291n1, 293n1, 294n2, 297n1, 308n8, 311n40
American University in Cairo Press (AUC Press) 43–4, 48, 55, 235, 258, 276n2, 277n6, 280n3, 281n22, 282n4, 282n5, 282n8, 282n13, 283n14, 283n16, 283n19, 285n1, 285n3, 285n10, 287n7, 287n32, 288n9, 288n10, 289n17, 290n46, 291n3, 293n1, 293n6, 293n9, 294n20, 294n22, 296n95, 296n96, 296n101, 296n102, 297n4, 297n6, 297n8, 297n10, 297n12, 298n25, 298n27, 300n4, 300n12, 304n13, 306n1, 306n14, 308n8, 308n9, 309n14, 309n18
Amin, Nora 125
Amireh, Amal 56, 284n62
Amrika umm al-dunya (America Mother of the World) 31–2, 47, 281n23
Amrikanli 74, 82–4, 86, 279n1, 287n29, 287n31, 287n33, 287n34
An takun Abbas al-Abd (Being Abbas El Abd) 141–2, 296n95, 296n98
Anderson, Benedict 100, 290n45, 298n19
Anderson, Jon W. 276n2

Arab French Friendship Prize 52
Arab Human Development Report 99, 112, 116, 289n28, 290n38, 290n48, 291n1, 292n12
Arab Nationalism: A Critical Enquiry 288n13
Arabic language 10, 50, 65, 93, 98, 99–100, 103–6, 109, 111–13, 249, 291n65, 328n58
Arabic Sociolinguistics: Issues and Perspectives 290n36
Arafat, Yasser 77
Arandel, Christian 299n38
Armbrust, Walter 276n2, 300n6
Asfur, Gabir 72, 78–9, 81, 199
Ashbah wataniyya (Nationalistic Ghosts) 68–71, 286n27
Ashour, Radwa 49
ashwa'iyyat 153
Aslan, Ibrahim 54, 283n30
Atlas of the European Novel 144, 148, 297n3, 298n20
autonomous 8, 26–7, 30–1, 34, 36–7, 46, 55, 76, 81, 147, 222
autonomy 6, 8–9, 11–12, 17, 23, 26–8, 40, 81, 94, 96, 112, 208–9, 214, 227, 241, 259, 289n21
avant-garde 2, 12, 36, 44–5, 56, 63, 84, 123–6, 140, 143, 195, 212–14, 218
Awan al-ward (Time of Roses) 172, 192–3, 304n18
Awlad haratina (Children of Our Alley) 41–3, 45, 47, 49–51, 53–5, 57, 124, 149, 281n1, 282n2, 282n11, 293n4
Awraq al-narjis (Leaves of Narcissus) 45, 50–2, 126, 130, 133, 135, 137, 142, 284n46, 294n22, 295n44
Awraq shabb asha mundhu alf am 60
Az-Zinzana (The Cell) 35, 281n33

Bada'i' al-zuhur fi waka'i' al-umur 59
Badawi, Muhammad 283n34
Badran, Margo 291n3
Baha al-Din, Ahmad 29
Bahgat, Ahmed 286n23
Bahibb issima (I Love Cinema) 188, 194–5, 196–9, 200–7, 301n10, 304n25, 306n48
Bakhtin 85–6
Bakr, Salwa 48, 80, 243, 283n30, 312n55, 312n56
Banipal: Magazine of Modern Arab Literature 140, 296n93
Barakat, Hoda 45, 47–8, 51

328 *Index*

Barghouti, Mourid 45, 48–9, 51
Baron, Beth 291n3
Basquiat 215
Bayat, Assef 298n31, 299n38
Bayn al-Qasrayn 293n1
Bayrut Bayrut 25, 34, 39, 74, 253, 279n1
Baziʿ, Shawqi 284n47
Beckett, Samuel 98, 133
Ben Jelloun, Taher 235, 257, 308n10
blasphemy 19, 21, 126, 224, 279n14
Bok, Derek 278n23
Boktor, Leslie 296n99
Booker Prize 45, 52, 257
Booth, Marilyn 293n6, 294n20, 294n22, 297n7
Botiveau, Bernard 302n6
Boughigian, Anna 215
Bourdieu, Pierre 7–9, 12, 26–30, 33–4, 59, 114, 229, 277n18, 277n19, 280n7, 280n8, 280n9, 280n10, 281n19, 281n27, 292n28, 308n2, 308n3
Bowles, Paul 235, 257, 267, 308n10
British International School 102
British occupation, The 94, 189
British University 104

Cairo 1–2, 4–5, 10, 19, 25, 29, 31, 34–5, 50–1, 59, 62–3, 97, 115, 127, 138, 141–9, 151, 153, 156–7, 158–60, 164, 166, 172–5, 190, 193, 208, 211, 214–18, 224, 232–3, 234, 240, 253, 257–8, 279n1, 280n6, 281n22, 282n1, 286n28, 287n14, 290n59, 294n21, 294n22, 294n24, 295n24, 298n31, 299n38, 299n39, 300n13, 300n16, 303n7, 304n16, 307n36, 311n45
Cairo American College 102
Cairo Cosmopolitan 166, 277n6, 298n25, 299n39, 299n46, 299n64, 300n12, 300n13
Cairo from Edge to Edge 83, 146, 281n22, 287n32, 297n10
Cairo International Book Fair 15, 55, 69, 86, 255, 284n64, 305n30, 309n16
Cairo International Book Fair Prize 45
Cairo Magazine 68–9, 286n22, 296n99
Cairo Times 79, 284n54, 287n12, 287n16, 287n30, 298n16, 310n34
Cairo University 46, 79, 92–5, 116, 147, 200, 247, 279n1, 282n5, 288n10, 289n18, 289n20, 289n21, 289n22
Cairo University and the Making of Modern Egypt 288n10
Camp David Accords 101

Campagna, Joel 277n9
Campus Watch 278n22
Camus, A. 98
Canadian University 104
Cardinal, Philippe 298n21
CASA Program 269–70
Cavafy Prize 52
censorship 10–11, 13, 15–16, 18, 26, 59, 63, 65, 69–70, 76, 92, 112, 169, 175–8, 188, 195, 199–203, 205–7, 209–12, 221–2, 225–32, 240, 243–4, 246, 251, 261, 268, 275, 285n12, 306n3, 306n5, 306n6, 306n48, 307n1, 308n9, 310n34, 312n58; self 10, 169, 212, 228, 232; street 7, 188, 210–11, 226–7, 306n3, 306n5
Chahine, Youssef 192, 205
Choukri, Mohamed 12, 229, 232–5, 240, 243, 248–9, 257–60, 308n10, 309n17, 311n40, 312n58
Christians 92–3, 190, 192, 203–5, 248, 264, 273, 285, 299n38, 301n1, 302n3, 302n4, 302n5, 302n6, 303n7, 303n12
Colderbank, Tony 283n16, 294n20, 297n6
Colla, Eliott 298n17
Colonizing Egypt 289n17
Contemporary Image Collective Group 214
Coptic community 4, 125, 188–90, 192–3, 200, 203–7, 224–5, 301n1, 302n3, 302n4, 302n5, 302n6, 303n8, 303n9, 303n10, 303n12, 304n20; religious authorities 201–4
Country Higher Education Profiles: Egypt 289n19
Coupland, Douglas 142
cultural identity 181–2, 215, 217, 276n2, 292n7
cultural sovereignty 10, 104–5, 176–8, 306n7, 307n27, 307n32

Dali, Salvadore 133
Damascus 59, 279n1, 279n12, 285n1
Dar al-Hilal 25, 34, 36–7, 40, 279n1, 281n33, 289n21, 293n13, 293n14
Dar al-Mustaqbal al-Arabi 25, 33–4, 279n1, 283n16, 285n3, 287n5, 287n29, 293n8, 297n6
Dar al-Shuruq 34, 282n1
Davies, Humphrey 296n95, 296n101, 297n8
de Beauvoir, Simone 60
democratization 7, 206, 210
Denis, Eric 153, 158, 297n5, 299n39

Index 329

Desiring Arabs 299n53
Dhakirat al-jasad (*Memory in the Flesh*) 45, 50, 284n45
Dhat (*Zaat*) 25–6, 28, 33–4, 38–40, 46, 55–7, 74, 77, 86, 124–5, 146–7, 150–2, 161, 165–6, 253, 279n1, 280n4, 281n28, 283n16, 288n42, 293n8, 293n9, 297n6, 298n27
Distant View of a Minaret 268
Dramas of Nationhood: The Politics of Television in Egypt 174, 276n2, 293n1, 300n4, 300n7, 300n9, 300n13, 300n26, 304n15, 304n16, 304n19, 304n21
Draz, Ceza 287n24
Dream TV 69, 286n23

École Oasis Internationale 102
Education, Politics, and Religious Transformation in Egypt 102, 276n5, 290n52
Egypt in the Reign of Muhammad Ali 278n9, 289n17
Egypte/Monde 281n32
Egyptian elite 91, 94–6, 102–4, 106, 288n5
Egyptian State Merit Prize 45
Egyptian TV 171, 173–8, 192
Egyptian Writers between History and Fiction: Essays on Naguib Mahfouz, Sonallah Ibrahim and Gamal al-Ghitani 280n3, 285n10, 296n96, 297n12
Eickelman, Dale 276n2
El Amrani, Issandr 277n16
El Ghobashy, Mona 277n9, 298n16
El Saadawi, Nawal 305n31
El-Batran, Manal 299n38
Elsadda, Huda 115–16
Elsheshtawy, Yasser 298n25
Entre scribes et écrivains: Le Champ littéraire dans l'Egypte contemporaine (*Between Scribes and Writers: The Literary Field in Contemporary Egypt*) 276n2, 276n4, 278n10, 285n3, 298n18
Espace Karim Francis 214–16
extremism 102, 189, 303n7
Ezzat, Heba Raouf 118–19, 122, 292n36

Fadl, Fathi 35, 37, 281n33
Fahmy, Khaled 278n9, 289n17
Farag, Alfrid 287n11
Farag, Iman 291n62
Farghali, Ibrahim 125, 283n14
Fathi, Ibrahim 282n5
Fathi, Yasmine 299n47
Fawzi, Hani 188, 193–5, 206, 305n29

Fawzi, Usama 188, 195, 202, 204, 305n29
Fayiq, Muhammad 34
Feminists Islam and Nation: Gender and the Making of Modern Egypt 291n3
Fight Club 142
Fischer, Ernest 76
Flaubert, Gustave 8, 26, 59
Found in Cairo 208–9, 211, 213, 215, 217, 221–3, 225–7, 307n21, 307n25, 307n26, 307n31, 307n38
Frankfurt Book Fair 213
French University 104
Friends of Sonallah Ibrahim Society 82
Fuda, Farag 17, 230
fundamentalism 13–14, 172, 189, 192, 206, 210, 290n51
Fusul 282n5

Galeano, Eduardo 83
gamaʿa al-Islamiyya 102
Gelfant, Blanche Housman 297n1
gender 9–10, 12, 41, 46–7, 107–11, 113–24, 126, 172, 180–1, 194, 214, 276n2, 290n59, 291n1, 291n3, 291n6, 292n7, 292n8, 292n9, 292n27, 295n25, 297n1, 310n34; relations 9, 115, 180–1, 291n3; studies 10, 12, 107–11, 113–20, 291n1, 297n1
Gender in Translation: Cultural Identity and the Politics of Transmission 292n7, 292n27
General Egyptian Book Organization (GEBO) 18, 294n22
General Organization for Cultural Palaces (GOCP) 14, 18–19, 278n4, 279n16, 293n17, 294n18
Generation X 142
George Antonius Memorial Lecture 75, 84, 286n3, 287n7, 287n8, 287n33
German School 102
German University 104
Ghannam, Farha 174, 298n31, 300n12
Gharib, Samir 126, 293n16, 312n66
Ghazoul, Ferial 17, 41, 45, 85, 235, 244, 258, 278n1, 278n5, 278n11, 282n5, 282n6, 282n8, 283n19, 284n61, 287n24, 288n40, 292n10, 294n19, 308n11, 309n18, 310n35, 311n45, 312n58, 312n62, 312n63
Gibril, Muhammad 283n30
globalization 34, 38–9, 91–3, 95, 97, 99, 101, 103, 105, 121, 150, 165, 174, 177, 300n12
Goncourt Prize 45, 257

330 Index

Gordon, Larry 291n65
Gulf War 107, 128–9, 175

hadith 201, 222, 224, 227–8, 305n31
Haeri, Niloofar 99, 290n40, 290n41
Hafez, Sabry 124, 278n12, 279n14, 286n15, 293n10, 293n12, 309n17
Hajar 116
Hajis mawt 126–7, 135, 137–8, 140–2, 294n23, 296n73
Hamid, Alaa 35
Hamid, Mahmud 126, 278n1, 293n17
Hamid, Marwan 148, 191
Hanafi, Hasan 119–21
Haqqi, Yahya 29, 280n16
hara (*alley*) 43, 144–51, 153, 159, 161, 163, 165, 167, 281n1, 297n1
Harafish 149
Harb, Talaʿat 281n29
Harith al-miyah (*The Tiller of Water*) 45, 47
Harlow, Barbara 258, 283n19
Harvard Law School 104
Hasan, Farkhunda 195
Hasan, Husni 125
Haydar, Haydar 18–21, 66, 211, 278n12, 282n11, 286n15, 305n32, 305n38
Haykal, Muhammad Hasanayn 29, 281n1, 303n9
Herald Tribune, the 290n57
Herrera, Linda 290n59
Heshmat, Gamal 14
Higher Council for Culture 18, 72, 76–8, 200, 202, 206
Himmich, Bensalem 45, 49–50
Histoire de la littérature romanesque de l'Egypte moderne 280n13
Holy Council of the Coptic Orthodox Church, the 204
Homo Academicus 229, 277n18, 308n2
Huraʾ mataha qutiyya 294n24
Husayn, Adil 19
Husni, Faruq 14–18, 44, 72, 87, 126, 211
Hussein, Taha 2, 6, 29, 52

Ibdaʿ 126
Ibid, Atif 14
Ibn Iyas 59–60
Ibn Khaldun 49–50
Ibn Khaldun Center for Development Studies 190, 286n17, 301n1
Ibn Mandhur 109
Ibrahim, Saad Eddin 20, 67, 69, 78, 120, 190, 225, 286n17, 287n14, 301n1, 311n52

Ibrahim, Sonallah 9, 25–7, 33, 35–7, 40, 46–7, 55–7, 72, 75, 77–8, 80, 82–3, 85–8, 124, 140–1, 146–7, 150, 158–9, 166, 212–13, 216, 233, 258, 268, 279n1, 280n3, 280n4, 280n14, 281n21, 281n22, 281n24, 281n28, 283n16, 283n17, 283n18, 285n10, 286n1, 286n2, 286n3, 287n5, 287n7, 287n11, 287n23, 287n24, 287n26, 287n29, 287n32, 288n40, 288n42, 293n8, 293n9, 296n96, 297n6, 297n10, 297n12, 298n27, 309n14
Ibtisamat al-qiddisin (*The Smile of Saints*) 283n14
Idris, Yusuf 45–6, 191, 233, 258, 269, 298n26
Idriss, Samah 246
Ihdar istiqlal al-jamiʿat 289n21
ijtihad 91–2, 118, 217, 292n36
Imagined Communities 55–6, 100, 290n45, 298n19
Imarat Yaʿqubyan (*The Yacoubian Building*) 56–7, 146–8, 160–2, 165–6, 191, 285n66, 297n8
In the Eye of the Sun 52
infitah 96, 101, 124–5, 127, 165, 210, 298n27
International Conference on the Arab Novel 72
International School of Choueifat 102
Intimate Selving in Arab Families 293n3
Islamic culture 91, 112, 181, 192, 271
Islamic Research Academy (IRA) 201, 205, 305n30, 305n31
Islamic Trend 3, 7, 10, 101–2, 302n4
Islamist 3–4, 10, 14–15, 17–20, 34, 36, 62, 64, 67, 97, 100, 118–19, 121, 178, 182, 210–11, 230, 277n9, 302n4
Islamization 92, 101, 165, 110, 302n4
Ismat, Adil 125–7, 135, 138, 294n23
Israel 30, 39, 46, 48–9, 62, 72–4, 77, 80, 97, 101, 107, 178, 181, 189, 199, 210, 254, 274–5, 278n22, 281n22, 304n13, 304n16, 308n5
Issa, Ibrahim 9, 58, 62–3, 66–71, 86, 285n2, 285n12, 286n24, 286n27, 286n28
Issa, Sheikh Imam 1, 2
Izz al-Din, Mansura 140, 283n31

Jackson, Nancy Beth 290n57
Jacquemond, Richard 54, 56, 59, 140, 210, 226, 244–5, 251, 276n2, 276n4, 278n10, 279n1, 280n6, 281n32, 282n2, 284n62, 284n65, 285n3, 285n4, 293n16, 296n92,

Index

298n18, 306n3, 307n37, 310n36, 311n47, 312n59, 312n66
Jahin, Salah 2, 6
janasa 109–10
Jannat al-shayatin 294n24
jins 108–9, 111, 115–16
Journal of Modern Education 93
Joyce, James 73, 133, 244
junusa 110–11

Kaplan, Cora 291n6
Kassem, Maye 277n13
Kepel, Gilles 285n67
Khalifa, Kamal 215
Khalifeh, Sahar 45
Khashab wa nahas 294n22
Khayrallah, Mahmud 284n42
Khoury, Elias 258
Kifaya (Enough) 1–2, 4–5
King Faysal Prize 45, 282n12
Kitabat al-banat 126
Kuppinger, Petra 298n31

La ahad yanam fi l-Iskandariya (*No One Sleeps in Alexandria*) 125, 293n13
Lamsa min alam gharib 294n24
Langohr, Vickie 302n3, 303n8, 303n10, 303n12
Laylat urs (*Wedding Night*) 45, 53,
Le champ littéraire égyptien depuis 1967 59, 279n1, 280n6, 285n3, 285n4, 285n9, 296n92
Le Monde 285n67, 293n16
Leadership for Education and Development Program (LEAD) 97, 290n34
Les règles de l'art (*The Rules of Art*) 8, 26, 59, 277n19, 280n9
Levinson, Charles 287n12
l-Id, Yumna 287n11
L'Islam en questions 298n21
liberal arts 93–4, 96, 98, 105, 246, 260, 262, 268, 270
liberal education 10, 13, 91–3, 95–6, 98, 104–6, 230, 232–3, 236–7, 239–40, 242–3, 246, 248, 261–5, 311n52
Lindsey, Ursula 178, 300n25
Linz, Mark 55, 282n4, 282n5, 284n64
Lisan al-Arab 104
Literary Voices 14, 20
Los Angeles Times 105, 291n65
Love Story 165
Lusus mutaqaʿidun (*Thieves in Retirement*) 146–7, 152–3, 158, 165–6, 297n7, 297n13

Lutfi, Huda 208, 214, 218–20, 222, 306n17, 308n18, 308n21, 308n23, 308n25, 308n26, 308n31, 308n34, 308n38, 310n27, 310n36
Lutfy Al-Sayyid Marsot, Afaf 278n9, 289n17
Lycée Français du Caire 102

Ma yaʿrifuhu Amin 127, 138, 141, 294n24, 296n91
Madbuli 35
Magic and the Image 215
Mahfouz, Naguib 3, 7, 17, 32, 41, 43–4, 47, 50, 52–3, 56–7, 76, 123, 144, 148–9, 167, 184, 230, 233, 240, 248, 257, 265–6, 280n3, 282n2, 282n3, 282n11, 285n10, 293n2, 293n4, 296n96, 297n2, 297n12, 298n22, 298n24
Mamdouh, Alia 45, 48, 283n33
mamluk 59–60, 70
Manazil al-ruh 294n22
Manshiyyat Nasir 146, 152–3, 156, 158
Maqtal al-rajul al-kabir (*The Assassination of the Big Man*) 58, 63–9, 285n2, 285n13, 286n21
Marsot, Afaf Lutfy Al-Sayyid 278n9, 289n17, 321
Masculine Domination 292n28
Mashaynaha khutan 289n21
Mashrabiyya, Gallery 214, 216, 221
Massad, Joseph 162, 278n22, 299n53
Mehrez, Samia 256, 260–3, 267–71, 280n14, 281n22, 282n5, 284n52, 285n10, 287n7, 288n42, 291n2, 293n6, 293n9, 296n96, 297n12, 298n18, 298n27, 307n18, 309n14, 312n57
Memory of Fire Trilogy 83
Merit publishing house 69, 141
MESA (Middle East Studies Association) 31, 242, 251, 311n50, 311n51
Metamorphosis of Narcissus 133
Middle East Report 277n8, 277n9, 290n59, 297n5, 298n31, 301n1, 302n3, 308n6
Miller, Catherine 159, 299n46
Min awwil il-satr (*The Beginning of the Line*) 69
Minister of Culture 2–3, 14, 19, 44, 50, 66, 72, 77–80, 85–7, 126, 205, 211, 221, 282n5, 287n26, 288n46, 288n49
ministry of culture 15, 17, 80–1, 87, 147, 200, 205, 209–10, 212–13, 221, 278n1, 285n1, 305n30, 307n32, 309n12
Misr International University 104
Mitchell, Richard P. 277n9

Mitchell, Timothy 289n17
Modern English School 103
modernization 16–17, 27, 100, 111–12
modernizing 10, 97, 276n3, 289n17
Monroe, Marilyn 138, 217
Moretti, Franco 144, 148, 297n3, 298n20
Mosteghanemi, Ahlam 45, 50, 233, 258
Mubarak, Gamal 5, 286n28
Mubarak, Hosni 16, 71, 190, 286n28, 308n1
Muharram, Mustafa 178, 180, 186
Muntasir, Salah 230, 248, 308n4
Muslim Brothers 2, 4–6, 14, 20, 204, 212, 277n9
Muslim community 189, 205, 207, 224
Muslim religious authorities 201, 203–5
Mustagab, Muhammad 54

Nabil, Mustafa 36
Nagui, Iffat 215
Naguib Mahfouz AUC Award 12, 31–2, 41, 43–9, 51–6, 86, 130, 282n5, 282n9, 283n18, 283n23, 283n29, 283n33, 283n35, 285n50, 285n51, 285n56
nahda (Arab cultural renaissance) 1, 6, 9, 16, 18, 100, 302n5
Nahdat Misr 304n24
Najib Mahfudh yatadhakkar (*Naguib Mahfouz Remembers*) 149, 298n24
Najmat Aghustus 39, 74, 253, 279n1
Nasser, Gamal Abdel 16, 34, 50, 60, 94–5, 145, 147, 152–3, 158, 173, 195, 199, 209–10, 226, 280n14, 282n1, 284n40, 303n9
nasserist 18, 25, 31, 34, 38
National Council for Human Rights 116
National Council for Women 114–16, 172, 181, 184–7
national imaginary 123–6, 128, 130, 135, 140, 143, 148, 172, 209
national imaginings 189, 207, 276
National Translation Project 80
nationalism 74, 113, 117, 121, 188–9, 273, 288n13, 306n1, 306n2
nationalist 9, 32, 46–51, 55–6, 68, 94, 97, 99–100, 111, 113, 119–20, 128, 172, 175–8, 184, 189–90, 215, 274, 279n12, 281n29, 302n4, 302n6, 303n9
nationalization 94, 158
Negus, Steve 79
Nelson, Cynthia 297n1
New Internationalist 290n57
New Left Review 278n12, 286n15
New York Review of Books 278n12, 286n15

Nigm, Ahmad Fuad 1–2, 6
niqab (face veiling) 96
Nitaq, I, II 213, 218
Nobel Prize 7, 17, 43, 45, 77, 123, 230, 240, 254, 269
nouveau riches 95, 164, 180
Nuqtat nur (*A Spot of Light*) 125, 293n14
Nur, Ayman 5, 78, 277n15, 287n14
Nur, Hasan 18

objectification of the self 26, 39, 59, 281n28, 288n42, 293n9, 298n27
Ottoman 16, 59–60, 145, 274
Out of Place 92, 288n7, 311n45

Pacini, Andrea 301n1, 302n5,
Palahniuk, Chuck 142
pan-Arab 175–6, 178, 300n14, 302n4, 302n6
Picasso, 215, 231
Pipes, Daniel 278n22
Plath, Sylvia, 133, 149
polygamy 180–4, 186, 301n29, 301n31
pornographic 14–15, 126, 152, 212, 234, 236, 258, 263, 267–9, 312n62
pornography 14, 212, 234–5, 257–8
post-colonial 160, 162
President Mubarak 1, 3, 5, 7, 17, 69, 86, 100, 230
Prince, Mona 126–7, 130, 294n21
Prophet Muhammad 182, 201, 222, 227, 230, 282n1, 305n31
Protestant 92–3, 193, 203–4, 206, 306n45
Public Culture 298n17, 300n5
public sphere 172, 182, 188–9, 193, 203, 205–7, 223, 238, 243, 246, 276n2, 303n7
Putting Islam to Work: Education, Politics, and Religious Transformation in Egypt 102, 276n5, 290n52

Qabbani, Nizar 51
Qabla wa baʿd (*Before and After*) 278n1
Qasim, Abdel Hakim 258
Qasr al-Shawq 293n1
Qissat hubb (*City of Love and Ashes*) 45
Qitʿat al-tin al-akhira 294n21
Qurʾan 65, 99, 109, 177, 201, 278n3, 279n14, 289n16, 294n23, 305n31, 313n70

Raʾaytu Ramallah (*I Saw Ramallah*) 45, 48–9

Index 333

Rakha, Youssef 287n35, 288n43, 296n95, 296n97, 296n100, 296n101, 297n106
Rama wa l-tinnin 44, 52
Ramadan 44, 50, 171–4, 177–8, 180–1, 183, 185, 192, 300n25, 300n27; TV serials 171n3, 178, 300n27
Ramadan, Abd al-Munʿim 282n14, 283n34
Ramadan, Somaya 42–4, 125–6, 282n11, 294n20, 294n22
Raymond, André 145, 297n4, 297n5, 298n25
Reading between the "Red Lines": The Repression of Academic Freedom in Egyptian Universities 289n21, 307n1, 308n6, 308n8, 322
Readings, Bill 278n22
Reid, Donald Malcolm 93, 288n10, 289n18, 289n20, 289n21, 289n22, 289n25
Remaking Women: Feminism and Modernity in the Middle East 289n17, 291n3
Representations of the Intellectual 88, 288n51
Rethinking Translation Discourse, Subjectivity, Ideology 284n62, 291n2, 291n5
Rhoads, Gary 278n23
Ribiere, Jean-Pierre 155–6, 281n22, 287n32, 297n10
Rifaat, Alifa 268
Risq, Abd al- Fattah 283n30
Riwayat al-Hilal 36
Rodenbeck, Max 278n12, 286n15
Rodinson, Maxime 230, 288n8, 308n1, 308n5, 308n6, 308n9
Roy, Arundhati 77
Russell, Jane 76
Ruz al-Yusuf 35–6, 62, 183, 281n31, 285n1, 301n30, 301n36, 306n14, 306n45, 308n9, 309n16

St Antony's College, Oxford 75–6, 82–3
Saʿid, Mahmud 215, 306n14
Saʿidi fil-gamiʿa il-amrikiyya (An Upper Egyptian at the American University in Cairo) 97
Sacred Language Ordinary People 99, 290n40, 299n43
Sadat, Anwar 3, 17–19, 62, 96, 124, 145, 152, 189, 210–11, 226, 300n27, 302n4
Said, Edward 49, 72, 75, 88, 91, 106, 241–2, 245–6, 248, 271, 278n22, 288n1, 288n7, 288n51, 311n45, 311n46, 311n49, 312n67, 313n74

Said, Mohsen Elmahdy 289n19
Salah al-Din, Muhsin 21, 279n17
Saleh, Tayeb 47, 52, 72, 81, 85, 233, 247, 258
Salih, Fakhri 282n5
Samaha, Hanan 287n30
Saqiyat al-Sawi Cultural Center 214
Saramago 77
Sartre, John Paul 61
satellite television 11, 14, 68–9, 175, 296n98, 300n15
Sawiris Literary Award 12, 45
Sawt al-Umma 15, 68, 86, 288n36, 301n34, 301n35, 305n33
Sayed, Fatma H. 100–1, 290n46, 290n49, 290n51
Schleifer, Abdallah 176, 300n14, 300n23
Season of Migration to the North 47, 245, 268, 312n58
secular players 4, 7, 16, 18
secularists 118–19, 121–2
Shaʿban, Yasir 15, 126, 278n1, 278n4
Shaath, Randa 154–57
Shafik, Viola 192, 276n2, 304n13, 304n16, 304n23
Shahin, Abd al-Sabur 278n3
Shakry, Omnia 289n17
Shalaby, Khairy 45, 53–4, 283n30, 284n57, 284n59
Sharaf 25–9, 31, 33–40, 74, 86–7, 253–4, 279n1, 280n2, 280n11, 281n17, 281n20, 281n26, 281n33, 288n45
Shehata, Samer 277n8
Shenouda III (Coptic Patriarch) 302n4, 303n9, 303n11
Shihab, Mufid 266
Shirdi, Muhammad Mustafa 266
Shukri, Girgis 14
Siddiq, Muhammad 240, 267–8, 311n43
Simon, Sherry 110, 113, 292n7
Singerman, Diane 166, 277n6, 298n25, 299n64
Sixth of October University 102
Slaughter, Sheila 278n23
social mobility 145, 151, 162, 181
Sorbonne 50–1, 298n13
Souief, Ahdaf 49, 52, 233, 284n52
Soviet Union, The 92, 209
Space, Culture and Power: New Identities in Globalizing Cities 297n11
Spivak, Gayatri 110, 292n8, 292n9, 292n11
Starrett, Gregory 3, 101, 276n5, 290n52
Statcher, Joshua 277n8

334 Index

State Encouragement Prize 45
Stories of Our Alley 42, 149
Strelitz, Larry 174, 300n11, 300n24
studio Imad al-Din 214
Sufi, Sufism 64–5, 125, 214, 216, 220–1, 225–8
Sukhur al-sama' (*The Rocks of Heaven*) 125
Sultan al-Uways Prize 45, 52, 282n12
Sura wa ayquna wa ahdun qadim (*The Image, the Icon, and the Covenant*) 45, 283n14

Taher, Bahaa 54, 86–7, 125, 140, 191, 293n14
Tallima, Abd al Mun'im 282n5
Tantawi, Muhammad, head of al-Azhar 19
Taqrir Misr wa-l- naw' al-ijtima' 114–15
Tawfik, Mohamed 146–7, 162, 165–6, 297n9, 298n15, 299n55, 299n56, 299n57, 299n60, 299n61
TBS (Transnational Broadcasting Studies) 300n11, 300n13, 300n14, 300n17, 300n25
Telmissany, May 125, 293n11, 294n20
Thalath haqa'ib li l-safar (*Three Suitcases for Departure*) 126–7, 130, 140–1, 294n21, 295n26
thanawiyya amma 102, 296n98
The American City Novel 297n2
The Changing Consumer Cultures of Modern Egypt: Cairo's Urban Reshaping 296n101, 298n27, 306n14
The Map of Love 52
The Misfits 138–9
The Old in the New 215
The Student Movement and National Politics in Egypt 289n21
The Translation Studies Reader 284n63, 292n8, 293n45
The Translator's Invisibility: A History of Translation 291n4
The Urban Challenge in Africa: Growth and Management of its Large Cities 297n5
The View from Within 235, 258, 283n19, 309n18
The Women's Awakening in Egypt: Culture Society and the Press 291n3
Tifl shaqi ismuhu Antar (*A Naughty boy called Antar*) 146–7, 162–3, 165–6, 297n9, 299n55, 299n57, 299n60
Tilka l-ra'iha (*The Smell of It*) 25, 28–9, 35, 39, 73–4, 76, 140–1, 234, 253, 279n1, 280n14, 280n16, 286n1, 287n7, 309n14
Tomiche, Nada 280n13
Townhouse Gallery, the 208, 217–18, 223–6
Transforming Education in Egypt: Western Influence and Domestic Policy Reform 100
translation studies 12, 107, 284n63, 292n8, 293n45
Tucker, Judith, 291n3
Tuyur al-anbar (*Birds of Amber*) 125, 293n13

ulama 16, 94, 227
Umm Kulthum 2, 6, 172, 217
UNDP 99, 101, 112, 116, 289n28
UNESCO 30, 32, 99, 101, 254, 281n21
United States Agency for International Development 97
United States, the 11, 13, 30–1, 39, 46–7, 63–4, 83, 93, 95, 97, 102, 105, 152, 181, 183, 190, 210, 214, 221, 238–9, 240, 241, 254, 256, 274, 278n22, 292n8, 302n3, 303n11, 303n12
University of Fuad I 92
Uways, Layla 84

Van der Veer, Peter 209, 306n2
Venuti, Lawrence 54, 284n62, 284n63, 291n2, 291n4, 291n5, 292n8, 293n45

Wa'il, Abd al-Fattah 35, 288n36
Wahid, Abd al-Maguid 284n45
Wali, Yusuf 18
Walima li a'shab al-bahr (*Banquet for Seaweed*) 19, 66, 279n12, 279n14, 282n11, 305n32, 305n38
Warda 74, 125, 140, 279n1
Wasfi, Huda 282n5
Watson, Charles R. 92
Wazin, Abdu 284n37
Wells, William 218
Weyland, Petra 297n11
Wikalat Atiyya (*The Lodging House*) 45, 53
Williams, Caroline 298n25
Williams, Ester 76
Winegar, Jessica 211, 276n2, 306n1, 306n7, 307n27, 307n32
Women and Gender in Islam: Historical Roots of a Modern Debate 291n3
Women and Memory 215
Women and Memory Forum 115–18

Women in Nineteenth Century Egypt 291n3
Women Islam and the State 291n3
Woolf, Virginia 294n22
World Bank 101, 114–15, 289n29
Writers and Artists for Change 1–4, 6

Yasir Suleiman 290n36
Yawmiyyat al-wahat (*Oasis Diary*) 75
Yevtushenko, Yevgeni 76

Yousry, Mahmoud 297n5
Youssef, Saadi 77

Zaki, Sahar 286n28
Zeidan, David 302n4, 302n5, 303n7
Zikri, Mustafa 125, 127, 138, 140, 294n24
Zuhur, Sherifa 276n2
Zuqaq al midaqq (*Midaq Alley*) 148–9, 167, 298n22, 298n23, 299n66

CPSIA information can be obtained
at www.ICGtesting.com
Printed in the USA
JSHW021512211219
3107JS00008B/41